Einfache Englische Grammatik mit Übungen

Vadym Zubakhin

Einfache Englische Grammatik mit Übungen

Das Erste Englische Lesebuch Inklusive

Einfache Englische Grammatik mit Übungen
von Vadym Zubakhin

Audiodateien: www.lppbooks.com/English/FirstEnglishReader_audio
Homepage: www.audiolego.com

Umschlaggestaltung: Audiolego Design
Umschlagfoto: Canstockphoto

1. Ausgabe
Copyright © 2019 Language Practice Publishing
Copyright © 2019 Audiolego
Alle Rechte vorbehalten. Das Werk ist urheberrechtlich geschützt.

Table of contents
Inhaltsverzeichnis

Englisches alphabet 10

Vokalgruppen 10

Konsonantengruppen 11

Die englischen Laute in der Internationalen Lautschrift 12

So steuern Sie die Geschwindigkeit der Audiodateien 14

1 The Plural / Der Plural 15

Reading comprehension Text 1 Robert has a dog 18

2 The indefinite Article / Der unbestimmte Artikel 20

3 The definite Article / Der bestimmte Artikel 23

    No article / Kein Artikel 27

    Bestimmte versus unbestimmte versus kein Artikel 28

Reading comprehension Text 2 They live in San Francisco (the USA) 30

4 Verb Conjugation in Present Simple / Konjugation der Verben im Präsens 32

5 The irregular Verbs have and be / Die unregelmäßige Verben have und be 33

6 Questions with auxiliary or modal Verbs / Fragesätze mit Hilfs- oder Modalverben 34

Reading comprehension Text 3 Are they Germans? 36

7 Modal Verbs and the Infinitive / Modale Hilfsverben und der Infinitiv 38

    can / können 39

    may / dürfen, können 40

    must / müssen 41

    need / brauchen 42

    will / werden 42

Reading comprehension Text 4 Can you help, please? 46

8 There is and There are / Es gibt 48

Reading comprehension Text 5 Robert lives in the USA now 50

9 The Genitive / Der Genitiv 52

Reading comprehension Text 6 Robert has many friends 54

10 The personal Pronoun / Das Personalpronomen 56

    Die possessive Form 56

Die Objektform 56

Reading comprehension Text 7 David buys a bike 59

11 The Adjective / Das Adjektiv 61

Bildung des Komparativs einsilbiger Adjektive 61

Bildung des Superlativs einsilbiger Adjektive 62

Bildung des Komparativs mehrsilbiger Adjektive 62

Bildung des Superlativs mehrsilbiger Adjektive 63

Gleichheit 63

Reading comprehension Text 8 Linda wants to buy a new DVD 66

12 The Prepositions of place / Die Präpositionen des Ortes 68

Reading comprehension Text 9 Paul listens to German songs 72

13 The Imperative / Der Imperativ 74

Bildung des verneinten Imperativs 75

Reading comprehension Text 10 Paul buys textbooks on design 77

14 Adverbs of manner / Adverbien der Art und Weise 79

15 Adverbs of frequency / Adverbien der Häufigkeit 80

16 Adverbs of time / Adverbien der Zeit 81

17 Adverbs of place / Adverbien des Ortes 83

Reading comprehension Text 11 Robert wants to earn some money (part 1) 85

18 Conversion / Wortartenwechsel 87

19 Question words / Fragewörter 88

Reading comprehension Text 12 Robert wants to earn some money (part 2) 90

20 The Prepositions of direction / Die Präpositionen der Richtung 92

Reading comprehension Text 13 The name of the hotel 95

21 The negative words / Die verneinende Wörter 97

22 Have got 98

23 Much little, many few, a lot of 99

Reading comprehension Text 14 Aspirin 102

24 Numbers / Zahlen 104

Decimals / Dezimalzahlen 106

Years / Jahre 106

Reading comprehension Text 15 Nancy and the kangaroo 107

25 The Prepositions of time / Die temporale Präpositionen 109

Reading comprehension Text 16 Parachutists 112

26 Some und any 115

27 Would like 117

Reading comprehension Text 17 Turn the gas off! 118

28 Present Simple / Präsens 120

29 Short answers / Kurzantworten 124

Reading comprehension Text 18 A job agency 126

30 Present Progressive (Continuous) / Verlaufsform des Präsens 129

Reading comprehension Text 19 David and Robert wash the truck (part 1) 132

31 Present Progressive versus Present Simple 134

Reading comprehension Text 20 David and Robert wash the truck (part2) 137

32 Present Participle and Gerund / Partizip I und Gerundium 140

Reading comprehension Text 21 A lesson 141

33 Past Simple / Imperfekt oder Präteritum 143

Reading comprehension Text 22 Paul works at a publishing house 147

34 Past Progressive (Continuous) / Verlaufsform der Vergangenheit 150

Reading comprehension Text 23 Cat rules 153

35 Past Progressive versus Past Simple 156

Reading comprehension Text 24 Teamwork 158

36 Future / Futur 161

    Present Progressive mit festgelegten persönlichen Handlungen 161

    Present Simple mit festgelegten öffentlichen Handlungen 161

    Futur I mit Meinung, Hoffnung, Unsicherheit, spontaner Entschluss 161

Reading comprehension Text 25 Robert and David are looking for a new job 166

37 Present Perfect / Perfekt 170

Reading comprehension Text 26 Applying to "San Francisco News" 173

38 Present Perfect versus Past Simple 176

Reading comprehension Text 27 The police patrol (part 1) 177

39 Word order / Die Wortstellung 181

Reading comprehension Text 28 The police patrol (part 2) 182

40 Too either, so neither 186

Reading comprehension Text 29 School for Foreign Students (SFS) and au pair 190

Keys / Lösungen 194

Wörterbuch Englisch-Deutsch 212

Wörterbuch Deutsch-Englisch 224

Die unregelmäßigen Verben 235

Wichtige Adjektive 241

Körperliche Eigenschaften 242

Gegenteile 243

Die 1300 wichtigen englischen Wörter 244

Days of the week 244

Months 244

Seasons of the year 244

Family 244

Appearance and qualities 244

Emotions 245

Clothes 245

House and furniture 246

Kitchen 247

Tableware 247

Food 248

Meat and fish 249

Fruit 249

Vegetables 249

Beverages 250

Cooking 250

Housekeeping 250

Body care 251

Weather 251

Transport 252

City 252

School 253

Professions 254

Actions 255

Music 256

Sports 257

Body 257

Nature 258

Pet 258

Animals 259

Birds 259

Flowers 260

Trees 260

Sea 260

Colors 261

Size 261

Materials 261

Airport 261

Geography 262

Crimes 263

Numbers 263

Ordinal numbers 264

Appendix / Anhang 265

Index / Register 267

Bibliography / Bibliografie 268

Buchtipps 269

Englisches Alphabet

Die englische Sprache wird im lateinischen Alphabet geschrieben. Es besteht aus denselben 26 Buchstaben, aus denen auch das deutsche Alphabet besteht. Sie werden jedoch anders ausgesprochen.

Sonderzeichen (außer: Apostroph, z.B. He'll…), Akzente und diakritische Zeichen kennt die englische Schrift nicht.

Buchstabe	Name	Aussprache (IPA)	Buchstabe	Name	Aussprache (IPA)
A	*a*	/eɪ/	O	*o*	/oʊ/
B	*bee*	/biː/	P	*pee*	/piː/
C	*cee*	/siː/	Q	*cue*	/kjuː/
D	*dee*	/diː/	R	*ar*	/ɑr/
E	*i*	/iː/	S	*ess*	/ɛs/
F	*ef*	/ɛf/	T	*tee*	/tiː/
G	*gee*	/dʒiː/	U	*u*	/juː/
H	*aitch*	/eɪtʃ/	V	*vee*	/viː/
I	*ei*	/aɪ/	W	*double-u*	/ˈdʌbljuː/
J	*jay*	/dʒeɪ/	X	*ex*	/ɛks/
K	*kay*	/keɪ/	Y	*wy*	/waɪ/
L	*el*	/ɛl/	Z	*zed*	/zɛd/, zee im Amerikanischen Englisch /ziː/
M	*em*	/ɛm/			
N	*en*	/ɛn/			

Vokalgruppen

En	De	Beschreibung	Beispiele
ai	ey	langes e, das in 'i' übergeht	air (Lüft)
aw	o:	offenes, langes o	paw (Pfote)
ei	ey	langes e, das in 'i' übergeht	eight (acht),
ei	ei	wie in Eifer	either [UK] (weder)

En	De	Beschreibung	Beispiele
ei	i:	langes i, wie in Lied	deceit (Betrug)
ea	i:	langes i, wie in Lied	eat (essen)
ea	ä	offenes, kurzes ä	beaver (Biber)
ee	i:	langes i, wie in Lied	bee (Biene)
ie	ie	langes i, wie in Lied	believe (glauben)
ia	eia	das i (ei) und das a (ä) getrennt ausgesprochen	liability (Verpflichtung)
ia	iä	kurzes i und kurzes ä	billiard (Billard)
eu	ju	wie in jung	Euro (Euro)
ew	ju	wie in jung	new (neu)
ue	ju:	wie in jung	due (gültig)
oo	u	langes u, wie in Jugend	foot (Fuß)

Konsonantengruppen

En	De	Beschreibung	Beispiele
ch	tsch	wie checken	chat (Unterhaltung)
ch	k	wie Kranz	Chemical (chemisch)
ck	k	wie Nacken	lock (Schloss)
gh	f	wie in kaufen	laugh (lachen), enough (genug)
gh	-	ohne Betonung	through (durch)
ng	ng	wie springen	sing (singen)
qu	kw	wie Quitte, mit schwach betontem w	quit (beenden)
sh	sch	wie lauschen	cash (Bargeld)
sp	sp	ein echtes sp	sport (Sport)
st	st	ein echtes st	stock (Aktienkapital)
th		weicher Laut	the (der, die, das)
th		harter Laut	theater (Theater)

Die englischen Laute in der Internationalen Lautschrift

Vokale

	Beispiele	Aussprache
ʌ	nut [nʌt] come [kʌm]	leicht geschlossenes aber ungerundetes a
ɑː	start [stɑːt] park [pɑːk]	
æ	bat [bæt] cat [kæt]	
ə	printer [ˈprɪntə]	wie das End-e in Katze, bitte
e	pet [pet] get [get]	ä wie in Bär, Käse
ɜː	earn [ɜːn] firm [fɜːm]	etwa wie ir in Wirt, aber offener
ɪ	bin [bɪn] big [bɪg]	kurzes i wie in Tisch
iː	meet [miːt] sea [siː]	langes i wie in biegen
ɔ	box [bɔks] want [wɔnt]	
ɔː	door [dɔː] source [sɔːs]	wie oo in boot
ʊ	cook [kʊk] good [gʊd]	kurzes u wie in Nummer
uː	two [tuː] cool [kuːl]	langes u wie in Blut, aber offener

Vokale, silbig

	Beispiele	Aussprache
aɪ	bike [baɪk] kind [kaɪnd]	etwa wie ei in Rein
aʊ	house [haʊs] round [raʊnd]	
əʊ	home [həʊm] go [gəʊ]	von /ə/ zu /ʊ/ gleiten
eə	care [keə] bear [beə]	
eɪ	game [geɪm] day [deɪ]	
ɪə	dear [dɪə] beer [bɪə]	von /ɪ/ zu /ə/ gleiten
ɔɪ	oil [ɔɪl] boy [bɔɪ]	etwa wie eu in neu
ʊə	poor [pʊə] tour /tʊə/	

Konsonanten

	Beispiele	Aussprache
j	year [jiə] few [fjuː]	wie j in Junge
w	want [wɔnt] way [weɪ]	
ŋ	gang [gæŋ] king [kɪŋ]	wie ng in lang
r	carry [ˈkæri] room [ruːm]	
s	sad [sæd] face [feɪs]	stimmloses s wie in Pasta
z	is /ɪz/ zero [ˈzɪərəʊ]	stimmhaftes s wie in Hase
ʃ	cash [kæʃ] station [ˈsteɪʃn]	wie sch in Schale
tʃ	chain [tʃeɪn] much [mʌtʃ]	wie tsch in Tschüss
ʒ	conclusion [kənˈkluːʒn]	
dʒ	jam [dʒæm] general [ˈdʒenrəl]	wie in Job
θ	month [mʌnθ] thanks [θæŋks]	
ð	this [ðɪs] father [ˈfɑːðə]	
v	drive [draɪv] very [ˈverɪ]	etwa wie w in wir

Betonungszeichen

ː bedeutet, dass der vorhergehende Vokal lang zu sprechen ist

ˈ Hauptbetonung (bedeutet, dass die nachfolgende Silbe betont gesprochen wird)

ˌ Nebenbetonung (bedeutet, dass die nachfolgende Silbe betont gesprochen wird)

So steuern Sie die Geschwindigkeit der Audiodateien

Das Buch ist mit den Audiodateien ausgestattet. Die Adresse der Homepage des Buches, wo Audiodateien zum Anhören und Herunterladen verfügbar sind, ist am Anfang des Buches auf der bibliographischen Beschreibung vor dem Copyright-Hinweis aufgeführt.

Wir empfehlen Ihnen, den kostenlosen VLC-Mediaplayer zu verwenden, die Software, die zur Steuerung der Wiedergabegeschwindigkeit aller Audioformate verwendet werden kann. Die Steuerung der Geschwindigkeit ist auch einfach und erfordert nur wenige Klicks oder Tastatureingaben.

Android: Nach der Installation vom VLC Media Player klicken Sie auf die Audiodatei am Anfang eines Kapitels oder auf der Homepage des Buches, wenn Sie ein Papierbuch lesen. Wählen Sie "Open with VLC". Wenn Sie Schwierigkeiten beim Öffnen von Audiodateien mit VLC haben, ändern Sie die Standard-App für den Musik-Player. Gehen Sie zu Einstellungen>Apps, wählen Sie VLC und klicken Sie auf "Open by default" oder "Set default".

Kindle Fire: Nach der Installation vom VLC Media Player klicken Sie auf eine Audiodatei am Anfang eines Kapitels oder auf der Homepage des Buches, wenn Sie ein Papierbuch lesen. Wählen Sie "Complete action using>VLC".

iOS: Nach der Installation vom VLC Media Player kopieren Sie den Link zu der Audiodatei am Anfang eines Kapitels oder auf der Homepage des Buches, wenn Sie ein Papierbuch lesen, und fügen Sie ihn in den Download-Bereich des VLC Media Players ein. Nachdem der Download abgeschlossen ist, gehen Sie zu "Alle Dateien" und starten Sie die Audiodatei.

Windows: Starten Sie den VLC Media Player und klicken Sie auf die Audiodatei am Anfang eines Kapitels oder auf der Homepage des Buches, wenn Sie ein Papierbuch lesen. Gehen Sie nun in die Wiedergabe (Playback) und navigieren Sie die Geschwindigkeit.

MacOS: Starten Sie den VLC Media Player und klicken Sie auf die Audiodatei am Anfang eines Kapitels oder auf der Homepage des Buches, wenn Sie ein Papierbuch lesen. Nun, navigieren Sie zum Playback und öffnen die Optionen von Geschwindigkeit. Navigieren Sie die Geschwindigkeit.

1

The Plural / Der Plural

Um im Englischen aus der Einzahl (Singular) eines Nomens die Mehrzahl (Plural) zu bilden, braucht man am Ende des Nomens einfach nur ein *-s* anzuhängen.

book [bʊk] - books [bʊks] (das Buch - die Bücher)

cup [kʌp] - cups [kʌps] (die Tasse - die Tassen)

bike [baɪk] - bikes [baɪks] (das Fahrrad - die Fahrräder)

lake [leɪk] - lakes [leɪks] (der See - die Seen)

Bei einigen Wörtern, die folgende (Doppel-)Konsonanten bzw. den folgenden Vokal am Ende haben *o, s, ss, x, sh oder ch*, setzt man für eine angenehmere Aussprache ein *-e* vor das *-s*.

bus [bʌs] - buses [ˈbʌsɪz] (der Bus - die Busse)

bush [bʊʃ] - bushes [ˈbʊʃɪz] (der Busch - die Büsche)

peach [piːtʃ] - peaches [ˈpiːtʃɪz] (der Pfirsich - die Pfirsiche)

box [bɔks] - boxes [ˈbɔksɪz] (die Schachtel - die Schachteln)

potato [pəˈteɪtoʊ] - potatoes [pəˈteɪtoʊz] (die Kartoffel - die Kartoffeln)

Es gibt eine Ausnahme bei Wörtern, die nach einem Konsonanten auf *-y* enden. Bei diesen Wörtern wird aus dem *-y* ein *-ie*.

baby [ˈbeɪbɪ] - babies [ˈbeɪbɪz] (das Baby - die Babies)

lady [ˈleɪdɪ] - ladies [ˈleɪdɪz] (die Dame - die Damen)

country [ˈkʌntrɪ] - countries [ˈkʌntrɪz] (das Land - die Länder)

Der Plural einiger Wörter ist unregelmäßig.

 child [tʃaɪld] - children [ˈtʃɪldrən] (das Kind - die Kinder)

 woman [ˈwʊmən] - women [ˈwɪmɪn] (die Frau - die Frauen)

 man [mæn] - men [men] (der Mann - die Männer)

 tooth [tuːθ] - teeth [tiːθ] (der Zahn - die Zähne)

 mouse [maʊs] - mice [maɪs] (die Maus - die Mäuse)

 foot [fʊt] - feet [fiːt] (der Fuß - die Füße)

 goose [guːs] - geese [giːs] (die Gans - die Gänse)

Es gibt Worte, die es nur in einer Form gibt.

 hair [heə] - das Haar

 fruit [fruːt] - das Obst, die Früchte

 sheep [ʃiːp] - das Schaf, die Schafe

 fish [fɪʃ] - der Fisch, die Fische

 information [ˌɪnfəˈmeɪʃn] - die Information, die Informationen

 furniture [ˈfɜːnɪtʃə] - die Möbel

 luggage [ˈlʌgɪdʒ] - das Gepäck

 trousers [ˈtraʊzəz] - die Hose, die Hosen

 clothes [kloʊðz] - die Kleidung

 scissors [ˈsɪzəz] - die Schere, die Scheren

 news [njuːz] - die Nachrichten

 stairs [steəz] - die Treppe

Bei einigen Wörtern ändert sich die Rechtschreibung im Plural. *F* oder *fe* am Wortende, wird zu *ves*.

knife [naɪf] - knives [naɪvz] (das Messer - die Messer)

life [laɪf] - lives [laɪvz] (das Leben - die Leben)

wife [waɪf] - wives [waɪvz] (die Ehefrau - die Ehefrauen)

thief [θiːf] - thieves [θiːvz] (der Dieb - die Diebe)

Es gibt Ausnahme:

roof [ruːf] - roofs [ruːfs] (das Dach - die Dächer)

Exercise 1-1 Put the nouns into the plural.
Übung 1-1 Setze die Nomen in den Plural.

1. cat ... cats
2. dog ....
3. book ....
4. box ....
5. player ....
6. computer ....
7. kiss ....
8. game ....
9. tomato ....
10. beach ....

Exercise 1-2 Put the nouns into the plural.
Übung 1-2 Setze die Nomen in den Plural.

1. baby babies
2. hair -
3. child ....
4. life ....
5. lady ....
6. fish ....
7. wife ....
8. man ....
9. woman ....
10. tooth ....

Reading comprehension

Robert has a dog
Robert hat einen Hund

A

Words
Vokabeln

1. and [ænd] - und
2. bed [bed] - das Bett
3. beds [bedz] - die Betten
4. big [bɪg] - groß
5. bike [baɪk] - das Fahrrad
6. black [blæk] - schwarz
7. blue [bluː] - blau
8. book [bʊk] - das Buch
9. cat [kæt] - die Katze
10. dog [dɔg] - der Hund
11. dream [driːm] - der Traum
12. eye [aɪ] - das Auge
13. eyes [aɪz] - die Augen
14. four [fɔː] - vier
15. green [griːn] - grün
16. have [hæv] - haben; he/she/it has [hæz] - er/sie/es hat; He has a book. - Er hat ein Buch.
17. he [hiː] - er
18. his [hɪz] - sein, seine; his bed - sein Bett
19. hotel [həʊˈtel] - das Hotel
20. hotels [həʊˈtelz] - die Hotels
21. I [aɪ] - ich
22. little [lɪtl] - klein
23. many [ˈmenɪ] - viele
24. my [maɪ] - mein, meine, mein
25. new [njuː] - neu
26. nice [naɪs] - schön
27. nose [nəʊz] - die Nase
28. not [nɔt] - nicht
29. notebook [ˈnəʊtbʊk] - das Notizbuch
30. notebooks [ˈnəʊtbʊks] - die Notizbücher
31. one [wʌn] - ein
32. park [pɑːk] - der Park
33. parks [pɑːks] - die Parks
34. pen [pen] - der Stift
35. pens [pens] - die Stifte
36. room [ruːm] - das Zimmer
37. rooms [ruːmz] - die Zimmer
38. shop [ʃɔp] - der Laden

39. shops [ʃɔps] - die Läden
40. star [stɑː] - der Stern
41. street [striːt] - die Straße
42. streets [striːts] - die Straßen
43. student [ˈstjuːd(ə)nt] - der Student
44. students [ˈstjuːd(ə)nts] - die Studenten
45. table [ˈteɪbl] - der Tisch
46. tables [ˈteɪblz] - die Tische
47. text [tekst] - der Text
48. that [ðæt] - jener, jene, jenes
49. these [ðiːz] - diese (Pl.)
50. those [ðəʊz] - jene (Pl.)
51. they [ðeɪ] - sie
52. this [ðɪz] - dieser, diese, dieses
53. this book - dieses Buch
54. too [tuː] - auch
55. window [ˈwɪndəʊ] - das Fenster
56. windows [ˈwɪndəʊz] - die Fenster
57. word [wəːd] - das Wort, die Vokabel
58. words [wəːdz] - die Wörter, die

 B

Robert has a dog

1.This student has a book. 2.He has a pen too.

3.San Francisco has many streets and parks. 4.This street has new hotels and shops. 5.This hotel has four stars. 6.This hotel has many nice big rooms.

7.That room has many windows. 8.And these rooms do not have many windows. 9.These rooms have four beds. 10.And those rooms have one bed. 11.That room does not have many tables. 12.And those rooms have many big tables.

13.This street does not have hotels. 14.That big shop has many windows.

15.These students have notebooks. 16.They have pens too. 17.Robert has one little black notebook. 18.Paul has four new green notebooks.

19.This student has a bike. 20.He has a new blue bike. 21.David has a bike too. 22.He has a nice black bike. 23.Paul has a dream. 24.I have a dream too. 25.I do not have a dog. 26.I have a cat. 27.My cat has nice green eyes. 28.Robert does not have a cat. 29.He has a dog. 30.His dog has a little black nose.

Robert hat einen Hund

1.Dieser Student hat ein Buch. 2.Er hat auch einen Stift.

3.San Francisco hat viele Straßen und Parks. 4.Diese Straße hat neue Hotels und Läden. 5.Dieses Hotel hat vier Sterne. 6.Dieses Hotel hat viele schöne, große Zimmer.

7.Jenes Zimmer hat viele Fenster. 8.Und diese Zimmer haben nicht viele Fenster. 9.Diese Zimmer haben vier Betten. 10.Und diese Zimmer haben ein Bett. 11.Jenes Zimmer hat nicht viele Tische. 12.Und diese Zimmer haben viele große Tische.

13.In dieser Straße sind keine Hotels. 14.Dieser große Laden hat viele Fenster.

15.Diese Studenten haben Notizbücher. 16.Sie haben auch Stifte. 17.Robert hat ein kleines schwarzes Notizbuch. 18.Paul hat vier neue grüne Notizbücher.

19.Dieser Student hat ein Fahrrad. 20.Er hat ein neues blaues Fahrrad. 21.David hat auch ein Fahrrad. 22.Er hat ein schönes schwarzes Fahrrad. 23.Paul hat einen Traum. 24.Ich habe auch einen Traum. 25.Ich habe keinen Hund. 26.Ich habe eine Katze. 27.Meine Katze hat schöne grüne Augen. 28.Robert hat keine Katze. 29.Er hat einen Hund. 30.Sein Hund hat eine kleine schwarze Nase.

2

The indefinite Article / Der unbestimmte Artikel

Substantive müssen im Deutschen dekliniert werden, d.h. sie müssen entsprechend der vier Fälle (Nominativ, Genitiv, Dativ oder Akkusativ) gebeugt werden. Dass kann dazu führen, dass die deutsche Sprache beim Erlernen oft als schwer empfunden wird. Allerdings ist das Deutsche dabei nicht allein und es gibt noch einige weitere Sprachen, wie z.B. Finnisch, Russisch u.v.m., die durch ihre Grammatik, als schwer erlernbar empfunden werden können. Im Englischen haben wir es da zum Glück deutlich leichter, da den Substantiven lediglich Präpositionen beigefügt werden müssen, um sie grammatisch zu klären.

Anders, als im Deutschen werden auch Substantive im Englischen alle klein geschrieben. Lediglich Eigennamen bilden hier eine Ausnahme und werden auch im Englischen groß geschrieben.

Bestimmte und unbestimmte Artikel helfen uns, genauer festzulegen, ob es sich um irgendeine Person, irgendein Objekt handelt oder, ob es sich um eine bestimmte Person, ein bestimmtes Objekt handelt. Ist es *ein* Fischgeschäft oder ist es *das* stadtbekannte Fischgeschäft? Der, die, das bilden im Deutschen die bestimmten Artikel, ein und eine sind die unbestimmten Artikel. Wie sich bereits leicht von den Begriffen ableiten lässt, handelt es sich bei dem unbestimmten Artikel um einen Artikel, der das Substantiv nicht näher definiert bzw. bestimmt (eine Schule, ein Kind, ein Hammer). Der bestimmte Artikel hingegen definiert bzw. bestimmt das Substantiv genau (die Schule, das Kind, der Hammer).

Da im Deutschen die Substantive entsprechend der vier Fälle gebeugt, bzw. dekliniert werden, ergibt sich bereits für ein einziges Substantiv eine Vielzahl an Artikeln (der Vater, dem Vater, den Vater, des Vaters).

Im Englischen ist es da einfacher. Es gibt lediglich einen bestimmten Artikel, nämlich *the* und einen unbestimmten Artikel, nämlich *a*. Die Artikel brauchen sich auch nicht zu ändern, da die Substantive über die Präpositionen dekliniert werden.

Den englischen unbestimmten Artikel *a* übersetzen wir im Deutschen mit ein oder eine. So, wie im Deutschen auch wird der unbestimmte Artikel nur in Einzahl verwendet.

     a father [ə ˈfɑːðə] - ein Vater

     a mother [ə ˈmʌðə] - eine Mutter

     a cat [ə kæt] - eine Katze

Der Artikel wird dem Substantiv und den Beschreibungen des Substantivs vorangestellt.

     a girl [ə gɜːl] - ein Mädchen

     a clever girl [ə ˈklevə gɜːl] - ein kluges Mädchen

     a clever and pretty girl [ə ˈklevər ənd ˈprɪti gɜːl] - ein kluges und hübsches Mädchen

Wenn man nun unbestimmte Dinge in der Mehrzahl beschreiben möchte, kann man nicht den unbestimmten Artikel verwenden, sondern muss auf anzahlbeschreibende Begriffe zurückgreifen, wie z.B. a couple of (ein paar), some (einige, etwas), a lot of (viel, viele), many (viele) usw.

Im Englischen ist es genau, wie im Deutschen so, dass der unbestimmte Artikel nur dann verwendet wird, wenn es sich um zählbare Objekte/Personen handelt. Um es etwas anschaulicher zu machen: anstatt *ein Zucker*, würde man von einem *Teelöffel Zucker* sprechen, statt *eine Milch*, würde man sagen *etwas Milch* oder statt *ein Rauch*, würde man festhalten, dass es sich um *sehr viel Rauch* handelt und sich somit bestimmenden Maßangaben bedienen.

Falsch	Richtig	
a sugar	a teaspoon of sugar	ein Teelöffel Zucker
a milk	some milk	etwas Milch
a smoke	a lot of smoke	ganz viel Rauch

Für den unbestimmten Artikel a im Englischen gibt es eine kleine, aber nicht unwesentliche Besonderheit, um die Aussprache zu erleichtern, d.h. sobald auf den unbestimmten Artikel a ein Wort folgt, das mit einem Vokal beginnt, wird aus a - an.

an apple [ən ˈæpl] - ein Apfel

a sweet apple [ə swiːt ˈæpl] - ein süßer Apfel

a man [ə mæn] - ein Mann

an old man [ən oʊld mæn] - ein alter Mann

Die Ausnahmen dafür sind Wörter deren Aussprache mit [ju] beginnt.

a university [ə juːnɪˈvɜːsɪtɪ] - eine Universität

a Euro [ə jʊro] - ein Euro

Sprechabsichten

▶ vor Substantiven, die bis dahin im Gespräch noch nicht erwähnt wurden

I have a new book. - Ich habe ein neues Buch.

▶ vor Substantiven, die den Beruf, den Rang, die Nationalität oder die Religion beschreiben

Brian is a teacher. - Brian ist Lehrer.

His uncle is a lawyer. - Sein Onkel ist Anwalt.

His wife is a Christian. - Seine Frau ist Christin.

▶ als Verallgemeinerung

    A shark is a dangerous animal. - Haie sind gefährliche Tiere. (Ein Hai ist ein gefährliches Tier)

    A car is an expensive vehicle. - Autos sind teure Fahrzeuge. (Ein Auto ist ein teures Fahrzeug)

Exercise 2 Put in a, an or some, but only where necessary.

Übung 2 Setze a, an oder some ein, aber nur, wenn notwendig.

Wortschatz: this [ðis] - das, is [iz] - ist, some [sʌm] - etwas / einige, dog [dɔg] - Hund, book [buk] - Buch, water [ˈwɔːtə] - Wasser, cup [kʌp] - Tasse, apple [ˈæpl] - Apfel, orange [ˈɔrindʒ] - Orange, money [ˈmʌni] - Geld, old [ould] - alt, new [njuː] - neu, big [big] - gross

1. This is a dog.
2. This is an old dog.
3. This is .... book.
4. This is .... old book.
5. This is .... water.
6. This is .... cup.
7. This is .... old cup.
8. This is .... apple.
9. This is .... big apple.
10. This is .... money.
11. This is .... orange.
12. This is .... big orange.

3

The definite Article / Der bestimmte Artikel

Der bestimmte Artikel *the* ist etwas unkomplizierter und kann unabhängig von Singular oder Plural, sowie bestimmter oder unbestimmter Anzahl und Art des Substantivs eingesetzt werden.

    the tree / the trees - der Baum / die Bäume

    the table / the tables - der Tisch / die Tische

    the cup / the cups - die Tasse / die Tassen

Jedoch kommt es auch bei der Aussprache des bestimmten Artikels darauf an, ob das darauffolgende Wort mit einem Vokal beginnt oder nicht. Wenn das nächste Wort mit einem Vokal beginnt, dann wird aus dem kurzen offenen *e* von *the* in der Aussprache ein *i*. Diese Besonderheit bezieht sich aber eher auf das britische Englisch und wird im amerikanischen Englisch zunehmend mehr ignoriert.

> the apple [ðɪ ˈæpəl] - der Apfel
>
> the sweet apple [ðə swiːt ˈæpəl] - der süße Apfel
>
> the man [ðə mæn] - der Mann
>
> the old man [ðɪ oʊld mæn] - der alte Mann

Bestimmte Artikel werden in der Regel dann verwendet, wenn alle Gesprächsbeteiligten wissen, worum es sich bei dem bestimmten Begriff handelt.

Sprechabsichten

▶ wenn der Begriff vorher bereits mit einem unbestimmten Artikel oder ohne Artikel verwendet wurde

> I have a book. The book is interesting. - Ich habe ein Buch. Das Buch ist interessant.
>
> They live in a house. The house is big. - Sie wohnen in einem Haus. Das Haus ist groß.
>
> She has some pens. The pens are new. - Sie hat einige Kugelschreiber. Die Kugelschreiber sind neu.

▶ wenn von allgemein bekannten Dingen die Rede ist

> The weather is nice. - Das Wetter ist schön.
>
> The sky is blue. - Der Himmel ist blau.
>
> The sun is shining. - Die Sonne scheint.

▶ bei Verallgemeinerungen

>The tiger is a big animal. - Der Tiger ist ein großes Tier. (Tiger sind groß)

>The winter is very cold in Canada. - Der Winter in Kanada ist sehr kalt. (Winter in Kanada sind sehr kalt)

▶ bei Substantivierung von Adjektiven in der Mehrzahl

>the old and the young - die Alten und die Jungen

>the stupid and the intelligent - die Dummen und die Intelligenten

▶ bei (Himmels-)Richtungen in Verbindung mit Präpositionen

>The park is on the left. - Der Park ist links.

>Finland is in the north. - Finnland ist im Norden.

>Spain is in the south. - Spanien ist im Süden.

▶ in bestimmten Redewendungen

>the right answer / direction - die richtige Antwort / Richtung

>the usual tasks / days - die üblichen Aufgaben / Tage

>the previous version of Windows - die vorherige Version von Windows

▶ bei Flüssen und Meeren sowie bei Eigennamen in der Mehrzahl

>The Baltic Sea is cold. - Die Ostsee ist kalt.

>The Atlantic is a big ocean. - Der Atlantik ist ein großer Ozean.

>The Bahamas are exotic. - Die Bahamas sind exotisch.

>The Netherlands are beautiful. - Die Niederlande sind schön.

>The United States are big. - Die Vereinigten Staaten sind groß.

▶ bei Eigennamen, die Republic, Union, Föderation oder Kingdom beinhalten

The United Kingdom is an island state. - Das Vereinigte Königreich ist ein Inselstaat.

The Irish Republic is a European country. - Die Irische Republik ist ein europäischer Staat.

Exercise 3-1 Put in a, an, the or some, but only where necessary.

Übung 3-1 Setze a, an, the oder some ein, aber nur, wenn notwendig.

Wortschatz: this [ðis] - das, is [iz] - ist, some [sʌm] - etwas / einige, dog [dɔg] - Hund, book [buk] - Buch, paper [ˈpeipə] - Papier, water [ˈwɔːtə] - Wasser, cup [kʌp] - Tasse, apple [ˈæpl] - Apfel, orange [ˈɔrindʒ] - Orange, old [ould] - alt, new [njuː] - neu, big [big] - gross, little [ˈlitl] - klein, car [kɑː] - Wagen, interesting [ˈintrəstiŋ] - interessant, white [wait] - weiss, clean [kliːn] - sauber / rein, cat [kæt] - Katze, house [ˈhaus] - Haus

1. This is a dog. The dog is little.
2. This is an old car. The car is clean.
3. This is ………… interesting book. ………… book is new.
4. This is ………… paper. ………… paper is white.
5. This is ………… water. ………… water is clean.
6. This is ………… cup. ………… cup is big.
7. This is ………… orange. ………… orange is little.
8. This is ………… apple. ………… apple is big.
9. This is ………… cat. ………… cat is white.
10. This is ………… old house. ………… house is little.

Exercise 3-2 Put in a, an or the, but only where necessary.

Übung 3-2 Setze a, an oder the ein, aber nur, wenn notwendig.

1. ………… sun is ………… star.
2. ………… United Kingdom is in Europe.
3. ………… dog is ………… animal.
4. ………… Bahamas are in ………… south.
5. ………… Atlantic is ………… big ocean.

6. This is .... right answer.
7. .... sky is blue.
8. .... United States are big.
9. .... Federal Republic of Germany is in .... European Union.
10. The hotel is on .... right.

No article / Kein Artikel

Im Deutschen, wie auch im Englischen wird in manchen Fällen weder ein bestimmter, noch ein unbestimmter Artikel gebraucht. Vor abstrakten Wörtern und Substantiven, die eine Einheit bezeichnen, wie z.B. Wind oder auch Eigennamen wird im Englischen kein Artikel verwandt. Die deutsche Sprache kann in diesen beiden Punkten abweichen.

Sprechabsichten

▶ im Allgemeinen vor abstrakten Begriffen und bei unteilbaren Einzahlwörtern

Im Englischen verwendet man keinen Artikel vor abstrakten Begriffen und Substantiven, wie z.B. Wasser, Luft, Feuer usw. Im Deutschen kann man hingegen einen Artikel setzen, wenn man möchte.

Music is important to me. - Musik ist wichtig für mich.

He learns at school. - Er lernt in (der) Schule.

▶ bei bestimmten Eigennamen

Im Englischen werden Feiertagen (Weihnachten, Ostern usw.), Monaten (Januar, Juli usw.), Tagen (Montag, Freitag usw.), sowie Mahlzeiten (Mittagessen, Abendessen usw.) keine Artikel vorangestellt. Auch Straßennamen, Seen und Berge im Singular werden nicht von Artikeln begleitet:

Lake Starnberg is in Germany. - Der Starnberger See ist in Deutschland.

Mount Everest is the highest mountain in the world. - Der Mount Everest ist der höchste Berg der Erde.

My birthday is in January. - Mein Geburtstag ist im Januar.

Let's meet on Sunday. - Wollen wir uns am Sonntag treffen.

Ausnahmen

▶ Seen und Bergen im Plural

The Alps are high. - Die Alpen sind hoch.

The Great Lakes are in the US. - Die Großen Seen sind in den USA.

▶ Mahlzeiten mit Adjektiv

This is a delicious breakfast. - Das ist ein leckeres Frühstück.

We had a vegetarian dinner. - Wir hatten ein vegetarisches Abendessen.

Zusammenfassung bestimmte versus unbestimmte versus kein Artikel

	ohne Artikel	unbestimmter Artikel	bestimmter Artikel	
	Einzahl und Mehrzahl	Einzahl	Einzahl	Mehrzahl
Verallgemeinerungen	Dogs are clever animals.	A dog is a clever animal.	The dog is a clever animal.	The clever and the silly.
allgemein bekannte Begriffe			the sky the moon	
genauer definierte Begriffe			the boy with a book	the people in the room
noch nicht erwähnt		I have a cat.		
bereits erwähnt			The cat is black.	The eyes are green.

	ohne Artikel	unbestimmter Artikel	bestimmter Artikel	
	Einzahl und Mehrzahl	Einzahl	Einzahl	Mehrzahl
unteilbare Begriffe	sugar, milk, oil		The ice of Antarctica	
Berufe, Titel, Ränge	Dr. Tanner, Princess Diana	He is a policeman.	Mr. Kent, the policeman, is a serious person.	The police are after him.
Institutionen	to learn at university	a university (Gebäude)	the university (Gebäude)	the universities in this region
(Jahres-) Zeitangaben	in winter, at noon	on a windy day	the day after tomorrow	the days I spent with you
(Himmels-) Richtungen			to the south	
Eigennamen (von u.a. Mahlzeiten)	we have dinner at six	a delicious dinner		
Preis- und Zeitausdrücke		5 Euro a liter		

Exercise 3-3 Put in a, an, the or some, but only where necessary.

Übung 3-3 Setze a, an, the oder some ein, aber nur, wenn notwendig.

Wortschatz: learn [lɜːn] - lernen, school [skuːl] - Schule, I [ˈai] - ich, my [mai] - mein, birthday [ˈbɜːθdei] - Geburtstag, in [in] - in, May [mei] - Mai, like [ˈlaik] - mögen, need [niːd] - brauchen, Monday [ˈmʌndei] - Montag, after [ˈɑːftə] - nach, Sunday [ˈsʌndei] - Sonntag, breakfast [ˈbrekfəst] - Frühstück, nice [nais] - schön / nett, milk [milk] - Milch

1. The cat is a little animal.
2. I like music.
3. I learn at ……………… school.
4. I learn at …………… new school.
5. My birthday is in …………… May.
6. I like ……………… Christmas.
7. I need ……………… new car.
8. I like ………… interesting books.
9. I need ……………… clean water.
10. …. Monday is after ….. Sunday.

11. I like .... breakfast.

12. It is .... nice breakfast.

13. My house is in ..... Wall Street.

14. .... milk is white.

Reading comprehension

They live in San Francisco (the USA)
Sie wohnen in San Francisco (USA)

Words
Vokabeln

1. American [əˈmerɪkən] - Amerikaner
2. big [bɪg] - groß
3. brother [ˈbrʌðə] - der Bruder
4. buy [baɪ] - kaufen
5. Canada [ˈkænədə] - Kanada
6. Canadian [kəˈneɪdɪən] - Kanadier
7. city [ˈsɪtɪ] - die Stadt
8. from [frɔm] - aus
9. from the USA - aus den USA
10. German [ˈdʒɜːmən] - der Deutsche, die Deutsche
11. hungry [ˈhʌŋgrɪ] - hungrig; I am hungry. - Ich habe Hunger.
12. in [ɪn] - in
13. live [lɪv] - leben, wohnen
14. mother [ˈmʌðə] - die Mutter
15. now [naʊ] - jetzt, zurzeit, gerade
16. sandwich [ˈsæn(d)wɪtʃ] - das Sandwich
17. she [ʃiː] - sie
18. sister [ˈsɪstə] - die Schwester
19. supermarket [ˈsʊpəˌmɑːkɪt] - der Supermarkt
20. two [tuː] - zwei
21. USA - USA
22. we [wɪ] - wir
23. you [ju] - du

B

They live in San Francisco (USA)

1.San Francisco is a big city. 2.San Francisco is in the USA.

3.This is Robert. 4.Robert is a student. 5.He is in San Francisco now. 6.Robert is from Germany. 7.He is German. 8.Robert has a mother, a father, a brother and a sister. 9.They live in Germany.

10.This is Paul. 11.Paul is a student too. 12.He is from Canada. 13.He is Canadian. 14.Paul has a mother, a father and two sisters. 15.They live in Canada.

16.Robert and Paul are in a supermarket now. 17.They are hungry. 18.They buy sandwiches.

19.This is Linda. 20.Linda is American. 21.Linda lives in San Francisco too. 22.She is not a student.

23.I am a student. 24.I am from Germany. 25.I am in San Francisco now. 26.I am not hungry.

27.You are a student. 28.You are German. 29.You are not in Germany now. 30.You are in the USA.

31.We are students. 32.We are in the USA now.

33.This is a bike. 34.The bike is blue. 35.The bike is not new.

36.This is a dog. 37.The dog is black. 38.The dog is not big.

39.These are shops. 40.The shops are not big. 41.They are little. 42.That shop has many windows. 43.Those shops do not have many windows.

44.That cat is in the room. 45.Those cats are not in the room.

Sie wohnen in San Francisco (USA)

1.San Francisco ist eine große Stadt. 2.San Francisco ist in den USA.

3.Das ist Robert. 4.Robert ist Student. 5.Er ist zurzeit in San Francisco. 6.Robert kommt aus Deutschland. 7.Er ist Deutscher. 8.Robert hat eine Mutter, einen Vater, einen Bruder und eine Schwester. 9.Sie leben in Deutschland.

10.Das ist Paul. 11.Paul ist auch Student. 12.Er kommt aus Kanada. 13.Er ist Kanadier. 14.Paul hat eine Mutter, einen Vater und zwei Schwestern. 15.Sie leben in Kanada.

16.Robert und Paul sind gerade im Supermarkt. 17.Sie haben Hunger. 18.Sie kaufen Sandwiches.

19.Das ist Linda. 20.Linda ist Amerikanerin. 21.Linda wohnt auch in San Francisco. 22.Sie ist kein Student.

23.Ich bin Student. 24.Ich komme aus Deutschland. 25.Ich bin zurzeit in San Francisco. 26.Ich habe keinen Hunger.

27.Du bist Student. 28.Du bist Deutsche. 29.Du bist zurzeit nicht in Deutschland. 30.Du bist in den USA.

31.Wir sind Studenten. 32.Wir sind zurzeit in den USA.

33.Dies ist ein Fahrrad. 34.Das Fahrrad ist blau. 35.Das Fahrrad ist nicht neu.

36.Dies ist ein Hund. 37.Der Hund ist schwarz. 38.Der Hund ist nicht groß.

39.Dies sind Läden. 40.Die Läden sind nicht groß. 41.Sie sind klein. 42.Dieser Laden hat viele Fenster. 43.Jene Läden haben nicht viele Fenster.

44.Die Katze ist im Zimmer. 45.Diese Katzen sind nicht im Zimmer.

Verb Conjugation in Present Simple / Konjugation der Verben im Präsens

Verben werden im Deutschen auch gerne als Tuwörter bezeichnet. Durch diese Bezeichnung wird uns direkt klar, worin ihre Aufgabe besteht.

Abgesehen von der 3. Person Singular, die durch ein angehängtes –s abweicht, entspricht die finite Form in der Gegenwart exakt dem Infinitiv (Grundform).

to run - rennen

Präsens	Singular	Einzahl	Plural	Mehrzahl
1. Person	I run	ich renne	we run	wir rennen
2. Person	you run	du rennst	you run	ihr rennt, Sie rennen
3. Person	he / she / it runs	er / sie / es rennt	they run	sie rennen

to hunt - jagen

Präsens	Singular	Einzahl	Plural	Mehrzahl
1. Person	I hunt	ich jage	we hunt	wir jagen
2. Person	you hunt	du jagst	you hunt	ihr jagt, Sie jagen
3. Person	he / she / it hunts	er / sie / es jagt	they hunt	sie jagen

to drink - trinken

Präsens	Singular	Einzahl	Plural	Mehrzahl
1. Person	I drink	ich trinke	we drink	wir trinken
2. Person	you drink	du trinkst	you drink	ihr trinkt, Sie trinken
3. Person	he / she / it drinks	er / sie / es trinkt	they drink	sie trinken

Durch die obige Tabellen fällt auf, dass es in der englischen Sprache keine Höflichkeitsform, bzw. die Möglichkeit eine Person zu siezen gibt (Wie heißen Sie?). Im Englischen wird dafür alternativ die 2. Person Singular/Plural benutzt. In anderen Worten: Sobald man 'you' sagt, meint man sowohl 'du', als auch 'Sie'.

Exercise 4 Put the ending -s where necessary.
Übung 4 Setze die Endung -s ein, aber nur, wenn notwendig.

Wortschatz: cat [kæt] - Katze, book [buk] - Buch, too [tuː] - auch, park [pɑːk] - Park

1. (like) I like this cat.
2. (like) He likes this cat too.
3. (drink) She ………………………… some milk.
4. (drink) I ………………………… some water.
5. (learn) He ………………………… on Monday.
6. (learn) We ………………………… on Monday too.
7. (need) I ………………………… a book.
8. (need) She ………………………… a book too.
9. (run) He ………………………… in park.
10. (run) They ………………………… in park too.

5

The irregular Verbs have and be / Die unregelmäßige Verben have und be

Es gibt zwei Verben, die vollkommen unregelmäßig sind, deren finite Formen sich auch im Präsens vollkommen vom Infinitiv (Grundform) unterscheiden: be (sein) und have (haben).

to be

Präsens	Singular	Einzahl	Plural	Mehrzahl
1. Person	I am	ich bin	we are	wir sind
2. Person	you are	du bist / Sie sind	you are	ihr seid, Sie sind
3. Person	he / she / it is	er / sie / es ist	they are	sie sind

to have

Präsens	Singular	Einzahl	Plural	Mehrzahl
1. Person	I have	ich habe	we have	wir haben
2. Person	you have	du hast / Sie haben	you have	ihr habt, Sie haben
3. Person	he / she / it has	er / sie / es hat	they have	sie haben

Exercise 5 Put the verbs in brackets in the correct form.

Übung 5 Setze die Verben in Klammern in die richtige Form.

1. (have) He has a house.
2. (be) I am in the park
3. (have) You .... a house.
4. (have) She .... a house too.
5. (be) You .... in the house.
6. (be) We .... in the house too.
7. (have) We .... a cat.
8. (have) They .... a cat too.
9. (be) She .... a students.
10. (be) I .... a student too.

6

Questions with auxiliary or modal Verbs / Fragesätze mit Hilfs- oder Modalverben

Die meisten Sätze, die wir im Alltag formulieren sind Aussagesätze. Das heißt wir machen eine Aussage bzw. eine Feststellung. Daneben gibt es auch noch Frage- und Befehlssätze. Die Struktur eines Aussagesatzes im Englischen ist wie folgt

Subjekt - Verb/Prädikat - Objekt

Mit Subjekt wird dabei die handelnde Person in einem aktivischen Satz bezeichnet. Das Prädikat steht für das Verb, also die ausgeführte Handlung des Subjekts. Das Objekt ist dann der Gegenstand oder die Person, auf die sich das Verb/Prädikat bezieht.

>Subjekt - Verb/Prädikat - Objekt
>
>I have a book. - Ich habe ein Buch.

Um sich das Ganze etwas leichter zu machen, kann man sich schlicht die Formel S-P-O bzw. S-V-O merken, da sich diese immer wiederholt. Es gibt natürlich auch hier Ausnahmen, die wir später noch näher behandeln werden.

Im Englischen gelten dieselbe Regeln, wie im Deutschen, wenn es um die Inversion (Umkehrung der normalen Reihenfolge) Subjekt-Verb geht.

>She is French. - Sie ist Französin.
>
>Is she French? - Ist sie Französin?

Wenn der Satz bereits über ein der folgende sechs Hilfs- oder Modalverben verfügt, dann folgt das Subjekt genau, wie im Deutschen auf dieses Modal- oder Hilfsverb

can - können, may - dürfen, must - müssen, be - sein, will - werden, shall - sollen

>She can swim. - Sie kann schwimmen.
>
>Can she swim? - Kann sie schwimmen?
>
>He is a student. - Er ist Student.
>
>Is he a student? - Ist er Student?

Exercise 6 Make questions as in the example.

Übung 6 Bilde Fragen nach dem Beispiel.

>Wortschatz: his [hɪz] - sein, birthday [ˈbɜːθdeɪ] - Geburtstag, in [ɪn] - in, May [meɪ] - Mai, breakfast [ˈbrekfəst] - Frühstück, tasty [ˈteɪsti] - lecker, this [ðɪs] - diese, man [mæn] - Mann, woman [ˈwumən] - Frau, teacher [ˈtiːtʃə] - Lehrer, doctor [ˈdɔktə] - Arzt

1. The car is little. ... Is the car little?
2. His birthday is in May. ....
3. The book is interesting. ....
4. The cat is white. ....

5. The house is clean. ....
6. The breakfast is tasty. ....
7. This man is a teacher. ....
8. This woman is a doctor. ....
9. This car is clean. ....
10. The doctor is in the house. ....

Reading comprehension

Are they Germans?
Sind sie Deutsche?

Words
Vokabeln

1. all [ɔːl] - alle
2. animal [ˈænɪm(ə)l] - das Tier
3. at [æt] - am, beim
4. boy [bɔɪ] - der Junge
5. café [ˈkæfeɪ] - das Café
6. CD player [ˌsiːˈdiːˌpleɪə] - der CD-Spieler
7. her [həː] book - ihr Buch
8. house [haʊs] - das Haus
9. how [haʊ] - wie
10. it [ɪt] - es
11. man [mæn] - der Mann
12. map [mæp] - die Karte
13. no [nəʊ] - nein
14. on [ɔn] - auf
15. our [ˈaʊə] - unser
16. Spanish [ˈspænɪʃ] - spanisch
17. where [(h)weə] - wo
18. woman [ˈwʊmən] - die Frau
19. yes [jes] - ja
20. you [juː] - du/ihr

Are they Germans?	**Sind sie Deutsche?**
- I am a boy. I am in the room.	- Ich bin ein Junge. Ich bin im Zimmer.
- Are you American?	- Bist du Amerikaner?
- No, I am not. I am German.	- Nein, ich bin nicht Amerikaner. Ich bin Deutscher.
- Are you a student?	- Bist du Student?
- Yes, I am. I am a student.	- Ja, ich bin Student.
- This is a woman. The woman is in the room too.	- Das ist eine Frau. Die Frau ist auch im Zimmer.
- Is she German?	- Ist sie Deutsche?
- No, she is not. She is American.	- Nein, sie ist nicht Deutsche. Sie ist Amerikanerin.
- Is she a student?	- Ist sie Studentin?
- No, she is not. She is not a student.	- Nein, sie ist nicht Studentin.
- This is a man. He is at the table.	- Das ist ein Mann. Er sitzt am Tisch.
- Is he American?	- Ist er Amerikaner?
- Yes, he is. He is American.	- Ja, er ist Amerikaner.
- These are students. They are in the park.	- Das sind Studenten. Sie sind im Park.
- Are they all Americans?	- Sind sie alle Amerikaner?
- No, they are not. They are from Germany, the USA and Canada.	- Nein, sie sind nicht alle Amerikaner. Sie kommen aus Deutschland, den USA und Kanada.
- This is a table. It is big.	- Das ist ein Tisch. Er ist groß.
- Is it new?	- Ist er neu?
- Yes, it is. It is new.	- Ja, er ist neu.
- This is a cat. It is in the room.	- Das ist eine Katze. Sie ist im Zimmer.
- Is it black?	- Ist sie schwarz?
- Yes, it is. It is black and nice.	- Ja, das ist sie. Sie ist schwarz und schön.
- These are bikes. They are at the house.	- Das sind Fahrräder. Sie stehen beim Haus.
- Are they black?	- Sind sie schwarz?
- Yes, they are. They are black.	- Ja, sie sind schwarz.
- Do you have a notebook?	- Hast du ein Notizbuch?
- Yes, I have.	- Ja.
- How many notebooks have you?	- Wie viele Notizbücher hast du?
- I have two notebooks.	- Ich habe zwei Notizbücher.
- Does he have a pen?	- Hat er einen Stift?
- Yes, he has.	- Ja.
- How many pens have he?	- Wie viele Stifte hat er?
- He has one pen.	- Er hat einen Stift.
- Does she have a bike?	- Hat sie ein Fahrrad?
- Yes, she has.	- Ja.
- Is her bike blue?	- Ist ihr Fahrrad blau?

- No, it is not. Her bike is not blue. It is green.	- *Nein, es ist nicht blau. Es ist grün.*
- Do you have a Spanish book? - No, I do not. I do not have a Spanish book. I have no books.	- *Hast du ein spanisches Buch?* - *Nein, ich habe kein spanisches Buch. Ich habe keine Bücher.*
- Does she have a cat? - No, she does not. She does not have a cat. She has no animal.	- *Hat sie eine Katze?* - *Nein, sie hat keine Katze. Sie hat kein Tier.*
- Do you have a CD player? - No, we do not. We do not have a CD player.	- *Habt ihr einen CD-Spieler?* - *Nein, wir haben keinen CD-Spieler.*
- Where is our map? - Our map is in the room. - Is it on the table? - Yes, it is.	- *Wo ist unsere Karte?* - *Unsere Karte ist im Zimmer.* - *Liegt sie auf dem Tisch?* - *Ja, sie liegt auf dem Tisch.*
- Where are the boys? - They are in the café. - Where are the bikes? - They are at the café. - Where is Paul? - He is in the café too.	- *Wo sind die Jungs?* - *Sie sind im Café.* - *Wo sind die Fahrräder?* - *Sie stehen vor dem Café.* - *Wo ist Paul?* - *Er ist auch im Café.*

7

Modal Verbs and the Infinitive / Modale Hilfsverben und der Infinitiv

Der Infinitiv ist die Grundform des Verbs. Der Infinitiv ist, was wir in einem Wörterbuch finden. Der Infinitiv wird mit to signalisiert.

I want to be a doctor. - Ich will Arzt werden.

They like to play tennis. - Sie lieben es Tennis zu spielen.

Der Infinitiv mit modalen Hilfsverben can (können), may (dürfen), must (müssen), need (brauchen), shall (sollen), will (werden) verwendet man ohne 'to'.

I can play tennis. - Ich kann Tennis spielen.

We can read now. - Wir können jetzt lesen.

I must cook now. - Ich muss jetzt kochen.

Modale Hilfsverben haben kein *-s* in der 3. Person Singular.

He can swim. - Er kann schwimmen.

She must cook. - Sie muss kochen.

Bei Fragen muss ein modales Hilfsverb vor dem Subjekt stehen. Bei verneinten Aussagen mit *not* muss das Hilfsverb stets vor diesem platziert werden.

Can she play tennis? - Kann sie Tennis spielen?

She cannot play tennis. - Sie kann nicht Tennis spielen.

Must I cook today? - Muss ich heute kochen?

You need not cook today. - Du brauchst heute nicht zu kochen.

can / können

	Singular		Plural	
1. Person	I can	ich kann	we can	wir können
2. Person	you can	du kannst	you can	Sie können / ihr könnt
3. Person	he / she / it can	er / sie / es kann	they can	sie können

Can kann mit not zusammen oder getrennt geschrieben sein:

Can we play now? - Können wir jetzt spielen?

We cannot play now. - Wir können jetzt nicht spielen.

Can he swim? - Kann er schwimmen?

He can not swim. - Er kann nicht schwimmen.

Sprechabsichten

▶ Fähigkeit

I can swim. - Ich kann schwimmen.

▶ Unfähigkeit

    She cannot swim. - Sie kann nicht schwimmen.

▶ Bitte um Erlaubnis

    Can I take this cup, please? - Kann ich diese Tasse nehmen, bitte?

▶ Vorschlag / Angebot

    You can take a cup and a spoon. - Sie können eine Tasse und ein Löffel nehmen.

▶ Zukünftige Möglichkeit

    She can go to Spain in summer. - Sie kann in Sommer nach Spanien fahren.

▶ Höfliche Bitte

    Can you help me, please? - Können Sie mit, bitte, helfen?

▶ Höfliche Frage

    Can I buy a ticket here? - Kann ich eine Fahrkarte hier kaufen?

may / dürfen, können

	Singular		Plural	
1. Person	I may	ich darf	we may	wir dürfen
2. Person	you may	du darfst	you may	Sie dürfen / ihr dürft
3. Person	he / she / it may	er / sie / es darf	they may	sie dürfen

Das modale Hilfsverb may hat zwei Bedeutungen. May bedeutet etwas dürfen bzw. die Erlaubnis haben. Es drückt aber auch Unsicherheit aus.

Sprechabsichten

▶ Bitte um Erlaubnis

    May I take a cup, please? - Kann ich eine Tasse nehmen, bitte?

▶ Möglichkeit

> I may go to Spain in June. - Ich kann nach Spanien im Juni fahren.

▶ Unsicherheit

> He may not be at home. I saw him at school two minutes ago. - Er kann nicht zu Hause sein. Ich habe ihn in der Schule vor zwei Minuten gesehen.

must / müssen

	Singular		Plural	
1. Person	I must	ich muss	we must	wir müssen
2. Person	you must	du musst	you must	Sie müssen / ihr müsst
3. Person	he / she / it must	er / sie / es muss	they must	sie müssen

Das modale Hilfsverb must entspricht dem deutschen Verb müssen.

Sprechabsichten

▶ Notwendigkeit

> I must clean my room. - Ich muss mein Zimmer putzen.
>
> Must you wash the window too? - Muss du das Fenster auch waschen?

Wenn es keine Notwendigkeit gibt, wird nicht *must not* sondern *need not* benutzt:

> I need not wash the window. - Ich brauche das Fenster nicht zu waschen.

▶ Verbot

> She must not smoke. - Sie darf nicht rauchen.
>
> You must not forget it. - Du darfst das nicht vergessen.

▶ Annahme

> They must be in hotel now. - Sie sind jetzt wahrscheinlich im Hotel.

need / brauchen

	Singular		Plural	
1. Person	I need	ich brauche	we need	wir brauchen
2. Person	you need	du brauchst	you need	Sie brauchen / ihr braucht
3. Person	he / she / it need(s)	er /sie /es braucht	they need	sie brauchen

Das Verb need ist vielseitig und kann daher als Vollverb, wie auch als Hilfsverb verwendet werden. Sobald need, als Vollverb benutzt wird, wird der 3. Person Singular ein -s angehängt.

Beispiele Vollverb

I need a computer. - Ich brauche einen Rechner.

She needs a new book. - Sie braucht ein neues Buch.

Beispiele Hilfsverb

She need not wash the window. - Sie braucht das Fenster nicht zu waschen.

Need we stay in this hotel so long? - Müssen wir in diesem Hotel so lange bleiben?

will / werden

	Singular		Plural	
1. Person	I will	ich werde	we will	wir werden
2. Person	you will	du wirst	you will	Sie werden / ihr werdet
3. Person	he / she / it will	er / sie / es wird	they will	sie werden

Das modale Hilfsverb will, wird zur Konstruktion der Zukunftszeiten benutzt.

I will read. - Ich werde lesen.

Will you cook? - Wirst du kochen?

I will not cook. - Ich werde nicht kochen.

Exercise 7-1 Compose questions and answers with can.

Übung 7-1 Setze Fragen und Antworten mit can zusammen.

Wortschatz: the cat / play (die Katze / spielen), the dolphin / read (der Delphin / lesen), the teacher / read (der Lehrer / lesen), the dolphin / swim (der Delphin / schwimmen), a child / buy a house (ein Kind / ein Haus kaufen), children / drink milk (Kinder / Milch trinken), the cat / clean the house (die Katze / das Haus reinigen), the student / read (der Student / read), a child / ask questions (ein Kind / Fragen stellen), the teacher / use a book (der Lehrer / ein Buch benutzen)

1. Can the cat play? The cat can play.
2. Can the dolphin read? The dolphin cannot read.
3. ....
4. ....
5. ....
6. ....
7. ....
8. ....
9. ....
10. ....

Exercise 7-2 Answer the questions with can or must not.

Übung 7-2 Beantworte die Fragen mit can oder must not.

Wortschatz: skip classes / den Unterricht schwänzen, night club / Nachtclub, smoke / rauchen, play Tennis / Tennis spielen, cook / kochen

1. May students skip classes? Students must not skip classes.
2. May the cat drink milk? The cat can drink milk.
3. May teachers skip classes? ....
4. May teachers go to night clubs? ....
5. May children go to night clubs? ....
6. May children play? ....
7. May parents play tennis? ....
8. May students ask questions? ....
9. May children smoke? ....
10. May parents cook? ....

Exercise 7-3 Answer the questions with I am not sure. Use may not and may to express a possibility or uncertainty.

Übung 7-3 Beantworte die Fragen mit I am not sure (ich bin nicht sicher). Benutze may not und may um Möglichkeit oder Unsicherheit auszudrücken.

1. Will you read a book? (cook pizza) I am not sure. I may not read. I may cook pizza.
2. Is Robert at home? (be the park) I am not sure. He may not be at home. He may be in the park.
3. Are the children in the garden? (be the house) ....
4. Will you play tennis? (clean the house) ....
5. Will Anna cook tonight? (wash the windows) ....
6. Are these books new? (be old) ....
7. Is this man German? (be Italian) ....
8. Will you go to Spain? (go Italy) ....
9. Will they buy a car? (buy a house) ....
10. Is she in the house? (be in the garden) ....
11. Are they Spanish? (be German) ....
12. Will the children drink cola? (drink milk) ....
13. Is this woman Italian? (be Spanish) ....

Exercise 7-4 Answer the questions with must, must not or need not.

Übung 7-4 Beantworte die Fragen mit must, must not oder need not.

Wortschatz: teachers / teach (Lehrer / lehren), teachers / drink milk (Lehrer / Milch trinken), children / learn (Kinder / lernen), teachers / use books (Lehrer / Bücher benutzen), children / cook (Kinder / kochen), students / skip classes (Studenten / Schule schwänzen), children / go to a night club (Kinder / in Nachtklub gehen), students / go to school on weekends (Studenten / on Wochenende in die Schule gehen), parents / buy milk for children (Eltern / für Kinder Milch kaufen), children / drink milk (Kinder / Milch trinken), parents / drink milk (Eltern / Milch trinken)

1. Must teachers teach children? Teachers must teach children.
2. Must teachers drink milk? Teachers need not drink milk.
3. Must children learn? ....
4. Must teachers use books? ....
5. Must children cook? ....
6. Can students skip classes? ....
7. Can children go to a night club? ....
8. Must students go to school on weekends? ....
9. Must parents buy milk for children? ....
10. Must children drink milk? ....
11. Must parents drink milk? ....

Reading comprehension

Can you help, please?
Können Sie bitte helfen?

Words
Vokabeln

1. address [əˈdres] - die Adresse
2. bank [bæŋk] - die Bank
3. but [bət] - aber
4. can [kən] - können; I can read. - Ich kann lesen.
5. for [fə] - für
6. go [gəʊ] - gehen, fahren; I go to the bank. - Ich gehe zur Bank.
7. help [help] - die Hilfe; to help [help] - helfen
8. learn [lə:n] - lernen
9. may [meɪ] - dürfen, können
10. must [məst] not - nicht dürfen
11. must [məst] - müssen
12. I must go. - Ich muss gehen.
13. place [pleɪs] - legen, der Platz
14. play [pleɪ] - spielen
15. please [pli:z] - bitte
16. read [ri:d] - lesen
17. sit [sɪt] - sitzen, setzen
18. speak [spi:k] - sprechen
19. take [teɪk] - nehmen
20. thank [θæŋk] - danken
21. thank you, thanks - danke
22. write [raɪt] - schreiben

Can you help, please?

- Can you help me, please?
- Yes, I can.
- I cannot write the address in English. Can you write it for me?
- Yes, I can.
- Thank you.

Können Sie bitte helfen?

- *Können Sie mir bitte helfen?*
- *Ja, das kann ich.*
- *Ich kann die Adresse nicht auf Englisch schreiben. Können Sie sie für mich schreiben?*
- *Ja, das kann ich.*
- *Danke.*

- Can you play tennis?
- No, I cannot. But I can learn. Can you help me to learn?
- Yes, I can. I can help you to learn to play tennis.
- Thank you.

- Can you speak English?
- I can speak and read English but I cannot write.
- Can you speak German?
- I can speak, read and write German.
- Can Linda speak German too?
- No, she cannot. She is American.
- Can they speak English? Yes, they can a little. They are students and they learn English.
- This boy cannot speak English.

- Where are they?
- They play tennis now.
- May we play too?
- Yes, we may.

- Where is Robert?
- He may be at the café.

- Sit at this table, please.
- Thank you. May I place my books on that table?
- Yes, you may.

- May Paul sit at his table?
- Yes, he may.

- May I sit on her bed?
- No, you must not.
- May Linda take his CD player?
- No. She must not take his CD player.

- May they take her map?
- No, they may not.

- You must not sit on her bed.
- She must not take his CD player.
- They must not take these notebooks.

- I must go to the bank.
- Must you go now?
- Yes, I must.

- *Kannst du Tennis spielen?*
- *Nein. Aber ich kann es lernen. Kannst du mir dabei helfen?*
- *Ja, ich kann dir helfen, Tennis spielen zu lernen.*
- *Danke.*

- *Sprichst du Englisch?*
- *Ich kann Englisch sprechen und lesen, aber nicht schreiben.*
- *Sprichst du Deutsch?*
- *Ich kann Deutsch sprechen, lesen und schreiben.*
- *Kann Linda auch Deutsch?*
- *Nein, sie kann kein Deutsch. Sie ist Amerikanerin.*
- *Sprechen sie Englisch?*
- *Ja, ein bisschen. Sie sind Studenten und lernen Englisch.*
- *Dieser Junge spricht kein Englisch.*

- *Wo sind sie?*
- *Sie spielen gerade Tennis.*
- *Können wir auch spielen?*
- *Ja, das können wir.*

- *Wo ist Robert?*
- *Er ist vielleicht im Café.*

- *Setzen Sie sich an diesen Tisch, bitte.*
- *Danke. Kann ich meine Bücher auf diesen Tisch legen?*
- *Ja.*

- *Darf Paul sich an seinen Tisch setzen?*
- *Ja, das darf er.*

- *Darf ich mich auf ihr Bett setzen?*
- *Nein, das darfst du nicht.*
- *Darf Linda seinen CD-Spieler nehmen?*
- *Nein, sie darf seinen CD-Spieler nicht nehmen.*

- *Dürfen sie ihre Karte nehmen?*
- *Nein, das dürfen sie nicht.*

- *Du darfst dich nicht auf ihr Bett setzen.*
- *Sie darf seinen CD-Spieler nicht nehmen.*
- *Sie dürfen diese Notizbücher nicht nehmen.*

- *Ich muss zur Bank gehen.*
- *Musst du jetzt gehen?*
- *Ja.*

- Must you learn German?
- I need not learn German. I must learn English.

- Must she go to the bank?
- No. She need not go to the bank.

- May I take this bike?
- No, you must not take this bike.
- May we place these notebooks on her bed?
- No. You must not place the notebooks on her bed.

- *Musst du Deutsch lernen?*
- *Ich muss nicht Deutsch lernen. Ich muss Englisch lernen.*

- *Muss sie zur Bank gehen?*
- *Nein, sie muss nicht zur Bank gehen.*

- *Darf ich dieses Fahrrad nehmen?*
- *Nein, du darfst dieses Fahrrad nicht nehmen.*
- *Dürfen wir diese Notizbücher auf ihr Bett legen?*
- *Nein, ihr dürft die Notizbücher nicht auf ihr Bett legen.*

8

There is and There are / Es gibt

There is bedeutet es gibt. Bei mehreren Personen oder Sachen benutzt man there are.

There is a book on the table. - Es gibt ein Buch auf dem Tisch.

There are some books on the table. - Es gibt einige Bücher auf dem Tisch.

There is a bus at five o'clock. - Es gibt einen Bus um fünf Uhr.

Ort (on the table) und Zeit (at five o'clock) stehen immer nach dem Objekt (a book, books, a bus).

Um eine Frage zu stellen, muss man die Wortstellung ändern.

Is there a book on the table? - Gibt es ein Buch auf dem Tisch?

Are there any books on the table? - Gibt es einige Bücher auf dem Tisch?

Mann benutzt there is not/no oder there are not/no um ein negativer Satz zu bilden.

There is not a book on the table. - Es gibt kein Buch auf dem Tisch.

There are not books on the table. - Es gibt keine Bücher auf dem Tisch.

Man kann Fragen mit Is there…? oder Are there…? mit Kurzantworten beantworten:

Yes, there is. / No, there is not.

Yes, there are. / No, there are not.

Exercise 8-1 Compose negative answers.

Übung 8-1 Bilde verneinte Antworten.

1. Are there children in the park? There are not children in the park.
2. Are there books on the table? ....
3. Is there a table in the garden? ....
4. Is there milk on the table? ....
5. Are there cars in the street? ....
6. Are there cats in the school? ....
7. Are there teachers in the night club? ....
8. Is there a cup on the table? ....
9. Are there children in the room? ....

Exercise 8-2 Compose questions with how many. Answer them.

Übung 8-2 Setze Fragen mit how many / wie viele zusammen. Beantworte sie.

1. (children in the park / ten) How many children are there in the park? There are ten children in the park.
2. (books on the table / five) ....
3. (cars in the street / three) ....
4. (cats in the school / no) ....
5. (teachers in the night club / no) ....
6. (cups on the table / four) ....
7. (students in the room / two) ....
8. (people in the garden / six) ....
9. (houses in the street / ten) ....
10. (buses in the street / no) ....

Reading comprehension

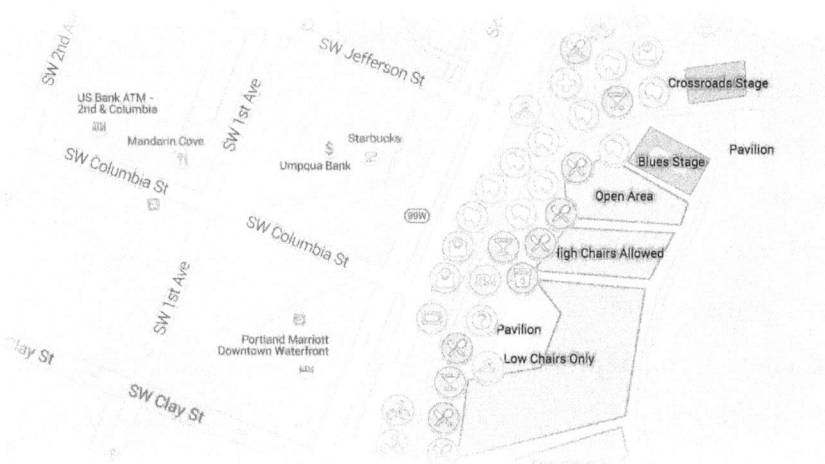

Robert lives in the USA now
Robert wohnt jetzt in den USA

Words
Vokabeln

1. breakfast ['brekfəst] - das Frühstück; have breakfast - frühstücken
2. chair [tʃeə] - der Stuhl
3. drink [drɪŋk] - trinken
4. eat [iːt] - essen
5. eight [eɪt] - acht
6. farm [faːm] - der Bauernhof
7. five [faɪv] - fünf
8. furniture ['fəːnɪtʃə] - die Möbel
9. girl [gəːl] - das Mädchen
10. good [gʊd] (Adj.), well [wel] (Adv.) - gut
11. like [laɪk], love - mögen, lieben
12. listen ['lɪs(ə)n] - hören; I listen to music. - Ich höre Musik.
13. music ['mjuːzɪk] - die Musik
14. need [niːd] - brauchen
15. newspaper ['njuːsˌpeɪpə] - die Zeitung
16. people ['piːpl] - die Menschen
17. seven ['sev(ə)n] - sieben
18. six [sɪks] - sechs
19. some [sʌm] - ein paar
20. square [skweə] - der Platz
21. tea [tiː] - der Tee
22. there [ðeə] - dort
23. three [θriː] - drei
24. want [wɔnt] - wollen

Robert lives in the USA now

Linda reads English well. I read English too. The students go to the park. She goes to the park too.

We live in San Francisco. Paul lives in San Francisco now too. His father and mother live in

Robert wohnt jetzt in den USA

Linda liest gut Englisch. Ich lese auch Englisch. Die Studenten gehen in den Park. Sie geht auch in den Park.

Wir wohnen in San Francisco. Paul wohnt jetzt auch in San Francisco. Sein Vater und seine Mutter leben in

Canada. Robert lives in San Francisco now. His father and mother live in Germany.	*Kanada. Robert wohnt jetzt in San Francisco. Sein Vater und seine Mutter leben in Deutschland.*
The students play tennis. Paul plays well. Robert does not play well.	*Die Studenten spielen Tennis. Paul spielt gut. Robert spielt nicht gut.*
We drink tea. Linda drinks green tea. David drinks black tea. I drink black tea too.	*Wir trinken Tee. Linda trinkt grünen Tee. David trinkt schwarzen Tee. Ich trinke auch schwarzen Tee.*
I listen to music. Sarah listens to music too. She likes to listen to good music.	*Ich höre Musik. Sarah hört auch Musik. Sie hört gerne gute Musik.*
I need six notebooks. David needs seven notebooks. Linda needs eight notebooks.	*Ich brauche sechs Notizbücher. David braucht sieben Notizbücher. Linda braucht acht Notizbücher.*
Sarah wants to drink. I want to drink too. Paul wants to eat.	*Sarah will etwas trinken. Ich will auch etwas trinken. Paul will etwas essen.*
There is a newspaper on the table. Paul takes it and reads. He likes to read newspapers.	*Dort liegt eine Zeitung auf dem Tisch. Paul nimmt sie und liest. Er liest gerne Zeitung.*
There is some furniture in the room. There are six tables and six chairs there.	*Im Zimmer gibt es Möbel. Es gibt dort sechs Tische und sechs Stühle.*
There are three girls in the room. They are eating breakfast.	*Es sind drei Mädchen im Zimmer. Sie frühstücken.*
Sarah is eating bread and drinking tea. She likes green tea.	*Sarah isst Brot und trinkt Tee. Sie mag grünen Tee.*
There are some books on the table. They are not new. They are old.	*Auf dem Tisch liegen ein paar Bücher. Sie sind nicht neu. Sie sind alt.*
- Is there a bank in this street? - Yes, there is. There are five banks in this street. The banks are not big.	*- Ist in dieser Straße eine Bank?* *- Ja. Es gibt fünf Banken in dieser Straße. Sie sind nicht groß.*
- Are there people in the square? - Yes, there are. There are some people in the square.	*- Sind Menschen auf dem Platz?* *- Ja, auf dem Platz sind ein paar Menschen.*
- Are there bikes at the café? - Yes, there are. There are four bikes at the café. They are not new.	*- Stehen Fahrräder vor dem Café?* *- Ja, es stehen vier Fahrräder vor dem Café. Sie sind nicht neu.*
- Is there a hotel in this street? - No, there is not. There are no hotels in this street.	*- Gibt es in dieser Straße ein Hotel?* *- Nein, es gibt keine Hotels in dieser Straße.*
- Are there any big shops in that street? - No, there are not. There are no big shops in that	*- Gibt es in dieser Straße große Läden?* *- Nein, es gibt keine großen Läden in dieser Straße.*

street.

- Are there any farms in the USA?
- Yes, there are. There are many farms in the USA.

- Gibt es in den USA Bauernhöfe?
- Ja, es gibt viele Bauernhöfe in den USA.

- Is there any furniture in that room?
- Yes, there is. There are four tables and some chairs there.

- Sind Möbel in diesem Zimmer?
- Ja, es sind dort vier Tische und einige Stühle.

9

The Genitive / Der Genitiv

Nach dem Genitiv-Objekt wird im Deutschen mit *wessen* gefragt. Das bedeutet, dass jemand oder etwas, jemand anderem oder etwas anderem gehört. Der Genitiv wird im Zusammenhang mit Personen oder Personifizierungen, durch das Anhängen eines *'s* an die besitzende Person gebildet.

> Whose cup is this? This is Tom's cup. - Wessen Tasse ist das? Das ist Toms Tasse.

> Whose book is this? This is the man's book. - Wessen Buch ist das? Das ist ein Buch des Mannes.

Bei regelmäßigen Pluralformen wird nur ein Apostroph angehängt.

> The students' books are new. - Die Bücher der Studenten sind neu.

> The parents' house is big. - Das Haus der Eltern ist groß.

Bei unregelmäßigen Pluralformen wird *'s* angehängt

> The children's bikes are blue. - Die Fahrräder der Kinder sind blau.

> The people's bags are in the car. - Die Taschen der Menschen sind im Auto.

Wenn es sich nicht um Personen oder Personifizierungen handelt, sondern um Dinge, Mengenangaben, Orte usw., dann wird der Genitiv im Englischen durch die Präposition *of* gebildet.

The cover of the book is red. - Der Buchumschlag ist rot.

The windows of the house are big. - Die Fenster des Hauses sind groß.

The head of the company has a red car. - Der Geschäftsleiter hat ein rotes Auto.

Der of-Genitiv kann auch für Personen verwendet werden. Allerdings sollte man sich bewusst machen, dass es als schlechter Stil gilt, wenn man mehrere *ofs* aufeinanderfolgen lässt.

Exercise 9 Answer the questions as in the example.

Übung 9 Beantworte die Fragen nach dem Beispiel.

1. Whose children are they? (Anna) They are Anna's children.
2. Whose books are on the table? (those students) They are................................
3. Whose cat is in the garden? (Tom) This is................................
4. Whose computer is this? (Otto) This is................................
5. Whose bags are these? (my parents) These are................................
6. Whose cups are these? (teachers) They are................................
7. Whose car is this? (Linda) This is................................
8. Whose parents are in the garden? (this boy) They are................................
9. Whose baby is this? (that woman) This is................................
10. Whose radio is this? (this man) This is................................
11. Whose house is this? (my friend) This is................................
12. Whose bikes are these? (my friends) These are................................

Reading comprehension

Robert has many friends
Robert hat viele Freunde

Words
Vokabeln

1. agency ['eɪdʒənsɪ] - die Agentur
2. as well [æzwel] - auch
3. car [ka:] - das Auto
4. CD [ˌsi:'di:] - die CD
5. clean [kli:n] - sauber
6. coffee ['kɔfɪ] - der Kaffee
7. come [kʌm]/ go [gəʊ] - kommen / gehen
8. computer [kəm'pju:tə] - der Computer
9. cooker ['kʊkə] - der Herd
10. dad [dæd] - der Vater
11. David's book - Davids Buch
12. door [dɔ:] - die Tür
13. free [fri:] - frei; free time - die Freizeit, freie Zeit
14. friend [frend] - der Freund
15. into ['ɪntə] - in
16. job [dʒɔb] - die Arbeit
17. job agency - die Arbeitsvermittlung
18. know [nəʊ] - kennen, wissen
19. many ['menɪ] - viele
20. much [mʌtʃ] - viel
21. under ['ʌndə] - unter
22. work [wə:k] - Arbeit; have a lot of work - viel zu tun haben

Robert has many friends

Robert hat viele Freunde

Robert has many friends. Robert's friends go to the café. They like to drink coffee. Robert's friends drink a lot of coffee.

Robert hat viele Freunde. Roberts Freunde gehen ins Café. Sie trinken gerne Kaffee. Roberts Freunde trinken viel Kaffee.

Paul's dad has a car. The dad's car is clean but old. Paul's dad drives a lot. He has a good job and he has a lot of work now.

Pauls Vater hat ein Auto. Das Auto seines Vaters ist sauber, aber alt. Pauls Vater fährt viel Auto. Er hat eine gute Arbeit und im Moment viel zu tun.

David has a lot of CDs. David's CDs are on his

David hat viele CDs. Davids CDs liegen auf seinem Bett.

bed. David's CD player is on his bed as well.

Robert reads American newspapers. There are many newspapers on the table in Robert's room.

Nancy has a cat and a dog. Nancy's cat is in the room under the bed. Nancy's dog is in the room as well.

There is a man in this car. This man has a map. The man's map is big. This man drives a lot.

I am a student. I have a lot of free time. I go to a job agency. I need a good job.

Paul and Robert have a little free time. They go to the job agency as well. Paul has a computer. The agency may give Paul a good job.

Linda has a new cooker. Linda's cooker is good and clean. Linda cooks breakfast for her children. Nancy and David are Linda's children. Linda's children drink a lot of tea. The mother drinks a little coffee. Nancy's mother can speak very few German words. She speaks German very little. Linda has a job. She has little free time.

Robert can speak English little. Robert knows very few English words. I know a lot of English words. I can speak English a little. This woman knows a lot of English words. She can speak English well.

George works at a job agency. This job agency is in San Francisco. George has a car. George's car is in the street. George has a lot of work. He must go to the agency. He drives there. George comes into the agency. There are a lot of students there. They need jobs. George's job is to help the students.

There is a car at the hotel. The doors of this car are not clean. Many students live in this hotel. The rooms of the hotel are little but clean. This is Robert's room. The window of the room is big and clean.

Davids CD-Spieler ist auch auf seinem Bett.

Robert liest amerikanische Zeitungen. Auf dem Tisch in Roberts Zimmer liegen viele Zeitungen.

Nancy hat eine Katze und einen Hund. Nancys Katze ist im Zimmer unter dem Bett. Nancys Hund ist auch im Zimmer.

In dem Auto ist ein Mann. Der Mann hat eine Karte. Die Karte des Mannes ist groß. Dieser Mann fährt viel Auto.

Ich bin Student. Ich habe viel Freizeit. Ich gehe zu einer Arbeitsvermittlung. Ich brauche einen guten Job.

Paul und Robert haben ein bisschen freie Zeit. Sie gehen auch zu der Arbeitsvermittlung. Paul hat einen Computer. Die Agentur wird ihm vielleicht eine gute Arbeit geben.

Linda hat einen neuen Herd. Lindas Herd ist gut und sauber. Linda macht Frühstück für ihre Kinder. Nancy und David sind Lindas Kinder. Lindas Kinder trinken viel Tee. Die Mutter trinkt ein bisschen Kaffee. Nancys Mutter kann nur ein paar Wörter auf Deutsch. Sie spricht sehr wenig Deutsch. Linda hat Arbeit. Sie hat wenig Freizeit.

Robert spricht wenig Englisch. Er kennt nur sehr wenige englische Wörter. Ich kenne viele englische Wörter. Ich spreche ein bisschen Englisch. Diese Frau kennt viele englische Wörter. Sie spricht gut Englisch.

George arbeitet in einer Arbeitsvermittlung. Diese Arbeitsvermittlung ist in San Francisco. George hat ein Auto. Georges Auto steht an der Straße. George hat viel Arbeit. Er muss in die Agentur gehen. Er fährt mit dem Auto dorthin. George kommt in die Agentur. Dort sind viele Studenten. Sie brauchen Arbeit. Georges Arbeit ist, den Studenten zu helfen.

Vor dem Hotel steht ein Auto. Die Türen des Autos sind nicht sauber. In diesem Hotel wohnen viele Studenten. Die Zimmer des Hotels sind klein, aber sauber. Das ist Roberts Zimmer. Das Fenster des Zimmers ist groß und sauber.

10

The personal Pronoun / Das Personalpronomen

Pronomen werden im Deutschen auch gerne als „Fürwörter" bezeichnet. Auf diese Weise wird auch schnell ihre Bedeutung klar, denn Pronomen stehen für etwas.

1. Person: I - ich, we - wir

2. Person: you - du / Sie (Sing) / ihr / Sie (Pl)

3. Person: he - er, she - sie (Sing), it - es, they - sie (Pl)

Bei Personen im Singular nimmt man entweder he oder she. Bei Tieren und Sachen im Singular steht it.

Die possessive Form des Personalpronomens

Person	Fragewörter	1. Sing.	2. Sing.	3. Sing.	1. Plur.	2. Plur.	3. Plur.
Possessiv	whose	my	your	his / her / its	our	your	their
	wessen	mein	dein	sein / ihr / sein	unser	Ihr, euer	ihr

Die Objektform des Personalpronomens wird nach allen Präpositionen und in allen Fällen benutzt

Person	Objektiv *(Dativ, Akkusativ)*	Personalpronomen nach Präposition
1. Singular	me	Anna plays tennis with me.
	mir, mich	Anna spielt Tennis mit mir.
2. Singular	you	Anna plays tennis with you.
	dir, dich	Anna spielt Tennis mit dir.
3. Singular	him	Anna plays tennis with him.
	ihm, ihn	Anna spielt Tennis mit ihm.
	her	Anna plays tennis with her.

Person	Objektiv *(Dativ, Akkusativ)*	Personalpronomen nach Präposition
	ihr, sie	Anna spielt Tennis mit ihr.
	it	Anna plays tennis with it.
	ihm, es	Anna spielt Tennis mit ihm.
1. Plural	us	Anna plays tennis with us.
	uns	Anna spielt Tennis mit uns.
2. Plural	you	Anna plays tennis with you.
	Ihnen, Sie, euch	Anna spielt Tennis mit euch.
3. Plural	them	Anna plays tennis with them.
	ihnen, sie	Anna spielt Tennis mit ihnen.
Fragewörter	whom (who)	Whom / Who can you beat?
	wem, wen	Wen kannst du besiegen?

Die Objektform des Personalpronomens mit Dativ und Akkusativ

	Nominativ	Dativ	Akkusativ
1. Person Singular	*I* have a book. Ich habe ein Buch.	Give *me* a book, please. Geben Sie mir ein Buch, bitte.	You know *me*. Sie kennen mich.
2. Person Singular	*You* have a book. Du hast ein Buch.	I give *you* books sometimes. Ich gebe dir Bücher manchmal.	I know *you*. Ich kenne dich.
3. Person Singular	*He* has a book. Er hat ein Buch.	Give *him* a book, please. Geben Sie ihm ein Buch, bitte.	I know *him*. Ich kenne ihn.
	She has a book. Sie hat ein Buch.	Give *her* a book, please. Geben Sie ihr ein Buch, bitte.	I know *her*. Ich kenne sie.
	It is a pussycat. Es ist ein Kätzchen.	Give *it* some milk, please. Geben Sie ihm bisschen Milch, bitte.	I like *it*. Ich mag es.

	Nominativ	Dativ	Akkusativ
1. Person Plural	*We* have some books. Wir haben einige Bücher.	Give *us* some books, please. Geben Sie uns einige Bücher, bitte.	You know *us*. Sie kennen uns.
2. Person Plural	*You* have some books. Sie haben einige Bücher.	I give *you* books sometimes. Ich gebe Ihnen manchmal einige Bücher.	I know *you*. Ich kenne Sie.
3. Person Plural	*They* have some books. Sie haben einige Bücher.	Give *them* some books, please. Geben Sie ihnen einige Bücher, bitte.	I know *them*. Ich kenne sie.

Exercise 10-1 Compose the sentences as in the example.

Übung 10-1 Bilde die Sätze nach dem Beispiel.

1. This is my book. Give it to me, please.
2. These are their cups. Give them to them, please.
3. This is her cat. Give ....
4. This is his radio. ....
5. This is my computer. ....
6. These are our bags. ....
7. These are their batteries. ....
8. These are his bananas. ....
9. This is her lamp. ....
10. This is my pizza. ....
11. These are our cups. ....
12. These are their pens. ....

Exercise 10-2 Compose the sentences as in the example.

Übung 10-2 Bilde die Sätze nach dem Beispiel.

Wortschatz: show / zeigen, know / kennen, understand / verstehen, help / helfen, tell / sagen, the truth / Wahrheit, invite / einladen, visit / besuchen, on Sunday / am Sonntag, ask / fragen, this question / diese Frage, trust / vertrauen

1. (give / I / this book) Give me this book, please.

2. (I / sometimes / see / she) I sometimes see her.
3. (show / she / the garden) ....
4. (I / know / they) ....
5. (She / understand / I) ....
6. (They / sometimes / help / he) ....
7. (tell / we / the truth) ....
8. (I / sometimes / invite / she / to play tennis) ....
....
9. (visit / we / on Sunday) ....
10. (ask / he / this question) ....
11. (trust / I) ....

Reading comprehension

David buys a bike
David kauft ein Fahrrad

Words
Vokabeln

1. bathroom [ˈbaːθruːm] - das Bad, das Badezimmer; bath [baːθ] - die Badewanne
2. bathroom table - der Badezimmertisch
3. bus [bʌs] - der Bus; go by [baɪ] bus - mit dem Bus fahren
4. centre [ˈsentə] - das Zentrum; city centre - das Stadtzentrum
5. face [feɪs] - das Gesicht
6. firm [fəːm] - die Firma
7. firms - die Firmen
8. go by bike, ride [raɪd] a bike - Fahrrad fahren, mit dem Fahrrad fahren
9. home [həʊm] - das Zuhause; go home - nach Hause gehen

10. kitchen [ˈkɪtʃɪn] - die Küche
11. make [meɪk] - machen; coffee-maker - die Kaffeemaschine
12. morning [ˈmɔːnɪŋ] - der Morgen
13. office [ˈɔfɪs] - das Büro
14. one by one - einer nach dem anderen
15. queue [kjuː] - die Schlange
16. Saturday [ˈsætədeɪ] - der Samstag
17. snack [snæk] - der Imbiss
18. sport [spɔːt] - der Sport; sport shop [spɔːt ʃɔp] - das Sportgeschäft
19. sport bike [spɔːt baɪk] - das Sportfahrrad
20. then [ðen] - dann; after that - danach
21. time [taɪm] - die Zeit
22. today [təˈdeɪ] - heute
23. wash [wɔʃ] - waschen
24. washer [ˈwɔʃə] - die Waschmaschine
25. with [wɪð] - mit
26. worker [ˈwəːkə] - der Arbeiter

David buys a bike

It is Saturday morning. David goes to the bathroom. The bathroom is not big. There is a bath, a washer and a bathroom table there. David washes his face. Then he goes to the kitchen. There is a tea-maker on the kitchen table. David eats his breakfast. David's breakfast is not big. Then he makes some coffee with the coffee-maker and drinks it. He wants to go to a sport shop today. David goes into the street. He takes bus seven. It takes David a little time to go to the shop by bus.

David goes into the sport shop. He wants to buy a new sport bike. There are a lot of sport bikes there. They are black, blue and green. David likes blue bikes. He wants to buy a blue one. There is a queue in the shop. It takes David a lot of time to buy the bike. Then he goes to the street and rides the bike. He rides to the city centre. Then he rides from the city centre to the city park. It is so nice to ride a new sport bike!

It is Saturday morning but George is in his office. He has a lot of work today. There is a queue to George's office. There are many students and workers in the queue. They need a job. They go one by one into George's room. They speak with George. Then he gives addresses of firms.

It is snack time now. George makes some coffee with the coffee maker. He eats his snack and drinks some coffee. There is no queue to his office now. George can go home. He goes into the street. It is so nice today! George goes home. He takes his children and goes to the city park. They have a nice time there.

David kauft ein Fahrrad

Es ist Samstagmorgen. David geht ins Bad. Das Badezimmer ist nicht groß. Dort gibt es eine Badewanne, eine Waschmaschine und einen Badezimmertisch. David wäscht sich das Gesicht. Dann geht er in die Küche. Auf dem Küchentisch steht ein Teekessel. David frühstückt. Davids Frühstück ist nicht groß. Dann macht er Kaffee mit der Kaffeemaschine und trinkt ihn. Er will heute in ein Sportgeschäft. David geht auf die Straße. Er nimmt den Bus 7. David braucht nicht lange, um mit dem Bus zum Laden zu fahren.

David geht in das Sportgeschäft. Er will sich ein neues Sportfahrrad kaufen. Es gibt viele Sportfahrräder. Sie sind schwarz, blau und grün. David mag blaue Fahrräder. Er will ein blaues kaufen. Im Laden ist eine Schlange. David braucht lange, um das Fahrrad zu kaufen. Dann geht er auf die Straße und fährt mit dem Fahrrad. Er fährt ins Stadtzentrum. Dann fährt er vom Zentrum in den Stadtpark. Es ist so schön, mit einem neuen Sportfahrrad zu fahren!

Es ist Samstagmorgen, aber George ist in seinem Büro. Er hat heute viel zu tun. Vor Georges Büro ist eine Schlange. In der Schlange stehen viele Studenten und Arbeiter. Sie brauchen Arbeit. Sie gehen einer nach dem anderen in Georges Büro. Sie sprechen mit George. Dann gibt er ihnen Adressen von Firmen.

Jetzt ist Zeit für einen Imbiss. George macht Kaffee mit der Kaffeemaschine. Er isst seinen Imbiss und trinkt Kaffee. Jetzt ist keine Schlange mehr vor seinem Büro. George kann nach Hause gehen. Er geht auf die Straße. Es ist so ein schöner Tag! George geht nach Hause. Er holt seine Kinder ab und geht in den Stadtpark. Dort haben sie eine schöne Zeit.

The Adjective / Das Adjektiv

Adjektive werden auch Wie-Wörter genannt, da sie beschreiben wie eine Person oder ein Gegenstand ist. Im Englischen werden Adjektive nach Geschlecht, Zahl und Fall nicht dekliniert. Das heißt, wir brauchen nicht auf das Geschlecht der Person achten, auch nicht auf Einzahl oder Mehrzahl.

A kind man lives in this house. - Ein guter Mann wohnt in diesem Haus.

A kind woman lives in this house. - Eine gute Frau wohnt in diesem Haus.

These kind people are from the USA. - Diese gute Leute sind aus der USA.

I sometimes talk to these kind people. - Ich spreche manchmal mit diesen guten Leuten.

Bildung des Komparativs einsilbiger Adjektive

Die Bildung der Steigerung (des Komparativs) hängt im Englischen von der Anzahl der Silben ab. Wenn das Adjektiv nur eine Silbe hat, dann wird die erste Steigerungsform durch das Anhängen der Endung -er an das Adjektiv gebildet.

Grundform		Komparativ	
fast	schnell	faster	schneller
small	klein	smaller	kleiner
big	groß	bigger	größer

The red car is fast. The blue car is faster. - Das rote Auto ist schnell. Das blaue Auto ist schneller.

The red car is small. The blue car is smaller. - Das rote Auto ist klein. Das blaue Auto ist kleiner.

The red cup is big. The blue cup is bigger. - Die rote Tasse ist groß. Die blaue Tasse ist größer.

Wenn man im Englischen etwas vergleichen möchte, benutzt man den Vergleichspartikel than (als) und den Komparativ:

The blue car is faster than the red car. - Das blaue Auto ist schneller als das rote Auto.

The blue car is smaller than the red car. - Das blaue Auto ist kleiner als das rote Auto.

Bildung des Superlativs einsilbiger Adjektive

Der Superlativ wird mit dem bestimmten Artikel *the* gebildet. Bei der Bildung des Superlativs kommt es ebenfalls auf die Anzahl der Silben an. Bei Adjektiven mit nur einer Silbe wird der Superlativ durch das Anhängen der Endung -est gebildet.

Grundform		Komparativ		Superlativ	
fast	schnell	faster	schneller	the fastest	am schnellsten
small	klein	smaller	kleiner	the smallest	am kleinsten
big	groß	bigger	größer	the biggest	am größten
old	alt	older	älter	the oldest/eldest	am ältesten

Der Komparativ und der Superlativ zweisilbiger Adjektive, die auf -y, -er, -le oder -ow enden, wird auch durch das Anhängen der Endungen -er und -est gebildet:

I am clever. He is cleverer. She is the cleverest. - Ich bin klug. Er ist klüger. Sie ist am klügsten.

Dabei verwandelt sich das -y am Ende eines Adjektivs in ein -i:

My task is easy. His task is easier. Her task is the easiest. - Meine Aufgabe ist leicht. Seine Aufgabe ist leichter. Ihre Aufgabe ist am leichtesten.

Bildung des Komparativs mehrsilbiger Adjektive

Bei Adjektiven mit zwei oder mehr Silben wird der Komparativ mit dem Zusatz more (mehr) gebildet.

Grundform	Komparativ
beautiful	more beautiful
schön	schöner
interesting	more interesting
interessant	interessanter

Bildung des Superlativs mehrsilbiger Adjektive

Bei Adjektiven mit zwei oder mehr Silben wird der Superlativ mit dem Zusatz the most gebildet.

Grundform	Komparativ	Superlativ
beautiful	more beautiful	the most beautiful
schön	schöner	am schönsten
interesting	more interesting	the most interesting
interessant	interessanter	am interessantesten

Ausnahmen

Grundform		Komparativ		Superlativ	
good well	gut	better	besser	the best	am besten
bad	schlecht	worse	schlechter	the worst	am schlechtesten
much many	viel viele	more	mehr	the most	am meisten
little	wenig	less	weniger	the least	am wenigsten
far	weit	further	weiter	the furthest	am weitesten

Gleichheit

Gleichheit mit *as .. as*:

She is as tall as her mother. - Sie ist so groß wie ihre Mutter.

London is not as old as Rome. - London ist nicht so alt wie Rom.

This car is as fast as a small airplane. - Dieses Auto ist so schnell wie ein kleines Flugzeug.

Bei Vergleichen im Zusammenhang mit den Sinneswahrnehmungen sehen, schmecken, hören, riechen, wird der Vergleich nicht mit *as .. as* gebildet, sondern mit *like*:

She looks like her mother. - Sie sieht aus wie ihre Mutter.

Her skin feels like a peach. - Ihre Haut fühlt sich an wie Pfirsich.

Their voices sound like a single voice. - Ihre Stimmen hören sich an wie eine Stimme.

This fruit tastes like lemon. - Diese Frucht schmeckt wie eine Zitrone.

My new perfume smells like an apple. - Mein neues Parfüm duftet wie ein Apfel.

Exercise 11-1 Answer the questions as in the example.

Übung 11-1 Beantworte die Fragen nach dem Beispiel.

Wortschatz: hungry / hungrig, expensive / teuer, heavy / schwer, friendly / freundlich, beautiful / schön

1. Whose books are newer? (Anna, Linda, Tom) Anna's books are newer than Linda's books. But Tom's books are the newest.
2. Whose car is faster? (Otto, Anna, Robert)..
   ....
3. Whose cat is hungrier? (Tom, Linda, Daniel) ....
   ....
4. Whose computer is more expensive? (Otto, Emma, Anna)..
   ....
5. Whose bags are heavier? (Daniel, Linda, Finn) ....
   ....
6. Whose cup is bigger? (Max, Daniel, Otto) ....
   ....
7. Whose parents are friendlier? (Julia, Paul, Max) ....
   ....
8. Whose baby is more beautiful? (Paul, Finn, Julia)..

9. Whose radio is smaller? (Linda, Emma, Finn) ....

10. What city is older? (Milan, Detroit, Luxor) ....

Exercise 11-2 Write sentences about Finn, Emma and Tom.

Übung 11-2 Bilde die Sätze über Finn, Emma und Tom.

Wortschatz: clever / klug, driver / Fahrer, friendly / freundlich, generous / großzügig, ambitious / ehrgeizig, neat / ordentlich, punctual / pünktlich

Finn	Emma	Tom
1. I am 28.	1. I am 25.	1. I am 59.
2. I am 1 meter 88 tall.	2. I am 1 meter 68 tall.	2. I am 1 meter 83 tall.
3. I am very generous.	3. I am not that generous.	3. I am generous.
4. I am ambitious.	4. I am not that ambitious.	4. I am very ambitious.
5. I am neat.	5. I am very neat.	5. I am not that neat.
6. I am clever.	6. I am not that clever.	6. I am very clever.
7. I am a good driver.	7. I am not a good driver.	7. I am a very good driver.
8. I am happy.	8. I am very happy.	8. I am not that happy.
9. I am friendly.	9. I am very friendly.	9. I am not that friendly.
10. I am punctual.	10. I am not that punctual.	10. I am very punctual.

1. Finn is older than Emma. Tom is the eldest.
2. Tom is taller than Emma. Finn is the tallest.
3. ....
4. ....
5. ....
6. ....
7. ....

....
8. ....
....
9. ....
....
10. ....
....

Reading comprehension

Linda wants to buy a new DVD
Linda will eine neue DVD kaufen

Words
Vokabeln

1. adventure [əd'ventʃə] - das Abenteuer
2. ask [aːsk] - bitten, fragen
3. big / bigger / the biggest - groß / größer / am größten
4. box [bɔks] - die Kiste
5. cup [kʌp] - die Tasse
6. DVD [ˌdiviˈdiː] - die DVD
7. favourite ['feɪv(ə)rɪt] - Lieblings-
8. favourite film - der Lieblingsfilm
9. fifteen [ˌfɪfˈtiːn] - fünfzehn
10. film [fɪlm] - der Film
11. friendly ['frendlɪ] - freundlich
12. give, hand [hænd] - geben
13. go away [əˈweɪ] - weggehen
14. hour [aʊə] - die Stunde
15. interesting ['ɪntrəstɪŋ] - interessant

16. last, take [lɑːst | teɪk] - dauern; The movie lasts more than three hours. - Der Film dauert mehr als 3 Stunden.
17. long [lɒŋ] - lang
18. more [mɔː] - mehr
19. say [seɪ] - sagen
20. shop assistant [ˈʃɒpəˌsɪstənt] - der Verkäufer, die Verkäuferin
21. show [ʃəʊ] - zeigen
22. than [ðən] - als; George is older than Linda. - George ist älter als Linda.
23. that [ðət] - dass; I know that this book is interesting. - Ich weiß, dass dieses Buch interessant ist.
24. twenty [ˈtwentɪ] - zwanzig
25. videocassette [ˌvɪdɪəʊkəˈset] - die Videokassette
26. video-shop [ˈvɪdɪəʊʃɒp] - die Videothek
27. young [jʌŋ] - jung

Linda wants to buy a new DVD

David and Nancy are Linda's children. Nancy is the youngest child. She is five years old. David is fifteen years older than Nancy. He is twenty. Nancy is much younger than David.

Nancy, Linda and David are in the kitchen. They drink tea. Nancy's cup is big. Linda's cup is bigger. David's cup is the biggest.

Linda has a lot of videocassettes and DVDs with interesting films. She wants to buy a newer film. She goes to a video-shop. There are many boxes with videocassettes and DVDs there. She asks a shop assistant to help her. The shop assistant hands Linda some cassettes. Linda wants to know more about these films but the shop assistant goes away.

There is one more shop assistant in the shop and she is friendlier. She asks Linda about her favorite films. Linda likes romantic films and adventure films. The film "Titanic" is her favorite film. The shop assistant shows Linda a DVD with the newest Hollywood film "The German Friend". It is about romantic adventures of a man and a young woman in the USA.

She shows Linda a DVD with the film "The Firm" as well. The shop assistant says that the film "The Firm" is one of the most interesting films. And it is one of the longest films as well. It is more than three hours long. Linda likes longer films. She says that "Titanic" is the most interesting and the longest film that she has. Linda buys a DVD with the film "The Firm". She thanks the shop assistant and goes.

Linda will eine neue DVD kaufen

David und Nancy sind Lindas Kinder. Nancy ist die Jüngste. Sie ist fünf. David ist fünfzehn Jahre älter als Nancy. Er ist zwanzig. Nancy ist viel jünger als David.

Nancy, Linda und David sind in der Küche. Sie trinken Tee. Nancys Tasse ist groß. Lindas Tasse ist größer. Davids Tasse ist am größten.

Linda hat viele Videokassetten und DVDs mit interessanten Filmen. Sie will einen neueren Film kaufen. Sie geht in eine Videothek. Dort sind viele Kisten mit Videokassetten und DVDs. Sie bittet einen Verkäufer, ihr zu helfen. Der Verkäufer gibt Linda ein paar Filme. Linda will mehr über diese Filme wissen, aber der Verkäufer geht weg.

Es gibt eine andere Verkäuferin im Laden und sie ist freundlicher. Sie fragt Linda nach ihren Lieblingsfilmen. Linda mag romantische Filme und Abenteuerfilme. Der Film ‚Titanic' ist ihr Lieblingsfilm. Die Verkäuferin zeigt Linda eine DVD mit dem neusten Hollywoodfilm 'Der deutsche Freund'. Er handelt von den romantischen Abenteuern eines Mannes und einer jungen Frau in den USA.

Sie zeigt Linda auch eine DVD mit dem Film ‚Die Firma'. Die Verkäuferin sagt, dass der Film ‚Die Firma' einer der interessantesten Filme ist. Und auch einer der längsten. Er dauert mehr als drei Stunden. Linda mag längere Filme. Sie sagt, dass ‚Titanic' der interessanteste und der längste Film ist, den sie hat. Linda kauft die DVD mit dem Film 'Die Firma'. Sie bedankt sich bei der Verkäuferin und geht.

The Prepositions of place / Die Präpositionen des Ortes

On - auf

The book is on the table. - Das Buch ist auf dem Tisch.

In - in

Linda is in the room. - Linda ist im Zimmer.

At, near, by, close to - an, neben, in der Nähe von

Mark is at the table. - Mark ist am Tisch.

The café is near the park. - Das Café ist neben dem Park.

Under - unter

My bag is under the table. - Meine Tasche ist unter dem Tisch.

Above - über

There is a lamp above the table. - Es gibt eine Lampe über dem Tisch.

Between - zwischen

The hotel is between the café and the park. - Das Hotel ist zwischen dem Café und dem Park.

Among - unter

There are two Americans among these students. - Es gibt zwei Amerikaner unter diesen Studenten.

On (to) the left - links

The hotel is on the left. - Das Hotel ist links.

On (to) the right - rechts

The furniture shop is on the right. - Das Möbelgeschäft ist rechts.

Behind - hinter, hinten

The job agency is behind the hotel. - Die Arbeitsvermittlung ist hinter dem Hotel.

In front of - vor

The bus stop is in front of the hotel. - Die Bushaltestelle ist vor dem Hotel.

In the middle (of) - in der Mitte (von)

There is a table in the middle of the room. - Es gibt einen Tisch in der Mitte des Raumes.

Wir benutzen at in verschiedenen Situationen:

▶ um auf einen Platz hinzuweisen, dass sich in der Nähe von etwas befindet

at the table - am Tisch

at the door - an der Tür

▶ um auf einen Arbeitsplatz hinzuweisen

at work - am Arbeitsplatz

▶ mit school / college / university

at school - in der Schule

at college - an der Hochschule

▶ um auf einen Platz hinzuweisen, wo Leute zusammenkommen

at home - zu Hause

at a concert - auf einem Konzert

at a party - auf einer Party

▶ um auf einen öffentlichen Platz, einen Laden oder eine Verkehrsanlage z.B. eine Haltestelle oder Station hinzuweisen

at the doctor's - beim Arzt

at the florist's - beim Blumenhändler

at the station - an der Station

at the airport - im Flughafen

Exercise 12 Insert a preposition.

Übung 12 Füge eine Präposition ein.

1. The cat is .... the room.

2. The cups are .... the table.

3. The students are .... the room.

4. The bus stop is .... the shop.

5. The dog is .... the table.

6. The lamp is .... the table.

7. There is a teacher .... those students.

8. The shop is .... the station and the school.

9. The park is ....

10. The café is ....

11. The hotel is .... the school.

12. The school is .... of the hotel.

13. The bed is .... of the room.

14. The park is .... the school.

15. The cat is .... the car.

16. The balloon is .... the school.

17. There is a German student .... those Polish students.

18. The bus stop is .... the station and the shop.

19. The school is ....

20. The park is ....

21. The shop is .... the station.

22. The station is .... of the shop.

71

23. ☐ ● ☐ ☐ ☐ The cat is .... of the room.

Reading comprehension

Paul listens to German songs
Paul hört deutsche Musik

Words
Vokabeln

1. about [əˈbaʊt] - etwa
2. bag [bæg] - die Tasche
3. be ashamed [bi əˈʃeɪmd] - sich schämen; he is ashamed - er schämt sich
4. because [bɪˈkɔz] - weil
5. before [bɪˈfɔː] - vor
6. begin [bɪˈgɪn] - anfangen
7. bread [bred] - das Brot
8. butter [ˈbʌtə] - die Butter
9. call on the phone - anrufen
10. call [kɔːl] - rufen; call centre [kɔːl ˈsentə] - das Callcenter
11. day [deɪ] - der Tag
12. dorms [dɔːmz] - das Studentenwohnheim
13. every [ˈevrɪ] - jeder, jede, jedes
14. family [ˈfæm(ə)lɪ] - die Familie
15. hat [hæt] - der Hut
16. head [hed] - der Kopf; to head, to go - gehen
17. jump [dʒʌmp] - springen; der Sprung
18. like [ˈlaɪk] - gefallen; I like that. - Das gefällt mir.
19. minute [ˈmɪnɪt] - die Minute
20. name [neɪm] - der Name; nennen
21. nearness [ˈnɪənəs] - die Nähe

22. near [nɪə], nearby [ˌnɪəbaɪ], next [nekst] - in der Nähe
23. out of order [ˈaʊt əv ˈɔːdə] - außer Betrieb
24. phrase [freɪz] - der Satz
25. run [rʌn] - rennen, joggen, laufen
26. simple [ˈsɪmpl] - einfach
27. sing [sɪŋ] - singen; singer [ˈsɪŋə] - der Sänger
28. telefone [ˈtelɪfəʊn] - das Telefon; to telephone - telefonieren
29. very [ˈverɪ] - sehr

B

Paul listens to German songs

Carol is a student. She is twenty years old. Carol is from Spain. She lives in the student dorms. She is a very nice girl. Carol has a blue dress on. There is a hat on her head.

Carol wants to telephone her family today. She heads to the call centre because her telephone is out of order. The call centre is in front of the café. Carol calls her family. She speaks with her mother and father. The call takes her about five minutes. Then she calls her friend Angela. This call takes her about three minutes.

Robert likes sport. He runs every morning in the park near the dorms. He is running today too. He jumps as well. His jumps are very long. Paul and David are running and jumping with Robert. David's jumps are longer. Paul's jumps are the longest. He jumps best of all. Then Robert and Paul run to the dorms and David runs home.

Robert has his breakfast in his room. He takes bread and butter. He makes some coffee with the coffee-maker. Then he butters the bread and eats.

Robert lives in the dorms in San Francisco. His room is near Paul's room. Robert's room is not big. It is clean because Robert cleans it every day. There is a table, a bed, some chairs and some more furniture in his room. Robert's books and notebooks are on the table. His bag is under the table. The chairs are at the table. Robert takes some CDs in his hand and heads to Paul's because Paul wants to listen to German music.

Paul is in his room at the table. His cat is under the table. There is some bread before the cat. The cat eats the bread. Robert hands the CDs to Paul. There is the best German music on the CDs. Paul wants to know the names of the German singers as well. Robert names his favorite singers. He names Blümchen, Nena and Herbert Grönemeyer. These

Paul hört deutsche Musik

Carol ist Studentin. Sie ist zwanzig. Carol kommt aus Spanien. Sie wohnt im Studentenwohnheim. Sie ist ein sehr nettes Mädchen. Carol hat ein blaues Kleid an. Auf dem Kopf hat sie einen Hut.

Carol will heute ihre Familie anrufen. Sie geht ins Callcenter, weil ihr Telefon außer Betrieb ist. Das Callcenter ist vor dem Café. Carol ruft ihre Familie an. Sie spricht mit ihrer Mutter und ihrem Vater. Der Anruf dauert etwa fünf Minuten. Dann ruft sie ihre Freundin Angela an. Dieser Anruf dauert etwa drei Minuten.

Robert mag Sport. Er geht jeden Morgen im Park in der Nähe des Studentenwohnheims joggen. Heute läuft er auch. Er springt auch. Er springt sehr weit. Paul und David laufen und springen mit Robert. David springt weiter. Paul springt am weitesten. Er springt am besten von allen. Dann laufen Robert und Paul zum Studentenwohnheim und David nach Hause.

Robert frühstückt in seinem Zimmer. Er holt Brot und Butter. Er macht Kaffee mit der Kaffeemaschine. Dann bestreicht er das Brot mit Butter und isst.

Robert wohnt im Studentenwohnheim in San Francisco. Sein Zimmer ist in der Nähe von Pauls Zimmer. Roberts Zimmer ist nicht groß. Es ist sauber, weil Robert es jeden Tag sauber macht. In seinem Zimmer stehen ein Tisch, ein Bett, ein paar Stühle und ein paar andere Möbel. Roberts Bücher und Notizbücher liegen auf dem Tisch. Seine Tasche ist unter dem Tisch. Die Stühle stehen am Tisch. Robert nimmt ein paar CDs in die Hand und geht zu Pauls Zimmer, weil Paul deutsche Musik hören will.

Paul sitzt in seinem Zimmer am Tisch. Seine Katze ist unter dem Tisch. Vor der Katze liegt etwas Brot. Die Katze isst das Brot. Robert gibt Paul die CDs. Auf den CDs ist die beste deutsche Musik. Paul will auch die Namen der deutschen Sänger wissen. Robert nennt seine Lieblingssänger. Er nennt Jan Delay, Nena und

| names are new to Paul. | Herbert Grönemeyer. Diese Namen sind Paul neu. |

He listens to the CDs and then begins to sing the German songs! He likes these songs very much. Paul asks Robert to write the words of the songs. Robert writes the words of the best German songs for Paul. Paul says that he wants to learn the words of some songs and asks Robert to help. Robert helps Paul to learn the German words. It takes a lot of time because Robert cannot speak English well. Robert is ashamed. He cannot say some simple phrases! Then Robert goes to his room and learns English.

Er hört die CDs an und beginnt dann, die deutschen Lieder zu singen! Ihm gefallen die Lieder sehr. Paul bittet Robert, den Text der Lieder aufzuschreiben. Robert schreibt die Texte der besten deutschen Lieder für Paul auf. Paul sagt, dass er die Texte von ein paar Liedern lernen will, und bittet Robert um Hilfe. Robert hilft Paul, die deutschen Texte zu lernen. Es dauert sehr lange, weil Robert nicht gut Englisch spricht. Robert schämt sich. Er kann nicht einmal ein paar einfache Sätze sagen! Dann geht Robert in sein Zimmer und lernt Englisch.

13

The Imperative / Der Imperativ

Im Englischen wird der Imperativ für die 2. Person Singular und Plural verwendet. Dabei gleicht der Imperativ der Infinitivform. Die Personalpronomen können dabei weggelassen werden.

2. Person Singular (du / Sie)

Sing with me Linda. - Sing mit mir, Linda.

2. Person Plural (ihr / Sie)

Sing with me kids. - Singt mit mir, Kinder.

Die erste Person Plural kann in gewisser Weise auch eine Imperativ-Form bilden.

Let us (let's) + Verb

Let us go to the new bar tonight. - Lass uns heute Abend in die neue Bar gehen.

Let's sing a song. - Lasst uns ein Lied singen.

Wir verwenden den Imperativ

▶ als Befehl

Come to the blackboard. - Komm an die Tafel.

▶ als Vorschlag

> Let's sing a song and have fun. - Lass uns ein Lied singen und Spass haben.
>
> Come join our group. - Komm in unsere Gruppe.

▶ als Ermunterung

> Have a nice cup of tea and relax. - Trink eine schöne Tasse Tee und entspann dich.
>
> Make yourself at home. - Fühl dich wie zu Hause.

Bildung des verneinten Imperativs

Die Verneinung des Imperativ wird in den allermeisten Fällen mit do not (don't) gebildet.

> Don't forget it! - Vergiss es nicht!
>
> Don't be shy. - Sei nicht schüchtern.

Um ein Wunsch, dass jemand etwas tut, auszudrücken, verwendet man die Formel I want you to.

> I want you to help me. - Ich will, dass du mir hilfst.
>
> Sam wants Linda to help him. - Sam will, dass Linda ihm hilft.
>
> They want me to help them. - Sie wollen, dass ich ihnen helfe.

Man kann auch höflich sagen I would like you to.

> I would like you to help me. - Ich möchte, dass du mir hilfst.
>
> Sam would like Linda to help him. - Sam möchte, dass Linda ihm hilft.
>
> They would like me to help them. - Sie möchten, dass ich ihnen helfe.

Exercise 13-1 Compose the sentences as in the example.

Übung 13-1 Bilde die Sätze nach dem Beispiel.

> Wortschatz: lend - verleihen, cook - kochen, play - spielen, dance - tanzen, help - helfen, show - zeigen, trust - vertrauen, have - trinken/essen

1. I want Sam to come today. I say to him: Sam, come today, please!

2. You want Marta to lend you a book. You say to her: Marta, lend me this book, please.

3. Sam wants his mother to cook pizza. Sam says to her:

   Mom, ...

4. I want to play tennis with Marta. I say to her:

   Marta, let's ....

5. Linda wants you to dance with her. She says to you:

   ....

6. Anna wants Bill to help her. She says to him:

   ....

7. Emma wants Tom to show her the city. She says to him:

   ....

8. Finn wants Linda to trust him. He says to her:

   ....

9. Marta wants you to have an apple. She says to you:

   ....

Exercise 13-2 Compose negative sentences as in the example.

Übung 13-2 Bilde Verneinungen nach dem Beispiel.

1. I don't want Sam to come today. I say to him: Sam, don't come today, please!

2. Sam doesn't want his mother to cook pizza. Sam says to her:

   Mom, ...

3. Anna doesn't want Bill to help her. She says to him:

   ....

4. Finn doesn't want Linda to trust Bill. He says to her:

   ....

5. Marta doesn't want you to forget it. She says to you:

   ....

6. Tom doesn't want me to be shy. He says to me:

   ....

Reading comprehension

Paul buys textbooks on design
Paul kauft Fachbücher über Design

A

Words
Vokabeln

1. any [ˈenɪ] - irgendwelche
2. bye [baɪ] - tschüss
3. choose [tʃuːz] - wählen, aussuchen
4. college [ˈkɔlɪdʒ] - die Universität, die Uni
5. cost [kɔst] - kosten
6. design [dɪˈzaɪn] - das Design
7. explain [ɪkˈspleɪn] - erklären
8. fine [faɪn] - gut
9. hello [ˈheˈləʊ] - hallo
10. him [hɪm] - ihm
11. kind [kaɪnd], type [taɪp] - die Art
12. language [ˈlæŋgwɪdʒ] - die Sprache
13. lesson [ˈles(ə)n] - die Aufgabe, Lektion
14. look [lʊk] - schauen, betrachten
15. native language [ˈneɪtɪv ˈlæŋgwɪdʒ] - die Muttersprache
16. only [ˈəʊnlɪ] - nur
17. pay [peɪ] - zahlen
18. picture [ˈpɪktʃə] - das Foto
19. program [ˈprəʊgrʌm] - das Programm
20. really [ˈrɪəlɪ] - wirklich
21. see [siː] - sehen
22. study [ˈstʌdɪ] - studieren
23. textbook [ˈtekstbʊk] - das Fachbuch

B

Paul buys textbooks on design

Paul is Canadian and English is his native language. He studies design at college in San Francisco.
It is Saturday today and Paul has a lot of free time. He wants to buy some books on design. He goes to the nearby book shop. They may have some textbooks on design. He comes into the shop and looks at the tables with books. A

Paul kauft Fachbücher über Design

Paul ist Kanadier und seine Muttersprache ist Englisch. Er studiert Design an der Universität in San Francisco.
Heute ist Samstag und Paul hat viel Freizeit. Er will ein paar Bücher über Design kaufen. Er geht zum Buchladen in der Nähe. Der könnte Fachbücher über Design haben. Er kommt in den Laden und betrachtet den Tisch mit Büchern. Eine Frau kommt

woman comes to Paul. She is a shop assistant.

"Hello. Can I help you?" the shop assistant asks him.

"Hello," Paul says, "I study design at college. I need some textbooks. Do you have any textbooks on design?" Paul asks her.

"What kind of design? We have some textbooks on furniture design, car design, sport design, internet design," she explains to him.

"Can you show me some textbooks on furniture design and internet design?" Paul says to her.

"You can choose the books from the next tables. Look at them. This is a book by Italian furniture designer Palatino. This designer explains the design of Italian furniture. He explains the furniture design of Europe and the USA as well. There are some fine pictures there," the shop assistant explains.

"I see there are some lessons in the book too. This book is really fine. How much is it?" Paul asks her.

"It costs 52 dollars. And with the book you have a CD. There is a computer program for furniture design on the CD," the shop assistant says to him.

"I really like it," Paul says.

"You can see some textbooks on internet design there," the woman explains to him, "This book is about the computer program Microsoft Office. And these books are about the computer program Flash. Look at this red book. It is about Flash and it has some interesting lessons. Choose, please."

"How much is this red book?" Paul asks her.

"This book, with two CDs, costs only 43 dollars," the shop assistant says to him.

"I want to buy this book by Palatino about furniture design and this red book about Flash. How much must I pay for them?" Paul asks.

"You need to pay 95 dollars for these two books," the shop assistant says to him.

Paul pays. Then he takes the books and the CDs.

"Bye," the shop assistant says to him.

"Bye," Paul says to her and goes.

zu Paul. Sie ist eine Verkäuferin.

„Hallo, kann ich Ihnen helfen?", fragt ihn die Verkäuferin.

„Hallo", sagt Paul. „Ich studiere Design an der Universität. Ich brauche ein paar Fachbücher. Haben Sie irgendwelche Fachbücher über Design?", fragt Paul.

„Welche Art von Design? Wir haben Fachbücher über Möbeldesign, Autodesign, Sportdesign oder Internetdesign", erklärt sie ihm.

„Können Sie mir Fachbücher über Möbeldesign und Internetdesign zeigen?", fragt Paul.

„Sie können sich Bücher von den nächsten Tischen aussuchen. Schauen Sie sie sich an. Dies ist ein Buch von dem italienischen Möbeldesigner Palatino. Dieser Designer erklärt das Design italienischer Möbel. Er erklärt auch europäisches und amerikanisches Möbeldesign. In dem Buch sind einige gute Bilder", erklärt die Verkäuferin.

„Ich sehe, dass das Buch auch Aufgaben enthält. Dieses Buch ist wirklich gut. Wie viel kostet es?", fragt Paul.

„Es kostet zweiundfünfzig Dollar. Und mit dem Buch kommt eine CD. Auf der CD ist ein Computerprogramm für Möbeldesign", sagt die Verkäuferin.

„Das gefällt mir wirklich", sagt Paul.

„Dort können Sie sich ein paar Fachbücher über Internetdesign anschauen", erklärt ihm die Frau. „Dieses Buch ist über das Computerprogramm Microsoft Office. Und diese Bücher sind über das Computerprogramm Flash. Schauen Sie sich dieses rote Buch an. Es ist über Flash und es enthält einige interessante Lektionen. Suchen Sie sich eins aus."

„Wie viel kostet das rote Buch?", fragt Paul.

„Dieses Buch mit zwei CDs kostet nur dreiundvierzig Dollar", sagt die Verkäuferin.

„Ich möchte das Buch von Palatino über Möbeldesign und das rote Buch über Flash kaufen. Wie viel muss ich dafür zahlen?", fragt Paul.

„Sie müssen fünfundneunzig Dollar für diese zwei Bücher zahlen", sagt die Verkäuferin.

Paul zahlt. Dann nimmt er die Bücher und die CDs.

„Tschüss", sagt die Verkäuferin zu ihm.

„Tschüss", sagt Paul und geht.

14

Adverbs of manner / Adverbien der Art und Weise

Die Adverbien lassen sich in zwei Gruppen gliedern: die regelmäßigen Adverbien und die ursprünglichen Adverbien. Um ein regelmäßiges Adverb im Englischen zu bilden, hängen wir dem Adjektiv einfach die Endung -ly an.

nice - nicely

She is so nice. - Sie ist so nett.

She sings nicely. - Sie singt angenehm.

normal - normally

This is a normal day. - Das ist ein normaler Tag.

I normally sleep seven hours. - Ich schlafe normalerweise sieben Stunden.

warm - warmly

The tea is warm. - Der Tee ist warm.

She smiled at me warmly. - Sie lächelte mich herzlich an.

Aber das Adverb von good lautet well.

She is a good singer. - Sie ist eine gute Sängerin.

She sings well. - Sie singt gut.

Exercise 14 Compose adverbs from the adjectives as in the example.

Übung 14 Bilde Adverbien von der Adjektiven nach dem Beispiel.

Wortschatz: cheap / cheaply - billige / billig, bad / badly - schlechte / schlecht, slow / slowly - langsame / langsam, easy / easily - leichte / leicht, angry / angrily - wütende / wütend, happy / happily - glückliche / glücklich

1. This is a cheap shop. You can buy here cheaply.

   Das ist ein billiger Laden. Man kann hier billig kaufen.

2. He is a bad player. He plays ....
3. She is a slow worker. She works ....
4. This is an easy work. I can do it ....
5. My mom is angry with me. She speaks ....to me.
6. This girl is happy. She smiles ....

15

Adverbs of frequency / Adverbien der Häufigkeit

always - immer

usually - gewöhnlich

regularly - regelmäßig

normally / generally - normalerweise

often - oft

sometimes - manchmal

occasionally - gelegentlich

rarely / seldom - selten

never - nie

Adverbien der Häufigkeit folgen immer auf das Hilfsverb.

I am seldom late. - Ich komme selten zu spät.

They can sometimes visit us. - Sie können uns manchmal besuchen.

He will always love her. - Er wird sie immer lieben.

She has never dated a boy before. - Sie hat noch nie zuvor mit einem Jungen ausgegangen.

Wenn es im Satz kein Hilfsverb gibt, dann wird das Adverb dem Vollverb vorangestellt.

I often visit my grandma. - Ich besuche oft meine Oma.

We usually eat very late. - Wir essen normalerweise sehr spät.

I sometimes feel quite lonely. - Ich fühle mich manchmal ziemlich einsam.

Exercise 15 Put the words in the logical order from *never* to *always*.

Übung 15 Setze die Wörter in die logische Reihenfolge, von never bis always.

sometimes - manchmal, always - immer, ~~seldom - selten~~, usually - normalerweise, ~~never - nie~~, often - oft, occasionally - gelegentlich

never - seldom ....

....

16

Adverbs of time / Adverbien der Zeit

when - wann

then - dann, damals

a long time ago - längst

two years ago - vor zwei Jahren

three months ago - vor drei Monaten

last week - letzte Woche

the day before yesterday - vorgestern

yesterday - gestern

six hours ago - vor sechs Stunden

an hour and a half ago - vor anderthalb Stunde

half an hour ago - vor einer halben Stunde

five minutes ago - vor fünf Minuten

now - jetzt

soon - bald

in five minutes - nach fünf Minuten

in an hour - nach einer Stunde

in the morning - am Morgen

by day - am Tag	tomorrow - morgen
in the evening - am Abend	the day after tomorrow - übermorgen
at night - Nachts	in two days - nach zwei Tagen
before noon - am Vormittag	next week - nächste Woche
at noon - am Mittag	in three months - nach drei Monaten
in the afternoon - am Nachmittag	in two years - nach zwei Jahren

Adverbien der Zeit stehen meistens am Ende des Satzes.

The bus arrives soon. - Der Bus kommt bald an.

I must work in another city next week. - Ich soll nächste Woche in einer anderen Stadt arbeiten.

Let's go to the lake tomorrow. - Lassen wir uns morgen zum See gehen.

I am always at home in the evening. - Ich bin immer zu Hause am Abend.

Exercise 16 Put the adverbs in the logical order from *two years ago* to *in two years*.

Übung 16 Setze die Adverbien in die logische Reihenfolge, von *two years ago* bis *in two years*.

~~two years ago - vor zwei Jahren~~, in five minutes - nach fünf Minuten, six hours ago - vor sechs Stunden, three months ago - vor drei Monaten, in an hour - nach einer Stunde, next week - nächste Woche, in two days - nach zwei Tagen, last week - letzte Woche, five minutes ago - vor fünf Minuten, soon - bald, in three months - nach drei Monaten, yesterday - gestern, now - jetzt, in two years - nach zwei Jahren, tomorrow - morgen

two years ago ....

....

....

....

....

17

Adverbs of place / Adverbien des Ortes

around - um ... herum

below - unten

downstairs - unten

here - hier

there - dort

inside - drinnen

outside - draußen

close by - nah

far away - weit weg

Tourists walk around the monument. - Touristen gehen um das Denkmal herum.

The shop is downstairs. - Der Laden ist unten.

The children are outside. - Die Kinder sind draußen.

Wenn zusammen benutzt stehen Adverbien des Ortes meistens vor Adverbien der Zeit. Die Reihenfolge der Ortsangaben und Zeitangaben ist also nach folgender Formel einfach zu merken

wo + wann

The children are outside now. - Die Kinder sind jetzt draußen.

I must work here next week. - Ich soll nächste Woche hier arbeiten.

I was there an hour ago. - Ich war dort vor einer Stunde.

Exercise 17 Correct the sentences as in the example.

Übung 17 Korrigiere die Sätze wie im Beispiel.

1. I read ~~on Sundays outside~~. I read outside on Sundays.
2. The cat sleeps by day inside. ....
   ....
3. The cat is in the evening outside. ....

4. The children play in the afternoon here. ....

5. We never go at night to the park. ....

6. Linda often plays tennis in the morning at school. ....

7. Tom works on Sundays at the station. ....

8. The students are usually after the lessons in the park. ....

9. Sam is often by day at home. ....

10. Emma is always in the morning at work. ....

Reading comprehension

Robert wants to earn some money (part 1)
Robert will ein bisschen Geld verdienen (Teil 1)

Words
Vokabeln

1. after [ˈɑːftə] - nach
2. answer [ˈɑːn(t)sə] - antworten, erwidern; die Antwort
3. be continued - Fortsetzung folgt
4. better [ˈbetə] - besser
5. box [bɔks] - die Kiste
6. day [deɪ] - der Tag; daily [ˈdeɪlɪ] - täglich, jeden Tag
7. earn [əːn] - verdienen; I earn 10 dollars per hour. - Ich verdiene zehn Dollar pro Stunde.
8. energy [ˈenədʒɪ] - die Energie
9. finish [ˈfɪnɪʃ] - das Ende; to finish - beenden
10. hard [hɑːd] - schwer
11. hour [aʊə] - die Stunde; hourly [ˈaʊəlɪ] - stündlich
12. list [lɪst] - die Liste
13. load [ləʊd] - beladen; loader [ˈləʊdə] - der Verlader
14. note [nəʊt] - die Notiz
15. number [ˈnʌmbə] - die Nummer
16. o'clock [əˈklɔk] - Uhr; It is two o'clock. - Es ist zwei Uhr.
17. OK [əʊˈkeɪ], well [wel] - gut, alles klar
18. one more [wʌn mɔː] - noch einen
19. part [pɑːt] - der Teil
20. personnel department [ˌpɜːsəˈnel dɪˈpɑːtmənt] - die Personalabteilung
21. quick, quickly [kwɪk | ˈkwɪklɪ] - schnell
22. transport [trænˈspɔːt] - der Transport
23. truck [trʌk] - der Lastwagen
24. understand [ˌʌndəˈstænd] - verstehen
25. usual [ˈjuːʒ(ə)l] - normal
26. usually [ˈjuːʒ(ə)lɪ] - normalerweise

B

Robert wants to earn some money (part 1)

Robert has free time daily after college. He wants to earn some money. He heads to a job agency. They give him the address of a transport firm. The transport firm *Rapid* needs a loader. This work is really hard. But they pay 11 dollars per hour. Robert wants to take this job. So he goes to the office of the transport firm.

"Hello. I have a note for you from a job agency," Robert says to a woman in the personnel department of the firm. He gives her the note.

"Hello," the woman says, "My name is Margaret Bird. I am the head of the personnel department. What is your name?"

"My name is Robert Genscher" Robert says.

"Are you American?" Margaret asks.

"No. I am German," Robert answers.

"Can you speak and read English well?" she asks.

"Yes, I can," he says.

"How old are you, Robert?" she asks.

"I am twenty years old," Robert answers.

"Do you want to work at the transport firm as a loader?" the head of the personnel department asks him.

Robert is ashamed to say that he cannot have a better job because he cannot speak English well. So he says: "I want to earn 11 dollars per hour."

"Well-well," Margaret says, "Our transport firm usually does not have much loading work. But now we really need one more loader. Can you load quickly boxes with 20 kilograms of load?"

"Yes, I can. I have a lot of energy," Robert answers.

"We need a loader daily for three hours. Can you work from four to seven o'clock?" she asks.

"Yes, my lessons finish at one o'clock," the student answers to her.

"When can you begin the work?" the head of the personnel department asks him.

"I can begin now," Robert answers.

"Well. Look at this loading list. There are some names of firms and shops in the list," Margaret explains, "Every firm and shop has some numbers. They are numbers of the boxes. And these are numbers of the trucks where you must

Robert will ein bisschen Geld verdienen (Teil 1)

Robert hat jeden Tag nach der Universität freie Zeit. Er will ein bisschen Geld verdienen. Er geht in eine Arbeitsvermittlung. Sie geben ihm die Adresse einer Transportfirma. Die Transportfirma Rapid braucht einen Verlader. Diese Arbeit ist wirklich schwer. Aber sie bezahlen elf Dollar pro Stunde. Robert will den Job annehmen. Also geht er zum Büro der Transportfirma.

„Hallo. Ich habe eine Notiz für Sie von einer Arbeitsvermittlung", sagt Robert zu einer Frau in der Personalabteilung der Firma. Er gibt ihr die Notiz.

„Hallo", sagt die Frau. „Ich bin Margaret Bird. Ich bin die Leiterin der Personalabteilung. Wie heißen Sie?"

„Ich heiße Robert Genscher", sagt Robert.

„Sind Sie Amerikaner?", fragt Margaret.

„Nein, ich bin Deutscher", antwortet Robert.

„Können Sie gut Englisch sprechen und schreiben?", fragt sie.

„Ja", sagt er.

„Wie alt sind Sie?", fragt sie.

„Ich bin zwanzig", antwortet Robert.

„Wollen Sie in der Transportfirma als Verlader arbeiten?", fragt ihn die Leiterin der Personalabteilung.

Robert schämt sich, zu sagen, dass er keine bessere Arbeit haben kann, weil er nicht gut Englisch spricht. Deswegen sagt er: „Ich möchte elf Dollar pro Stunde verdienen."

„Na gut", sagt Margaret. „Normalerweise hat unsere Transportfirma nicht viel Verladearbeit. Aber gerade brauchen wir wirklich noch einen Verlader. Können Sie schnell Kisten mit zwanzig Kilogramm Ladung verladen?"

„Ja, das kann ich. Ich habe viel Energie", antwortet Robert.

„Wir brauchen einen Verlader für drei Stunden täglich. Können Sie von vier bis sieben Uhr arbeiten?", fragt sie.

„Ja, mein Unterricht endet um ein Uhr", antwortet der Student.

„Wann können Sie anfangen, zu arbeiten?", fragt ihn die Leiterin der Personalabteilung.

„Ich kann jetzt anfangen", erwidert Robert.

„Gut. Schauen Sie sich diese Ladeliste an. Dort stehen Namen von Firmen und Läden", erklärt Margaret. „Bei jeder Firma und jedem Laden stehen ein paar Nummern. Das sind die Nummern der Kisten. Und das sind die Nummern der Lastwägen, auf die Sie die Kisten laden

load these boxes. The trucks come and go hourly. So you need to work quickly. OK?"

"OK," Robert answers, not understanding Margaret well.

"Now take this loading list and go to the loading door number three," the head of the personnel department says to Robert. Robert takes the loading list and goes to work.

(to be continued)

müssen. Die Lastwägen kommen und gehen stündlich. Sie müssen also schnell arbeiten. Alles klar?"

„Alles klar", antwortet Robert, ohne Margaret richtig zu verstehen.

„Nehmen Sie jetzt diese Ladeliste und gehen Sie zur Ladetür Nummer drei", sagt die Leiterin der Personalabteilung zu Robert. Robert nimmt die Ladeliste und geht arbeiten.

(Fortsetzung folgt)

18

Conversion / Wortartenwechsel

Im Englischen kann man einige Wörter als Verb und als Nomen verwenden.

I work with students. My work is interesting. - Ich arbeite mit Studenten. Meine Arbeit ist interessant.

The teacher questions a student. The student answers all the questions. - Der Lehrer befragt einen Student. Der Student beantwortet alle Fragen.

Can you name the capital of Germany? The name of the capital is Berlin. - Können Sie die Hauptstadt der Bundesrepublik Deutschland nennen? Die Hauptstadt heißt Berlin.

Exercise 18 Use each word as a verb and as a noun.

Übung 18 Benutze jedes Wort als ein Verb und als ein Nomen.

Wortschatz: ~~work - arbeiten / Arbeit~~, help - helfen / Hilfe, fear - Angst haben / Angst, hope - hoffen / Hoffnung, smile - lächeln / Lächeln, attack - angreifen / Angriff, visit - besuchen / Besuch, call - anrufen / Anruf

1. I sometimes work outside. My work is good.
2. Can you help me? I need your ....
3. I know about her fear. She .... dogs.
4. Tom hopes to find a job. It is also Emma's ....
5. Linda sometimes smiles to Finn. Her .... is nice.
6. This small dog often attacks other dogs. Those .... are very short.

7. Anna's friend often visits her. She likes his ....

8. Sam must call his mother. His .... are important to her.

19

Question words / Fragewörter

Die meisten Fragewörter im Englischen beginnen mit einem W. Sie werden daher auch W-Fragewörter genannt.

What? Was?

What is this? - Was ist das?

Who? Wer?

Who is this woman? - Wer ist diese Frau?

Where? Wo?

Where is the bathroom? - Wo ist das Badezimmer?

When? Wann?

When is your birthday? - Wann ist dein Gerburtstag?

Why? Warum?

Why are children sad? - Warum sind die Kinder traurig?

How? Wie?

How can I help you? - Wie kann ich Ihnen helfen?

How much? How many? Wie viel?

How many books must you buy? - Wie viel Bücher musst du kaufen?

Which? Welcher? / Welche? / Welches?

Which student lives in this house? - Welcher Student wohnt in diesem Haus?

Whose? Wessen?

Whose book is this? - Wessen Buch ist das?

Weitere Fragen, die man mit dem deutschen Fragewort *wie* bildet, werden im Englischen mit *how* gestellt. How wird von einem Adjektiv oder Adverb gefolgt:

How long must he study? - Wie lange muss er studieren?

How far is the bookshop? - Wie weit ist das Buchladen?

How often do you read books? - Wie oft liest du Bücher?

How old is he? - Wie alt ist er?

How tall is he? - Wie groß ist er?

Exercise 19 Make questions with What? Who? Where? When? Why? How? Which? Whose?
Übung 19 Bilde Fragen mit What? Who? Where? When? Why? How? Which? Whose?

1. is in the cup What is in the cup?
2. is in the bag What ....
3. is in the box ....
4. is at school ....
5. must you go in the morning ....
6. must you start your work ....
7. is on the bus ....
8. cup is on the table ....
9. car is faster, the red or the blue ....
10. pen is this ....
11. can play tennis ....
12. must do it ....
13. is the bus stop ....
14. must Linda come home ....
15. are you angry ....
16. is not Sam at work ....
17. can I help you with this work now ....

18. student is the best ....
19. is this cheese made in England ....
20. is this bread made in Germany ....

Reading comprehension

Robert wants to earn some money (part 2)
Robert will ein bisschen Geld verdienen (Teil 2)

Words
Vokabeln

1. back [bæk] - zurück
2. bad [bæd] - schlecht
3. be sorry [bi ˈsɔri] - leid tun; I am sorry. [ˈaɪ əm ˈsɔri] - Es tut mir leid.
4. bring [brɪŋ] - bringen
5. correct [kəˈrekt], correctly [kəˈrektli] - richtig; to correct - korrigieren
6. incorrectly [ɪnkəˈrektli] - falsch
7. drive [draɪv] - fahren
8. driver [ˈdraɪvə] - der Fahrer
9. get up - aufstehen; Get up! - Steh auf!
10. glad [glæd] - froh
11. hate [heɪt] - hassen
12. here [hɪə] (a place) - hier (Ort)
13. here [hɪə] (a direction) - hierher (Richtung)
14. here is - hier ist
15. instead of [ɪnˈsted ɔv] - anstelle von
16. instead of you - an deiner Stelle
17. meet [mi:t] - treffen, kennenlernen
18. mister, Mr. [ˈmɪstə] - Herr, Hr.
19. mom [mɔm], mother - Mama, die Mutter

20. Monday [ˈmʌndeɪ] - Montag
21. reason [ˈriːz(ə)n] - der Grund
22. son [sʌn] - der Sohn
23. teacher [ˈtiːtʃə] - der Lehrer
24. their [ðeə] - ihr
25. walk [wɔːk] - gehen
26. your [jə] - dein

Robert wants to earn some money (part 2)

There are many trucks at the loading door number three. They are coming back bringing back their loads. The head of the personnel department and the head of the firm come there. They come to Robert. Robert is loading boxes in a truck. He is working quickly.
"Hey, Robert! Please, come here," Margaret calls him, "This is the head of the firm, Mr. Profit."
"I am glad to meet you," Robert says coming to them.
"I too," Mr. Profit answers, "Where is your loading list?"
"It is here," Robert gives him the loading list.
"Well-well," Mr. Profit says looking in the list, "Look at these trucks. They are coming back bringing back their loads because you load the boxes incorrectly. The boxes with books go to a furniture shop instead of the book shop, the boxes with videocassettes and DVDs go to a café instead of the video shop, and the boxes with sandwiches go to a video shop instead of the café! It is bad work! Sorry but you cannot work at our firm," Mr. Profit says and walks back to the office.
Robert cannot load boxes correctly because he can read and understand very few English words. Margaret looks at him. Robert is ashamed.
"Robert, you can learn English better and then come again. OK?" Margaret says.
"OK," Robert answers, "Bye Margaret."
"Bye Robert," Margaret answers.
Robert walks home. He wants to learn English better now and then take a new job.

It is time to go to college

Monday morning a mother comes into the room to wake up her son.
"Get up, it is seven o'clock. It is time to go to college!"
"But why, Mom? I don't want to go."

Robert will ein bisschen Geld verdienen (Teil 2)

An der Ladetür Nummer 3 stehen viele Lastwagen. Sie kommen mit ihrer Ladung zurück. Die Leiterin der Personalabteilung und der Firmenchef kommen dorthin. Sie gehen zu Robert. Robert lädt Kisten in einen Lastwagen. Er arbeitet schnell.
„Hey Robert! Komm bitte hierher!", ruft Margaret.
„Das ist der Chef der Firma, Herr Profit."
„Es freut mich, Sie kennenzulernen", sagt Robert auf sie zugehend.
„Mich auch", antwortet Hr. Profit. „Wo ist Ihre Ladeliste?"
„Hier ist sie." Robert gibt ihm die Ladeliste.
„Na gut", sagt Hr. Profit, während er auf die Liste schaut. „Sehen Sie diese Lastwagen? Sie bringen ihre Fracht zurück, weil Sie die Kisten falsch verladen haben. Die Kisten mit Büchern werden zu einem Möbelladen gebracht anstelle von einem Buchladen, die Kisten mit Videos und DVDs zu einem Café anstelle von einer Videothek und die Kisten mit Sandwiches zu einer Videothek anstelle von einem Café! Das ist schlechte Arbeit! Es tut mir leid, aber Sie können nicht in unserer Firma arbeiten", sagt Hr. Profit und geht zurück in sein Büro.
Robert kann die Kisten nicht richtig verladen, weil er nur sehr wenig Englisch lesen und verstehen kann. Margaret sieht ihn an. Robert schämt sich.
„Robert, du kannst dein Englisch verbessern und dann wiederkommen, ok?", sagt Margaret.
„Ok", antwortet Robert. „Tschüss Margaret".
„Tschüss Robert", antwortet Margaret.
Robert geht nach Hause. Er will jetzt sein Englisch verbessern und sich dann eine neue Arbeit suchen.

Es ist an der Zeit, in die Uni zu gehen

An einem Montagmorgen kommt eine Mutter ins Zimmer, um ihren Sohn aufzuwecken.
„Steh auf, es ist sieben Uhr. Es ist an der Zeit, in die Uni zu gehen!"
„Aber warum, Mama? Ich will nicht gehen."
„Nenne mir zwei Gründe, warum du nicht gehen

"Name me two reasons why you don't want to go," the mother says to the son.
"The students hate me for one and the teachers hate me too!"
"Oh, they are not reasons not to go to college. Get up!"
"OK. Name me two reasons why I must go to college," he says to his mother.
"Well, for one, you are 55 years old. And for two, you are the head of the college! Get up now!"

willst", sagt die Mutter zu ihrem Sohn.
„Die Studenten hassen mich und die Lehrer auch!"
„Oh, das sind keine Gründe, um nicht in die Uni zu gehen. Steh auf!"
„Ok. Nenn mir zwei Gründe, warum ich in die Uni muss", sagt er zu seiner Mutter.
„Gut, einerseits, weil du fünfundfünfzig Jahre alt bist. Und andererseits, weil du der Direktor der Universität bist! Steh jetzt auf!"

The Prepositions of direction / Die Präpositionen der Richtung

From - von, aus

I come from the shop. - Ich komme von dem Laden.

This train comes from London. - Dieser Zug kommt von London.

Take the book from the shelf, please. - Nimm das Buch aus der Regal, bitte.

To - zu (zu einer Person, zu einem Gebäude oder Platz), nach / in (in einen Ort, in ein Land)

Give this book to Dennis, please. - Geben Sie das Buch zu Dennis, bitte.

They go to work. - Sie gehen zur Arbeit.

I would like to go to Spain. - Ich möchte nach Spanien fahren.

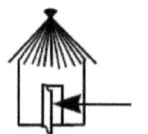

Into - in / hinein (in einen Raum/ein Gebäude hinein)

Some people come into the hotel. - Einige Leute kommen ins Hotel hinein.

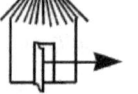

Out of - aus etwas (heraus / hinaus)

She goes out of the hotel. - Sie geht aus dem Hotel hinaus.

The children take their books out of their bags. - Die Kinder nehmen ihre Bücher aus ihren Taschen heraus.

Up - nach oben (herauf / hinauf)
The lift goes up. - Der Fahrstuhl fährt nach oben herauf.
The balloon goes up. - Der Ballon fliegt hinauf.

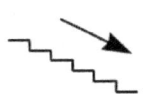
Down - nach unten (herunter / hinunter)
Go down to the ground floor, please. - Gehen Sie nach unten zum Erdgeschoss, bitte.

Over, above - über
The balloon flies above the house. - Der Ballon fliegt über das Haus.
Dennis can jump over a chair. - Dennis kann ein Stuhl überspringen.

Under - unter
The car goes under the bridge. - Der Wagen fährt unter der Brücke.

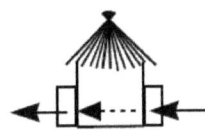
Through - durch
They go through the hall. - Sie gehen durch die Halle.

Round - um ... herum
They go round the house. - Sie gehen um das Haus herum.

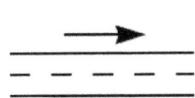
Along - entlang
You can go to the park along this street. - Sie können zum Park entlang dieser Strasse gehen.

Across - über
They go across the road. - Sie gehen über die Strasse.

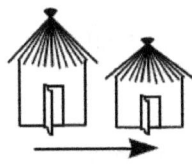
Past - an ... vorbei
She goes past some shops. - Sie geht an einigen Läden vorbei.

Exercise 20 Insert a preposition.

Übung 20 Füge eine Präposition ein.

1. The children go ………………………… school in the morning.

2. The children come ………………………… school in the afternoon.

3. A girl comes ……………… the café and sits down near a window.

4. Some people go ………………………………………… the café.

5. I must go ………………………………………… to my room now.

6. Sam goes ………………………… to the kitchen in the morning.

7. My cat can jump ………………………………… a small table.

8. Anna's cat runs ……………… the table and goes ……………… another room.

9. You can go to the station ……………………… the park.

10. Tourists go ………………………………………… the monument.

11. Students go ……………… the university ……………… a big street.

12. They go ……………………………… the street near the university.

13. Students go ……………………… some book shops every morning.

94

Reading comprehension

The name of the hotel
Der Name des Hotels

Words

1. advert [ədˈvəːt] - die Werbung
2. again [əˈgen] - wieder
3. already [ɔːlˈredɪ] - schon
4. angry [ˈæŋgrɪ] - wütend
5. another [əˈnʌðə] - ein anderer, eine andere, ein anderes
6. away [əˈweɪ] - weg
7. bridge [brɪdʒ] - die Brücke
8. down [daʊn] - nach unten
9. evening [ˈiːvnɪŋ] - der Abend
10. find [faɪnd] - finden
11. foot [fʊt] - der Fuß
12. on foot - zu Fuß
13. lake [leɪk] - der See
14. lift [lɪft] - der Aufzug
15. night [naɪt] - die Nacht
16. now [naʊ] - jetzt, zurzeit, gerade
17. open [ˈəʊpən] - öffnen
18. over [ˈəʊvə], across [əˈkrɔs] - über
19. past [paːst] - vorbei
20. Poland [ˈpəʊlənd] - Polen
21. round [raʊnd] - rund
22. see [siː] - sehen
23. show [ʃəʊ] - zeigen
24. silly [ˈsɪlɪ] - dumm
25. sleep [sliːp] - schlafen
26. smile [smaɪl] - das Lächeln
27. to smile - lächeln
28. stand [stænd] - stehen
29. stop [stɔp] - anhalten
30. surprise [səˈpraɪz] - die Überraschung
31. to surprise - überraschen
32. surprised - überrascht, verwundert
33. taxi [ˈtæksɪ] - das Taxi
34. taxi driver [ˈtæksi ˈdraɪvə] - der Taxifahrer
35. then [ðen] - dann
36. through [θruː] - hindurch
37. tired [ˈtaɪəd] - müde
38. walk [wɔːk] - gehen
39. way [weɪ] - der Weg

B

The name of the hotel

This is a student. His name is Kasper. Kasper is from Poland. He cannot speak English. He wants to learn English at a college in the USA. Kasper lives in a hotel in San Francisco now.
He is in his room now. He is looking at the map. This map is very good. Kasper sees streets, squares and shops on the map. He goes out of the room and through the long corridor to the lift. The lift takes him down. Kasper goes through the big hall and out of the hotel. He stops near the hotel and writes the name of the hotel into his notebook.
There is a round square and a lake at the hotel. Kasper goes across the square to the lake. He walks round the lake to the bridge. Many cars, trucks and people go over the bridge. Kasper goes under the bridge. Then he walks along a street to the city centre. He goes past many nice buildings.
It is evening already. Kasper is tired and he wants to go back to the hotel. He stops a taxi, then opens his notebook and shows the name of the hotel to the taxi driver. The taxi driver looks in the notebook, smiles and drives away. Kasper cannot understand it. He stands and looks in his notebook. Then he stops another taxi and shows the name of the hotel to the taxi driver again. The driver looks in the notebook. Then he looks at Kasper, smiles and drives away too.
Kasper is surprised. He stops another taxi. But this taxi drives away too. Kasper cannot understand it. He is surprised and angry. But he is not silly. He opens his map and finds the way to the hotel. He comes back to the hotel on foot.
It is night. Kasper is in his bed. He is sleeping. The stars are looking into the room through the window. The notebook is on the table. It is open. "Ford is the best car". This is not the name of the hotel. This is an advert on the building of the hotel.

Der Name des Hotels

Das ist ein Student. Er heißt Kasper. Kasper kommt aus Polen. Er spricht kein Englisch. Er will an einer Universität in den USA Englisch lernen. Kasper wohnt zurzeit in einem Hotel in San Francisco.
Gerade ist er in seinem Zimmer. Er schaut auf die Karte. Diese Karte ist sehr gut. Kasper sieht Straßen, Plätze und Läden auf der Karte. Er geht aus dem Zimmer und durch den langen Gang zum Aufzug. Der Aufzug bringt ihn nach unten. Kasper geht durch die große Halle und aus dem Hotel. Er hält in der Nähe des Hotels an und schreibt den Namen des Hotels in sein Notizbuch.

Beim Hotel gibt es einen runden Platz und einen See. Kasper geht über den Platz zum See. Er geht um den See zur Brücke. Viele Autos, Lastwägen und Menschen überqueren die Brücke. Kasper geht unter der Brücke hindurch. Dann geht er eine Straße entlang zum Stadtzentrum. Er geht an vielen schönen Gebäuden vorbei.
Es ist schon Abend. Kasper ist müde und will zurück ins Hotel gehen. Er hält ein Taxi an, öffnet dann sein Notizbuch und zeigt dem Taxifahrer den Namen des Hotels. Der Taxifahrer schaut in das Notizbuch, lächelt und fährt weg. Kasper versteht nichts. Er steht da und schaut in sein Notizbuch. Dann hält er ein anderes Taxi an und zeigt dem Taxifahrer wieder den Namen des Hotels. Der Fahrer schaut in das Notizbuch. Dann schaut er Kasper an, lächelt und fährt auch weg. Kasper ist verwundert. Er hält ein anderes Taxi an. Aber auch dieser Taxifahrer fährt weg. Kasper kann das nicht verstehen. Er ist verwundert und wütend. Aber er ist nicht dumm. Er öffnet seine Karte und findet den Weg zum Hotel. Er kehrt zu Fuß zum Hotel zurück.
Es ist Nacht. Kasper ist in seinem Bett. Er schläft. Die Sterne schauen durch das Fenster ins Zimmer. Das Notizbuch liegt auf dem Tisch. Es ist offen. „Ford ist das beste Auto". Das ist nicht der Name des Hotels. Das ist Werbung am Hotelgebäude.

21

The negative words and their antonyms / Die verneinende Wörter und ihre Antonyme

Verneinung	Antonym
no - nein, kein	all / every - alle / jede
not - nicht	-
none - kein	some / all - etwas / ganze
nobody, no-one - niemand	everybody, everyone - jeder, alle, jederman
nothing - nichts	everything / something - alles / etwas
nowhere - nirgendwo	everywhere / somewhere - überall / irgendwo
never - nie	always - immer

I have no book. - Ich habe kein Buch.

Nobody can do it. - Niemand kann das machen.

I never play tennis. - Ich spiele nie Tennis.

How many sandwiches are there on the table? None. (~~There are none sandwiches~~) - Wie viele Sandwichs gibt es auf dem Tisch? Keine.

How much money have you got? None. (~~I have none money~~) - Wie viel Geld hast du? Kein.

Exercise 21 Compose negative sentences as in the example.

Übung 21 Bilde Verneinungen nach dem Beispiel.

1. I always work outside. I never work outside.
2. How many apples can you give me? None. / I can give you no apples.
3. Every child can do it. No ....
4. Somebody lives in this house. ....
5. Everything in this room is mine. ....

6. Linda's cat can go everywhere. ....
7. Finn goes somewhere at night. ....
8. You see a taxi everywhere in this city. ....
9. Tom always reads books. ....
10. There is something on the table. ....
11. Emma is always angry. ....
12. There is somebody in the garden. ....
13. We know something about Bill. ....
14. Every student has a job. ....
15. Some children play in the park at night. ....
16. How much money can you give me? ....
17. How many apples are there on the table? ....

22

Have got

Anstatt have kann man im Präsens have got benutzen:

I have a book. = I have got a book. - Ich habe ein Buch.

She has a cat. = She has got a cat. - Sie hat eine Katze.

Do you have a dog? = Have you got a dog? - Haben Sie ein Hund?

Does he have a brother? = Has he got a brother? - Hat er einen Bruder?

I do not have a dog. = I have not got a dog. - Ich habe kein Hund.

He does not have a brother. = He has not got a brother. - Er hat keinen Bruder.

Exercise 22 Compose the sentences as in the example. Use have got / has got.
Übung 22 Bilde die Sätze nach dem Beispiel. Benutze have got / has got.

1. Sam friends Sam has got friends.
2. I not books I have not got books.

3. You books? Have you ....
4. Linda free time? ....
5. Finn not apples ....
6. They children ....
7. They a cat? ....
8. Marta not money ....
9. Bill not a job ....
10. I a dog ....
11. Emma a car? ....
12. Tom not a radio ....

23

Much little, many few, a lot of

Man benutzt many (viele) und few (wenige) mit zählbaren Substantiven.

> Few people can play piano well. - Wenige Leute können gut Klavier spielen.

> Are there many rooms in this house? - Gibt es viele Zimmer in diesem Haus?

Man benutzt much (viel) und little (wenig) mit unzählbaren Substantiven.

> She need not cook much food. She often eats in a café. - Sie braucht nicht viel Essen zu kochen. Sie isst oft im Café.

> I have little free time today. I cannot go to a café. - Ich habe heute wenig Freizeit. Ich kann nicht ins Café gehen.

Man verwendet a lot of (viel/viele) mit unzählbaren und zählbaren Substantiven.

> I have a lot of free time. - Ich habe viel Freizeit.

> You have a lot of books. - Du hast viele Bücher.

Many und much werden hauptsächlich in Fragen und in Sätzen mit negativer Bedeutung verwendet. Vergleiche a lot of und many/much:

> A lot of people learn a language. But not many of them like to learn grammar. - Viele Menschen lernen eine Sprache. Aber nicht viele von ihnen lernen die Grammatik gern.
>
> Is there much work in the garden? Yes, a lot. - Gibt es viel Arbeit im Garten? Ja, viel.

A few und a little bedeuten einige/etwas. Vergleiche:

> He has got few friends. He is unhappy. - Er hat nur wenige Freunde. Er ist unglücklich/unzufrieden.
>
> I have got a few friends. I am happy. - Ich habe einige Freunde. Ich bin glücklich.
>
> We have got a little money. We can buy some food. - Wir haben etwas Geld. Wir können ein bisschen Lebensmittel kaufen.
>
> They have got little money. They can buy almost nothing. - Sie haben wenig Geld. Sie können fast nichts kaufen.

Exercise 23-1 Change the sentences as in the example. Use much, many, a lot of.
Übung 23-1 Ändere die Sätze nach dem Beispiel. Benutze much, many, a lot of.

1. Sam has got friends. Sam has got a lot of friends.
2. Are there books on the table? Are there many books on the table?
3. There are not apples in the box. ....
4. Linda has got free time. ....
5. There is not water in the cup. ....
6. There is not money on the table. ....
7. There are children in the park. ....
8. There are not dogs in the park. ....
9. There are not big trees there. ....
10. Have you got friends? ....
11. They drink tea. ....
12. She eats fast-food. ....

Exercise 23-2 Change the sentences as in the example. Use little, few.

Übung 23-2 Ändere die Sätze nach dem Beispiel. Benutze little, few.

1. Sam has got friends. Sam has got few friends.
2. I have got free time. ....
3. There are shops in this street. ....
4. Finn has got money. ....
5. There are trees in this park. ....
6. Anna drinks water. ....
7. I have got grammar books. ....
8. Sam speaks German. ....
9. There are tables in the class-room. ....

Exercise 23-3 Answer the questions. Use a little, a few.

Übung 23-3 Beantworte die Fragen. Benutze a little, a few.

1. Has Sam got friends? A few.
2. Have you got free time? ....
3. Have they got books? ....
4. Has Tom got free time? ....
5. Has Marta got apples? ....
6. Has Emma got money? ....
7. Have they got water? ....

Exercise 23-4 Compose the sentences as in the example. Use a little, a few, little, few.

Übung 23-4 Bilde die Sätze nach dem Beispiel. Benutze a little, a few, little, few.

1. I am happy. I have got a little money.
2. Bill is unhappy. He has got .... money.
3. Sam can play tennis. He has got .... free time.
4. Emma cannot play tennis. She has got .... free time.
5. Tom can cook a steak. He has got .... meat.
6. You cannot cook a steak. You have got .... meat.
7. I can play football. I have got .... friends.
8. He cannot play football. He has got .... friends.
9. She can learn English fast. She has got .... good books.

10. He cannot learn English fast. He has got ………………………………… good books.

Reading comprehension

Aspirin
Aspirin

A

Words

1. answer [ˈɑːn(t)sə] - die Lösung
2. aspirin [ˈæspərɪn] - das Aspirin
3. at last [ət lɑːst] - schließlich
4. at one o'clock [ət wʌn əˈklɔk] - um eins
5. break [breɪk], pause - die Pause
6. chemical [ˈkemɪk(ə)l] (adj) - chemisch
7. chemicals - die Chemikalien
8. chemistry [ˈkemɪstrɪ] - die Chemie
9. classroom [ˈklɑːsrʊm] - das Klassenzimmer
10. crystal [ˈkrɪstəl] - das Kristall
11. desk [desk] - der Schreibtisch
12. dorms [dɔːmz] - das Studentenwohnheim
13. for [fə] - für
14. get [get] (something) - (etwas) erhalten
15. get [get] (somewhere) - ankommen
16. grey [greɪ] - grau
17. guy [gaɪ] - der Junge
18. half [hɑːf] - halb
19. of course [əv kɔːs] - natürlich
20. often [ˈɔf(t)ən] - oft
21. paper [ˈpeɪpə] - das Papier
22. past [pɑːst] - nach
23. at half past eight - um halb neun
24. pharmacy [ˈfɑːməsɪ] - die Apotheke
25. pill [pɪl] - die Tablette
26. sheet [ʃiːt] (of paper) - das Blatt
27. sit down [sɪt daʊn] - sich hinsetzen
28. smart [smɑːt] - intelligent
29. some [sʌm] - einige
30. something [ˈsʌmθɪŋ] - etwas
31. stinking [ˈstɪŋkɪŋ] - stinkend
32. task [tɑːsk] - die Aufgabe
33. ten [ten] - zehn
34. test [test] - die Prüfung
35. to test - prüfen
36. to pass [pɑːs] a test - eine Prüfung bestehen

37. that [ðæt] *(conj)* - dass
38. think [θɪŋk] - denken
39. try [traɪ] - versuchen

40. watch [wɔtʃ] - die Uhr
41. white [(h)waɪt] - weiß
42. wonderful [ˈwʌndəf(ə)l] - wunderbar

B

Aspirin

This is Robert's friend. His name is Paul. Paul is from Canada. English is his native language. He can speak French very well too. Paul lives in the dorms. Paul is in his room now. Paul has a chemistry test today. He looks at his watch. It is eight o'clock. It is time to go.

Paul goes outside. He goes to the college. The college is near the dorms. It takes him about ten minutes to go to the college. Paul comes to the chemical classroom. He opens the door and looks into the classroom. There are some students and the teacher there. Paul comes into the classroom.

"Hello," he says.

"Hello," the teacher and the students answer.

Paul comes to his desk and sits down. The chemistry test begins at half past eight. The teacher comes to Paul's desk.

"Here is your task," the teacher says. Then he gives Paul a sheet of paper with the task, "You must make aspirin. You can work from half past eight to twelve o'clock. Begin, please," the teacher says.

Paul knows this task. He takes some chemicals and begins. He works for ten minutes. At last he gets something grey and stinking. This is not good aspirin. Paul knows that he must get big white crystals of aspirin. Then he tries again and again. Paul works for an hour but he gets something grey and stinking again.

Paul is angry and tired. He cannot understand it. He stops and thinks a little. Paul is a smart guy. He thinks for a minute and then finds the answer! He stands up.

"May I have a break for ten minutes?" Paul asks the teacher.

"Of course, you may," the teacher answers.

Paul goes outside. He finds a pharmacy near the college. He comes in and buys some pills of aspirin. In ten minutes he comes back to the classroom. The students sit and work. Paul sits

Aspirin

Das ist ein Freund von Robert. Er heißt Paul. Paul kommt aus Kanada. Seine Muttersprache ist Englisch. Er spricht auch sehr gut Französisch. Paul wohnt im Studentenwohnheim. Paul ist gerade in seinem Zimmer. Paul hat heute eine Prüfung in Chemie. Er schaut auf die Uhr. Es ist acht Uhr. Es ist an der Zeit, zu gehen.

Paul geht nach draußen. Er geht zur Universität. Die Uni ist in der Nähe des Wohnheims. Er braucht etwa zehn Minuten bis zur Uni. Paul kommt zum Klassenzimmer. Er öffnet die Tür und schaut ins Klassenzimmer. Einige Studenten und der Lehrer sind da. Paul betritt das Klassenzimmer.

„Hallo", sagt er.

„Hallo", antworten der Lehrer und die Studenten.

Paul geht zu seinem Schreibtisch und setzt sich hin. Die Prüfung beginnt um halb neun. Der Lehrer kommt zu Pauls Tisch.

„Hier ist deine Aufgabe", sagt der Lehrer. Dann gibt er Paul ein Blatt Papier mit der Aufgabe. „Du musst Aspirin herstellen. Du kannst von halb neun bis zwölf Uhr arbeiten. Fang bitte an", sagt der Lehrer.

Paul weiß, wie diese Aufgabe geht. Er nimmt einige Chemikalien und beginnt. Er arbeitet zehn Minuten lang. Das Ergebnis ist grau und stinkt. Das ist nicht gutes Aspirin. Paul weiß, dass er große, weiße Aspirinkristalle erhalten muss. Dann versucht er es wieder und wieder. Paul arbeitet eine Stunde lang, aber das Ergebnis ist wieder grau und stinkend.

Paul ist wütend und müde. Er kann es nicht verstehen. Er macht eine Pause und denkt ein bisschen nach. Paul ist intelligent. Er denkt ein paar Minuten nach und findet dann die Lösung! Er steht auf.

„Kann ich zehn Minuten Pause machen?", fragt er den Lehrer.

„Ja, natürlich", antwortet der Lehrer.

Paul geht nach draußen. Er findet eine Apotheke in der Nähe der Uni. Er geht hinein und kauft ein paar Tabletten Aspirin. Nach zehn Minuten kommt er

down.

"May I finish the test?" Paul says to the teacher in five minutes.

The teacher comes to Paul's desk. He sees big white crystals of aspirin. The teacher stops in surprise. He stands and looks at aspirin for a minute.

"It is wonderful! Your aspirin is so nice! But I cannot understand it! I often try to get aspirin and I get only something grey and stinking," the teacher says, "You passed the test," he says.

Paul goes away after the test. The teacher sees something white at Paul's desk. He comes to the desk and finds the paper from the aspirin pills.

"Smart guy. Ok, Paul. Now you have a problem," the teacher says.

zurück ins Klassenzimmer. Die Studenten sitzen da und arbeiten. Paul setzt sich hin.

„Kann ich die Prüfung beenden?", fragt Paul den Lehrer nach fünf Minuten.

Der Lehrer kommt zu Pauls Tisch. Er sieht große, weiße Aspirinkristalle. Der Lehrer ist überrascht. Er bleibt stehen und schaut eine Weile auf das Aspirin.

„Wunderbar! Dein Aspirin ist gut! Aber ich kann das nicht verstehen! Ich versuche oft, Aspirin herzustellen, aber alles, was ich herausbekomme, ist grau und stinkt", sagt der Lehrer. „Du hast die Prüfung bestanden".

Paul geht nach der Prüfung weg. Der Lehrer sieht etwas Weißes auf Pauls Tisch. Er geht zum Tisch und findet das Papier der Aspirintabletten.

„Intelligenter Junge. Na ja, Paul, jetzt hast du ein Problem", sagt der Lehrer.

24

Numbers / Zahlen

	Cardinal numbers Grundzahlen	Ordinal numbers Ordnungszahlen
0	zero	zeroth
1	one	first
2	two	second
3	three	third
4	four	fourth
5	five	fifth
6	six	sixth
7	seven	seventh
8	eight	eighth
9	nine	ninth
10	ten	tenth

11	eleven	eleventh
12	twelve	twelfth
13	thirteen	thirteenth
14	fourteen	fourteenth
15	fifteen	fifteenth
16	sixteen	sixteenth
17	seventeen	seventeenth
18	eighteen	eighteenth
19	nineteen	nineteenth
20	twenty	twentieth
21	twenty-one	twenty-first
22	twenty-two	twenty-second
23	twenty-three	twenty-third
24	twenty-four	twenty-fourth
25	twenty-five	twenty-fifth
26	twenty-six	twenty-sixth
27	twenty-seven	twenty-seventh
28	twenty-eight	twenty-eighth
29	twenty-nine	twenty-ninth
30	thirty	thirtieth
31	thirty-one	thirty-first
40	forty	fortieth
50	fifty	fiftieth
60	sixty	sixtieth
70	seventy	seventieth
80	eighty	eightieth
90	ninety	ninetieth
100	one hundred	hundredth
500	five hundred	five hundredth
1,000	one thousand	thousandth

1,500	one thousand five hundred	one thousand five hundredth
100,000	one hundred thousand	hundred thousandth
1,000,000	one million	millionth

I have two books. - Ich habe zwei Bücher.

It is my second day in LA. - Es ist mein zweiter Tag in Los Angeles.

Two plus two is four. - Zwei plus zwei ist gleich vier.

Five minus four is one. - Fünf minus vier ist gleich eins.

Decimals / Dezimalzahlen

Written / Schriftlich	Said / Mündlich
0.2	point two
0.25	point two five
0.07	point zero seven
0.2596	point two five nine six
2.49	two point four nine

Years / Jahre

Written / Schriftlich	Spoken / Mündlich
2017	twenty seventeen or two thousand seventeen
2007	two thousand seven
2000	two thousand
1965	nineteen sixty-five
1907	nineteen o seven
1900	nineteen hundred

Exercise 24 Compose the sentences as in the example.

Übung 24 Bilde die Sätze nach dem Beispiel.

1. Two plus three is five.
2. Four plus two is ....
3. Five plus one is ....
4. Seven minus three is ....
5. Eight plus two is ....
6. Ten minus ten is ....
7. Ten minus one is ....
8. Two plus ten is ....
9. Twenty plus six is ....
10. Thirty plus fifty is ....
11. One thousand five hundred plus five hundred is ....
12. Point one plus point two is ....
13. Point six plus point four is ....

Reading comprehension

Nancy and the kangaroo
Nancy und das Känguru

Words

1. bookcase [ˈbʊkkeɪs] - das Bücherregal
2. bother [ˈbɔðə] - ärgern
3. cry [kraɪ] - weinen, schreien, rufen
4. doll [dɔl] - die Puppe
5. ear [ɪə] - das Ohr
6. fall [fɔːl] - der Fall
7. to fall - fallen
8. full [fʊl] - voll
9. hair [heə] - das Haar
10. happy [ˈhæpɪ] - glücklich
11. Hey! [heɪ] - Hey!
12. hit [hɪt], beat [biːt] - schlagen
13. ice-cream [ˌaɪsˈkriːm] - das Eis
14. its [ɪts] *(for neuter)* - sein
15. kangaroo [ˌkæŋ(ə)ˈruː] - das Känguru
16. let us, let's [let əz | lets] - lass uns

17. lion [ˈlaɪən] - der Löwe
18. me [miː] - mich
19. monkey [ˈmʌŋkɪ] - der Affe
20. Oh! [əʊ] - Oh!
21. okay [əʊˈkeɪ], well - okay, gut
22. pail [peɪl] - der Eimer
23. plan [plæn] - der Plan
24. to plan - planen
25. poor [pɔː | pʊə] - arm
26. pull [pʊl] - ziehen
27. quietly [ˈkwaɪətlɪ] - leise
28. strong [strɒŋ], strongly [stˈrɒŋlɪ] - stark
29. study [ˈstʌdɪ] - studieren
30. tail [teɪl] - der Schwanz
31. tiger [ˈtaɪɡə] - der Tiger
32. together [təˈɡeðə] - zusammen
33. toy [tɔɪ] - das Spielzeug
34. us [əs] - uns
35. water [ˈwɔːtə] - das Wasser
36. wet [wet] - nass
37. what [(h)wɒt] - was, welcher / welche / welches
38. What is this? - Was ist das?
39. What table? - Welcher Tisch?
40. when [(h)wen] - wenn
41. wide [waɪd], widely [ˈwaɪdlɪ] - weit
42. year [jɪə] - das Jahr
43. zebra [ˈziːbrə] - das Zebra
44. zoo [zuː] - der Zoo

Nancy and the kangaroo

Robert is a student now. He studies at a college. He studies English. Robert lives at the dorms. He lives next door to Paul's.
Robert is in his room now. He takes the telephone and calls his friend David.
"Hello," David answers the call.
"Hello David. It is Robert here. How are you?" Robert says.
"Hello Robert. I am fine. Thanks. And how are you?" David answers.
"I am fine too. Thanks. I will go for a walk. What are your plans for today?" Robert says.
"My sister Nancy asks me to take her to the zoo. I will take her there now. Let us go together," David says.
"Okay. I will go with you. Where will we meet?" Robert asks.
"Let us meet at the bus stop Olympic. And ask Paul to come with us too," David says.
"Okay. Bye," Robert answers.
"See you. Bye," David says.
Then Robert goes to Paul's room. Paul is in his room.
"Hello," Robert says.
"Oh, hello Robert. Come in, please," Paul says. Robert comes in.
"David, his sister and I will go to the zoo. Will you go together with us?" Robert asks.
"Of course, I will go too!" Paul says.

Nancy und das Känguru

Robert ist jetzt Student. Er studiert an der Universität. Er studiert Englisch. Robert wohnt im Studentenwohnheim. Er ist Pauls Nachbar.
Robert ist gerade in seinem Zimmer. Er nimmt sein Telefon und ruft seinen Freund David an.
David geht ans Telefon und sagt: „Hallo."
„Hallo David. Ich bin es, Robert. Wie geht's dir?", sagt Robert.
„Hallo Robert. Mir geht's gut. Danke. Und dir?", antwortet David.
„Mir geht's auch gut, danke. Ich werde einen Ausflug machen. Was hast du heute vor?", sagt Robert.
„Meine Schwester Nancy will mit mir in den Zoo gehen. Ich werde jetzt mit ihr dorthin gehen. Lass uns zusammen gehen", sagt David.
„Alles klar, ich komme mit. Wo treffen wir uns?", fragt Robert.
„Lass uns an der Bushaltestelle Olympic treffen. Und frag Paul, ob er auch mitkommen will", sagt David.
„Alles klar. Tschüss", antwortet Robert.
„Bis gleich", sagt David.
Dann geht Robert zu Pauls Zimmer. Paul ist in seinem Zimmer.
„Hallo", sagt Robert.
„Oh, hallo Robert. Komm rein", sagt Paul. Robert betritt das Zimmer.
„David, seine Schwester und ich gehen in den Zoo. Willst du mitkommen?", fragt Robert.
„Natürlich komme ich mit", sagt Paul.

Robert and Paul drive to the bus stop Olympic. They see David and his sister Nancy there.

David's sister is only five years old. She is a little girl and she is full of energy. She likes animals very much. But Nancy thinks that animals are toys. The animals run away from her because she bothers them very much. She can pull tail or ear, hit with a hand or with a toy. Nancy has a dog and a cat at home. When Nancy is at home the dog is under a bed and the cat sits on the bookcase. So she cannot get them.

Nancy, David, Robert and Paul come into the zoo.

There are many animals in the zoo. Nancy is very happy. She runs to the lion and to the tiger. She hits the zebra with her doll. She pulls the tail of a monkey so strong that all the monkeys run away crying. Then Nancy sees a kangaroo. The kangaroo drinks water from a pail. Nancy smiles and comes to the kangaroo very quietly. And then…

"Hey!! Kangaroo-oo-oo!!" Nancy cries and pulls its tail. The kangaroo looks at Nancy with wide open eyes. It jumps in surprise so that the pail with water flies up and falls on Nancy. Water runs down her hair, her face and her dress. Nancy is all wet.

"You are a bad kangaroo! Bad!" she cries.

Some people smile and some people say: "Poor girl." David takes Nancy home.

"You must not bother the animals," David says and gives an ice-cream to her. Nancy eats the ice-cream.

"Okay. I will not play with very big and angry animals," Nancy thinks, "I will play with little animals only." She is happy again.

Robert und Paul fahren bis zur Bushaltestelle Olympic. Dort sehen sie David und seine Schwester Nancy.

Davids Schwester ist erst fünf. Sie ist ein kleines Mädchen und voller Energie. Sie mag Tiere sehr gerne. Aber Nancy denkt, dass Tiere Spielzeug sind. Die Tiere rennen vor ihr weg, weil sie sie sehr ärgert. Sie zieht sie am Schwanz oder am Ohr, schlägt sie mit der Hand oder mit einem Spielzeug. Zu Hause hat Nancy einen Hund und eine Katze. Wenn Nancy zu Hause ist, sitzt der Hund unter dem Bett und die Katze auf dem Bücherregal. So kann Nancy sie nicht kriegen.

Nancy, David, Robert und Paul betreten den Zoo. Im Zoo gibt es sehr viele Tiere. Nancy ist glücklich. Sie rennt zu den Löwen und Tigern. Sie schlägt das Zebra mit ihrer Puppe. Sie zieht so stark am Schwanz eines Affen, dass alle Affen schreiend wegrennen. Dann sieht Nancy ein Känguru. Das Känguru trinkt Wasser aus einem Eimer. Nancy lächelt und nähert sich dem Känguru langsam. Und dann...

„Hey!!! Kängruu-uu-uu!", schreit Nancy und zieht es am Schwanz. Das Känguru sieht Nancy mit weit aufgerissenen Augen an. Vor Schreck macht es einen Satz, sodass der Wassereimer in die Luft fliegt und auf Nancy fällt. Wasser läuft über ihr Haar, ihr Gesicht und ihr Kleid. Nancy ist ganz nass.

„Du bist ein böses Känguru! Böse!", ruft sie.

Einige Leute lächeln und einige Leute sagen: „Armes Mädchen." David bringt Nancy nach Hause.

„Du darfst die Tiere nicht ärgern", sagt David und gibt ihr ein Eis. Nancy isst das Eis.

„Okay, ich werde nicht mehr mit sehr großen und wütenden Tieren spielen", denkt Nancy. „Ich werde nur noch mit kleinen Tieren spielen." Sie ist wieder glücklich.

25

The Prepositions of time / Die temporale Präpositionen

At - die Uhrzeit; die Nacht

I get up at seven o'clock. - Ich stehe um sieben Uhr auf.

He works at night. - Er arbeitet nachts.

Vergleiche: They work by day. - Sie arbeiten tags.

On - die Wochentage, Datum, Feiertage

See you on Sunday! - Bis Sonntag!

The film is on 19 May. - Der Film ist am neunzehnten Mai.

In - in, die Monate, Jahre, die Jahreszeiten

The bus comes in ten minutes. - Der Bus kommt in zehn Minuten an.

The concert begins in two hours. - Das Konzert beginnt in zwei Stunden.

Her birthday is in February. - Ihr Geburtstag ist im Februar.

She was born in 2017. - Sie ist 2017 geboren.

His birthday is in summer. - Sein Geburtstag ist im Sommer.

For - für einen Zeitraum

They played tennis for two hours. - Sie spielten Tennis zwei Stunden.

I have been in London for five days. - Ich bin fünf Tage in London.

Ago - vor

I was in Italy one month ago. - Ich war in Italien vor einem Monat.

They played tennis two days ago. - Sie spielten Tennis vor zwei Tagen.

Since - seit

I have been in London since April. - Ich bin in London seit April.

They have been working since nine o'clock. - Sie arbeiten seit neun Uhr.

Until / till - bis

Wait until I come back, please. - Warte bis ich zurückkomme, bitte.

We lived in Manchester until 2015. - Wir lebten in Manchester bis 2015.

From… to… - von… bis…

> They lived in Bristol from 2014 to 2016. - Sie lebten in Bristol von 2014 bis 2016.
>
> I was in London from Monday to Friday. - Ich war in London von Montag bis Freitag.

Before - vor

> I play tennis before breakfast. - Ich spiele Tennis vor dem Frühstück.

After - nach, nachdem

> She reads books after dinner. - Sie liest Bücher nach dem Abendessen.
>
> I can visit you after I come back from India. - Ich kann dich besuchen nachdem ich von Indien zurückkomme.

During - während

> I am listening carefully during the performance. - Ich höre aufmerksam zu während der Aufführung.
>
> They must not eat during the classes. - Sie dürfen während des Unterrichts nicht essen.

While - während

> He came home while his wife was cooking. - Er kam nach Hause während seine Frau kochte.

Exercise 25 Compose the sentences as in the example. Use prepositions of time.
Übung 25 Bilde die Sätze nach dem Beispiel. Benutze temporale Präpositionen.

1. I get up at six o'clock.
2. Linda gets up .... seven o'clock.
3. She drinks a cup of coffee .... going to university.
4. She studies .... eight .... three o'clock.
5. Linda works hard .... the classes.
6. She goes to the library .... the classes.
7. She usually works in the library .... two hours.

8. Linda phones some of her friends ………………………… working in the library.
9. She meets her friends ………………………… working in the library.
10. They go to a café and stay there ………………………… seven o'clock.
11. Linda comes home ………………………… half past seven.
12. She watches TV ………………………… eight ………………………… ten o'clock.
13. She has supper ………………………… watching TV.
14. She takes a bath ………………………… going to bed.

Reading comprehension

Parachutists
Die Fallschirmspringer

A

Words

1. after [ˈɑːftə] - nach
2. air [eə] - die Luft
3. airplane [ˈeəpleɪn] - das Flugzeug
4. airshow [ˈeəʃəʊ] - die Flugschau
5. angrily [ˈæŋɡrɪlɪ] - wütend
6. audience [ˈɔːdɪəns] - das Publikum
7. be [biː] - sein
8. believe [bɪˈliːv] - glauben; to not believe one's eyes - seinen Augen nicht trauen
9. by the way [baɪ ðə ˈweɪ] - übrigens
10. catch [kætʃ] - fangen
11. close [kləʊz] - schließen
12. clothes [kləʊðz] - die Kleidung
13. club [klʌb] - der Verein
14. daddy [ˈdædɪ] - Papa
15. do [duː] - machen
16. fallen [ˈfɔːlən] - abgestürzt
17. falling [ˈfɔːlɪŋ] - fallend
18. get off [ˈɡet ɒf] - aussteigen
19. great [ɡreɪt] - super, toll
20. if [ɪf] - ob
21. inside [ˌɪnˈsaɪd] - in
22. jacket [ˈdʒækɪt] - die Jacke
23. just [dʒʌst] - einfach
24. land [lænd] - landen
25. life [laɪf] - das Leben

26. life-saving trick - der Rettungstrick
27. member [ˈmembə] - das Mitglied
28. metal [ˈmet(ə)l] - das Metall
29. nine [naɪn] - neun
30. other [ˈʌðə] - andere, andere, andere
31. over [ˈəʊvə] - über
32. own [əʊn] - eigener, eigene, eigenes
33. parachute [ˈpærəʃuːt] - der Fallschirm
34. parachutist [ˈpærəˌʃuːtɪst] - der Fallschirmspringer
35. part [paːt] - der Teil
36. pilot [ˈpaɪlət] - der Pilot
37. prepare [prɪˈpeə] - vorbereiten
38. push [pʊʃ] - stoßen, ziehen
39. put on [ˈpʊt ɒn] - sich anziehen
40. dressed [drest] - angezogen
41. real [rɪəl] - wirklich
42. red [red] - rot
43. roof [ruːf] - das Dach
44. rubber [ˈrʌbə] - der Gummi
45. save [seɪv] - retten
46. seat [siːt] - der Sitz; take a seat [teɪk ə siːt] - sich hinsetzen
47. silent [ˈsaɪlənt], silently [ˈsaɪləntli] - leise
48. stuffed [stʌft] - ausgestopft; stuffed parachutist - die Fallschirmspringerpuppe
49. team [tiːm] - die Mannschaft
50. train [treɪn] - trainieren; trained - trainiert
51. trick [trɪk] - der Trick
52. trousers [ˈtraʊzəz] - die Hose
53. yellow [ˈjeləʊ] - gelb

B

Parachutists

It is morning. Robert comes to Paul's room. Paul is sitting at the table and writing something. Paul's cat Favorite is on Paul's bed. It is sleeping quietly.
"May I come in?" Robert asks.
"Oh, Robert. Come in please. How are you?" Paul answers.
"Fine. Thanks. How are you?" Robert says.
"I am fine. Thanks. Sit down, please," Paul answers.
Robert sits on a chair.
"You know I am a member of a parachute club. We are having an airshow today," Robert says, "I am going to make some jumps there."
"It is very interesting," Paul answers, "I may come to see the airshow."
"If you want I can take you there and you can fly in an airplane," Robert says.
"Really? That will be great!" Paul cries, "What time is the airshow?"
"It begins at ten o'clock in the morning," Robert answers, "David will come too. By the way we need help to push a stuffed parachutist out of the airplane. Will you help?"
"A stuffed parachutist? Why?" Paul says in surprise.
"You see, it is a part of the show," Robert says, "This is a life-saving trick. The stuffed parachutist

Die Fallschirmspringer

Es ist Morgen. Robert kommt in Pauls Zimmer. Paul sitzt am Tisch und schreibt etwas. Pauls Katze Favorite sitzt auf Pauls Bett. Sie schläft ruhig.
„Kann ich reinkommen?", fragt Robert.
„Oh, Robert. Komm rein. Wie geht's dir?", antwortet Paul.
„Gut, danke. Und dir?", sagt Robert.
„Danke, auch gut. Setz dich", antwortet Paul.
Robert setzt sich auf einen Stuhl.
„Du weißt doch, dass ich Mitglied in einem Fallschirmspringerverein bin. Wir haben heute eine Flugschau", sagt Robert. „Ich werde ein paar Sprünge machen".
„Das ist interessant", antwortet Paul. „Ich komme vielleicht zuschauen."
„Wenn du willst, kann ich dich mitnehmen und du kannst in einem Flugzeug mitfliegen", sagt Robert.
„Echt? Das wäre super!", ruft Paul. „Um wie viel Uhr ist die Flugschau?"
„Sie fängt um zehn Uhr morgens an", antwortet Robert. „David kommt auch. Übrigens, wir brauchen Hilfe, eine Fallschirmspringerpuppe aus dem Flugzeug zu werfen. Kannst du helfen?"
„Eine Fallschirmspringerpuppe? Warum?", fragt Paul überrascht.
„Ach, weißt du, das ist ein Teil der Schau", sagt

falls down. At this time a real parachutist flies to it, catches it and opens his own parachute. The "man" is saved!"

"Great!" Paul answers, "I will help. Let's go!"

Paul and Robert go outside. They come to the bus stop Olympic and take a bus. It takes only ten minutes to go to the airshow. When they get off the bus, they see David.

"Hello David," Robert says, "Let's go to the airplane."

They see a parachute team at the airplane. They come to the head of the team. The head of the team is dressed in red trousers and a red jacket.

"Hello Martin," Robert says, "Paul and David will help with the life-saving trick."

"Okay. The stuffed parachutist is here," Martin says. He gives them the stuffed parachutist. The stuffed parachutist is dressed in red trousers and a red jacket.

"It is dressed like you," David says smiling to Martin.

"We have no time to talk about it," Martin says, "Take it into this airplane."

Paul and David take the stuffed parachutist into the airplane. They take seats at the pilot. All the parachute team but its head gets into the airplane. They close the door. In five minutes the airplane is in the air. When it flies over San Francisco David sees his own house.

"Look! My house is there!" David cries.

Paul looks through the window at streets, squares, and parks of the city. It is wonderful to fly in an airplane.

"Prepare to jump!" the pilot cries. The parachutists stand up. They open the door.

"Ten, nine, eight, seven, six, five, four, three, two, one. Go!" the pilot cries.

The parachutists begin to jump out of the airplane. The audience down on the land sees red, green, white, blue, yellow parachutes. It looks very nice. Martin, the head of the parachute team is looking up too. The parachutists are flying down and some are landing already.

"Okay. Good work guys," Martin says and goes to the nearby café to drink some coffee.

The airshow goes on.

"Prepare for the life-saving trick!" the pilot cries.

David and Paul take the stuffed parachutist to the door.

"Ten, nine, eight, seven, six, five, four, three, two,

Robert. „Es ist ein Rettungstrick. Die Puppe fällt herunter. In dem Moment fliegt ein echter Fallschirmspringer zu ihr, fängt sie und öffnet seinen eigenen Fallschirm. Der „Mann" ist gerettet!"

„Toll!", antwortet Paul. „Ich helfe. Lass uns gehen!"

Paul und Robert gehen nach draußen. Sie kommen zur Bushaltestelle Olympic und nehmen einen Bus. Es dauert nur zehn Minuten bis zur Flugschau. Als sie aus dem Bus steigen, sehen sie David.

„Hallo David", sagt Robert. „Lass uns zum Flugzeug gehen."

Beim Flugzeug sehen sie eine Fallschirmspringermannschaft. Der Führer der Mannschaft hat eine rote Hose und eine rote Jacke an.

„Hallo Martin", sagt Robert. „Paul und David helfen beim Rettungstrick."

„Okay. Hier ist die Puppe", sagt Martin. Er gibt ihnen die Fallschirmspringerpuppe. Die Puppe trägt eine rote Hose und eine rote Jacke.

„Sie trägt die gleiche Kleidung wie du", sagt David und grinst Martin an.

„Wir haben keine Zeit, darüber zu reden", sagt Martin. „Nehmt sie mit in dieses Flugzeug."

Paul und David bringen die Puppe ins Flugzeug. Sie setzen sich neben den Piloten. Die ganze Fallschirmspringermannschaft außer ihrem Führer besteigt das Flugzeug. Sie schließen die Tür. Nach fünf Minuten ist das Flugzeug in der Luft. Als es über San Francisco fliegt, sieht David sein Haus.

„Schau! Da ist mein Haus!", ruft David.

Paul sieht aus dem Fenster auf Straßen, Plätze und Parks. Es ist toll, in einem Flugzeug zu fliegen.

„Zum Sprung bereit machen!", ruft der Pilot. Die Fallschirmspringer stehen auf. Sie öffnen die Tür.

„Zehn, neun, acht, sieben, sechs, fünf, vier, drei, zwei, eins! Los!", ruft der Pilot.

Die Fallschirmspringer beginnen, aus dem Flugzeug zu springen. Das Publikum auf dem Boden sieht rote, grüne, weiße, blaue und gelbe Fallschirme. Es sieht sehr schön aus. Martin, der Führer der Mannschaft, schaut auch nach oben. Die Fallschirmspringer fliegen nach unten und einige landen bereits.

„Okay, gute Arbeit, Jungs", sagt Martin und geht in ein Café in der Nähe, um Kaffee zu trinken.

Die Flugschau geht weiter.

„Für den Rettungstrick bereit machen!", ruft der Pilot.

David und Paul bringen die Puppe zur Tür.

„Zehn, neun, acht, sieben, sechs, fünf, vier, drei, zwei, eins! Los!", ruft der Pilot.

one. Go!" the pilot cries.

Paul and David push the stuffed parachutist through the door. It goes out but then stops. Its rubber "hand" catches on some metal part of the airplane.

"Go-go boys!" the pilot cries.

The boys push the stuffed parachutist very strongly but cannot get it out.

The audience down on the land sees a man dressed in red in the airplane door. Two other men are trying to push him out. People cannot believe their eyes. It goes on about a minute. Then the parachutist in red falls down. Another parachutist jumps out of the airplane and tries to catch it. But he cannot do it. The parachutist in red falls down. It falls through the roof inside of the café. The audience looks silently. Then the people see a man dressed in red run outside of the café. This man in red is Martin, the head of the parachutist team. But the audience thinks that he is that falling parachutist. He looks up and cries angrily, "If you cannot catch a man then do not try it!"

The audience is silent.

"Daddy, this man is very strong," a little girl says to her dad.

"He is well trained," the dad answers.

After the airshow Paul and David go to Robert.

"How is our work?" David asks.

"Ah... Oh, it is very good. Thank you," Robert answers.

"If you need some help just say," Paul says.

Paul und David stoßen die Puppe aus der Tür. Sie fällt heraus, bleibt dann aber hängen. Ihre Gummihand ist an einem Metallteil des Flugzeugs hängen geblieben.

„Los, auf, Jungs!", ruft der Pilot.
Die Jungs ziehen mit aller Kraft an der Puppe, aber sie bekommen sie nicht los.
Das Publikum unten auf dem Boden sieht einen Mann in Rot gekleidet in der Flugzeugtür. Zwei andere Männer versuchen, ihn herauszustoßen. Die Leute trauen ihren Augen nicht. Es dauert etwa eine Minute. Dann fällt der Fallschirmspringer in Rot nach unten. Ein anderer Fallschirmspringer springt aus dem Flugzeug und versucht, ihn zu fangen. Aber er schafft es nicht. Der Fallschirmspringer in Rot fällt weiter. Er fällt durch das Dach in das Café. Das Publikum sieht schweigend zu. Dann sehen die Leute einen in rot gekleideten Mann aus dem Café rennen. Der Mann in Rot ist Martin, der Führer der Fallschirmspingermannschaft. Aber das Publikum denkt, dass er der abgestürzte Fallschirmspringer ist. Er schaut nach oben und ruft wütend: „Wenn ihr einen Mann nicht fangen könnt, dann versucht es nicht!"
Das Publikum ist still.
„Papa, dieser Mann ist sehr stark", sagt ein kleines Mädchen zu ihrem Vater.
„Er ist gut trainiert", antwortet der Vater.
Nach der Flugschau gehen David und Paul zu Robert.
„Wie war unsere Arbeit?", fragt David.
„Ähm...Oh, sehr gut. Danke", antwortet Robert.
„Wenn du Hilfe brauchst, sag es einfach", sagt Paul.

26

Some und any

Some und any bedeuten etwas / einige, sie werden aber unterschiedlich benutzt.

In positiven Sätzen verwendet man normalerweise some.

I have some books. - Ich habe einige Bücher.

There is some water in the cup. - Es gibt etwas Wasser in der Tasse.

In Fragen und negativen Sätzen verwendet man any. In negativen Sätzen bedeutet not any immer kein/keine.

>Are there any chairs in the room? - Gibt es einige Stühle im Zimmer?

>There are not any chairs in the room. - Es gibt keine Stühle im Zimmer.

Wird als Antwort auf die Frage jedoch ein ‚ja' erwartet oder erhofft, verwendet man in der Frage some.

>Can you give me some tea, please? - Können Sie mir etwas Tee geben, bitte?

>There is no tea. Have some coffee, please. - Es gibt keinen Tee. Trinken Sie etwas Kaffee, bitte.

>Then, can I just have some water? - Dann, kann ich einfach etwas Wasser bekommen?

Any in positiven Sätzen bedeutet jeder / beliebig.

>You can take any books. - Sie können beliebige Bücher nehmen.

>Any student of our group can speak some English. - Jeder Student unserer Gruppe kann etwas Englisch sprechen.

Exercise 26 Compose the sentences as in the example. Use some, any.

Übung 26 Bilde die Sätze nach dem Beispiel. Benutze some, any.

1. Sam has got some friends. I have not got .... friends in this city.
2. Has Anna got .... classes today? She has not got .... classes today.
3. Have you got .... problems with this work? Yes, I have got .... problems.
4. Have they got .... pets at home? They have not got .... pets.
5. Are there .... animals in this wood? There are .... animals there.
6. Are there .... big shops in this street? There are not .... big shops there.

Would like

I would like oder I'd like drückt einen Wunsch, eine Bitte oder eine Höflichkeitsform aus. Um jemandem etwas anzubieten verwendet man Would you like ..?

Would you like some mineral water? - Möchten Sie etwas Mineralwasser?

I would like some coffee, please. - Ich möchte etwas Kaffee, bitte.

Would you like to dance with me? - Möchten Sie mit mir tanzen?

I would like just to listen to music. - Ich möchte nur Musik hören.

Would they like to go to the park? - Möchten sie in die Park gehen?

Yes, they would like that. - Ja, sie möchten das.

Would he like to play with us? - Möchte er mit uns spielen?

Yes, he would like that. - Ja, er möchten das.

Einen Wunsch kann man auch mit want ausdrücken. Want kann aber unhöflich wirken.

I want a banana. - Ich will eine Banane.

I want to dance. - Ich will tanzen.

Exercise 27 Compose the sentences as in the example. Use would like.
Übung 27 Bilde die Sätze nach dem Beispiel. Benutze would like.

1. (water?) Would you like some water?
2. (banana.) I would like a banana.
3. (an apple?) ....
4. (a cup of coffee.) I would ....
5. (some tea.) ....
6. (to dance?) ....
7. (to play tennis.) ....

8. (to go to a café ?) ....
9. (to go to the park.) ....

Reading comprehension

Turn the gas off!
Mach das Gas aus!

Words

1. careful ['keəf(ə)l] - sorgfältig
2. eleven [ɪ'lev(ə)n] - elf
3. everything ['evrɪθɪŋ] - alles
4. feeling ['fiːlɪŋ] - das Gefühl
5. fill up [fɪl ʌp] - füllen
6. fire ['faɪə] - das Feuer
7. forget ['fəget] - vergessen
8. forty-four ['fɔːti fɔː] - vierundvierzig
9. freeze [friːz] - erstarren
10. gas [gæs] - das Gas
11. immediately [ɪ'miːdɪətlɪ] - sofort
12. kettle ['ketl] - der Kessel
13. kilometer [kɪ'lɔmɪtə] - der Kilometer
14. kindergarten ['kɪndəˌgaːt(ə)n] - der Kindergarten
15. living ['lɪvɪŋ] - wohnhaft
16. meanwhile [ˌmiːn'waɪl] - in der Zwischenzeit
17. moment ['məʊmənt] - der Moment
18. order ['ɔːdə] - befehlen
19. pale [peɪl] - blass
20. phone handset ['hændset] - der Telefonhörer
21. pussycat ['pʊsɪkæt] - die Miezekatze
22. quick [kwɪk], quickly ['kwɪklɪ] - schnell
23. railway ['reɪlweɪ] station - der Bahnhof
24. ring [rɪŋ] - das Klingeln; to ring - klingeln
25. secretary ['sekrət(ə)rɪ] - die Sekretärin
26. sly [slaɪ], slyly ['slaɪlɪ] - schlau
27. so [səʊ] - deswegen
28. spread [spred] - übergreifen
29. strange [streɪndʒ] - fremd
30. suddenly ['sʌd(ə)nlɪ] - plötzlich
31. tap [tæp] - der Wasserhahn
32. tell [tel], say ['seɪ] - sagen
33. ticket ['tɪkɪt] - die Fahrkarte
34. train [treɪn] - der Zug
35. turn [təːn] - drehen
36. turn on - anmachen
37. turn off - ausmachen
38. twenty ['twentɪ] - zwanzig
39. voice [vɔɪs] - die Stimme

40. warm [wɔ:m] - warm
41. warm up [wɔ:m ʌp] - aufwärmen
42. who [hu:] - wer
43. will [wɪl] - werden

 B

Turn the gas off!

It is seven o'clock in the morning. David and Nancy are sleeping. Their mother is in the kitchen. The mother's name is Linda. Linda is forty-four years old. She is a careful woman. Linda cleans the kitchen before she goes to work. She is a secretary. She works twenty kilometers away from San Francisco. Linda usually goes to work by train.
 She goes outside. The railway station is nearby, so Linda goes there on foot. She buys a ticket and gets on a train. It takes about twenty minutes to go to work. Linda sits in the train and looks out of the window.
Suddenly she freezes. The kettle! It is standing on the cooker and she forgot to turn the gas off! David and Nancy are sleeping. The fire can spread on the furniture and then... Linda turns pale. But she is a smart woman and in a minute she knows what to do. She asks a woman and a man, who sit nearby, to telephone her home and tell David about the kettle.
 Meanwhile David gets up, washes and goes to the kitchen. He takes the kettle off the table, fills it up with water and puts it on the cooker. Then he takes bread and butter and makes sandwiches. Nancy comes into the kitchen.
 "Where is my little pussycat?" she asks.
 "I do not know," David answers, "Go to the bathroom and wash your face. We will drink some tea and eat some sandwiches now. Then I will take you to the kindergarten."
 Nancy does not want to wash. "I cannot turn on the water tap," she says slyly.
 "I will help you," her brother says. At this moment the telephone rings. Nancy runs quickly to the telephone and takes the handset.
 "Hello, this is the zoo. And who are you?" she says. David takes the handset from her and says, "Hello. This is David."
 "Are you David Tweeter living at eleven Queen street?" the voice of a strange woman asks.
 "Yes," David answers.

Mach das Gas aus!

Es ist sieben Uhr morgens. David und Nancy schlafen. Ihre Mutter ist in der Küche. Die Mutter heißt Linda. Linda ist vierundvierzig. Sie ist eine sorgfältige Frau. Linda putzt die Küche, bevor sie zur Arbeit geht. Sie ist Sekretärin. Sie arbeitet zwanzig Kilometer außerhalb von San Francisco. Linda fährt normalerweise mit dem Zug zur Arbeit.

Sie geht nach draußen. Der Bahnhof ist in der Nähe, deswegen geht Linda zu Fuß dorthin. Sie kauft eine Fahrkarte und steigt ein. Es dauert etwa zwanzig Minuten bis zu ihrer Arbeit. Linda sitzt im Zug und schaut aus dem Fenster.
Plötzlich erstarrt sie. Der Kessel! Er steht auf dem Herd und sie hat vergessen, das Gas auszumachen. David und Nancy schlafen. Das Feuer kann auf die Möbel übergreifen und dann... Linda wird blass. Aber sie ist eine intelligente Frau und kurz darauf weiß sie, was zu tun ist. Sie bittet eine Frau und einen Mann, die neben ihr sitzen, bei ihr zu Hause anzurufen und David über den Kessel zu informieren.
In der Zwischenzeit steht David auf, wäscht sich und geht in die Küche. Er nimmt den Kessel vom Tisch, füllt ihn mit Wasser und stellt ihn auf den Herd. Dann nimmt er Brot und Butter und macht Butterbrote. Nancy kommt in die Küche.
„Wo ist meine kleine Miezekatze?", fragt sie.
„Ich weiß es nicht", antworte David. „Geh ins Bad und wasch dein Gesicht. Wir trinken jetzt Tee und essen Brote. Dann bring ich dich in den Kindergarten."
Nancy will sich nicht waschen. „Ich kann den Wasserhahn nicht anmachen", sagt sie schlau.

„Ich helfe dir", sagt ihr Bruder. In diesem Moment klingelt das Telefon. Nancy rennt schnell zum Telefon und nimmt den Hörer ab.
„Hallo, hier ist der Zoo. Und wer ist da?", sagt sie. David nimmt ihr den Hörer weg und sagt: „Hallo, David hier."
„Bist du David Tweeter, wohnhaft in der Queen Straße elf?", fragt die Stimme einer fremden Frau.
„Ja", antwortet David.

"Go to the kitchen immediately and turn the gas off!" the woman's voice cries.
"Who are you? Why must I turn the gas off?" David says in surprise.
"Do it now!" the voice orders.
David turns the gas off. Nancy and David look at the kettle in surprise.
"I do not understand," David says, "How can this woman know that we will drink tea?"
"I am hungry," his sister says, "When will we eat?"
"I am hungry too," David says and turns the gas on again. At this minute the telephone rings again.
"Hello," David says.
"Are you David Tweeter who lives at eleven Queen street?" the voice of a strange man asks.
"Yes," David answers.
"Turn off the cooker gas immediately! Be careful!" the voice orders.
"Okay," David says and turns the gas off again.
"Let's go to the kindergarten," David says to Nancy feeling that they will not drink tea today.
"No. I want some tea and bread with butter," Nancy says angrily.
"Well, let's try to warm up the kettle again," her brother says and turns the gas on.
The telephone rings and this time their mother orders to turn the gas off. Then she explains everything. At last Nancy and David drink tea and go to the kindergarten.

„Geh sofort in die Küche und mach das Gas aus", ruft die Stimme der Frau.
„Wer sind Sie? Warum soll ich das Gas ausmachen?", fragt David überrascht.
„Mach es jetzt!", befielt die Stimme.
David macht das Gas aus. Nancy und David sehen verwundert auf den Kessel.
„Ich verstehe das nicht", sagt David. „Woher weiß diese Frau, dass wir Tee trinken wollten?"
„Ich habe Hunger", sagt seine Schwester. „Wann essen wir?"
„Ich habe auch Hunger", sagt David und macht das Gas wieder an. In diesem Moment klingelt das Telefon wieder.
„Hallo", sagt David.
„Bist du David Tweeter, wohnhaft in der Queen Straße elf?", fragt die Stimme eines fremden Mannes.
„Ja", antwortet David.
„Mach sofort das Gas aus! Sei vorsichtig!", befiehlt die Stimme.
„Okay", sagt David und macht das Gas wieder aus.
„Lass uns in den Kindergarten gehen", sagt David zu Nancy in dem Gefühl, dass sie heute keinen Tee trinken werden.
„Nein. Ich will Tee und Brot mit Butter", sagt Nancy wütend.
„Gut, lass uns versuchen, den Kessel wieder zu wärmen", sagt ihr Bruder und stellt das Gas an.
Das Telefon klingelt und dieses Mal befiehlt ihre Mutter, das Gas abzustellen. Dann erklärt sie alles. Endlich trinken Nancy und David Tee und gehen in den Kindergarten.

28

Present Simple / Präsens

Mit dem Present Simple werden Handlungen in der Gegenwart ausgedrückt, die

▶ regelmäßig oder wiederholt stattfinden

I play tennis almost every day. - Ich spiele Tennis fast jeden Tag.

She reads books about pirates. - Sie liest Bücher über Piraten.

▶ nacheinander ablaufen

> He wakes up at seven o'clock then goes to the bathroom and takes a shower. - Er wacht um sieben Uhr auf, geht ins Badezimmer und duscht sich.
>
> I have my breakfast, then I drink a cup of coffee. - Ich esse mein Frühstück, dann trinke ich eine Tasse Kaffee.

▶ allgemeine Gültigkeit besitzen

> My birthday is in May. - Mein Geburtstag ist im Mai.
>
> Rome is the capital of Italy. - Rom ist Italiens Hauptstadt.

▶ bereits festgelegt sind (z.B. Fahrplan, Programm)

> The concert begins at five o'clock. - Das Konzert beginnt um fünf Uhr.
>
> The bus arrives at nine o'clock. - Der Bus kommt um neun Uhr.

Das Present Simple wird aus dem Infinitiv (Grundform) des jeweiligen Verbs gebildet. In der 3. Person Singular wird zusätzlich ein -s oder -es angehängt.

> I read - we read - you read - he reads - she reads - it reads - they read

Bei Fragen im Present Simple benutzten wir das Hilfsverb do am Satzanfang. Vergleiche:

> **Bejahte Sätze**
>
> Subjekt + Verb
>
> You play tennis every day. - Du spielst Tennis jeden Tag.
>
> They work in London. - Sie arbeiten in London.
>
> **Fragen**
>
> Do/Does + Subjekt + Infinitiv
>
> Do you play tennis every day? - Spielst du Tennis jeden Tag?
>
> Do they work in London? - Arbeiten sie in London?

In der 3. Person Singular verwenden wir das Hilfsverb does anstatt do. Gleichzeitig verliert das Verb die Endung -s/-es.

She reads books at home. - Sie liest Bücher zu Hause.

Does she read books at home? - Liest sie Bücher zu Hause?

He plays tennis every day. - Er spielt Tennis jeden Tag.

Does he play tennis every day? - Spielt er Tennis jeden Tag?

Verneinungen werden mit do not / does not und dem Infinitiv (Grundform) gebildet. Vergleiche:

Bejahte Sätze

Subjekt + Verb

You work in the garden. - Du arbeitest im Garten.

He works in the garden. - Er arbeitet im Garten.

Verneinte Sätze

Subjekt + do not/does not + Infinitiv

You do not work in the garden. - Du arbeitest im Garten nicht.

He does not work in the garden. - Er arbeitet im Garten nicht.

Wenn der Satz aber über ein der sechs Hilfs- oder Modalverben (can - können, may - dürfen, must - müssen, be - sein, will - werden, shall - sollen) verfügt, wird do/does als das Hilfsverb nicht genutzt. Dann folgt in Fragen das Subjekt genau, wie im Deutschen auf dieses Modal- oder Hilfsverb. Bei verneinten Aussagen mit *not* muss das Hilfsverb stets vor diesem platziert werden.

She can swim. - Sie kann schwimmen.

Can she swim? - Kann sie schwimmen?

She cannot swim. - Sie kann nicht schwimmen.

He is a student. - Er ist Student.

Is he a student. - Ist er Student?

He is not a student. - Er ist kein Student.

Exercise 28-1 Compose questions as in the example.

Übung 28-1 Bilde Fragen nach dem Beispiel.

1. You live in the US. Do you live in the US?
2. You play tennis. ....
3. Emma speaks German. ....
4. Tom can swim. ....
5. Bill works hard. ....
6. Anna must help Bill. ....
7. This man is a bus driver. ....
8. He works on weekends. ....
9. Linda likes cooking. ....
10. Linda's children like her pizza. ....
11. Finn can help Linda. ....
12. Finn is Linda's friend. ....
13. He lives in this street. ....
14. Shops open at nine o'clock. ....
15. Sam wakes up at seven o'clock. ....
16. He studies at university. ....
17. Sam is a good student. ....

Exercise 28-2 Compose negative sentences as in the example.

Übung 28-2 Bilde Verneinungen nach dem Beispiel.

1. You live in the US. You do not live in the US.
2. You play tennis. ....
3. Emma speaks German. ....
4. Tom can swim. ....
5. Bill works hard. ....
6. Anna must help Bill. ....
7. This man is a bus driver. ....
8. He works on weekends. ....
9. Linda likes cooking. ....
10. Linda's children like her pizza. ....

11. Finn can help Linda. ....

12. Finn is Linda's friend. ....

13. He lives in this street. ....

14. Shops open at nine o'clock. ....

15. Sam wakes up at seven o'clock. ....

16. He studies at university. ....

17. Sam is a good student. ....

29

Short answers / Kurzantworten

Viele Fragen können im Deutschen ganz einfach mit ja oder nein beantwortet werden. Es ist aber oft sinnvoll und aussagekräftiger, wenn man mit einer kompletten Kurzantwort antwortet.

Bist du müde?

Ja, bin ich.

Was im Deutschen eine Nettigkeit ist bzw. der besseren Verständigung dient, ist im Englischen unerlässlich und somit sind Kurzantworten auch im alltäglichen Sprachgebrauch nicht nur üblich, sondern nahezu schon Pflicht. Genau, wie im Deutschen wird dabei das Hilfsverb der Frage in der Antwort wieder aufgegriffen und die Struktur des Satzes gleicht der, eines Aussagesatzes.

Fragesatz - Bejahende Kurzantwort - Verneinende Kurzantwort

Are you hungry? - Yes, I am. - No, I am not.

Is she a student? - Yes, she is. - No, she is not.

Do you play the piano? - Yes, I do. - No, I do not.

Does he live in the US? - Yes, he does. - No, he does not.

Can she swim? - Yes, she can. - No, she cannot.

Exercise 29 Compose positive and negative short answers as in the example.

Übung 29 Bilde bejahende und verneinende Kurzantworten nach dem Beispiel.

1. Can you help me? Yes, I can. No, I cannot.
2. Can you play tennis? ....
3. Does Emma speak German? ....
4. Do you live in Germany? ....
5. Do they study English? ....
6. Is he a student? ....
7. Are they Americans? ....
8. Are you happy? ....

Reading comprehension

A job agency
Eine Arbeitsvermittlung

Words

1. agree [əˈgriː] - einverstanden sein
2. all-round [ˌɔːlˈraʊnd] - vielseitig, alles könnend
3. also [ˈɔːlsəʊ] - auch
4. arm [aːm] - der Arm
5. as [æz] - da, wie
6. cable [ˈkeɪbl] - das Kabel
7. carefully [ˈkeəf(ə)lɪ] - vorsichtig
8. listen carefully - genau zuhören
9. confused [kənˈfjuːzd] - verwirrt
10. consult [kənˈsʌlt] - beraten
11. consultant [kənˈsʌlt(ə)nt] - der Berater
12. current [ˈkʌr(ə)nt] - der Strom
13. deadly [ˈdedlɪ] - tödlich
14. electric [ɪˈlektrɪk] - elektrisch
15. experience [ɪkˈspɪərɪəns] - die Erfahrung
16. fifteen [ˌfɪfˈtiːn] - fünfzehn
17. floor [flɔː] - der Boden
18. grey-headed [greɪ ˈhedɪd] - grauhaarig
19. half [haːf] - halb
20. helper [ˈhelpə] - der Helfer
21. individually [ˌɪndɪˈvɪdʒʊəlɪ] - einzeln
22. know each other [nəʊ ˈiːtʃˈʌðə] - sich kennen
23. let [let] - lassen
24. manual work [ˈmænjʊəl ˈwɜːk] - die Handarbeit
25. mattress [ˈmætrəs] - die Matratze
26. mental [ˈment(ə)l] work - die Kopfarbeit
27. number [ˈnʌmbə] - die Nummer
28. per hour [pɜː ˈaʊə] - pro Stunde
29. position [pəˈzɪʃən] - die Position
30. publishing [ˈpʌblɪʃɪŋ] - der Verlag
31. recommend [ˌrekəˈmend] - empfehlen
32. running [ˈrʌnɪŋ] - führen
33. seriously [ˈsɪərɪəslɪ] - ernst
34. shake [ʃeɪk] - zittern
35. sixty [ˈsɪkstɪ] - sechzig
36. story [ˈstɔːrɪ] - die Geschichte
37. strong [strɒŋ], strongly [ˈstrɒŋlɪ] - stark
38. sure [ʃɔː | ʃʊə] - klar, sicher
39. the same [seɪm] - der/die/das Gleiche
40. at the same time - gleichzeitig
41. town [taʊn] - die Stadt
42. was [wɒz] - war
43. worry [ˈwʌrɪ] - sich Sorgen machen
44. Do not worry! - Mach dir keinen Kopf!

B

A job agency

One day Paul goes to Robert's room and sees that his friend is lying on the bed shaking. Paul sees some electrical cables running from Robert to the electric kettle. Paul believes that Robert is under a deadly electric current. He quickly goes to the bed, takes the mattress and pulls it strongly. Robert falls to the floor. Then he stands up and looks at Paul in surprise.
"What was it?" Robert asks.
"You were on electrical current," Paul says.
"No, I was listening to the music," Robert says and shows his CD player.
"Oh, I am sorry," Paul says. He is confused.
"It's okay. Do not worry," Robert answers quietly cleaning his trousers.
"David and I go to a job agency. Do you want to go with us?" Paul asks.
"Sure. Let's go together," Robert says.
They go outside and take the bus number seven. It takes them about fifteen minutes to go to the job agency. David is already there. They come into the building. There is a long queue to the office of the job agency. They stand in the queue. In half an hour they come into the office. There is a table and some bookcases in the room. A gray-headed man is sitting at the table. He is about sixty years old.
"Come in guys!" he says friendly, "Take seats, please."
David, Robert and Paul sit down.
"My name is George Estimator. I am a job consultant. Usually I speak with visitors individually. But as you are all students and know each other I can consult you all together. Do you agree?"
"Yes, sir," David says, "We have three or four hours of free time every day. We need to find jobs for that time, sir."
"Well. I have some jobs for students. And you take off your player," Mr. Estimator says to Robert.
"I can listen to you and to music at the same time," Robert says.
"If you seriously want to get a job take the

Eine Arbeitsvermittlung

Eines Tages kommt Paul in Roberts Zimmer und sieht seinen Freund zitternd auf dem Bett liegen. Paul sieht einige Stromkabel, die von Robert zum Wasserkocher führen. Paul glaubt, dass Robert einen tödlichen Stromschlag abbekommen hat. Er geht schnell zum Bett, nimmt die Matratze und zieht stark daran. Robert fällt auf den Boden. Dann steht er auf und sieht Paul verwundert an.
„Was war das denn?", fragt Robert.
„Du standest unter Strom", sagt Paul.
„Nein, ich habe Musik gehört", sagt Robert und zeigt auf seinen CD-Spieler.
„Oh, Entschuldigung", sagt Paul. Er ist verwirrt.
„Schon gut, mach dir keinen Kopf", sagt Robert ruhig und macht seine Hose sauber.
„David und ich gehen zu einer Arbeitsvermittlung. Willst du mitkommen?", fragt Paul.
„Klar, lass uns zusammen gehen", sagt Robert.
Sie gehen nach draußen und nehmen den Bus Nummer 7. Sie brauchen etwa fünfzehn Minuten bis zur Arbeitsvermittlung. David ist schon dort. Sie betreten das Gebäude. Vor dem Büro der Arbeitsvermittlung ist eine lange Schlange. Sie stellen sich an. Nach einer halben Stunde betreten sie das Büro. Im Zimmer sind ein Stuhl und ein paar Bücherregale. Am Tisch sitzt ein grauhaariger Mann. Er ist etwa sechzig.

„Kommt rein, Jungs", sagt er freundlich. „Setzt euch, bitte".
David, Robert und Paul setzen sich.
„Ich bin Georg Estimator. Ich bin Arbeitsberater. Normalerweise spreche ich einzeln mit Besuchern. Aber da ihr alle Studenten seid und euch kennt, kann ich euch zusammen beraten. Seid ihr einverstanden?"

„Ja", sagt David. „Wir haben drei, vier Stunden frei pro Tag. Wir brauchen für diese Zeit einen Job."
„Gut, ich habe ein paar Jobs für Studenten. Und du, mach deinen CD-Spieler aus", sagt Herr Estimator zu Robert.
„Ich kann gleichzeitig Ihnen zuhören und Musik hören", sagt Robert.
„Wenn du ernsthaft einen Job willst, mach die Musik aus und hör mir genau zu", sagt Herr Estimator. „Also, was

player off and listen carefully to what I say;" Mr. Estimator says, "Now guys say what kind of job do you need? Do you need mental or manual work?"

"I can do any work," Paul says, "I am strong. Want to arm?" he says and puts his arm on Mr. Estimator's table.

"It is not a sport club here but if you want..." Mr. Estimator says. He puts his arm on the table and quickly pushes down Paul's arm, "As you see son, you must be not only strong but also smart."

"I can work mentally too, sir," Paul says again. He wants to get a job very much. "I can write stories. I have some stories about my native town."

"This is very interesting," Mr. Estimator says. He takes a sheet of paper, "The publishing house "All-round" needs a young helper for a writing position. They pay nine dollar per hour."

"Cool!" Paul says, "Can I try?"

"Sure. Here are their telephone number and their address," Mr. Estimator says and gives a sheet of paper to Paul.

"And you guys can choose a job on a farm, in a computer firm, on a newspaper or in a supermarket. As you do not have any experience I recommend you to begin to work in a farm. They need two workers," Mr. Estimator says to David and Robert.

"How much do they pay?" David asks.

"Let me see…" Mr. Estimator looks into the computer, "They need workers for three or four hours a day and they pay seven dollars per hour. Saturdays and Sundays are days off. Do you agree?" he asks.

"I agree," David says.

"I agree too," Robert says.

"Well. Take the telephone number and the address of the farm," Mr. Estimator says and gives a sheet of paper to them.

"Thank you, sir," the boys say and go outside.

für einen Job wollt ihr denn. Wollt ihr Hand- oder Kopfarbeit?

„Ich kann jede Arbeit machen", sagt Paul. „Ich bin stark. Wollen Sie es testen?", fragt er und stützt seinen Arm auf Herrn Estimators Tisch auf.

„Das hier ist kein Sportverein, aber wenn du willst...", sagt Herr Estimator. Er stützt seinen Arm auf den Tisch auf und drückt Pauls Arm schnell nach unten. „Wie du siehst, musst du nicht nur stark, sondern auch schlau sein."

„Ich kann auch Denkarbeit machen", sagt Paul. Er will unbedingt einen Job. „Ich kann Geschichten schreiben. Ich habe ein paar Geschichten über meine Heimatstadt."

„Das ist sehr interessant", sagt Herr Estimator. Er greift nach einem Blatt Papier. „Der Verlag „All-Round" braucht einen jungen Helfer als Schreiber. Sie zahlen neun Dollar pro Stunde."

„Super", sagt Paul. „Kann ich das versuchen?"

„Natürlich. Hier sind Telefonnummer und Adresse", sagt Herr Estimator und gibt Paul ein Blatt Papier.

„Und ihr Jungs könnt zwischen einem Job auf einem Bauernhof, in einer Computerfirma, bei einer Zeitung oder im Supermarkt wählen. Da ihr keine Erfahrung habt, empfehle ich euch, mit der Arbeit auf dem Bauernhof anzufangen. Sie brauchen zwei Arbeiter", sagt Herr Estimator zu David und Robert.

„Wie viel zahlen sie?", fragt David.

„Mal sehen..." Herr Estimator schaut auf den Computer. „Sie brauchen Arbeiter für drei oder vier Stunden am Tag und zahlen sieben Dollar pro Stunde. Samstag und Sonntag sind frei. Seid ihr einverstanden?", fragt er.

„Ja, bin ich", sagt David.

„Ich auch", sagt Robert.

„Gut, nehmt die Telefonnummer und die Adresse des Bauernhofs", sagt Herr Estimator und gibt ihnen eine Blatt Papier.

„Dankeschön, Herr Estimator", sagen die Jungs und gehen nach draußen.

Present Progressive (Continuous) / Verlaufsform des Präsens

Das Present Progressive bilden wir aus einer Form von to be (am, is, are) und dem Verb mit der Endung -ing. Diese Zeitform nennt man auch das Present Continuous.

Bejahte Sätze

Subjekt + to be + Ving

I am reading a book. - Ich lese gerade ein Buch.

Anna is reading a book. - Anna liest gerade ein Buch.

We are reading a book. - Wir lesen gerade ein Buch.

Fragen

to be + Subjekt + Ving

Am I reading a book? - Lese ich gerade ein Buch?

Is Anna reading a book? - Liest Anna gerade ein Buch?

Are they reading a book? - Lesen wir gerade ein Buch?

Verneinte Sätze

Subjekt + to be not + Ving

I am not reading. - Ich lese gerade nicht.

Anna is not reading. - Anna liest gerade nicht.

We are not reading. - Wir lesen gerade nicht.

Das Present Progressive verwenden wir mit Handlungen, die

▶ im Moment des Sprechens geschehen (jetzt gerade)

Look! They are playing tennis. - Schau mal! Sie spielen gerade Tennis.

I cannot meet you now. I am working. Let's meet later. - Ich kann nicht mit dir jetzt treffen. Ich arbeite gerade. Lass uns später treffen.

Are you having breakfast? - Isst du gerade dein Frühstück?

It is raining. The sun is not shining. - Es regnet. Die Sonne scheint nicht.

▶ jetzt gerade geschehen, jedoch nicht unbedingt im Moment des Sprechens

I am learning English a lot. - Ich lerne Englisch viel.

We are building a swimming pool. - Wir bauen das Schwimmbad.

▶ nur vorübergehend stattfinden (befristete Handlungen deren Frist gerade andauert)

I am learning English a lot this week. - Ich lerne Englisch viel diese Woche.

We are building a swimming pool in the garden this summer. - Wir bauen das Schwimmbad im Garten diesen Sommer.

Es gibt einige Verben, die keine progressive-Form haben. Bei diesen Verben geht es um Zustand und nicht um Handlung. Hier sind einige von ihnen.

▶ Gefühle

hate - hassen, like - mögen, love - lieben, prefer - bevorzugen, want - wollen, wish - wünschen

▶ Sinnesempfindungen

feel - fühlen, hear - hören, see - sehen, seem / appear - scheinen, smell - riechen, sound - klingen, taste - schmecken

▶ Verständigung

agree - zustimmen, deny - verweigern, mean - bedeuten, promise - versprechen, satisfy - zufriedenstellen, surprise - überraschen

▶ Denken

believe - glauben, imagine - sich vorstellen, know - wissen, mean - meinen, realize - begreifen, recognize - erkennen, remember - merken, understand - verstehen

▶ andere Zustände

be - sein, belong - gehören, concern - betreffen, depend - abhängen, involve - umfassen, need - brauchen, owe - schulden, own / possess - besitzen

Exercise 30-1 Compose the sentences as in the example. Use the Present Progressive.

Übung 30-1 Bilde die Sätze nach dem Beispiel. Benutze das Present Progressive.

1. (I / eat / an apple) I am eating an apple.
2. (Finn / play / tennis) ....
3. (Sam / help / me) ....
4. (Anna / cook / pizza) ....
5. (Linda / swim) ....
6. (Tom / work / in the garden) ....
7. (We / study / English / hard today) ....
8. (The children / play / in the park) ....
9. (The students / have / breakfast) ....
10. (Emma / drive / a car) ....

Exercise 30-2 What is happening at the moment?

Übung 30-2 Was gerade passiert?

1. (I / drink / tea) I am (not) drinking tea.
2. (I / play / tennis) ....
3. (the teacher / help / me) ....
4. (I / swim) ....
5. (I / work / in the garden) ....
6. (I / learn / English) ....
7. (I / learn / German) ....
8. (it / rain) ....
9. (the sun / shine) ....

Reading comprehension

David and Robert wash the truck (part 1)
David und Robert waschen den Laster (Teil 1)

Words

1. along [əˈlɒŋ] - entlang
2. arrive [əˈraɪv] - ankommen
3. at first [ət ˈfɜːst] - erst
4. bigger [ˈbɪgə] - größer
5. box [bɒks] - die Kiste
6. brake [breɪk] - die Bremse
7. to brake - bremsen
8. check [tʃek] - kontrollieren
9. clean [kliːn] - sauber machen, putzen
10. close [kləʊz] - nahe
11. closer [ˈkləʊsə] - näher
12. driving license [ˈdraɪvɪŋ ˈlaɪsns] - der Führerschein
13. eighth [eɪtθ] - achter
14. employer [ɪmˈplɔɪə] - der Arbeitgeber
15. engine [ˈendʒɪn] - der Motor
16. far [fɑː] - weit
17. field [fiːld] - das Feld
18. fifth [fɪfθ] - fünfter
19. float [fləʊt] - treiben
20. fourth [fɔːθ] - vierter
21. front [frʌnt] - vorn
22. front wheels [frʌnt ˈwiːlz] - die Vorderräder
23. further [ˈfəːðə] - weiter
24. load [ləʊd] - laden
25. lot [lɒt] - viel
26. machine [məˈʃiːn] - die Maschine
27. meter [ˈmiːtə] - der Meter
28. ninth [naɪnθ] - neunter
29. owner [ˈəʊnə] - der Besitzer
30. pitch [ˈpɪtʃ]- schaukeln
31. quite [kwaɪt] - ziemlich
32. road [rəʊd] - die Straße
33. sea [siː] - das Meer
34. seashore [ˈsiːʃɔː] - die Küste
35. second [ˈsek(ə)nd] - zweiter
36. seed [siːd] - das Saatgut
37. seventh [ˈsev(ə)nθ] - siebter
38. ship [ʃɪp] - das Schiff

39. sixth [sɪksθ] - sechster
40. slowly [ˈsləʊlɪ] - langsam
41. start [staːt] - anfangen
42. step [ˈstep] - treten
43. strength [streŋθ] - die Stärke
44. suitable [ˈsjuːtəbl] - passend
45. tenth [tenθ] - zehnter
46. third [θəːd] - dritter

47. unload [ʌnˈləʊd] - abladen
48. use [juːz] - benutzen
49. wait [weɪt] - warten
50. wash [ˈwɔʃ] - waschen, putzen
51. wave [weɪv] - die Welle
52. wheel [(h)wiːl] - das Rad
53. yard [jaːd] - der Hof

B

David and Robert wash the truck (part 1)

David and Robert are working on a farm now. They work three or four hours every day. The work is quite hard. They must do a lot of work every day. They clean the farm yard every second day. They wash the farm machines every third day. Every fourth day they work in the farm fields.
Their employer's name is Daniel Tough. Mr. Tough is the owner of the farm and he does most of the work. Mr. Tough works very hard. He also gives a lot of work to David and Robert.
"Hey boys, finish cleaning the machines, take the truck and go to the transport firm Rapid," Mr. Tough says, "They have a load for me. Load boxes with the seed in the truck, bring them to the farm, and unload in the farm yard. Do it quickly because I need to use the seed today. And do not forget to wash the truck".
"Okay," David says. They finish cleaning and get into the truck. David has a driving license so he drives the truck. He starts the engine and drives at first slowly through the farm yard, then quickly along the road. The transport firm Rapid is not far from the farm. They arrive there in fifteen minutes. They look for the loading door number ten there.
David drives the truck carefully through the loading yard. They go past the first loading door, past the second loading door, past the third, past the fourth, past the fifth, past the sixth, past the seventh, past the eighth, then past the ninth loading door. David drives to the tenth loading door and stops.
"We must check the loading list first," Robert says who already has some experience with loading lists at this transport firm. He goes to the

David und Robert waschen den Laster (Teil 1)

David und Robert arbeiten jetzt auf einem Bauernhof. Sie arbeiten drei, vier Stunden am Tag. Die Arbeit ist ziemlich schwer. Sie müssen jeden Tag viel arbeiten. Sie machen den Hof jeden zweiten Tag sauber. Sie putzen die Maschinen jeden dritten Tag. Jeden vierten Tag arbeiten sie auf den Feldern.

Ihr Arbeitgeber heißt Daniel Tough. Herr Tough ist der Besitzer des Bauernhofs und macht die meiste Arbeit. Herr Tough arbeitet sehr hart. Er gibt David und Robert auch viel Arbeit.
„Hey Jungs, macht die Maschinen fertig sauber und fahrt dann mit dem Laster zur Transportfirma Rapid", sagt Herr Tough. „Sie haben eine Ladung für mich. Ladet die Kisten mit dem Saatgut auf den Laster, bringt sie zum Bauernhof und ladet sie auf dem Hof ab. Beeilt euch, denn ich brauche das Saatgut heute. Und vergesst nicht, den Laster zu waschen."
„Okay", sagt David. Sie machen die Maschine fertig sauber und steigen in den Laster. David hat einen Führerschein, deswegen fährt er. Er macht den Motor an, fährt erst langsam durch den Hof und dann schnell die Straße entlang. Die Transportfirma Rapid ist nicht weit vom Bauernhof. Sie kommen dort nach fünfzehn Minuten an. Dort suchen sie die Verladetür Nummer zehn.
David fährt den Laster vorsichtig über den Hof. Sie fahren an der ersten Verladetür vorbei, an der zweiten, an der dritten, an der vierten, an der fünften, an der sechsten, an der siebten, an der achten und dann an der neunten. David fährt zur zehnten Verladetür und hält an.

„Wir müssen erst die Ladeliste kontrollieren", sagt Robert, der schon Erfahrung mit den Ladelisten in dieser Firma hat. Er geht zum Verlader, der an der Tür

loader who works at the door and gives him the loading list. The loader loads quickly five boxes into their truck. Robert checks the boxes carefully. All numbers on the boxes have numbers from the loading list.

"Numbers are correct. We can go now," Robert says.

"Okay," David says and starts the engine, "I think we can wash the truck now. There is a suitable place not far from here".

In five minutes they arrive to the seashore.

"Do you want to wash the truck here?" Robert asks in surprise.

"Yeah! It is a nice place, isn't it?" David says.

"And where will we take a pail?" Robert asks.

"We do not need any pail. I will drive very close to the sea. We will take the water from the sea," David says and drives very close to the water. The front wheels go in the water and the waves run over them.

"Let's get out and begin washing," Robert says.

"Wait a minute. I will drive a bit closer," David says and drives one or two meters further, "It is better now."

Then a bigger wave comes and the water lifts the truck a little and carries it slowly further into the sea.

"Stop! David, stop the truck!" Robert cries, "We are in the water already! Please, stop!"

"It will not stop!!" David cries stepping on the brake with all his strength, "I cannot stop it!!"

The truck is slowly floating further in the sea pitching on the waves like a little ship.

(to be continued)

arbeitet, und gibt ihm die Ladeliste. Der Verlader lädt schnell fünf Kisten in ihren Laster. Robert kontrolliert die Kisten sorgfältig. Alle Kisten haben Nummern von der Ladeliste.

„Die Nummern stimmen. Wir können jetzt gehen", sagt Robert.

„Okay", sagt David und macht den Motor an. „Ich denke, wir können jetzt den Laster waschen. Nicht weit von hier ist ein passender Ort".

Nach fünf Minuten kommen sie an die Küste.

„Willst du den Laster hier waschen?", fragt Robert überrascht.

„Ja! Schöner Platz, nicht?", sagt David.

„Und woher bekommen wir einen Eimer?", fragt Robert.

„Wir brauchen keinen Eimer. Ich fahre ganz nah ans Meer. Wir nehmen das Wasser aus dem Meer", sagt David und fährt ganz nah ans Wasser. Die Vorderräder stehen im Wasser und die Wellen umspülen sie.

„Lass uns aussteigen und anfangen, zu waschen", sagt Robert.

„Warte kurz, ich fahre noch etwas näher ran", sagt David und fährt ein, zwei Meter weiter. „So ist es besser".

Da kommt eine größere Welle und das Wasser hebt den Laster ein bisschen nach oben und trägt ihn langsam weiter ins Meer.

„Stopp! David, halte den Laster an!", ruft Robert. „Wir sind schon im Wasser! Bitte, halte an!"

„Er hält nicht an!", ruft David und tritt mit aller Kraft die Bremse. „Ich kann ihn nicht anhalten."

Der Laster treibt langsam weiter aufs Meer und schaukelt auf den Wellen wie ein kleines Schiff.

(Fortsetzung folgt)

31

Present Progressive versus Present Simple

Wir wählen das Present Progressive oder das Present Simple um die Handlungen genauer zu beschreiben. Der wichtige Unterschied ist jedoch, dass beim Present Progressive sagt man, dass die Handlung gerade passiert oder die Handlung ist befristet. Beim Present Simple allerdings wird ausgesagt, dass etwas regelmäßig oder immer getan wird.

Sam is walking home. - Sam geht gerade nach Hause.

He walks home from the bus stop every day. - Er geht nach Hause von der Bushaltestelle jeden Tag.

He drives a car, but he is not driving now. - Er fährt Auto, aber gerade fährt er nicht.

Does Sam drive a car? Yes, he does. - Fährt Sam Auto? Ja, das tut er.

Is he driving a car? No, he is not. - Fährt Sam gerade ein Auto? Nein, das tut er nicht.

Auch für allgemeingültige Tatsachen, deren Dauer unerheblich ist, wird das Present Simple benutzt. Wir wählen das Present Progressive für befristete Handlungen deren Frist gerade andauert. Vergleiche:

They work in the garden. - Sie arbeiten im Garten. (oft oder manchmal)

They are working in the garden in summer. - Sie arbeiten im Garten im Sommer. (es ist Sommer jetzt)

They work in the garden in summer. - Sie arbeiten im Garten im Sommer. (es ist Herbst jetzt)

They are having breakfast in the garden from eight to nine o'clock. - Sie frühstücken im Garten von acht bis neun Uhr. (es ist gerade zwischen acht und neun Uhr)

They have breakfast in the garden from eight to nine o'clock. - Sie frühstücken im Garten von acht bis neun Uhr. (es ist elf Uhr)

Look! They are having breakfast in the garden. - Schau mal! Sie frühstücken im Garten.

Verben, die auf -e enden, verlieren in der -ing Form das -e.

to have - having, to give - giving, to make - making etc.

Verben mit kurzem Vokal am Ende und nachfolgendem Konsonanten (Mitlaut) verdoppeln den Konsonanten.

to run - running, to stop - stopping, to cut - cutting, to sit - sitting etc.

Exercise 31 Answer the questions. Use the Present Progressive Tense or the Present Simple Tense.

Übung 31 Beantworte die Fragen. Benutze das Present Progressive oder das Present Simple.

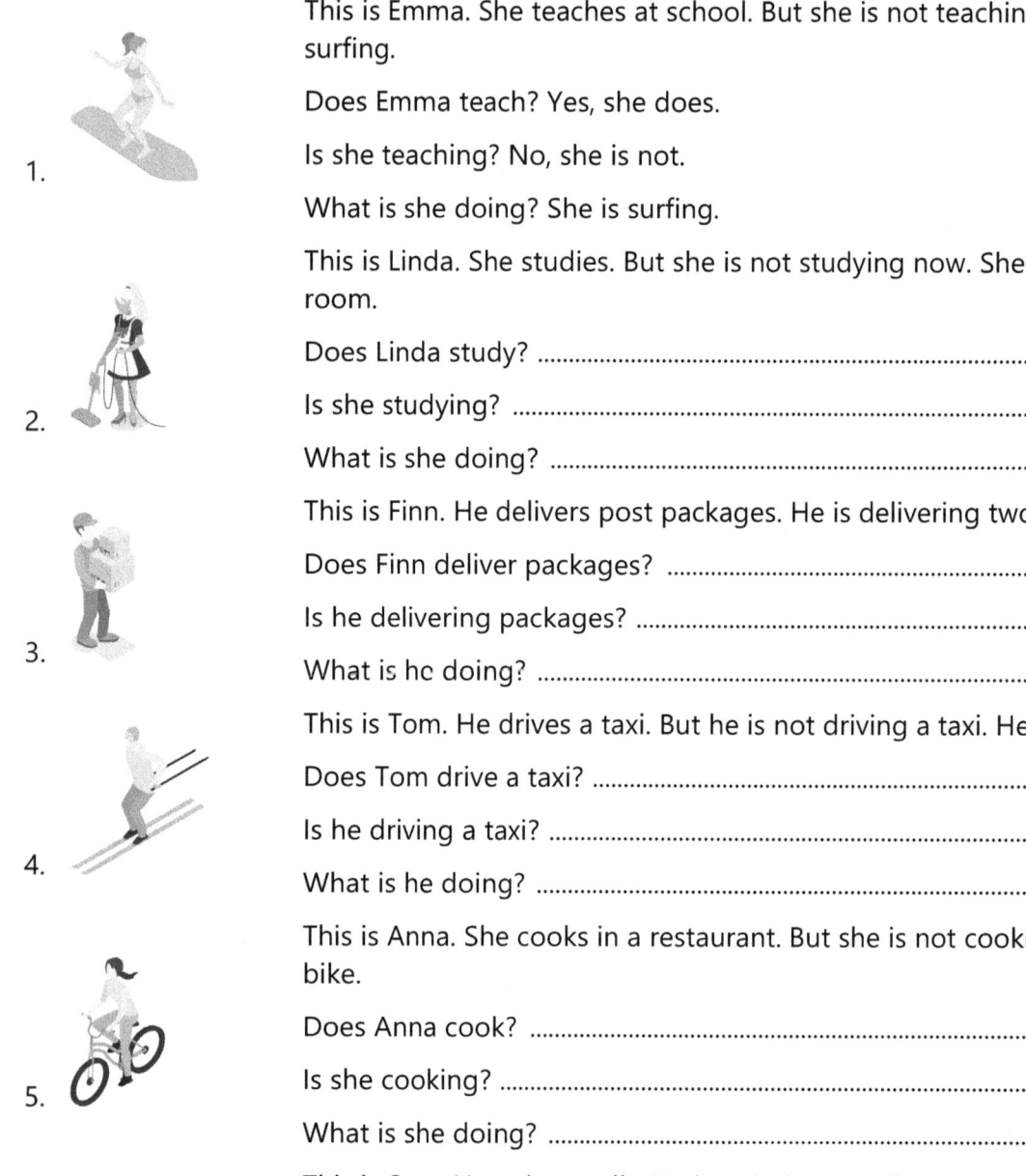

1. This is Emma. She teaches at school. But she is not teaching now. She is surfing.

   Does Emma teach? Yes, she does.

   Is she teaching? No, she is not.

   What is she doing? She is surfing.

2. This is Linda. She studies. But she is not studying now. She is cleaning a room.

   Does Linda study? ....

   Is she studying? ....

   What is she doing? ....

3. This is Finn. He delivers post packages. He is delivering two packages now.

   Does Finn deliver packages? ....

   Is he delivering packages? ....

   What is he doing? ....

4. This is Tom. He drives a taxi. But he is not driving a taxi. He is skiing.

   Does Tom drive a taxi? ....

   Is he driving a taxi? ....

   What is he doing? ....

5. This is Anna. She cooks in a restaurant. But she is not cooking. She is riding a bike.

   Does Anna cook? ....

   Is she cooking? ....

   What is she doing? ....

6. This is Sam. He paints walls. He is painting a wall now.

   Does Sam paint houses? ....

   Is he painting a house? ....

   What is he doing? ....

7. This is Denis. He repairs cars. But he is not repairing a car. He is skateboarding.

Does Denis repair cars? ....

Is he repairing a car? ....

What is he doing? ....

Reading comprehension

David and Robert wash the truck (part2)
David und Robert waschen den Laster (Teil 2)

A

Words

1. accident ['æksɪd(ə)nt] - der Unfall
2. ago [əˈgəʊ] - vor
3. a year ago - vor einem Jahr
4. bird [bɜːd] - der Vogel
5. ceremony [ˈserɪmənɪ] - die Feier
6. cleaned [kliːnd] - gesäubert
7. constant [ˈkɒn(t)stənt] - beständig
8. control [kənˈtrəʊl] - die Kontrolle
9. dear [dɪə] - lieber, liebe
10. enjoy [ɪnˈdʒɔɪ] - Spaß haben, genießen
11. example [ɪgˈzɑːmpl] - das Beispiel
12. for example [fər ɪgˈzɑːmpl] - zum Beispiel
13. feed [fiːd] - füttern
14. fire [ˈfaɪə] - feuern
15. floating [ˈfləʊtɪŋ] - treiben
16. flow [fləʊ] - der Fluss
17. happen [ˈhæp(ə)n] - passieren
18. happened [ˈhæpənd] - passiert
19. inform [ɪnˈfɔːm] - informieren, mitteilen
20. journalist [ˈdʒɜːn(ə)lɪst] - der Journalist
21. killer [ˈkɪlə] - der Mörder
22. laugh [lɑːf] - lachen
23. left [left] - links
24. money [ˈmʌnɪ] - das Geld
25. never [ˈnevə] - nie
26. oil [ɔɪl] - das Öl
27. photograph [ˈfəʊtəgrɑːf] - fotografieren; photographer [fəˈtɒgrəfə] - der Fotograf

28. rehabilitate [ˌriːhəˈbɪlɪteɪt] - gesund pflegen
29. rehabilitation [ˌriːhəˈbɪlɪteɪʃn] - die Genesung, Rehabilitation
30. rescue [ˈreskjuː] - retten
31. rescue service [ˈsəːvɪs] - der Rettungsdienst
32. right [raɪt] - rechts
33. set free [set friː] - freisetzen
34. shore [ʃɔː] - die Küste
35. situation [ˌsɪtjʊˈeɪʃən] - die Situation
36. speech [spiːtʃ] - die Rede
37. steer [stɪə] - lenken
38. swallow [ˈswɔləʊ] - (hinunter)schlucken
39. swim [swɪm] - schwimmen
40. tanker [ˈtæŋkə] - der Tanker
41. tomorrow [təˈmɔrəʊ] - morgen
42. twenty-five [ˈtwenti faɪv] - fünfundzwanzig
43. wanted [ˈwɔntɪd] - wollte
44. were [wə] - waren
45. whale [weɪl] - der Wal
46. killer whale [ˈkɪlə weɪl] - der Schwertwal
47. wind [wɪnd] - der Wind
48. wonderful [ˈwʌndəfəl] - wunderbar

B

David and Robert wash the truck (part 2)

The truck is floating slowly further in the sea pitching on the waves like a little ship. David is steering to the left and to the right stepping on the brake and gas. But he cannot control the truck. A strong wind is pushing it along the seashore. David and Robert do not know what to do. They are just sitting, looking out of the windows. The sea water begins to run inside.
"Let's go out and sit on the roof," Robert says. They sit on the roof.
"What will Mr. Tough say, I wonder?" Robert says.
The truck is floating slowly about twenty meters away from the shore. Some people on the shore stop and look at it in surprise.
"Mr. Tough may fire us," David answers.

Meanwhile the head of the college Mr. Kite comes to his office. The secretary says to him that there will be a ceremony today. They will set free two sea birds after rehabilitation. Workers of the rehabilitation centre cleaned oil off them after the accident with the tanker Gran Pollución. The accident happened one month ago. Mr. Kite must make a speech there. The ceremony begins in twenty-five minutes.
Mr. Kite and his secretary take a taxi and in ten minutes arrive to the place of the ceremony. These two birds are already there. Now they are not so white as usually. But they can swim

David und Robert waschen den Laster (Teil 2)

Der Laster treibt langsam weiter aufs Meer und schaukelt auf den Wellen wie ein kleines Schiff. David lenkt nach links und nach rechts, während er auf die Bremse und aufs Gas tritt. Aber er kann den Laster nicht kontrollieren. Ein starker Wind trägt ihn die Küste entlang. David und Robert wissen nicht, was sie tun sollen. Sie sitzen einfach da und schauen aus dem Fenster. Das Meerwasser beginnt, in den Laster zu laufen.
„Lass uns nach draußen gehen und uns aufs Dach setzen", sagt Robert.
Sie setzen sich aufs Dach.
„Ich frage mich, was Herr Tough sagen wird", sagt Robert.
Der Laster treibt langsam etwa zwanzig Meter von der Küste entfernt. Einige Leute an der Küste bleiben stehen und schauen verwundert.
„Herr Tough wird uns wohl feuern", antwortet David.

In der Zwischenzeit kommt der Direktor der Universität, Herr Kite, in sein Büro. Die Sekretärin sagt ihm, dass es heute eine Feier gibt. Sie werden zwei Vögel nach deren Genesung freisetzen. Arbeiter des Rehabilitationszentrums haben sie nach dem Unfall mit dem Tanker Gran Pollución von Öl gesäubert. Der Unfall passierte vor einem Monat. Herr Kite muss dort eine Rede halten. Die Feier beginnt in fünfundzwanzig Minuten. Herr Kite und seine Sekretärin nehmen ein Taxi und kommen nach zehn Minuten am Ort der Feier an. Die zwei Vögel sind bereits da. Jetzt sind sie nicht so weiß wie normalerweise. Aber sie können wieder schwimmen und fliegen. Es sind viele Menschen, Journalisten und

and fly again now. There are many people, journalists, photographers there now. In two minutes the ceremony begins. Mr. Kite begins his speech.

"Dear friends!" he says, "The accident with the tanker Gran Pollución happened at this place a month ago. We must rehabilitate many birds and animals now. It costs a lot of money. For example the rehabilitation of each of these birds costs 5,000 dollars! And I am glad to inform you now that after one month of rehabilitation these two wonderful birds will be set free."

Two men take a box with the birds, bring it to the water and open it. The birds go out of the box and then jump in the water and swim. The photographers take pictures. The journalists ask workers of the rehabilitation centre about the animals.

Suddenly a big killer whale comes up, quickly swallows those two birds and goes down again. All the people look at the place where the birds were before. The head of the college does not believe his eyes. The killer whale comes up again looking for more birds. As there are no other birds there, it goes down again. Mr. Kite must finish his speech now.

"Ah...," he chooses suitable words, "The wonderful constant flow of life never stops. Bigger animals eat smaller animals and so on... ah... what is that?" he says looking at the water. All the people look there and see a big truck floating along the shore pitching on the waves like a ship. Two guys sit on it looking at the place of the ceremony.

"Hello Mr. Kite," Robert says, "Why are you feeding killer whales with birds?"

"Hello Robert," Mr. Kite answers, "What are you doing there boys?"

"We wanted to wash the truck," David answers.

"I see," Mr. Kite says. Some of the people begin to enjoy this situation. They begin to laugh.

"Well, I will call the rescue service now. They will get you out of the water. And I want to see you in my office tomorrow," the head of the college says and calls the rescue service.

Fotografen da. Zwei Minuten später beginnt die Feier. Herr Kite beginnt seine Rede.

„Liebe Freunde", sagt er. „Vor einem Monat passierte an dieser Stelle der Unfall mit dem Tanker Gran Pollución. Wir müssen jetzt viele Vögel und Tiere gesund pflegen. Das kostet viel Geld. Die Rehabilitation dieser zwei Vögel zum Beispiel kostet fünftausend Dollar. Und es freut mich, Ihnen mitteilen zu können, dass diese zwei wunderbaren Vögel nach einem Monat Rehabilitation freigesetzt werden."

Zwei Männer nehmen die Kiste mit den Vögeln, bringen sie zum Wasser und öffnen sie. Die Vögel kommen aus der Kiste, springen ins Wasser und schwimmen. Die Fotografen machen Fotos. Die Journalisten befragen Arbeiter des Rehabilitationszentrums über die Tiere.

Plötzlich taucht ein großer Schwertwal auf, schluckt schnell die zwei Vögel hinunter und verschwindet wieder. Alle Leute sehen auf die Stelle, an der die Vögel zuvor gewesen waren. Der Direktor der Universität traut seinen Augen nicht. Der Schwertwal taucht wieder auf und sucht nach mehr Vögeln. Da es keine Vögel mehr gibt, verschwindet er wieder. Herr Kite muss seine Rede beenden.

„Ähm..." Er sucht nach passenden Worten. „Der wundervolle, beständige Fluss des Lebens hört nie auf. Größere Tiere essen kleinere Tiere und so weiter... Ähm... Was ist das?", fragt er aufs Wasser schauend. Alle schauen aufs Wasser und sehen einen großen Laster, der die Küste entlang treibt und auf den Wellen schaukelt wie ein Schiff. Zwei Jungen sitzen auf ihm und schauen zum Platz der Feier.

„Hallo Herr Kite", sagt Robert. „Warum füttern Sie Schwertwale mit Vögeln?"

„Hallo Robert", antwortet Herr Kite. „Was macht ihr da, Jungs?"

„Wir wollten den Laster waschen", sagt David.

„Alles klar", sagt Herr Kite. Einige Leute beginnen, an der Situation ihren Spaß zu haben. Sie fangen an, zu lachen.

„Gut, ich rufe jetzt den Rettungsdienst. Der wird euch aus dem Wasser holen. Und ich möchte euch morgen in meinem Büro sehen", sagt der Direktor der Universität und ruft den Rettungsdienst.

Present Participle and Gerund / Partizip I und Gerundium

Die Endung -ing wird nicht nur mit Verlaufsformen benutzt. Die Endung -ing verwendet man auch um das Gerundium und das Partizip I zu bilden.

Das Gerundium ist eine Verbform, die als Nomen verwendet wird. Zum Beispiel reading - das Lesen, playing - das Spielen, running - das Rennen.

> I read every day. Reading is my hobby. - Ich lese jeden Tag. Das Lesen ist mein Hobby.
>
> He teaches German. Teaching is really important for him. - Er unterrichtet Deutsch. Das Unterrichten ist ihm wirklich wichtig.
>
> I study hard. Studying takes a lot of time. - Ich studiere fleißig. Das Studieren nimmt viel Zeit.

Das Partizip I ist eine Verbform, die von einem Verb mit der Endung -ing gebildet ist und adjektivischen Charakter hat. Zum Beispiel reading - lesende(r/s), playing - spielende(r/s), running - rennende(r/s).

> This reading man is my friend. - Dieser lesende Mann ist mein Freund.
>
> Look at those playing children! - Schau dir mal diese spielende Kinder an!
>
> We know that dancing girl. - Wir kennen jenes tanzende Mädchen.

Exercise 32 Compose the sentences as in the example.

Übung 32 Bilde die Sätze nach dem Beispiel.

1. (eat) This eating girl is my sister. She must stop eating so much.
2. (read) This .... boy is my friend. He really likes ....
3. (dance) Look at that .... woman. She is crazy about ....
4. (sing) That .... girl has a nice voice. She dreams of .... a new hit.
5. (drive) That .... man must stop. His .... is dangerous.

6. (surf) Those .... boys want me to surf too. But I am afraid of ....
7. (cook) The food of this .... man is really tasty. He is good at ....
8. (cook) The food of that .... woman is bad. She hates ....
9. (swim) Those .... people are fit. Are you interested in ....?

Reading comprehension

A lesson
Eine Unterrichtsstunde

A

Words

1. always [ˈɔːlweɪz] - immer
2. attention [əˈtenʃən] - die Aufmerksamkeit
3. pay attention to - achten auf
4. between [bɪˈtwiːn] - zwischen
5. boyfriend [ˈbɔɪfrend] - der Freund
6. care [keə] - sich kümmern um
7. children [ˈtʃɪldrən] - die Kinder
8. class [klaːs] - die Klasse
9. else [els] - anders, sonst
10. empty [ˈemptɪ] - leer
11. girlfriend [ˈɡɜːlfrend] - die Freundin
12. happiness [ˈhæpɪnəs] - das Glück
13. health [helθ] - die Gesundheit
14. important [ɪmˈpɔːt(ə)nt] - wichtig
15. instead [ɪnˈsted] - stattdessen
16. jar [dʒaː] - der Krug
17. less [les] - weniger
18. loose [luːs] - verlieren
19. medical [ˈmedɪk(ə)l] - medizinisch
20. parent [ˈpeər(ə)nt] - die Eltern
21. pour [pɔː] - schütten, gießen
22. really [ˈrɪəlɪ] - wirklich
23. remain [rɪˈmeɪn] - bleiben
24. sand [sænd] - der Sand
25. slightly [ˈslaɪtlɪ] - leicht
26. small [smɔːl] - klein
27. spend [spend] - ausgeben, verwenden
28. still [stɪl] - noch, weiterhin

29. stone [stəʊn] - der Stein
30. television [ˈtelɪvɪʒ(ə)n] - der Fernseher
31. thing [θɪŋ] - das Ding, die Sache
32. this stuff [stʌf] - diese Dinge
33. which [wɪtʃ] - der, die, das *(konj.)*
34. without [wɪˈðaʊt] - ohne
35. without a word [wɪðˈaʊt ə ˈwɜːd] - wortlos

A lesson

The head of the college is standing before the class. There are some boxes and other things on the table before him. When the lesson begins he takes a big empty jar and without a word fills it up with big stones.
"Do you think the jar is already full?" Mr. Kite asks students.
"Yes, it is," agree students.
Then he takes a box with very small stones and pours them into the jar. He shakes the jar slightly. The little stones, of course, fill up the room between the big stones.
"What do you think now? The jar is already full, isn't it?" Mr. Kite asks them again.
"Yes, it is. It is full now," the students agree again. They begin to enjoy this lesson. They begin to laugh.
Then Mr. Kite takes a box of sand and pours it into the jar. Of course, the sand fills up all the other room.
"Now I want that you to think about this jar like a man's life. The big stones are important things - your family, your girlfriend and boyfriend, your health, your children, your parents - things that if you loose everything and only they remain, your life still will be full. Little stones are other things which are less important. They are things like your house, your job, your car. Sand is everything else - small stuff. If you put sand in the jar at first, there will be no room for little or big stones. The same goes for life. If you spend all of your time and energy on the small stuff, you will never have room for things that are important to you. Pay attention to things that are most important to your happiness. Play with your children or parents. Take time to get medical tests. Take your girlfriend or boyfriend to a café. There will be always time to go to work, clean the house and watch television," Mr. Kite says, "Take care of the big stones first - things that are

Eine Unterrichtsstunde

Der Direktor der Universität steht vor der Klasse. Auf dem Tisch vor ihm liegen Kisten und andere Dinge. Als der Unterricht beginnt, nimmt er einen großen, leeren Krug und füllt ihn wortlos mit großen Steinen.

„Meint ihr, dass der Krug schon voll ist?", fragt Herr Kite die Studenten.
„Ja, das ist er", stimmen die Studenten zu.
Da nimmt er eine Kiste mit sehr kleinen Steinen und schüttet sie in den Krug. Er schüttelt den Krug leicht. Die kleinen Steine füllen natürlich den Platz zwischen den großen Steinen.
„Was meint ihr jetzt? Der Krug ist voll, oder nicht?", fragt Herr Kite wieder.
„Ja, das ist er. Er ist jetzt voll", stimmen die Studenten wieder zu. Der Unterricht beginnt, ihnen Spaß zu machen. Sie lachen.
Da nimmt Herr Kite eine Kiste mit Sand und schüttet ihn in den Krug. Der Sand füllt natürlich den restlichen Platz.
„Jetzt möchte ich, dass ihr in diesem Krug das Leben seht. Die großen Steine sind wichtige Dinge - eure Familie, eure Freundin oder euer Freund, Gesundheit, Kinder, Eltern - Dinge, die euer Leben, wenn ihr alles verliert und nur sie bleiben, weiterhin füllen. Kleine Steine sind andere Dinge, die weniger wichtig sind. Dinge wie euer Haus, Job, Auto. Der Sand ist alles andere - die kleinen Dinge. Wenn ihr zuerst Sand in den Krug füllt, bleibt kein Platz für kleine oder große Steine. Das Gleiche gilt fürs Leben. Wenn ihr eure ganze Zeit und Energie für die kleinen Dinge verwendet, werdet ihr nie Platz für die Dinge haben, die euch wichtig sind. Achtet auf Dinge, die für euer Glück am wichtigsten sind. Spielt mit euren Kindern oder Eltern. Nehmt euch die Zeit für medizinische Untersuchungen. Geht mit eurer Freundin oder eurem Freund ins Café. Es wird immer Zeit bleiben, um zu arbeiten, das Haus zu putzen oder fernzusehen", sagt Herr Kite. „Kümmert euch erst um die großen Steine - um die Dinge, die wirklich wichtig sind. Alles andere ist nur Sand." Er sieht die

really important. Everything else is just sand," he looks at the students, "Now Robert and David, what is more important to you - washing a truck or your lives? You float on a truck in the sea like on a ship just because you wanted to wash the truck. Do you think there is no other way to wash it?"
"No, we do not think so," David says.
"You can wash a truck in a washing station instead, can't you?" says Mr. Kite.
"Yes, we can," say the students.
"You must always think before you do something. You must always take care of the big stones, right?"
"Yes, we must," answer the students.

Studenten an. „Nun, Robert und David, was ist euch wichtiger - einen Laster zu waschen oder euer Leben? Ihr treibt auf einem Laster im Meer wie auf einem Schiff, nur weil ihr den Laster waschen wolltet. Glaubt ihr, dass es keine andere Möglichkeit gibt, ihn zu waschen?"

„Nein, das glauben wir nicht", sagt David.
„Man kann einen Laster stattdessen in einer Waschanlage waschen, nicht wahr?", sagt Herr Kite.
„Ja, das kann man", sagen die Studenten.
„Ihr müsst immer erst nachdenken, bevor ihr handelt. Ihr müsst euch immer um die großen Steine kümmern, okay?"
„Ja, das müssen wir", antworten die Studenten.

33

Past Simple / Imperfekt oder Präteritum

Das Past Simple beschreibt eine Handlung oder einen Vorgang, der in der Vergangenheit einmalig oder wiederholt abgeschlossen ist. Bei regelmäßigen Verben hängen wir einfach -ed an.

work/worked

I worked in the garden yesterday. - Ich habe gestern im Garten gearbeitet.

play/played

They played tennis on Sunday. - Sie haben am Sonntag Tennis gespielt.

ask/asked

He asked me about the book. - Er hat mich über das Buch gefragt.

Bei unregelmäßigen Verben verwenden wir die 2. Verbform (siehe die Liste der unregelmäßigen Verben, 2. Spalte).

come/came

They came late. - Sie haben spät gekommen.

do/did

I did my homework on Friday. - Ich habe meine Hausarbeit am Freitag gemacht.

eat/ate

He ate an apple in the morning. - Er hat einen Apfel am Morgen gegessen.

Fragen und Verneinungen werden mit did bzw. did not und dem Infinitiv (Grundform) gebildet.

Bejahte Sätze

Subjekt + Ved

I worked in the garden. - Ich habe im Garten gearbeitet.

Linda cooked pizza. - Linda hat eine Pizza gemacht.

Fragen

Did + Subjekt + Infinitiv

Did you work in the garden? - Hast du im Garten gearbeitet?

Did Linda cook pizza? - Hat Linda eine Pizza gemacht?

Verneinte Sätze

Subjekt + did not + Infinitiv

I did not work in the garden. - Ich habe im Garten nicht gearbeitet.

Linda did not cook pizza. - Linda hat keine Pizza gemacht.

Das Past Simple wird auch benutzt, um aufeinanderfolgende Handlungen in der Vergangenheit zu beschreiben. Diese Aufzählung von Vorgängen finden sich beispielsweise in Erzählungen.

get/got, go/went, have/had

She got up, went to the kitchen and had a cup of coffee. - Sie stand auf, ging in die Küche und trank eine Tasse Kaffee.

meet/met, speak/spoke

I met my friend and spoke to him. - Ich habe meinen Freund getroffen und mit ihm gesprochen.

Das Past Simple wird auch benutzt, um zu fragen, wann etwas passiert ist.

When did you finish this book? I finished it a week ago. - Wann hast du dieses Buch beendet? Ich habe es vor einer Woche beendet.

When did you come home? I came home at seven o'clock. - Wann bist du nach Hause gekommen? Ich bin um sieben Uhr nach Hause gekommen.

Das Signalwort für das Past Simple ist ein Zeitpunkt in der Vergangenheit. Zum Beispiel: ten minutes ago - vor zehn Minuten, yesterday - gestern, on Friday - am Freitag, a long time ago - längst.

Exercise 33-1 Complete the positive sentences as in the example.

Übung 33-1 Ergänze die bejahte Sätze nach dem Beispiel.

Wortschatz: can/could, must/had to, is/was, wake up/woke up

1. I live in the US. I lived in Canada five years ago.
2. Anna plays tennis on Sundays. She ………………………… tennis last Monday too.
3. Bill often works in his garden. He ………………………… in his garden yesterday.
4. Emma sometimes cooks pizza. She ………………………… pizza last weekend.
5. Tom can swim well. He ………………………… swim very little ten years ago.
6. Linda cleans her room weekly. She ………………………… her room two days ago.
7. She washes windows every month. She ………………………… windows last week.
8. This man is happy now. He ………………………… sad this morning.
9. This café opens at nine o'clock. But it ………………………… at ten o'clock last Tuesday.
10. My brother wants to live in Africa. He ………………………… to live in China a year ago.
11. This shop always closes at nine o'clock. But it ………………………… at eight last Friday.
12. Sam wakes up at seven o'clock. But he ………………………… at six o'clock last Sunday.

Exercise 33-2 Complete the sentences as in the example.

Übung 33-2 Ergänze die Sätze nach dem Beispiel.

1. I visited Madrid but I did not visit Barcelona.

2. Anna played tennis with Tom but she .... with Denis.
3. Sam had some soup but he .... a spoon.
4. Emma cooked pizza but she .... soup.
5. I went to the bank but I .... to the shop.
6. Bill worked on Monday but he .... yesterday.
7. Linda cleaned her room but she .... the kitchen.
8. My brother wanted to live in China but he .... to learn Chinese.
9. You called your friend but you .... your mom.

Exercise 33-3 Compose the questions as in the example.

Übung 33-3 Bilde die Fragen nach dem Beispiel.

1. I played golf on Sunday. And you? Did you play golf?
2. I worked on Saturday. And you? ....
3. I studied hard last week. And you? ....
4. I learned German language in summer. And you? ....
5. I cooked some soup this morning. And you? ....
6. I washed the windows last month. And you? ....
7. I rode a bike in the morning. And you? ....

Exercise 33-4 Compose the questions as in the example.

Übung 33-4 Bilde die Fragen nach dem Beispiel.

1. I woke up late. What time did you wake up?
2. I had my breakfast. What .... for breakfast?
3. I looked out of the window. Why .... out of the window?
4. I saw somebody. Who ....
5. I rode a bike. Where ....
6. I bought some apples. How many ....
7. I paid for the apples. How much ....
8. I met somebody. Who ....
9. I came home. When ....

Reading comprehension

Paul works at a publishing house
Paul arbeitet in einem Verlag

Words

1. answering machine [ˈɑːnsərɪŋ məʃiːn] - der Anrufbeantworter
2. at least [ət liːst] - wenigstens
3. beep [biːp] - der Piepton
4. call [ˈkɔːl] - anrufen
5. cold [kəʊld] *(adj)* - kalt
6. coldness [ˈkəʊldnəs] - die Kälte
7. company [ˈkʌmpənɪ] - die Firma
8. compose [kəmˈpəʊz] - entwerfen, verfassen
9. composition [ˌkɔmpəˈzɪʃən] - der Entwurf, der Text
10. co-ordination [kəʊˌɔːdɪˈneɪʃən] - die Koordination
11. creative [krɪˈeɪtɪv] - kreativ
12. customer [ˈkʌstəmə] - der Kunde
13. dark [daːk] - dunkel
14. develop [dɪˈveləp] - entwickeln
15. different [ˈdɪf(ə)r(ə)nt] - verschieden
16. difficult [ˈdɪfɪk(ə)lt] - schwer
17. especially [ɪsˈpeʃəlɪ] - vor allem
18. etc. [ɪtˈset(ə)rə] - usw.
19. funny [ˈfʌnɪ] - lustig
20. future [ˈfjuːtʃə] - zukünftig
21. get [get] - bekommen
22. hi [haɪ] - hallo
23. human [ˈhjuːmən] - der Mensch
24. magazine [ˌmægəˈziːn] - die Zeitschrift
25. newspaper [ˈnjuːsˌpeɪpə] - die Zeitung
26. nobody [ˈnəʊbədɪ] - niemand
27. nose [nəʊz] - die Nase
28. nothing [ˈnʌθɪŋ] - nichts
29. outdoors [ˌaʊtˈdɔːz] - draußen
30. playing [pleɪŋ] - spielen
31. possible [ˈpɔsəbl] - möglich
32. as often as possible - so oft wie möglich
33. produce [ˈprɔdjuːs] - herstellen
34. profession [prəˈfeʃ(ə)n] - der Beruf
35. rain [reɪn] - der Regen
36. ready [ˈredɪ] - fertig
37. record [ˈrekɔːd] - aufnehmen
38. refuse [rɪˈfjuːz] - ablehnen
39. rule [ruːl] - die Regel
40. sad [sæd] - traurig
41. sell [sel] - verkaufen
42. since [sɪn(t)s], as - da, weil

43. skill [skɪl] - die Fähigkeit
44. sleeping [ˈsliːpɪŋ] - schlafen
45. stairs [steəz] - die Treppe
46. story [ˈstɔːrɪ] - die Geschichte
47. talk [tɔːk] - sich unterhalten
48. text [tekst] - der Text
49. thirty [ˈθəːtɪ] - dreißig
50. walking [ˈwɔːkɪŋ] - laufen
51. world [wəːld] - die Welt

B

Paul works at a publishing house

Paul works as a young helper at the publishing house All-round. He does writing work.
"Paul, our firm's name is All-round," the head of the firm Mr. Fox says, "And this means we can do any text composition and design work for any customer. We get many orders from newspapers, magazines and from other customers. All of the orders are different but we never refuse any."
Paul likes this job a lot because he can develop creative skills. He enjoys creative works like writing compositions and design. Since he studies design at college it is a very suitable job for his future profession.
Mr. Fox has some new tasks for him today.
"We have some orders. You can do two of them," Mr. Fox says, "The first order is from a telephone company. They produce telephones with answering machines. They need some funny texts for answering machines. Nothing sells better than funny things. Compose four or five texts, please."
"How long must they be?" Paul asks.
"They can be from five to thirty words," Mr. Fox answers, "And the second order is from the magazine "Green world". This magazine writes about animals, birds, fish etc. They need a text about any home animal. It can be funny or sad, or just a story about your own animal. Do you have an animal?"
"Yes, I do. I have a cat. Its name is Favorite," Paul answers, "And I think I can write a story about its tricks. When must it be ready?"
"These two orders must be ready by tomorrow," Mr. Fox answers.
"Okay. May I begin now?" Paul asks.
"Yes, Paul," Mr. Fox says.

Paul brings those texts the next day. He has

Paul arbeitet in einem Verlag

Paul arbeitet als junger Helfer im Verlag All-Round. Er erledigt Schreibarbeiten.
„Paul, unsere Firma heißt All-Round", sagt der Firmenchef Herr Fox. „Und das heißt, dass wir für jeden Kunden jede Art von Text und Design entwickeln können. Wir bekommen viele Aufträge von Zeitungen, Zeitschriften und anderen Kunden. Alle Aufträge sind verschieden, aber wir lehnen nie einen ab."

Paul mag diesen Job sehr, da er kreative Fähigkeiten entwickeln kann. Kreative Arbeit wie Schreiben und Design gefällt ihm. Da er Design an der Universität studiert, ist es ein passender Job für seinen zukünftigen Beruf.
Heute hat Herr Fox neue Aufgaben für ihn.
„Wir haben einige Aufträge. Du kannst zwei davon erledigen", sagt Herr Fox. „Der erste Auftrag ist von einer Telefonfirma. Sie stellen Telefone mit Anrufbeantwortern her. Sie brauchen ein paar lustige Texte für die Anrufbeantworter. Nichts verkauft sich besser als etwas Lustiges. Entwirf bitte vier, fünf Texte."

„Wie lang sollen sie sein?", fragt Paul.
„Sie können fünf bis dreißig Wörter haben", antwortet Herr Fox. „Der zweite Auftrag ist von der Zeitung ‚Grüne Welt'. Diese Zeitung schreibt über Tiere, Vögel, Fische usw. Sie brauchen einen Text über irgendein Haustier. Er kann lustig oder traurig sein oder einfach eine Geschichte über dein eigenes Haustier. Hast du ein Haustier?"

„Ja, ich habe eine Katze. Sie heißt Favorite", antwortet Paul. „Und ich denke, ich kann eine Geschichte über ihre Streiche schreiben. Wann sollen die Texte fertig sein?"
„Diese zwei Aufträge sollen bis morgen fertig sein", antwortet Herr Fox.
„Gut. Kann ich anfangen?", fragt Paul.
„Ja", sagt Herr Fox.

Paul bringt die Texte am nächsten Tag. Er hat fünf Texte

five texts for the answering machines. Mr. Fox reads them:
1. "Hi. Now you say something."
2. "Hello. I am an answering machine. And what are you?"
3. "Hi. Nobody is at home now but my answering machine is. So you can talk to it instead of me. Wait for the beep."
4. "This is not an answering machine. This is a thought-recording machine. After the beep, think about your name, your reason for calling and a number which I can call you back. And I will think about calling you back."
5. "Speak after the beep! You have the right to be silent. I will record and use everything you say."
"It is not bad. And what about animals?" Mr. Fox asks. Paul gives him another sheet of paper. Mr. Fox reads:

Some rules for cats
Walking:
As often as possible, run quickly and as close as possible in front of a human, especially: on stairs, when they have something on their hands, in the dark, and when they get up in the morning. This will train their co-ordination.
In bed:
Always sleep on a human at night. So he or she cannot turn in the bed. Try to lie on his or her face. Make sure that your tail is right on their nose.
Sleeping:
To have a lot of energy for playing, a cat must sleep a lot (at least 16 hours per day). It is not difficult to find a suitable place to sleep. Any place where a human likes to sit is good. There are good places outdoors too. But you cannot use them when it rains or when it is cold. You can use open windows instead.
Mr. Fox laughs.
"Good work, Paul! I think the magazine "Green world" will like your composition," he says.

für den Anrufbeantworter. Herr Fox liest sie:

1. „Hallo. Jetzt musst du etwas sagen".
2. „Hallo, ich bin ein Anrufbeantworter. Und was bist du?"
3. „Hallo. Außer meinem Anrufbeantworter ist gerade niemand zu Hause. Du kannst dich mit ihm unterhalten. Warte auf den Piepton".
4. „Das ist kein Anrufbeantworter. Das ist ein Gedankenaufnahmegerät. Nach dem Piepton denke an deinen Namen, den Grund, aus dem du anrufst, und die Nummer, unter der ich dich zurückrufen kann. Und ich werde darüber nachdenken, ob ich dich zurückrufe."
5. „Sprechen Sie nach dem Piepton! Sie haben das Recht, Ihre Aussage zu verweigern. Ich werde alles, was Sie sagen, aufzeichnen und verwenden."
„Nicht schlecht. Und was ist mit den Tieren?", fragt Herr Fox. Paul gibt ihm ein anderes Blatt. Herr Fox liest:

Regeln für Katzen
Laufen:
Renne so oft wie möglich schnell und nahe an einem Menschen vorbei, vor allem: auf Treppen, wenn sie etwas tragen, im Dunkeln und wenn sie morgens aufstehen. Das trainiert ihre Koordination.

Im Bett:
Schlafe nachts immer auf dem Menschen, damit er sich nicht umdrehen kann. Versuche, auf seinem Gesicht zu liegen. Vergewissere dich, dass dein Schwanz genau auf seiner Nase liegt.
Schlafen:
Um genug Energie zum Spielen zu haben, muss eine Katze viel schlafen (mindestens sechzehn Stunden am Tag). Es ist nicht schwer, einen passenden Schlafplatz zu finden. Jeder Platz, an dem ein Mensch gerne sitzt, ist gut. Draußen gibt es auch viele gute Plätze. Du kannst sie aber nicht verwenden, wenn es regnet oder kalt ist. Du kannst stattdessen das offene Fenster verwenden.
Herr Fox lacht.
„Gute Arbeit, Paul! Ich denke, die Zeitung ‚Grüne Welt' wird deinen Entwurf mögen", sagt er.

Past Progressive (Continuous) / Verlaufsform der Vergangenheit

Das Past Progressive bilden wir aus was (Einzahl) oder were (Mehrzahl) und dem Verb mit der Endung -ing. Diese Zeitform nennt man auch das Past Continuous.

> Bejahte Sätze

Subjekt + was / were + Ving

I was working at five o'clock. - Um fünf Uhr arbeitete ich.

They were working at five o'clock. - Um fünf Uhr arbeiteten sie.

> Fragen

was / were + Subjekt + Ving

Was he working at five o'clock? - Arbeitete er um fünf Uhr?

Were they working at five o'clock? - Arbeiteten sie um fünf Uhr?

> Verneinte Sätze

Subjekt + was not / were not + Ving

I was not working at five o'clock. - Um fünf Uhr arbeitete ich nicht.

They were not working at five o'clock. - Um fünf Uhr arbeiteten sie nicht.

Das Past Progressive verwendet man mit Handlungen oder Ereignissen, die

> ▶ in der Vergangenheit über eine längere Zeit passierten
>
>   I was reading in the evening. - Am Abend habe ich gelesen.
>
> ▶ zu einem bestimmten Zeitpunkt in der Vergangenheit geschahen
>
>   I was reading a book when Anna came. - Ich las gerade ein Buch als Anna kam.

▶ zur gleichen Zeit passierten

I was reading a book while Anna was cooking. - Ich las ein Buch während Anna kochte.

Exercise 34-1 What were these people doing this morning?
Übung 34-1 Was haben diese Leute am Morgen gemacht?

1. Bill / the mountain park / ski
Bill was in the mountain park. He was skiing.

2. Linda / the office / work
Linda was ....

3. Robert and Emma / the beach / sunbathe
....

4. Sam / the wood / ride a bike
....

5. Denis / the park / sit on a bench
....

6. Anna / in the garden / work
....

Exercise 34-2 What was Anna doing yesterday?

Übung 34-2 Was hat Anna gestern gemacht?

1. 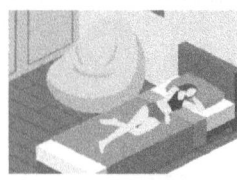 22:00 - 7:00 / sleep

   At 6:00 she was sleeping.

2.  7:00 - 7:20 / take a shower

   At 7:10 ....

3.  8:00 - 8:30 / ride a bike

   At 8:15 ....

4. 9:00 - 15:00 / work

   At 11 o'clock ....

5. 16:00 - 17:30 / sunbathe

   At 17 o'clock ....

6. 18:00 - 18:15 / talk with a friend

   At 18:05 ....

7. 20:00 - 21:30 / watch television

   At 21 o'clock ....

Exercise 34-3 Compose the sentences as in the example.

Übung 34-3 Bilde die Sätze nach dem Beispiel.

1. (what / Julia / do / when you saw her?) What was Julia doing when you saw her?
2. (what / mom / cook / when you came home?) ....

3. (where / Lea / go / when you met her?) ....

4. (the sun / shine / when you came to the beach?) ....

5. (you / work / at 10 o'clock?) ....

6. (you / watch TV / in the evening?) ....

7. (Emma / have lunch / at 2 o'clock?) ....

Reading comprehension

Cat rules
Katzenregeln

Words

1. although [ɔːlˈðəʊ] - obwohl, trotzdem
2. anything [ˈenɪθɪŋ] - etwas, nichts
3. behind [bɪˈhaɪnd] - hinter
4. bite [baɪt] - beißen
5. chance [tʃaːn(t)s] - die Chance
6. child [tʃaɪld] - das Kind
7. cooking [ˈkʊkɪŋ] - kochend
8. few [fjuː] - wenig; a few [fjuː] - ein paar

9. forget [fəˈget] - vergessen
10. fun [fʌn] - der Spaß
11. get [ˈget] - bekommen
12. guest [gest] - der Gast
13. hide [haɪd] - sich verstecken
14. hide-and-seek [ˌhaɪdəndˈsiːk] - das Versteckspiel
15. homework [ˈhəʊmwəːk] - die Hausaufgaben
16. keyboard [ˈkiːbɔːd] - die Tastatur
17. kiss [kɪs] - küssen
18. leg [leg] - das Bein
19. love [lʌv] - die Liebe
20. to love - lieben
21. mosquito [mɔsˈkiːtəʊ] - die Stechmücke
22. mystery [ˈmɪst(ə)rɪ] - das Rätsel
23. panic [ˈpænɪk] - die Panik; to panic - in Panik versetzen
24. planet [ˈplænɪt] - der Planet
25. plate [pleɪt] - der Teller
26. pretend [prɪˈtend] - vorgeben; so tun, als ob
27. reading [ˈriːdɪŋ] - lesend
28. rub [rʌb] - reiben
29. run away [rʌn əˈweɪ] - weglaufen
30. school [skuːl] - die Schule
31. season [ˈsiːz(ə)n] - die (Jahres)zeit
32. secret [ˈsiːkrət] - das Geheimnis
33. sometimes [ˈsʌmtaɪmz] - manchmal, ab und zu
34. steal [stiːl] - stehlen
35. step [step] - der Schritt; to step - treten
36. tasty [ˈteɪstɪ] - lecker
37. thinking [ˈθɪŋkɪŋ] - denken
38. toilet [ˈtɔɪlət] - die Toilette
39. weather [ˈweðə] - das Wetter

B

Cat rules

"The magazine "Green world" places a new order," Mr. Fox says to Paul next day, "And this order is for you, Paul. They like your composition and they want a bigger text about "Cat rules".
It takes Paul two days to compose this text. Here it is.

Some secret rules for cats

Although cats are the best and the most wonderful animals on this planet, they sometimes do very strange things. One of the humans managed to steal some cat secrets. They are some rules of life in order to take over the world! But how these rules will help cats is still a total mystery to the humans.
Bathrooms:
Always go with guests to the bathroom and to the toilet. You do not need to do anything. Just sit, look and sometimes rub their legs.
Doors:
All doors must be open. To get a door opened, stand looking sad at humans. When they open a door, you need not go through it. After you open in this way the outside door, stand in the door and think about something. This is

Katzenregeln

„Die Zeitschrift ‚Grüne Welt' hat uns einen neuen Auftrag erteilt", sagt Herr Fox am nächsten Tag zu Paul. „Und dieser Auftrag ist für dich. Ihnen hat dein Entwurf gefallen und sie wollen einen längeren Text über ‚Katzenregeln'."
Paul braucht zwei Tage für diesen Text. Hier ist er.

Geheime Regeln für Katzen

Obwohl Katzen die besten und wundervollsten Tiere auf diesem Planeten sind, tun sie manchmal sehr seltsame Dinge. Einem Menschen ist es gelungen, ein paar Katzengeheimnisse zu stehlen. Es sind Lebensregeln, um die Weltherrschaft zu übernehmen! Es bleibt jedoch ein Rätsel, wie diese Regeln den Katzen helfen sollen.

Badezimmer:
Gehe immer mit Gästen ins Badezimmer und auf die Toilette. Du musst nichts tun. Sitze einfach nur da, sieh sie an und reibe dich ab und zu an ihren Beinen.
Türen:
Alle Türen müssen offen sein. Um eine Tür zu öffnen, stelle dich mit einem traurigen Blick vor den Menschen. Wenn er eine Tür öffnet, musst du nicht durchgehen. Wenn du auf diese Weise die Haustür geöffnet hast, bleibe in der Tür stehen und denke nach. Das ist vor allem wichtig, wenn es

especially important when the weather is very cold, or when it is a rainy day, or when it is the mosquito season.

Cooking:
Always sit just behind the right foot of cooking humans. So they cannot see you and you have a better chance that a human steps on you. When it happens, they take you in their hands and give something tasty to eat.

Reading books:
Try to get closer to the face of a reading human, between eyes and the book. The best is to lie on the book.

Children's school homework:
Lie on books and copy-books and pretend to sleep. But from time to time jump on the pen. Bite if a child tries to take you away from the table.

Computer:
If a human works with a computer, jump up on the desk and walk over the keyboard.

Food:
Cats need to eat a lot. But eating is only half of the fun. The other half is getting the food. When humans eat, put your tail in their plate when they do not look. It will give you a better chance to get a full plate of food. Never eat from your own plate if you can take some food from the table. Never drink from your own water plate if you can drink from a human's cup.

Hiding:
Hide in places where humans cannot find you for a few days. This will make humans panic (which they love) thinking that you ran away. When you come out of the hiding place, the humans will kiss you and show their love. And you may get something tasty.

Humans:
Tasks of humans are to feed us, to play with us, and to clean our box. It is important that they do not forget who the head of the house is.

sehr kalt ist oder regnet oder in der Stechmückenzeit.

Kochen:
Setze dich immer genau hinter den rechten Fuß von kochenden Menschen. So können sie dich nicht sehen und die Chance ist größer, dass sie auf dich treten. Wenn das passiert, nehmen sie dich auf den Arm und geben dir etwas Leckeres zu essen.

Lesen:
Versuche, nahe an das Gesicht der lesenden Person zu kommen, zwischen Augen und Buch. Am besten ist es, sich auf das Buch zu legen.

Hausaufgaben der Kinder:
Lege dich auf Bücher und Hefte und tue so, als ob du schläfst. Springe von Zeit zu Zeit auf den Stift. Beiße, falls ein Kind versucht, dich vom Tisch zu verscheuchen.

Computer:
Wenn ein Mensch am Computer arbeitet, springe auf den Tisch und laufe über die Tastatur.

Essen:
Katzen müssen viel essen. Aber Essen ist nur der halbe Spaß. Die andere Hälfte ist, das Essen zu bekommen. Wenn Menschen essen, lege deinen Schwanz auf ihren Teller, wenn sie nicht hinsehen. Damit vergrößerst du deine Chancen, einen ganzen Teller Essen zu bekommen. Iss nie von deinem eigenen Teller, wenn du Essen vom Tisch nehmen kannst. Trink nie aus deiner eigenen Schüssel, wenn du aus der Tasse eines Menschen trinken kannst.

Verstecken:
Verstecke dich an Orten, an denen dich Menschen ein paar Tage lang nicht finden können. Das wird die Menschen in Panik versetzen (was sie lieben), weil sie glauben, dass du weggelaufen bist. Wenn du aus deinem Versteck hervorkommst, werden sie dich küssen und dir ihre Liebe zeigen. Und du bekommst vielleicht etwas Leckeres.

Menschen:
Die Aufgabe des Menschen ist, uns zu füttern, mit uns zu spielen und unsere Kiste sauber zu machen. Es ist wichtig, dass sie nicht vergessen, wer der Chef im Haus ist.

Past Progressive versus Past Simple

Robert was working in the garden near the house. He was also thinking about Emma. - Robert arbeitete im Garten neben dem Haus. Er dachte auch über Emma.

Robert's cat was waiting for him in the house. - Roberts Katze wartete gerade auf ihn im Haus.

At this moment the postman came. He gave Robert a letter from Emma. - In diesem Moment kam der Postbote. Er gab Robert einen Brief von Emma.

Robert opened the letter and read it. - Robert öffnete den Brief und las ihn.

And Robert's cat was still waiting for him. - Und Roberts Katze noch wartete auf ihn.

Das Past Progressive beschreibt Handlungen oder Ereignissen, die sich über eine gewisse Zeit erstrecken. Wir können sie als Prozesse oder Vorgänge bezeichnen. Zum Beispiel:

> Robert was working in the garden near the house.
>
> He was also thinking about Emma.
>
> Robert's cat was waiting for him in the house.

Das Past Simple beschreibt Handlungen oder Ereignisse, deren Dauer unerheblich oder sehr kurz ist. Zum Beispiel:

> At this moment the postman came.
>
> He gave Robert a letter from Emma.
>
> Robert opened the letter and read it.

Die Handlungen die nacheinander ablaufen brauchen das Present Simple oder das Past Simple.

Exercise 35 Compose the sentences as in the example. Choose the Past Progressive Tense or the Past Simple Tense.

Übung 35 Bilde die Sätze nach dem Beispiel. Wähle das Past Progressive oder das Past Simple.

Wortschatz: get out - aussteigen, wear - tragen (Kleidung), carry - tragen (in der Hand), listen - hören, wait - warten

1. When I saw (see) Julia she was playing (play) tennis.
2. Tom .... (swim) when the rain .... (start).
3. Mom .... (cook) when the children .... (come) home.
4. I .... (close) the door and .... (go) into the garden.
5. Emma .... (have) lunch when Sam .... (phone) her.
6. The car .... (stop) and a woman .... (get out). She .... (wear) a white dress.
7. I .... (see) Finn in the street. He .... (carry) a big red bag.

8. Anna .... (wake up) at 7 o'clock. Somebody .... (phone) her when she .... (have) breakfast.
9. I .... (play) the guitar. Lea .... (listen) At this moment the cat .... (start) to sing.
10. A big dog .... (run) in the park. Some children .... (run) home.
11. The rain .... (start) when the children .... (run) home from the park.
12. Mom .... (wait) for her children when they .... (come) home.
13. They .... (have) dinner and then they .... (watch) TV.

Reading comprehension

Teamwork
Gruppenarbeit

Words

1. against [əˈgen(t)st] - gegen
2. alien [ˈeɪliən] - der Außerirdische
3. beautiful [ˈbjuːtəfəl] - wunderschön
4. began [bɪˈgæn] - begann, begonnen
5. billion [ˈbɪliən] - Billionen
6. came [keɪm] - kam, gekommen
7. captain [ˈkæptɪn] - der Kapitän
8. central [ˈsentrl] - Haupt-, zentral
9. colleague [ˈkɔliːg] - der Kollege
10. continue [kənˈtɪnjuː] - fortführen

11. continued [kənˈtɪnjuːd] to watch - weiter schauen
12. dance [dɑːns] - tanzen
13. danced [dɑːnst] - getanzt *(part.)*
14. dancing [ˈdɑːnsɪŋ] - tanzend
15. destroy [dɪˈstrɔɪ] - zerstören
16. die [daɪ] - sterben
17. died - starb
18. earth [əːθ] - die Erde
19. either [ˈaɪðə] of you - einer von euch
20. fall [fɔːl] - fallen
21. fell [fel] - fiel
22. finished [ˈfɪnɪʃt] - fertig
23. flew away [fluː əˈweɪ] - flog weg
24. flower [ˈflaʊə] - die Blume
25. garden [ˈgɑːdn] - der Garten
26. had [həd] - hatte, gehabt
27. heard [həːd] - hörte, gehört
28. informed [ɪnˈfɔːmd] - informierte, mitgeteilt
29. killed [kɪld] - tötete, getötet *(part.)*
30. knew [njuː] - wusste
31. laser [ˈleɪzə] - der Laser
32. looked [lʊkt] - sah, schaute, geschaut
33. loved [ˈlʌvd] - liebte, geliebt
34. moved [muːvd] - bewegte sich
35. pointed [ˈpɔɪntɪd] - richtete
36. radar [ˈreɪdɑː] - der Radar
37. radio [ˈreɪdɪəʊ] - das Radio
38. remembered [rɪˈmembəd] - erinnerte sich
39. said [sed] - sagte
40. serial [ˈsɪərɪəl] - die Serie
41. shook [ʃʊk] - wackelte
42. short [ʃɔːt] - kurz
43. smiled [smaɪld] - lächelte, gelächelt
44. soon [suːn] - bald
45. space [speɪs] - das Weltall
46. spaceship [ˈspeɪsʃɪp] - das Raumschiff
47. stopped [stɔpt] - beendete
48. switched on [swɪtʃt ɔn] - machte an
49. take part [teɪk pɑːt] - teilnehmen
50. teach [tiːtʃ] - beibringen
51. thousand [ˈθaʊz(ə)nd] - tausend
52. TV-set [ˌtiːˈvɪset] - der Fernseher
53. until [(ə)nˈtɪl] - bis
54. war [wɔː] - der Krieg
55. went [went] away - verlassen
56. working [ˈwəːkɪŋ] - arbeitend

B

Teamwork

David wants to be a journalist. He studies at a college. He has a composition lesson today. Mr. Kite teaches students to write composition.
"Dear friends," he says, "some of you will work for publishing houses, newspapers or magazines, the radio or television. This means you will work in a team. Working in a team is not simple. Now I want that you try to make a journalistic composition in a team. I need a boy and a girl."
Many students want to take part in the team work. Mr. Kite chooses David and Carol. Carol is from Spain but she can speak English very well.
"Please, sit at this table. Now you are colleagues," Mr. Kite says to them, "You will write a short composition. Either of you will begin the composition and then give it to your colleague. Your colleague will read the

Gruppenarbeit

David will Journalist werden. Er studiert an der Universität. Heute hat er einen Schreibkurs. Herr Kite bringt den Studenten bei, Artikel zu schreiben.

„Liebe Freunde", sagt er, „ein paar von euch werden für Verlage, Zeitungen oder Zeitschriften, das Radio oder das Fernsehen arbeiten. Das bedeutet, dass ihr in einer Gruppe arbeiten werdet. Es ist nicht einfach, in einer Gruppe zu arbeiten. Ich möchte, dass ihr jetzt versucht, in einer Gruppe einen journalistischen Text zu schreiben. Ich brauche einen Jungen und ein Mädchen."
Viele Studenten wollen bei der Gruppenarbeit mitmachen. Herr Kite wählt David und Carol. Carol kommt aus Spanien, aber sie spricht sehr gut Englisch.

„Setzt euch bitte an diesen Tisch. Ihr seid jetzt Kollegen", sagt Herr Kite zu ihnen. „Ihr werdet einen kurzen Text schreiben. Einer von euch beginnt den Text und gibt ihn dann seinem Kollegen. Der Kollege liest den Text und führt ihn fort. Dann gibt euer Kollege ihn zurück, der Erste

composition and continue it. Then your colleague will give it back and the first one will read and continue it. And so on until your time is over. I give you twenty minutes."

Mr. Kite gives them paper and Carol begins. She thinks a little and then writes.

Team composition

Carol: Julia was looking through the window. The flowers in her garden were moving in the wind as if dancing. She remembered that evening when she danced with Billy. It was a year ago but she remembered everything - his blue eyes, his smile and his voice. It was a happy time for her but it was over now. Why was not he with her?

David: At this moment space captain Billy Brisk was at the spaceship White Star. He had an important task and he did not have time to think about that silly girl who he danced with a year ago. He quickly pointed the lasers of White Star at alien spaceships. Then he switched on the radio and talked to the aliens: "I give you an hour to give up. If in one hour you do not give up I will destroy you." But before he finished an alien laser hit the left engine of the White Star. Billy's laser began to hit alien spaceships and at the same time he switched on the central and the right engines. The alien laser destroyed the working right engine and the White Star shook badly. Billy fell on the floor thinking during the fall which of the alien spaceships he must destroy first.

Carol: But he hit his head on the metal floor and died at the same moment. But before he died he remembered the poor beautiful girl who loved him and he was very sorry that he went away from her. Soon people stopped this silly war on poor aliens. They destroyed all of their own spaceships and lasers and informed the aliens that people would never start a war against them again. People said that they wanted to be friends with the aliens. Julia was very glad when she heard about it. Then she switched on the TV-set and continued to watch a wonderful German serial.

David: Because people destroyed their own radars and lasers, nobody knew that spaceships of aliens came very close to the Earth. Thousands of aliens' lasers hit the Earth and

liest ihn und führt ihn fort. Und so weiter, bis die Zeit vorbei ist. Ihr habt zwanzig Minuten".

Herr Kite gibt ihnen Papier, und Carol fängt an. Sie denkt kurz nach und schreibt dann.

Gruppenarbeit

Carol: Julia sah aus dem Fenster. Die Blumen in ihrem Garten bewegten sich im Wind, als ob sie tanzten. Sie erinnerte sich an den Abend, an dem sie mit Billy getanzt hatte. Das war vor einem Jahr gewesen, aber sie erinnerte sich an alles - seine blauen Augen, sein Lächeln, seine Stimme. Es war eine glückliche Zeit für sie gewesen, aber sie war nun vorbei. Warum war er nicht bei ihr?

David: Zu dieser Zeit war Raumschiffkapitän Billy Brisk in seinem Raumschiff White Star. Er hatte eine wichtige Mission und keine Zeit, über dieses dumme Mädchen, mit dem er vor einem Jahr getanzt hatte, nachzudenken. Schnell richtete er den Laser der White Star auf die Raumschiffe Außerirdischer. Dann stellte er das Funkgerät an und sprach zu den Außerirdischen: „Ihr habt eine Stunde, um aufzugeben. Wenn ihr in einer Stunde nicht aufgebt, werde ich euch zerstören." Kurz bevor er seine Rede beendet hatte, traf jedoch ein Laser der Außerirdischen den linken Motor der White Star. Billys Laser begann, auf die Raumschiffe der Außerirdischen zu schießen, und gleichzeitig schaltete Billy den Hauptmotor und den rechten Motor an. Der Laser der Außerirdischen zerstörte den funktionierenden rechten Motor, und die White Star wackelte stark. Billy fiel auf den Boden und überlegte währenddessen, welches der Raumschiffe der Außerirdischen er zuerst zerstören musste.

Carol: Aber er schlug mit seinem Kopf auf dem metallenen Boden auf und war sofort tot. Bevor er starb, dachte er noch an das arme schöne Mädchen, das ihn liebte, und es tat ihm sehr leid, dass er es verlassen hatte. Kurz darauf beendeten die Menschen den dummen Krieg gegen die armen Außerirdischen. Sie zerstörten all ihre eigenen Raumschiffe und Laser und teilten den Außerirdischen mit, dass die Menschen nie wieder einen Krieg gegen sie beginnen würden. Die Menschen sagten, sie wollten Freunde der Außerirdischen sein. Julia war sehr froh, als sie davon hörte. Dann machte sie den Fernseher an und schaute eine tolle deutsche Serie weiter.

David: Da die Menschen ihre eigenen Radare und Laser zerstört hatten, wusste niemand, dass Raumschiffe der Außerirdischen der Erde sehr nahe kamen. Tausende Laser der Außerirdischen trafen die Erde und töten die

killed poor silly Julia and five billion people in a second. The Earth was destroyed and its turning parts flew away in space.	*arme, dumme Julia und fünf Billionen Menschen in einer Sekunde. Die Erde war zerstört, und ihre Teile flogen in den Weltraum hinaus.*
"I see you came to the finish before your time is over," Mr. Kite smiled, "Well, the lesson is over. Let us read and speak about this team composition during the next lesson."	*"Wie ich sehe, habt ihr euren Text fertig, bevor die Zeit um ist", sagte Herr Kite lächelnd. "Gut, der Unterricht ist vorbei. Lasst uns das nächste Mal diese Gruppenarbeit lesen und darüber sprechen."*

36

Future / Futur

Für zukünftige Handlungen, die von einer Person oder von mehreren Personen schon festgelegt sind, verwenden wir das Present Progressive oder going to + Infinitiv.

I am buying a new TV tomorrow. = I am going to buy a new TV tomorrow. - Ich kaufe einen neuen Fernseher morgen. (ich habe das Geld dafür gespart)

They are flying to Spain on Sunday. = They are going to fly to Spain on Sunday. - Sie fliegen am Sonntag nach Spanien. (sie haben schon die Flugkarten gekauft)

What are you doing afternoon? = What are you going to do afternoon? - Was machst du am Nachmittag?

I am playing football from five to seven o'clock. = I am going to play football from five to seven o'clock. - Ich spiele Fußball von fünf bis sieben Uhr. (ich habe es mir schon überlegt)

Für festgelegte öffentliche Handlungen in der Zukunft wie Öffnungszeiten, Fahrplan, Lehrplan usw. verwenden wir das Present Simple.

When does the bus arrive? - Wann kommt der Bus an?

The bus arrives at ten o'clock. - Der Bus kommt um zehn Uhr an.

Für Meinung, Hoffnung, Unsicherheit/Vermutung, spontaner Entschluss, Vorhersage, nicht beeinflussbares Geschehen in der Zukunft verwenden wir das Futur I. Das Futur I bilden wir aus will und dem Infinitiv (Grundform).

Bejahte Sätze

Subjekt + will + Infinitiv

I will read a book. - Ich werde ein Buch lesen.

Fragen

Will + Subjekt + Infinitiv

Will you read a book? - Wirst du ein Buch lesen?

Verneinte Sätze

Subjekt + will not (won't) + Infinitiv

I will not read a book. = I won't read a book. - I werde kein Buch lesen.

▶ Vermutung oder Hoffnung

I think I will read a book in the evening. - Ich denke, dass ich das Buch am Abend lesen werde.

▶ spontaner Entschluss

It is raining. I will give you an umbrella. - Es regnet. Ich werde dir einen Regenschirm geben.

▶ Vorhersage

Borussia will win the championship. - Borussia wird die Meisterschaft gewinnen.

▶ nicht beeinflussbares Geschehen in der Zukunft

She will be twenty years old tomorrow. - Morgen ist sie zwanzig Jahre alt.

Exercise 36-1 What are these people going to do next Sunday?

Übung 36-1 Was machen diese Leute am nächsten Sonntag?

1. Bill ski
   Bill is skiing.

2. Linda work
   Linda ....

3. Emma sunbathe on the beach
   ....

4. Sam ride a bike
   ....

5. Denis go to the park
   ....

6. Anna work in the garden
   ....

Exercise 36-2 Compose the questions about future as in the example.

Übung 36-2 Bilde die Fragen über die Zukunft nach dem Beispiel.

1. (what / Julia / do / on Sunday?) What is Julia doing on Sunday?
2. (what / mom / cook / tomorrow?) ....
   ....
3. (where / Lea / go / next weekend?) ....
   ....
4. (what time / Sam / come?) ....
   ....
5. (why / you / work / on Sunday?) ....

6. (what time / Emma / have lunch?) ....

Exercise 36-3 Compose the sentences about future. Use the Present Progressive Tense or the Present Simple Tense.

Übung 36-3 Bilde die Sätze über die Zukunft. Benutze das Present Progressive oder das Present Simple.

1. (the show / start / at 7 o'clock) The show starts at 7 o'clock.
2. (I / not / play tennis / tomorrow) I am not playing tennis tomorrow.
3. (what time / the bus / arrive?) ....
4. (who / meet / you / on the station?) ....
5. (what time / you / meet Emma?) ....
6. (the café / close / at 5 o'clock) ....
7. (my cooking class / finish / in December) ....
8. (I / cook / an big Thai dish / on Sunday) ....
9. (you / take / an English class / in January?) ....

Exercise 36-4 Compose the sentences about future. Use *going to*.

Übung 36-4 Bilde die Sätze über die Zukunft. Benutze going to.

1. (I / not / play tennis / tomorrow) I am not going to play tennis tomorrow.
2. (what time / Linda / work in the garden?) ....
3. (how many books / you / buy?) ....
4. (where / Emma / live in England?) ....
5. (when / she / come back?) ....
6. (Tom / not / wake up before 9 o'clock) ....

7. (what / mom / cook?) ....
8. (Sam / start a Chinese course) ....
9. (I / meet Anna / in the evening) ....
10. (how much time / you / spend in Spain?) ....

Exercise 36-5 Compose the negative sentences.

Übung 36-5 Bilde die verneinte Sätze.

1. I will play tennis. I won't play tennis.
2. Tom will come. ....
3. Emma will cook. ....
4. Sam will help Emma. ....
5. Bill will read the book. ....
6. Lea will wash windows. ....
7. Robert will drive the car. ....
8. We will go to the park. ....

Exercise 36-6 Are the sentences right or wrong? Correct wrong sentences.

Übung 36-6 Sind die Sätze richtig oder falsch? Korrigiere falsche Sätze.

1. I help you with this work, okay? **wrong** I will help you with this work, okay?
2. I sometimes help Anna. **right**
3. Tom probably comes in the evening. ....
   ....
4. Tom often comes in the evening. ....
   ....
5. I think Emma cooks pizza soon. ....
   ....
6. Emma occasionally cooks pizza. ....
   ....
7. We watch television tonight, okay? ....
   ....
8. We always watch television in evening. ....
   ....
9. Lea, you wash the window today after breakfast, please? ....

10. Lea seldom washes the window. ....

11. I will drive the car, okay? ....

12. My wife usually drives the car. ....

Reading comprehension

Robert and David are looking for a new job
Robert und David suchen einen neuen Job

Words

1. ad [æd] - das Inserat
2. advert [əd'və:t] - die Anzeige
3. age [eɪdʒ] - das Alter
4. aloud [ə'laʊd] - laut
5. art [a:t] - die Kunst
6. artist ['a:tɪst] - der Künstler
7. consultancy [kən'sʌltənsɪ] - die Beratung
8. dirty ['də:tɪ] - dreckig
9. doctor ['dɔktə] - der Arzt
10. dream [dri:m] - der Traum
11. to dream - träumen
12. engineer [ˌendʒɪ'nɪə] - der Ingenieur

13. estimate [ˈestɪmeɪt] - beurteilen
14. farmer [ˈfɑːmə] - der Bauer
15. food [fuːd] - das Essen
16. found [faʊnd] - gefunden
17. gift [gɪft] - die Begabung
18. idea [aɪˈdɪə] - die Idee
19. kitten [ˈkɪt(ə)n] - das Kätzchen
20. leader [ˈliːdə] - der Führer
21. method [ˈmeθəd] - die Methode
22. monotonous [məˈnɔtənəs] - monoton
23. nature [ˈneɪtʃə] - die Natur
24. neighbour [ˈneɪbə] - der Nachbar
25. personal [ˈpəːsən(ə)l] - persönlich
26. pet [pet] - das Haustier
27. programmer [ˈprəʊgræmə] - der Programmierer
28. puppy [ˈpʌpɪ] - der Welpe
29. questionnaire [kwestʃəˈneə] - der Fragebogen
30. rat [ræt] - die Ratte
31. recommend [ˌrekəˈmend] - empfehlen
32. recommendation [rekəmenˈdeɪʃn] - die Empfehlung
33. rubric [ˈruːbrɪk] - die Rubrik
34. serve [səːv] - bedienen
35. sly [slaɪ] - schlau
36. spaniel [ˈspænjel] - der Spaniel
37. Spanish [ˈspænɪʃ] - spanisch
38. translator [trænzˈleɪtə, trænsˈleɪtə] - der Übersetzer
39. travel [ˈtræv(ə)l] - reisen
40. vet [vet] - der Tierarzt
41. while [(h)waɪl] - während
42. writer [ˈraɪtə] - der Schriftsteller

B

Robert and David are looking for a new job

Robert and David are at David's home. David is cleaning the table after breakfast and Robert is reading adverts and ads in a newspaper. He is reading the rubric "Animals". David's sister Nancy is in the room too. She is trying to catch the cat hiding under the bed.
"There are so many pets for free in the newspaper. I think I will choose a cat or a dog. David, what do you think?" Robert asks David.
"Nancy, do not bother the cat!" David says angrily, "Well Robert, it is not a bad idea. Your pet will always wait for you at home and will be so happy when you come back home and give some food. And do not forget that you will have to walk with your pet in mornings and evenings or clean its box. Sometimes you will have to clean the floor or take your pet to a vet. So think carefully before you get an animal."
"Well, there are some ads here. Listen," Robert says and begins to read aloud:
"Found dirty white dog, looks like a rat. It may live outside for a long time. I will give it away for money."
Here is one more:
"Spanish dog, speaks Spanish. Give away for free. And free puppies half spaniel half sly neighbor's dog,"

Robert und David suchen einen neuen Job

Robert und David sind bei David zu Hause. David macht den Tisch nach dem Frühstück sauber, und Robert liest Anzeigen und Inserate in der Zeitung. Er liest die Rubrik ‚Tiere'. Davids Schwester Nancy ist auch im Zimmer. Sie versucht, die Katze, die sich unterm Bett versteckt, zu fangen.
„Es gibt so viele kostenlose Tiere in der Zeitung. Ich denke, ich werde mir eine Katze oder einen Hund aussuchen. Was meinst du, David?", fragt Robert.
„Nancy, hör auf, die Katze zu ärgern", sagt David wütend. „Na ja, Robert, das ist keine schlechte Idee. Dein Haustier wartet immer zu Hause auf dich und ist so glücklich, wenn du nach Hause kommst und ihm Futter gibst. Und vergiss nicht, dass du morgens und abends mit deinem Tier Gassi gehen oder seine Kiste sauber machen musst. Manchmal musst du den Boden putzen oder mit dem Tier zum Tierarzt gehen. Also, denk gut darüber nach, bevor du dir ein Haustier anschaffst."
„Also, hier sind ein paar Anzeigen. Hör zu", sagt Robert und beginnt, laut vorzulesen:
„Habe einen dreckigen, weißen Hund gefunden, sieht aus wie eine Ratte. Hat vielleicht lange auf der Straße gelebt. Ich gebe ihn für Geld her.
Und hier noch eine:
Spanischer Hund, spricht Spanisch. Gebe ihn kostenlos ab. Und kostenlose Welpen, halb Spaniel, halb schlauer Nachbarshund."

Robert looks at David, "How can a dog speak Spanish?"
"A dog may understand Spanish. Can you understand Spanish?" David asks smiling.
"I cannot understand Spanish. Listen, here is one more ad:
"Give away free farm kittens. Ready to eat. They will eat anything,"
Robert turns the newspaper, "Well, I think pets can wait. I will better look for a job," he finds the rubric about jobs and reads aloud,
"Are you looking for a suitable job? The job consultancy "Suitable personnel" can help you. Our consultants will estimate your personal gifts and will give you a recommendation about the most suitable profession."
Robert looks up and says: "David what do you think?"
"The best job for you is washing a truck in the sea and let it float," Nancy says and quickly runs out of the room.
"It is not a bad idea. Let's go now," David answers and takes carefully the cat out of the kettle, where Nancy put the animal a minute ago.
Robert and David arrive to the job consultancy "Suitable personnel" by their bikes. There is no queue, so they go inside. There are two women there. One of them is speaking on the telephone. Another woman is writing something. She asks Robert and David to take seats. Her name is Mrs. Sharp. She asks them their names and their age.
"Well, let me explain the method which we use. Look, there are five kinds of professions.
1. The first kind is man - nature. Professions: farmer, zoo worker etc.
2. The second kind is man - machine. Professions: pilot, taxi driver, truck driver etc.
3. The third kind is man - man. Professions: doctor, teacher, journalist etc.
4. The fourth kind is man - computer. Professions: translator, engineer, programmer etc.
5. The fifth kind is man - art. Professions: writer, artist, singer etc.
We give recommendations about a suitable profession only when we learn about you more. First let me estimate your personal gifts. I must know what you like and what you dislike. Then we will know which kind of profession is the most suitable for you. Please, fill up the

Robert sieht David an: „Wie kann ein Hund Spanisch sprechen?"
„Ein Hund kann Spanisch verstehen. Verstehst du Spanisch?", fragt David grinsend.
„Ich verstehe kein Spanisch. Hör zu, hier ist noch eine Anzeige:
Gebe kostenlos Kätzchen vom Bauernhof her. Fertig zum Essen. Sie essen alles."
Robert blättert die Zeitung um. „Na gut, ich denke, Tiere können warten. Ich suche besser einen Job." Er findet die Stellenanzeigen und liest laut:
„Suchen Sie nach einem passenden Job? Die Arbeitsvermittlung ‚Passende Mitarbeiter' kann Ihnen helfen. Unsere Berater beurteilen Ihre persönliche Begabung und erstellen Ihnen eine Empfehlung für den passendsten Beruf."
Robert sieht auf und sagt: „Was meinst du, David?"

„Der beste Job für euch ist, einen Laster im Meer zu waschen und ihn wegschwimmen zu lassen", sagt Nancy und rennt dann schnell aus dem Zimmer.
„Keine schlechte Idee. Lass uns gleich gehen", antwortet David und holt vorsichtig die Katze aus dem Kessel, in den Nancy sie kurz zuvor gelegt hatte.
Robert und David fahren mit dem Fahrrad zur Arbeitsvermittlung ‚Passende Mitarbeiter'. Es gibt keine Schlange und sie gehen hinein. Zwei Frauen sind da. Eine von ihnen telefoniert. Die andere schreibt etwas. Sie bittet Robert und David, Platz zu nehmen. Sie heißt Frau Sharp. Sie fragt sie nach ihren Namen und ihrem Alter.
„Gut, lasst mich euch die Methode, nach der wir arbeiten, erklären. Seht, es gibt fünf Berufskategorien:
1. Die Erste ist Mensch - Natur. Berufe: Bauer, Tierpfleger usw.
2. Die Zweite ist Mensch - Maschine. Berufe: Pilot, Taxifahrer, Lastwagenfahrer usw.
3. Die Dritte ist Mensch - Mensch. Berufe: Arzt, Lehrer, Journalist usw.
4. Die Vierte ist Mensch - Computer. Berufe: Übersetzer, Ingenieur, Programmierer usw.

5. Die Fünfte ist Mensch - Kunst. Berufe: Schriftsteller, Künstler, Sänger usw.
Wir erstellen Empfehlungen für passende Berufe erst, wenn wir euch besser kennengelernt haben. Lasst mich zuerst eure persönlichen Begabungen beurteilen. Ich muss wissen, was ihr mögt und was ihr nicht mögt. Dann wissen wir, welcher Beruf am besten zu euch passt. Füllt jetzt bitte den Fragebogen aus", sagt Frau Sharp und

questionnaire now," Mrs. Sharp says and gives them the questionnaires. David and Robert fill up the questionnaires.

Questionnaire
Name: David Tweeter

Watch machines - I do not mind
Speak with people - I like
Serve customers - I do not mind
Drive cars, trucks - I like
Work inside - I like
Work outside - I like
Remember a lot - I do not mind
Travel - I like
Estimate, check - I hate
Dirty work - I do not mind
Monotonous work - I hate
Hard work - I do not mind
Be leader - I do not mind
Work in team - I do not mind
Dream while working - I like
Train - I do not mind
Do creative work - I like
Work with texts - I like

Questionnaire
Name: Robert Genscher

Watch machines - I do not mind
Speak with people - I like
Serve customers - I do not mind
Drive cars, trucks - I do not mind
Work inside - I like
Work outside - I like
Remember a lot - I do not mind
Travel - I like
Estimate, check - I do not mind
Dirty work - I do not mind
Monotonous work - I hate
Hard work - I do not mind
Be leader - I hate
Work in team - I like
Dream while working - I like
Train - I do not mind
Do creative work - I like
Work with texts - I like

gibt ihnen die Fragebögen. David und Robert füllen die Fragebögen aus.

Fragebogen
Name: Robert Genscher

Maschinen beobachten - Habe ich nichts dagegen
Mit Menschen sprechen - Mag ich
Kunden bedienen - Habe ich nichts dagegen
Autos, Lastwagen fahren - Mag ich
Im Büro arbeiten - Mag ich
Draußen arbeiten - Mag ich
Mir viel merken - Habe ich nichts dagegen
Reisen - Mag ich
Bewerten, kontrollieren - Hasse ich
Dreckige Arbeit - Habe ich nichts dagegen
Monotone Arbeit - Hasse ich
Schwere Arbeit - Habe ich nichts dagegen
Führer sein - Habe ich nichts dagegen
In der Gruppe arbeiten - Habe ich nichts dagegen
Während der Arbeit träumen - Mag ich
Trainieren - Habe ich nichts dagegen
Kreative Arbeit - Mag ich
Mit Texten arbeiten - Mag ich

Fragebogen
Name: Robert Genscher

Maschinen beobachten - Habe ich nichts dagegen
Mit Menschen sprechen - Mag ich
Kunden bedienen - Habe ich nichts dagegen
Autos, Lastwagen fahren - Habe ich nichts dagegen
Im Büro arbeiten - Mag ich
Draußen arbeiten - Mag ich
Mir viel merken - Habe ich nichts dagegen
Reisen - Mag ich
Bewerten, kontrollieren - Habe ich nichts dagegen
Dreckige Arbeit - Habe ich nichts dagegen
Monotone Arbeit - Hasse ich
Schwere Arbeit - Habe ich nichts dagegen
Führer sein - Hasse ich
In der Gruppe arbeiten - Mag ich
Während der Arbeit träumen - Mag ich
Trainieren - Habe ich nichts dagegen
Kreative Arbeit - Mag ich
Mit Texten arbeiten - Mag ich.

Present Perfect / Perfekt

Das Present Perfekt bilden wir aus have/has und dem Perfekt Partizip des Hauptverbs. Das Perfekt Partizip nennt man auch das Partizip II oder die dritte Form des Verbs (V3). Das Perfekt Partizip bilden wir mit -ed bei regelmäßigen Verben oder wir finden es in der Liste der unregelmäßigen Verben in der 3. Spalte.

> Bejahte Sätze

Subjekt + have/has + V3

I have finished the work. - Ich habe die Arbeit beendet.

> Fragen

Have/has + Subjekt + V3

Have you learned the rule? - Hast du die Regel gelernt?

> Verneinte Sätze

Subjekt + have not/has not + V3

She has not invited me. - Sie hat mich nicht eingeladen.

Das Present Perfekt verwenden wir mit abgeschlossenen Handlungen und Ereignissen, die für Zuhörer noch unbekannt sind.

> I have bought a book by Tolkien. - Ich habe ein Buch von Tolkien gekauft.
>
> Andy come! The mother has cooked pizza. - Andy komm! Die Mutter hat eine Pizza gemacht.
>
> Have you seen Tom? - Hast du Tom gesehen?

Aber mit allgemein bekannten Tatsachen oder mit Zeitangaben in der Vergangenheit verwenden wir das Past Simple.

> Tolkien wrote several great books. - Tolkien hat einige tolle Bücher geschrieben.

The mother cooked pizza ten minutes ago. - Die Mutter hat eine Pizza vor zehn Minuten gekocht.

Did you see Tom in the morning? - Hast du Tom am Morgen gesehen?

Das Present Perfekt verwenden wir auch mit Handlungen und Ereignissen, die während einer noch nicht beendeten Zeitspanne dauern. Als eine Zeitspanne können wir die folgende Ausdrücke benutzen: today - heute, this week - diese Woche, this month - diesen Monat, for - seit, since - seit, just - gerade, recently - neulich, ever - jemals, never - nie u.Ä.m.

I have drunk two cups of tea today. - Ich habe heute zwei Tassen Tee getrunken.

He has played tennis two times this month. - Er hat diesen Monat zweimal Tennis gespielt

She has been in Berlin since Friday. - Sie ist in Berlin seit Freitag gewesen.

She has been in Berlin for three days. - Sie ist in Berlin seit drei Tagen.

We have never been to Africa. - Wir sind noch nie in Afrika gewesen.

Have you ever travelled by a ship? - Bist du jemals mit einem Schiff gefahren?

How long have you known him? - Wie lange kennst du ihn?

How long has she had her bike? - Wie lange hat sie ihren Fahrrad gehabt?

Exercise 37-1 Compose the sentences as in the example. Use the Present Perfect Tense.

Übung 37-1 Bilde die Sätze nach dem Beispiel. Benutze das Present Perfekt.

1. (cook) I have cooked pizza. Would you like to try it?
2. (buy) I .... some apples. Have one, please.
3. (finish) 'Tom, are you still working?' 'No, I...'
4. (buy) Look! Linda .... a new blue bike.
5. (watch) 'Let's go to the cinema.' 'No, thanks. I .... that film.'
6. (go) 'Where is Emma?' 'She .... home.'
7. (you wash) Your car looks great! .... it?
8. (take) I cannot find my pen. Somebody ....it.
9. (you see) Lea came back from Italy yesterday. ....her new hat?

Exercise 37-2 Compose the sentences as in the example. Use the Present Perfect Tense or the Past Simple Tense.

Übung 37-2 Bilde die Sätze nach dem Beispiel. Benutze das Present Perfekt oder das Past Simple.

1. (correct) I have corrected two mistakes in my work today.
2. (correct) I corrected five mistakes in my work yesterday.
3. (drink) I .... three cups of tea today.
4. (drink) I .... five cups of tea yesterday.
5. (watch) Tom .... two shows this week.
6. (watch) Tom .... a show last week.
7. (visit) Robert and Emma .... Emma's parents two times this year.
8. (visit) Robert and Emma .... Emma's parents three times last year.
9. (sing) My friend .... only one short song this evening.
10. (sing) My friend .... several songs on Sunday evening.

Exercise 37-3 Compose the sentences as in the example. Use the Present Perfect Tense.

Übung 37-3 Bilde die Sätze nach dem Beispiel. Benutze das Present Perfekt.

1. I am in Berlin. I have been in Berlin since Friday.
2. Tom lives in Boston. He has lived there for twenty years.
3. Emma works in a shop. She .... there since June.
4. Linda has a bike. She .... it since Sunday.
5. Sam is ill. He .... ill for three days.
6. I know Anna very well. I .... her for a long time.
7. Robert and Emma are married. They .... married since April.
8. They are in London. They .... there for five days.
9. I live in the UK. I .... here since 2005.
10. Lea works at school. She .... there for seven years.
11. I have a cat. I .... it for two years.
12. My cat is hungry. It .... hungry since morning.
13. I know Robert and Emma well. I .... them since 2015.
14. Finn is sad. He .... sad since the start of the lesson.

Reading comprehension

Applying to "San Francisco News"
Bewerbung bei den "San Francisco News"

A

Words

1. accompany [əˈkʌmpənɪ] - begleiten
2. apply [əˈplaɪ] - sich bewerben
3. arrived [əˈraɪvd] - angekommen
4. asked [ˈɑːskt] - gefragt
5. asterisk [ˈæst(ə)rɪsk] - das Sternchen
6. blank [blæŋk], empty [ˈemptɪ] - leer
7. could [kʊd] - könnte, kann
8. criminal [ˈkrɪmɪn(ə)l] - der Verbrecher
9. editor [ˈedɪtə] - der Herausgeber
10. education [ˌedjʊˈkeɪʃ(ə)n] - die Ausbildung
11. estimated - ausgewertet
12. female [ˈfiːmeɪl] - weiblich
13. field [fiːld] - das Feld
14. finance [ˈfaɪnæns, fɪˈnæns] - die Finanzwissenschaft
15. fluently [ˈfluːəntlɪ] - fließend
16. form [fɔːm] - das Formular
17. gave [geɪv] - gab
18. goodbye [gʊdˈbaɪ] - Auf Wiedersehen
19. information [ˌɪnfəˈmeɪʃ(ə)n] - die Information, die Angabe
20. learned [ˈləːnɪd] about - kennengelernt
21. leave [liːv] - verlassen
22. male [meɪl] - männlich
23. middle [ˈmɪdl] name - der zweite Name
24. Miss [mɪs] - Fräulein
25. nationality [ˌnæʃ(ə)ˈnælətɪ] - die Nationalität
26. patrol [pəˈtrəʊl] - die Patrouille, die Streife
27. police [pəˈliːs] - die Polizei
28. recommended [ˌrekəˈmendɪd] - empfohlen
29. report [rɪˈpɔːt] - berichten
30. reporter [rɪˈpɔːtə] - der Reporter
31. seventeen [ˌsev(ə)nˈtiːn] - siebzehn
32. sex [seks] - das Geschlecht
33. single [ˈsɪŋgl] - ledig
34. status [ˈsteɪtəs] - der Stand
35. family status - der Familienstand
36. took [tʊk] - nahm
37. twenty-one [ˈtwentɪ wʌn] - einundzwanzig
38. underline [ˈʌnd(ə)laɪn] - unterstreichen
39. week [wiːk] - die Woche
40. worked [wəːkt] - gearbeitet

B

Applying to "San Francisco News"

Mrs. Sharp estimated David's and Robert's answers in the questionnaires. When she learned about their personal gifts she could give them some recommendations about suitable professions. She said that the third profession kind is the most suitable for them. They could work as a doctor, a teacher or a journalist etc. Mrs. Sharp recommended them to apply for a job with the newspaper „San Francisco News". They gave a part time job to students who could compose police reports for the criminal rubric. So Robert and David arrived at the personnel department of the newspaper „San Francisco News" and applied for this job.

"We have been to the job consultancy "Suitable personnel" today," David said to Miss Slim, who was the head of the personnel department, "They have recommended us to apply to your newspaper."

"Well, have you worked as a reporter before?" Miss Slim asked.

"No, we have not," David answered.

"Please, fill up these personal information forms," Miss Slim said and gave them two forms. Robert and David filled up the personal information forms.

Personal information form

You must fill up fields with asterisk *. You can leave other fields blank.

First name* - *David*
Middle name
Last name* - *Tweeter*
Sex* (underline) - <u>Male</u> Female
Age* - *Twenty years old*
Nationality* - *US*
Family status (underline) - <u>single</u> married
Address* - *11 Queen street, San Francisco, USA*
Education - *I am studying Journalism in the third year at a college*
Where have you worked before? - *I worked for two months as a farm worker*
What experience and skills have you had?* - *I can drive a car, a truck and I can use a computer*
Languages* 0 - no, 10 - fluently - *Spanish - 8, English - 10*

Bewerbung bei den ‚San Francisco News'

Frau Sharp wertete Davids und Roberts Antworten im Fragebogen aus. Indem sie ihre persönlichen Begabungen kennenlernte, konnte sie ihnen Empfehlungen für passende Berufe geben. Sie sagte, dass die dritte Berufskategorie am besten zu ihnen passte. Sie könnten als Arzt, Lehrer oder Journalist arbeiten. Frau Sharp empfahl ihnen, sich um einen Job bei der Zeitung ‚San Francisco News' zu bewerben. Die hatte einen Nebenjob für Studenten zu vergeben, die Polizeiberichte in der Rubrik über Verbrechen verfassen konnten. Also gingen Robert und David in die Personalabteilung der Zeitung ‚San Francisco News' und bewarben sich um den Job.

„Wir waren heute bei der Arbeitsvermittlung Passende Mitarbeiter", sagte David zu Frau Slim, der Leiterin der Personalabteilung. „Sie haben uns empfohlen, uns bei Ihrer Zeitung zu bewerben."

„Habt ihr schon als Reporter gearbeitet?", fragte Frau Slim.

„Nein", antwortete David.

„Füllt bitte diese Formulare mit euren persönlichen Angaben aus", sagte Frau Slim und gab ihnen zwei Formulare. Robert und David füllten sie aus.

Persönliche Angaben

Alle mit einem Sternchen * markierten Felder müssen ausgefüllt werden. Die anderen Felder können leer gelassen werden.

Vorname - David
Zweiter Name
Nachname - Tweeter
Geschlecht (unterstreiche) - <u>männlich</u> weiblich
Alter - Zwanzig
Nationalität - Amerikaner
Familienstand (unterstreiche) - <u>ledig</u> verheiratet
Addresse - 11 Queen street, San Francisco, USA
Ausbildung - Ich studiere Journalismus im dritten Jahr an der Universität
Wo haben Sie zuvor gearbeitet? - Ich habe zwei Monate auf einem Bauernhof gearbeitet
Welche Erfahrung und Fähigkeiten haben Sie? - Ich kann Auto und Lastwagen fahren und mit dem Computer arbeiten.
Sprachen 0 - nein, 10 - fließend - Spanisch - 8, Englisch

Driving license* (underline) - No <u>Yes</u> Kind: BC, I can drive trucks
You need a job* (underline) - Full time <u>Part time</u>: 15 hours a week
You want to earn - 15 dollars per hour

Personal information form

You must fill up fields with asterisk *. You can leave other fields blank.

First name* - *Robert*
Middle name
Last name* - *Genscher*
Sex* (underline) - <u>Male</u> Female
Age* - *Twenty-one years old*
Nationality* - *German*
Family status (underline) - <u>Single</u> Married
Address* - *Room 218, student dorms, College Street 36, San Francisco, the USA.*
Education - *I study computer design in the second year at a college*
Where have you worked before? - *I worked for two months as a farm worker*
What experience and skills have you had?* - *I can use a computer*
Languages* 0 - no, 10 - fluently - *German - 10, English - 8*
Driving license* (underline) - <u>No</u> Yes Kind:
You need a job* (underline) - Full time <u>Part time</u>: 15 hours a week
You want to earn - *15 dollars per hour*

Miss Slim took their personal information forms to the editor of "San Francisco News".

"The editor has agreed," Miss Slim said when she came back, "You will accompany a police patrol and then compose reports for the criminal rubric. A police car will come tomorrow at seventeen o'clock to take you. Be here at this time, will you?"

"Sure," Robert answered.

"Yes, we will," David said, "Goodbye."

"Goodbye," Miss Slim answered.

- 10
Führerschein (unterstreiche) - Nein <u>Ja</u> Typ: BC Kann Lastwagen fahren.
Sie brauchen einen Job (unterstreiche) - Vollzeit <u>Teilzeit</u>: 15 Stunden die Woche
Sie wollen verdienen - 15 Dollar die Stunde

Persönliche Angaben

Alle mit einem Sternchen * markierten Felder müssen ausgefüllt werden. Die anderen Felder können leer gelassen werden.

Vorname - Robert
Zweiter Name
Nachname - Genscher
Geschlecht (unterstreiche) - <u>männlich</u> *weiblich*
Alter - einundzwanzig
Nationalität - Deutscher
Familienstand (unterstreiche) - <u>ledig</u> *verheiratet*
Addresse - Zimer 218, Studentenwohnheim, College Street 36, San Francisco, USA
Ausbildung - Ich studiere Computerdesign im zweiten Jahr an der Universität
Wo haben Sie zuvor gearbeitet? - Ich habe zwei Monate auf einem Bauernhof gearbeitet
Welche Erfahrung und Fähigkeiten haben Sie? - Ich kann mit dem Computer umgehen
Sprachen 0 - nein, 10 - fließend - Deutsch - 10, Englisch - 8
Führerschein (unterstreiche) - <u>Nein</u> *Ja Typ:*
Sie brauchen einen Job (unterstreiche) - Vollzeit <u>Teilzeit</u>*: 15 Stunden die Woche*
Sie wollen verdienen - 15 Dollar die Stunde

Frau Slim brachte die Formulare mit ihren persönlichen Angaben zum Herausgeber der ‚San Francisco News'.

„Der Herausgeber ist einverstanden", sagte Frau Slim, als sie zurückkam. „Ihr begleitet eine Polizeistreife und schreibt dann Berichte für die Kriminalrubrik. Morgen um siebzehn Uhr werdet ihr von einem Polizeiauto abgeholt. Seid pünktlich da, ok?"

„Klar", antwortete Robert.

„Ja, wir werden pünktlich sein", sagte David. „Auf Wiedersehen".

„Auf Wiedersehen", antwortete Frau Slim.

Present Perfect versus Past Simple

Das Past Simple verwenden wir mit Zeitangaben in der Vergangenheit, zum Beispiel: ten minutes ago - vor zehn Minuten, in the morning - am Morgen, yesterday - gestern, last week - letzte Woche, on Monday - am Montag, in January - im Januar.

When did you finish your work? - Wann hast du deine Arbeit beendet?

I finished it an hour ago. - Ich habe sie vor einer Stunde beendet.

Where was he on Monday? - Wo ist er am Montag gewesen?

He was in Spain that day. - Er ist in Spanien an diesen Tag gewesen.

Das Present Perfekt verwenden wir nicht mit Zeitangaben, die in der Vergangenheit beendeten.

How long have you been in Boston? - Seit wann bist du in Boston gewesen?

I have been in Boston since Sunday. - Ich bin seit Sonntag in Boston gewesen.

Have you finished your work? - Hast du deine Arbeit beendet?

I have just finished it. - Ich habe sie gerade beendet.

He is sun-tanned. Where has he been? - Er ist sonnengebräunt. Wo ist er gewesen?

He has been to Spain. - Er ist in Spanien gewesen.

Exercise 38 Compose the sentences as in the example. Use the Present Perfect Tense or the Past Simple Tense.

Übung 38 Bilde die Sätze nach dem Beispiel. Benutze das Present Perfekt oder das Past Simple.

1. (read) How many pages did you read yesterday?
2. (read) How many pages have you read?
3. (come) Tom .... ten minutes ago.
4. (cook) Mom .... pizza.
5. (play) When .... you .... tennis?

6. (learn) I .... English since May.
7. (learn) I .... English a lot in June.
8. (pay) .... you .... for parking?
9. (pay) I .... for parking five minutes ago.
10. (be) Finn .... happy when the lesson finished.
11. (be) Finn .... happy all day today.
12. (be) I .... hungry all day yesterday.
13. (be) I .... hungry since breakfast.
14. (have) Emma .... a blue bike a year ago.
15. (have) Emma .... a red bike since summer.

Reading comprehension

The police patrol (part 1)
Die Polizeistreife (Teil 1)

A

Words

1. accompanied [əˈkʌmpənid] - begleitet
2. afraid [əˈfreɪd] - ängstlich
3. alarm [əˈlɑːm] - der Alarm
4. barked [bɑːkt] - bellte
5. closed [kləʊzd] - geschlossen
6. cried [kraɪd] - gerufen
7. damn [dæm] - verdammt
8. did [dɪd] - tat
9. drove [drəʊv] - fuhr

10. dry [draɪ] *(adj)* - trocken; to dry - trocknen
11. everybody [ˈevrɪbɒdɪ] - alle
12. fasten [ˈfaːsən] - anschnallen
13. gun [gʌn] - die Waffe
14. handcuffs [ˈhændkʌfs] - die Handschellen
15. hid [hɪd] - versteckte
16. high [haɪ] - hoch
17. howling [ˈhaʊlɪŋ] - heulend
18. hundred [ˈhʌndrəd] - hundert
19. key [kiː] - der Schlüssel
20. limit [ˈlɪmɪt] - die Begrenzung
21. look around [əˈraʊnd] - sich umsehen
22. met [met] - getroffen, kennengelernt
23. microphone [ˈmaɪkrəfəʊn] - das Mikrofon
24. officer [ˈɒfɪsə], policeman [pəˈliːsmən] - der Polizist
25. opened - öffnete
26. price [praɪs] - der Preis
27. pursuit [pəˈsjuːt] - die Verfolgung
28. robbery [ˈrɒb(ə)rɪ] - der Diebstahl
29. rushed [rʌʃt] - raste
30. seat belts [siːt belts] - der Sicherheitsgurt
31. sergeant [ˈsaːdʒənt] - der Polizeihauptmeister
32. showed [ʃəʊd] - zeigte
33. siren [ˈsaɪərən] - die Sirene
34. speed [spiːd] - die Geschwindigkeit; to speed - rasen
35. speeder [ˈspiːdə] - der Raser
36. started [ˈstaːtɪd] (to drive) - fuhr los
37. stepped [stept] - trat
38. thief [θiːf] - der Dieb
39. thieves [θiːvz] - die Diebe
40. tried [traɪd] - versuchte
41. twelve [twelv] - zwölf
42. understood [ˌʌndəˈstʊd] - verstanden
43. waited [ˈweɪtɪd] - wartete
44. What is the matter [ˈmætə] ? - Was ist los?

The police patrol (part 1)

Robert and David arrived at the building of the newspaper "San Francisco News" at seventeen o'clock next day. The police car was waiting for them already. A policeman got out of the car.
"Hello. I am sergeant Frank Strict," he said when David and Robert came to the car.
"Hello. Glad to meet you. My name is Robert. We must accompany you," Robert answered.
"Hello. I am David. Were you waiting long for us?" David asked.
"No. I have just arrived here. Let us get into the car. We begin city patrolling now," the policeman said. They all got into the police car.
"Are you accompanying a police patrol for the first time?" sergeant Strict asked starting the engine.
"We have never accompanied a police patrol before," David answered.
At this moment the police radio began to talk: "Attention P11 and P07! A blue car is speeding along College street."
"P07 got it," sergeant Strict said in the

Die Polizeistreife (Teil 1)

Am nächsten Tag kamen Robert und David um siebzehn Uhr zum Gebäude der Zeitung ‚San Francisco News'. Das Polizeiauto wartete schon auf sie. Ein Polizist stieg aus dem Auto.

„Hallo. Ich bin Polizeihauptmeister Frank Strict", sagte er, als David und Robert zum Auto kamen.
"Hallo, schön, Sie kennenzulernen. Ich heiße Robert. Wir sollen Sie heute begleiten", antwortete Robert.
„Hallo, ich bin David. Haben Sie schon lange auf uns gewartet?", fragte David.
„Nein, ich bin gerade erst gekommen. Lasst uns einsteigen. Wir fangen jetzt mit der Streife in der Stadt an", sagte der Polizist. Sie stiegen alles ins Polizeiauto.
„Begleitet ihr zum ersten Mal eine Polizeistreife?", fragte Polizeihauptmeister Strict und machte den Motor an.
„Wir haben noch nie eine Polizeistreife begleitet", antwortete David.
In diesem Moment meldete sich der Polizeifunk: „Achtung P11 und P07! Ein blaues Auto fährt zu schnell auf der Universitätsstraße."
„P07 ist dran", sagte Polizeihauptmeister Strict ins

microphone. Then he said to the boys: "The number of our car is P07." A big blue car rushed past them with very high speed. Frank Strict took the mic again and said: "P07 is speaking. I see the speeding blue car. Begin pursuit," then he said to the boys, "Fasten your seat belts." The police car started quickly. The sergeant stepped on the gas up to the stop and switched on the siren. They rushed with the howling siren past buildings, cars and buses. Frank Strict made the blue car stop. Sergeant got out of the car and went to the speeder. David and Robert went after him.

"I am police officer Frank Strict. Show your driving license, please," the policeman said to the speeder.

"Here is my driving license," the driver showed his driving license, "What is the matter he said angrily.

"You were driving through the city with a speed of one hundred and twenty kilometers an hour. The speed limit is fifty," the sergeant said.

"Ah, this. You see, I have just washed my car. So I was driving a little faster to dry it up," the man said with a sly smile.

"Does it cost much to wash the car?" the policeman asked.

"Not much. It cost twelve dollars," the speeder said.

"You do not know the prices," sergeant Strict said, "It really costs you two hundred and twelve dollars because you will pay two hundred dollars for drying the car. Here is the ticket. Have a nice day," the policeman said. He gave a speeding ticket for two hundred dollars and the driving license to the speeder and went back to the police car.

"Frank, I think you have lots of experiences with speeders, haven't you?" David asked the policeman.

"I have met many of them," Frank said starting the engine, "At first they look like angry tigers or sly foxes. But after I speak with them, they look like afraid kittens or silly monkeys. Like that one in the blue car."

Meanwhile a little white car was slowly driving along a street not far from the city park. The car stopped near a shop. A man and a woman got out of the car and went up to the shop. It was closed. The man looked around. Then he quickly took

Mikrofon. Dann sagte er zu den Jungs: „Die Nummer unseres Autos ist P07." Ein großes blaues Auto raste mit hoher Geschwindigkeit an ihnen vorbei. Frank Strict nahm das Mikrofon und sagte: „Hier spricht P07. Ich sehe das rasende Auto. Nehme die Verfolgung auf". Dann sagte er zu den Jungs: „Bitte anschnallen!" Das Polizeiauto fuhr schnell los. Der Polizeihauptmeister trat das Gaspedal voll durch und machte die Sirene an. Mit heulender Sirene rasten sie an Gebäuden, Autos und Bussen vorbei. Frank Strict brachte das blaue Auto zum Anhalten. Der Polizeihauptmeister stieg aus dem Auto aus und ging zu dem Raser. David und Robert gingen ihm nach.

„Ich bin Polizeibeamter Frank Strict. Zeigen Sie mir bitte Ihren Führerschein", sagte der Polizist zu dem Raser.

„Hier ist mein Führerschein." Der Fahrer zeigte seinen Führerschein. „Was ist los?", fragte er wütend.

„Sie sind mit hundertzwanzig km/h durch die Stadt gefahren. Die Geschwindigkeitsbegrenzung ist fünfzig", sagte der Polizeihauptmeister.

„Ach so, das. Wissen Sie, ich habe gerade mein Auto gewaschen. Ich bin ein bisschen schneller gefahren, damit es trocknet", sagte der Mann mit einem schlauen Grinsen.

„Ist es teuer, Ihr Auto zu waschen?", fragte der Polizist.

„Nein. Es kostet zwölf Dollar", sagte der Raser.

„Sie kennen die Preise nicht", sagte Polizeihauptmeister Strict. „In Wirklichkeit kostet es Sie zweihundertzwölf Dollar, denn Sie werden zweihundert Dollar fürs Trocknen zahlen. Hier ist der Strafzettel. Einen schönen Tag noch", sagte der Polizist. Er gab dem Raser einen Strafzettel für Geschwindigkeitsüberschreitung über zweihundert Dollar und seinen Führerschein und ging zurück zum Polizeiauto.

„Frank, du hast viel Erfahrung mit Rasern, nicht wahr?", fragte David den Polizisten.

„Ich habe schon viele kennengelernt", sagte Frank und machte den Motor an. „Zu erst sehen sie wie wütende Tiger oder schlaue Füchse aus. Aber nachdem ich mit ihnen gesprochen habe, sehen sie wie ängstliche Kätzchen oder dumme Affen aus. Wie der im blauen Auto."

In der Zwischenzeit fuhr ein kleines, weißes Auto nicht weit vom Stadtpark langsam die Straße entlang. Das Auto hielt in der Nähe eines Ladens. Ein Mann und eine Frau stiegen aus und gingen zu dem Laden. Er war geschlossen. Der Mann sah sich um. Dann holte er

out some keys and tried to open the door. At last he opened it and they went inside.

"Look! There are so many dresses here!" the woman said. She took out a big bag and began to put in everything there. When the bag was full, she took it to the car and came back.

"Take everything quickly! Oh! What a wonderful hat!" the man said. He took from the shop window a big black hat and put it on.

"Look at this red dress! I like it so much!" the woman said and quickly put on the red dress. She did not have more bags. So she took more things in her hands, ran outside and put them on the car. Then she ran inside to bring more things.

The police car P07 was slowly driving along the city park when the radio began to talk: "Attention all patrols. We have got a robbery alarm from a shop near the city park. The address of the shop is 72 Park street."

"P07 got it," Frank said in the mic, "I am very close to this place. Drive there." They found the shop very quickly and drove up to the white car. Then they got out of the car and hid behind it. The woman in new red dress ran out of the shop. She put some dresses on the police car and ran back in the shop. The woman did it very quickly. She did not see that it was a police car!

"Damn it! I forgot my gun in the police station!" Frank said. Robert and David looked at the sergeant Strict and then surprised at each other. The policeman was so confused that David and Robert understood they must help him. The woman ran out of the shop again, put some dresses on the police car and ran back. Then David said to Frank: "We can pretend that we have guns."

"Let's do it," Frank answered, "But you do not get up. The thieves may have guns," he said and then cried, "This is the police speaking! Everybody who is inside the shop put your hands up and come slowly one by one out of the shop!" They waited for a minute. Nobody came out. Then Robert had an idea.

"If you will not come out now, we will set the police dog on you!" he cried and then barked like a big angry dog. The thieves ran out with hands up immediately. Frank quickly put handcuffs on them and got them to the police car. Then he said to Robert: "It was a great idea pretending that we have a dog! You see, I have forgotten my gun

schnell einige Schlüssel hervor und versuchte, die Tür zu öffnen. Schließlich öffnete er sie, und sie gingen hinein.

„Sieh, so viele Kleider", sagte die Frau. Sie holte eine große Tasche hervor und begann, alles hineinzupacken. Als die Tasche voll war, brachte sie sie zum Auto und kam zurück.

„Nimm schnell alles! Oh! Was für ein schöner Hut!", sagte der Mann. Er nahm einen großen schwarzen Hut aus dem Schaufenster und zog ihn auf.

„Sieh dir dieses rote Kleid an! Das finde ich toll!", sagte die Frau und zog schnell das rote Kleid an. Sie hatte keine Taschen mehr. Deswegen nahm sie mehr Sachen in die Hände, rannte nach draußen und packte sie ins Auto. Dann rannte sie nach drinnen, um noch mehr Dinge zu holen.

Das Polizeiauto P07 fuhr gerade langsam den Stadtpark entlang, als sich der Funk meldete: „Achtung, alle Einheiten. Wir haben einen Einbruchsalarm aus einem Laden in der Nähe des Stadtparks. Die Adresse des Ladens ist Parkstraße 72."

„P07 ist dran", sagte Frank ins Mikro. „Ich bin ganz in der Nähe. Fahre dorthin." Sie hatten den Laden schnell gefunden und fuhren zu dem weißen Auto. Dann stiegen sie aus dem Auto aus und versteckten sich dahinter. Die Frau im roten Kleid kam aus dem Laden gerannt. Sie legte einige Kleider auf das Polizeiauto und rannte zurück in den Laden. Die Frau tat das sehr schnell. Sie sah nicht, dass es ein Polizeiauto war.

„Verdammt! Ich habe meine Waffe auf der Polizeiwache vergessen!", sagte Frank. Robert und David sahen Polizeihauptmeister Strict und dann einander überrascht an. Der Polizist war so verwirrt, dass David und Robert verstanden, dass er Hilfe brauchte. Die Frau rannte wieder aus dem Laden, legte Kleider auf das Polizeiauto und rannte zurück. Dann sagte David zu Frank: „Wir können so tun, als ob wir Waffen haben."

„Lasst uns das machen", antwortete Frank. „Aber ihr steht nicht auf. Die Diebe haben vielleicht Waffen", sagte er und rief dann: „Hier spricht die Polizei! Alle, die im Laden sind, heben ihre Hände und kommen langsam einer nach dem anderen aus raus!"

Sie warteten eine Minute. Niemand kam. Dann hatte Robert eine Idee.

"Wenn ihr nicht rauskommt, hetzen wir den Polizeihund auf euch!", rief er und bellte wie ein großer, wütender Hund. Die Diebe kamen sofort mit erhobenen Händen herausgerannt. Frank legte ihnen schnell Handschellen an und brachte sie ins Polizeiauto. Dann sagte er zu Robert: „Das war eine gute Idee, so zu tun, als ob wir einen Hund hätten. Weißt du, ich habe meine Waffe

two times already. If they learn that I have forgotten it for the third time, they may fire me or make me do office work. You will not tell anybody about it, will you?"
"Sure, not!" Robert said.
"Never," David said.
"Thank you very much for helping me, guys!" Frank shook their hands strongly.

schon zweimal vergessen. Wenn sie herausfinden, dass ich sie zum dritten Mal vergessen habe, feuern sie mich vielleicht oder lassen mich Büroarbeit machen. Ihr erzählt es doch niemandem, oder?"
„Natürlich nicht!", sagte Robert.
„Nie", sagte David.
„Vielen Dank für eure Hilfe, Jungs!" Frank schüttelte ihnen kräftig die Hand.

39

Word order / Die Wortstellung

Die Reihenfolge des Objekts, Ortsangaben und Zeitangaben ist nach folgender Formel einfach zu merken

was + wo + wann

I read books in the garden on Sundays. - Ich lese Bücher im Garten an Sonntags.

Ort und Zeit stehen immer nach dem Objekt (books). Zeitangaben stehen am Ende eines Satzes (on Sundays). Stehen am Satzende eine Orts- und eine Zeitangabe, dann steht Ort (in the garden) vor Zeit (on Sundays).

I read books in the garden. - Ich lese Bücher im Garten.

I read books on Sundays. - Ich lese Bücher an Sonntags.

Exercise 39 Compose the sentences. Use the words in brackets.
Übung 39 Bilde die Sätze. Benutze die Wörter in Klammern.
(every month, the windows) (in the restaurant, every day, traditional dishes) (daily, two apples) (on Mondays, origami, at school) (in the garden, on weekends, a novel) (~~on Sundays, a bike, in the park~~) (two times a month, in the park, minigolf) (in summer, in the river) (to work, a new car) (in the garage, his old car, almost evey weekend)

1. I ride a bike in the park on Sundays.
2. Tom swims ....
3. Linda cooks ....

4. Finn writes ....
5. Anna drives ....
6. Sam eats ....
7. I play ....
8. Lea makes ....
9. Mom washes ....
10. Richard repairs ....

Reading comprehension

The police patrol (part 2)
Die Polizeistreife (Teil 2)

A

Words

1. answered - geantwortet
2. button [ˈbʌtn] - der Knopf
3. cash [kæʃ] - das Bargeld
4. cash register [kæʃ ˈredʒɪstə] - die Kasse; cashier [kæˈʃɪə], teller - der Kassierer
5. clever [ˈklevə] - schlau
6. either [ˈaɪðə], too, also - auch
7. excuse [ɪksˈkjuːs] - sich entschuldigen
8. Excuse me. - Entschuldigen Sie.
9. glass [glaːs] - das Glas
10. gone [gɔn] - weg
11. men [men] - die Männer
12. mine [maɪn] - mein
13. mobile [ˈməʊbaɪl] - das Handy
14. opened - geöffnet
15. phone [fəʊn] - das Telefon
16. to phone - anrufen
17. pocket [ˈpɔkɪt] - die Tasche
18. press [pres] - drücken
19. protect [prəˈtekt] - beschützen
20. rang [ræŋ] - klingelte
21. ricochet [ˈrɪkəʃeɪ] - abprallen
22. robber [ˈrɔbə] - der Dieb
23. robbery [ˈrɔb(ə)rɪ] - der Überfall
24. safe [seɪf] - der Tresor
25. saw [sɔː] - sahen
26. secretly [ˈsiːkrətlɪ] - heimlich
27. seldom [ˈseldəm] - selten

28. shopping center - das Einkaufszentrum
29. shot [ʃɔt] - schoss; angeschossen
30. somebody [ˈsʌmbədɪ] - jemand
31. stolen [ˈstəʊlən] - gestohlen
32. taken [ˈteɪkən] - gebracht
33. turned [tə:nd] - drehte
34. unconscious [ʌnˈkɔnʃəs] - bewusstlos
35. usual [ˈju:ʒ(ə)l] - gewöhnlich
36. whose [hu:z] - wessen
37. yesterday [ˈjestədeɪ] - gestern
38. yet [jet] - noch
39. yours sincerely [jɔ:z sɪnˈsɪəlɪ] - hochachtungsvoll

The police patrol (part 2)

Next day Robert and David were accompanying Frank again. They were standing near a big shopping centre when a woman came to them.
"Can you help me please?" she asked.
"Sure, madam. What has happened?" Frank asked.
"My mobile phone is gone. I think it has been stolen."
"Has it been used today?" the policeman asked.
"It had been used by me before I went out of the shopping centre," she answered.
"Let's get inside," Frank said. They went into the shopping centre and looked around. There were many people there.
"Let's try an old trick," Frank said taking out his own phone, "What is your telephone number?" he asked the woman. She said and he called her telephone number. A mobile telephone rang not far from them. They went to the place where it was ringing. There was a queue there. A man in the queue looked at the policeman and then quickly turned his head away. The policeman came closer listening carefully. The telephone was ringing in the man's pocket.
"Excuse me," Frank said. The man looked at him.
"Excuse me, your telephone is ringing," Frank said.
"Where?" the man said.
"Here, in your pocket," Frank said.
"No, it is not," the man said.
"Yes, it is," Frank said
"It is not mine," the man said.
"Then whose telephone is ringing in your pocket?" Frank asked.
"I do not know," the man answered.

Die Polizeistreife (Teil 2)

Am nächsten Tag begleiteten Robert und David Frank wieder. Sie standen neben einem großen Einkaufszentrum, als eine Frau zu ihnen kam.

„Können Sie mir bitte helfen?", fragte sie.
„Natürlich. Was ist passiert?", fragte Frank.

"Mein Handy ist weg. Ich glaube, es wurde gestohlen."
"Haben Sie es heute schon benutzt?", fragte der Polizist.
„Ich habe es benutzt, bevor ich das Einkaufszentrum verlassen habe", antwortete die Frau.
„Lasst uns reingehen", sagte Frank. Sie gingen ins Einkaufszentrum und sahen sich um. Viele Leute waren da.
„Lasst uns einen alten Trick versuchen", sagte Frank und holte sein eigenes Handy hervor. „Wie ist Ihre Nummer?", fragte er die Frau. Sie sagte sie ihm, und er wählte. Nicht weit von ihnen klingelte ein Handy. Sie gingen zu der Stelle, an der es klingelte. Dort war eine Schlange. Ein Mann in der Schlange sah den Polizisten an und schaute dann schnell weg. Der Polizist ging näher hin und horchte aufmerksam. Das Handy klingelte in der Tasche des Mannes.

„Entschuldigen Sie", sagte Frank. Der Mann sah ihn an.
„Entschuldigen Sie, Ihr Handy klingelt", sagte Frank.

„Wo?", sagte der Mann.
„Hier, in ihrer Tasche", sagte Frank.
„Nein, es klingelt nicht", sagte der Mann.
„Doch, es klingelt", sagte Frank.
„Das ist nicht meins", sagte der Mann.
„Wessen Telefon klingelt dann in Ihrer Tasche?", fragte Frank.
„Ich weiß es nicht", antwortete der Mann.

"Let me see, please," Frank said and took the telephone out of the man's pocket.	„Zeigen Sie es mir bitte", sagte Frank und holte das Handy aus der Tasche des Mannes.
"Oh, it is mine!" the woman cried.	„Oh, das ist meins!", rief die Frau.
"Take your telephone, madam," Frank said giving it to her.	„Hier, nehmen Sie Ihr Telefon", sagte Frank und gab es ihr.
"May I, sir?" Frank asked and put his hand in the man's pocket again. He took out another telephone, and then one more.	„Darf ich?", fragte Frank und steckte seine Hand wieder in die Tasche des Mannes. Er holte ein anderes Handy hervor und dann noch eins.
"Are they not yours either?" Frank asked the man.	„Gehören die auch nicht Ihnen?", fragte Frank den Mann.
The man shook his head looking away.	Der Mann schüttelte den Kopf und sah weg.
"What strange telephones!" Frank cried, "They ran away from their owners and jump into the pockets of this man! And now they are ringing in his pockets, aren't they?"	„Was für seltsame Handys!", rief Frank. „Sie sind ihren Besitzern davongelaufen und in die Tasche dieses Mannes gesprungen! Und jetzt klingeln sie in seiner Tasche, oder nicht?"
"Yes, they are," the man said.	„Ja, das tun sie", sagte der Mann.
"You know, my job is to protect people. And I will protect you from them. Get in my car and I will bring you to the place where no telephone can jump in your pocket. We go to the police station," the policeman said. Then he took the man by the arm and took him to the police car.	„Wie Sie wissen, ist es mein Job, Menschen zu beschützen. Und ich werde Sie vor ihnen beschützen. Steigen Sie in mein Auto, und ich bringe Sie an einen Ort, wo kein Telefon in Ihre Tasche springen kann. Wir fahren aufs Revier", sagte der Polizist. Dann nahm er den Mann am Arm und brachte ihn zum Auto.
"I like silly criminals," Frank Strict smiled after they had taken the thief to the police station.	„Ich mag dumme Verbrecher", sagte Frank Strict grinsend, nachdem sie den Dieb aufs Revier gebracht hatten.
"Have you met smart ones?" David asked.	„Hast du schon schlaue getroffen?", fragte David.
"Yes, I have. But very seldom," the policeman answered, "Because it is very hard to catch a smart criminal."	„Ja, das habe ich. Aber es passiert selten"; antwortete der Polizist. „Denn es ist sehr schwer, einen schlauen Verbrecher zu fangen."
Meanwhile two men came into the Express Bank. One of them took a place in a queue. Another one came up to the cash register and gave a paper to the cashier. The cashier took the paper and read:	In der Zwischenzeit betraten zwei Männer die Express Bank. Einer von ihnen stellte sich in der Schlange an. Ein Anderer ging zur Kasse und gab dem Kassierer einen Zettel. Der Kassierer nahm den Zettel und las.
"Dear Sir, this is a robbery of the Express Bank. Give me all the cash. If you do not, then I will use my gun. Thank you. Sincerely yours, Bob"	„Sehr geehrter Herr, das ist ein Überfall auf die Express Bank. Geben Sie mir alles Geld. Wenn Sie es nicht tun, werde ich meine Waffe benutzen. Danke. Hochachtungsvoll, Bob"
"I think I can help you," the cashier said pressing secretly the alarm button, "But the money had been locked by me in the safe yesterday. The safe has not been opened yet. I will ask somebody to open the safe and bring the money. Okay?"	„Ich denke, ich kann Ihnen helfen", sagte der Kassierer, während er heimlich den Alarmknopf drückte. „Aber das Geld wurde gestern von mir im Tresor eingeschlossen. Der Tresor wurde noch nicht geöffnet. Ich werde jemanden bitten, den Tresor zu öffnen und das Geld zu bringen. Okay?"
"Okay! But do it quickly!" the robber answered.	„Okay. Aber schnell!", antwortete der Dieb.
"Shall I make you a cup of coffee while the money is being put in bags?" the cashier asked.	„Hätten Sie gerne eine Tasse Kaffee, während das Geld in Taschen gepackt wird?", fragte der Kassierer.
"No, thank you. Just money," the robber	„Nein, danke. Nur Geld", antwortete der Dieb.

answered.

The radio in the police car P07 began to talk: "Attention all the patrols. We have got a robbery alarm from the Express Bank."

"P07 got it," sergeant Strict answered. He stepped on the gas up to the stop and the car started quickly. When they drove up to the bank, there was no other police car yet.

"We will make an interesting report if we go inside," David said.

"You guys do what you need. And I will come inside through the back door," sergeant Strict said. He took out his gun and went quickly to the back door of the bank. David and Robert came into the bank through the central door. They saw a man standing near the cash register. He put one hand in his pocket and looked around. The man, who came with him, stepped away from the queue and came up to him.

"Where is the money?" he asked Bob.

"Roger, the cashier has said that it is being put in bags," another robber answered.

"I am tired of waiting!" Roger said. He took out a gun and pointed it to the cashier, "Bring all the money now!" the robber cried at the cashier. Then he went to the middle of the room and cried: "Listen all! This is a robbery! Nobody move!" At this moment somebody near the cash register moved. The robber with the gun without looking shot at him. Another robber fell on the floor and cried: "Roger! You idiot! Damn it! You have shot me!"

"Oh, Bobby! I did not see that it was you!" Roger said. At this moment the cashier quickly ran out.

"The cashier has run away and the money has not been taken here yet!" Roger cried to Bob, "The police may arrive soon! What shall we do?"

"Take something big, break the glass and take the money. Quickly!" Bob cried. Roger took a metal chair and hit the glass of the cash register. It was of course not usual glass and it did not break. But the chair went back by ricochet and hit the robber on the head! He fell on the floor unconsciously. At this moment sergeant Strict ran inside and quickly put handcuffs on the robbers. He turned to David and Robert.

"I did say! Most criminals are just silly!" he said.

Der Funk im Polizeiauto P07 meldete sich: „Achtung, alle Einheiten. Überfallalarm in der Express Bank."

„P07 ist dran", antwortete Polizeihauptmeister Strict. Er trat aufs Gas, und das Auto fuhr schnell los. Als sie an der Bank ankamen, war noch kein anderes Polizeiauto da.

„Das wird ein interessanter Bericht, wenn wir reingehen", sagte David.

„Ihr Jungs macht, was ihr braucht. Ich gehe durch die Hintertür rein", sagte Polizeihauptmeister Strict. Er holte seine Waffe raus und ging schnell zur Hintertür der Bank. David und Robert betraten die Bank durch die Eingangstür. Sie sahen einen Mann in der Nähe der Kasse stehen. Er hatte eine Hand in seiner Tasche und sah sich um. Der Mann, der mit ihm gekommen war, ging aus der Schlange zu ihm.

„Wo ist das Geld?", fragte er Bob.

„Roger, der Kassierer hat gesagt, dass es in Taschen gepackt wird", antwortete der andere Dieb.

„Ich habe es satt, zu warten", sagte Roger. Er holte seine Waffe hervor und richtete sie auf den Kassierer. „Bringen Sie jetzt alles Geld!", schrie er. Dann ging er in die Mitte des Raums und rief: „Alle herhören! Das ist ein Überfall! Niemand bewegt sich!" In diesem Moment bewegte sich jemand in der Nähe der Kasse. Der Dieb mit der Waffe schoss auf ihn, ohne hinzuschauen. Der andere Dieb fiel auf den Boden und rief: „Roger! Du Vollidiot! Verdammt! Du hast mich angeschossen!"

„Oh, Bobby! Ich habe nicht gesehen, dass du das bist!", sagte Roger. In diesem Moment rannte der Kassierer schnell nach draußen.

„Der Kassierer ist weggerannt, und das Geld ist noch nicht hierher gebracht worden!", rief Roger Bob zu. „Die Polizei kann jeden Moment kommen! Was sollen wir machen?"

„Nimm etwas Großes, zerschlag das Glas und nimm das Geld! Schnell!", rief Bob. Roger nahm einen metallenen Stuhl und schlug auf das Glas der Kasse. Natürlich war es kein gewöhnliches Glas und zerbrach nicht. Doch der Stuhl prallte zurück und traf den Dieb am Kopf! Er fiel bewusstlos zu Boden. In diesem Moment kam Polizeihauptmeister Strict hereingerannt und legte den Dieben schnell Handschellen an. Er drehte sich zu David und Robert um.

„Hab ich es doch gesagt! Die meisten Verbrecher sind einfach nur dumm!", sagte er.

40

Too either, so neither

Too und either stehen am Satzende. Wir benutzen too in bejahten Sätzen.

I am hungry. - Ich bin hungrig.

I am hungry too. - Ich bin auch hungrig.

Tom worked yesterday. - Tom hat gestern gearbeitet.

I worked yesterday too. - Ich habe gestern auch gearbeitet.

Wir benutzen either in verneinten Sätzen.

I am not hungry. - Ich bin nicht hungrig.

I am not hungry either. - Ich bin auch nicht hungrig.

Tom did not work yesterday. - Tom hat gestern nicht gearbeitet.

I did not work yesterday either. - Ich habe gestern auch nicht gearbeitet.

So am I bedeutet I am too.

I am hungry. - Ich bin hungrig.

So am I. (nicht 'So I am') - Ich bin auch hungrig.

He is happy. - Er ist glücklich.

So am I. - Ich bin auch glücklich.

Anstatt am können wir die Hilfsverben (be, do, have, will) oder Modalverben (can, may, must, should) benutzen.

They are ready. - Sie sind bereit.

So are we. - Wir sind auch bereit.

She is happy. - Sie ist glücklich.

So is he. - Er ist auch glücklich.

I live in Germany. - Ich wohne in Deutschland.

So do I. - Ich wohne auch in Deutschland.

I have got a cat. - Ich habe eine Katze.

So have I. - Ich habe auch eine Katze.

They will go to a café . - Sie werden ins Café gehen.

So will I. - Ich werde auch ins Café gehen.

Tom can play the guitar. - Tom kann Gitarre spielen.

So can Anna. - Anna kann Gitarre auch spielen.

I may go to Spain. - Ich werde vielleicht nach Spanien fahren.

So may Tom. - Tom wird vielleicht nach Spanien auch fahren.

Neither am I bedeutet I am not either.

I am not hungry. - Ich bin nicht hungrig.

Neither am I. (nicht 'Neither I am') - Ich bin auch nicht hungrig.

He is not happy. - Er ist nicht glücklich.

Neither am I. - Ich bin auch nicht glücklich.

Hier können wir auch anstatt am die Hilfsverben (be, do, have, will) oder Modalverben (can, may, must, should) benutzen.

They are not ready. - Sie sind nicht bereit.

Neither are we. - Wir sind auch nicht bereit.

She is not happy. - Sie ist nicht glücklich.

Neither is he. - Er ist auch nicht glücklich.

I do not live in Germany. - Ich wohne nicht in Deutschland.

Neither do I. - Ich wohne auch nicht in Deutschland.

I have not got a cat. - Ich habe keine Katze.

Neither have I. - Ich habe auch keine Katze.

They will not go to a café . - Sie werden ins Café nicht gehen.

Neither will Emma. - Emma wird ins Café auch nicht gehen.

Tom cannot play the guitar. - Tom kann Gitarre nicht spielen.

Neither can Anna. - Anna kann Gitarre auch nicht spielen.

I may not go to Spain. - Ich werde vielleicht nach Spanien nicht fahren.

Neither may Tom. - Tom wird vielleicht nach Spanien auch nicht fahren.

Wenn die Situation es verlangt eine entgegengesetzte Antwort zu geben, benutzen wir einfach entweder bejahte oder verneinte form des Verbs.

They are ready. - Are they? We are not.

Sie sind bereit. - Wirklich? Wir sind nicht bereit.

They are not ready. - Aren't they? We are.

Sie sind nicht bereit. - Wirklich? Wir sind bereit.

She is happy. - Is she? He is not.

Sie ist glücklich.- Wirklich? Er ist nicht glücklich.

She is not happy. - Isn't she? He is.

Sie ist nicht glücklich. - Wirklich? Er ist glücklich.

Tom plays golf. - Does he? I don't.

Tom spielt Golf. - Wirklich? Ich spiele kein Golf.

Sam doesn't play tennis. - Doesn't he? I do.

Sam spielt kein Tennis. - Wirklich? Ich spiele Tennis.

Emma likes Bill. - Does she? Linda doesn't.

Emma mag Bill. - Wirklich? Linda mag ihn nicht.

I don't like Bill. - Don't you? I do.

Ich mag Bill nicht. - Wirklich? Ich mag ihn.

Exercise 40-1 Compose the sentences about yourself.

Übung 40-1 Bilde die Sätze über sich selbst.

1. I am hungry. - So am I.
2. Tom is not a student. ....
3. Emma cannot swim. ....
4. Bill can cook. ....
5. Sam lives in the USA. ....
6. I cooked pizza on Sunday. ....
7. Anna does not play golf. ....
8. I did not watch television yesterday. ....
9. I am tall. ....
10. I am not fit. ....
11. I am happy. ....
12. I am not friendly. ....
13. I was in Spain last week. ....
14. I will learn Spanish. ....
15. I will not go to the park next weekend. ....

Exercise 40-2 Compose the sentences with the opposite meaning about yourself.

Übung 40-2 Bilde die Sätze mit entgegengesetzter Bedeutung über sich selbst.

1. I am not hungry. - Are not you? I am.
2. He likes loud music. - Does he? I do not.
3. She does not work hard. ....
4. We eat more than we need. ....
5. They do not speak German. ....
6. Lea cannot play tennis. ....
7. Tom is not tall. ....
8. Anna has got a cat. ....
9. Sam has not got a bike. ....

10. Bill goes to work by bus. ....

11. Finn does not read much. ....

12. Linda dances a lot. ....

13. I will go to Italy. ....

14. I will not study today. ....

Reading comprehension

School for Foreign Students (SFS) and au pair
Schule für Austauschschüler (SAS) und Au-pair

Words

1. agreement [əˈgriːmənt] - die Vereinbarung
2. also [ˈɔːlsəʊ] - auch
3. called [kɔːld] - riefen an
4. change [tʃeɪndʒ] - die Änderung; to change - ändern
5. choose [tʃuːz] - auswählen, entscheiden für
6. chose [ʃəʊz] - entschied sich für
7. competition [ˌkɒmpəˈtɪʃ(ə)n] - die Ausschreibung, der Wettbewerb
8. country [ˈkʌntrɪ] - das Land
9. course [kɔːs] - der Kurs
10. date [deɪt] - das Datum
11. daughter [ˈdɔːtə] - die Tochter
12. elder [ˈeldə] - älter
13. e-mail [ˈiːmeɪl] - die E-Mail
14. hope [həʊp] - die Hoffnung; to hope - hoffen
15. host [həʊst] - der Gastgeber
16. the host family - die Gastfamilie
17. Internet site - die Website

18. join [dʒɔɪn] - kommen in
19. learning [ˈləːnɪŋ] - lernen
20. letter [ˈletə] - der Brief
21. lived [lɪvd] - lebte
22. nearest [ˈnɪərɪst] - nächste
23. North America and Eurasia [nɔːθ əˈmerɪkə ənd jʊəˈreɪʒə] - Nordamerika und Eurasien
24. once [wʌns] - einmal
25. participant [paːˈtɪsɪpənt] - der Teilnehmer
26. passed [pɑːst] - abgelaufen
27. pay [peɪ] - bezahlen, zahlen
28. paid [peɪd] - bezahlte, gezahlt
29. person [ˈpəːs(ə)n] - die Person
30. possibility [ˌpɔsəˈbɪləti] - die Möglichkeit
31. problem [ˈprɔbləm] - das Problem
32. sent [sent] - schickte
33. servant [ˈsəːv(ə)nt] - der Bedienstete
34. since [sɪn(t)s] *(temporal)* - seit
35. as, since [æz | sɪn(t)s] *(kausal)* - da, weil
36. standard [ˈstændəd] - der Standard, Standard-
37. the United States/the USA - die Vereinigten Staaten, die USA
38. twice [twaɪs] - zweimal
39. unfair [ʌnˈfeə] - ungerecht
40. village [ˈvɪlɪdʒ] - das Dorf
41. visited [ˈvɪzɪtɪd] - besuchte
42. wrote [rəʊt] - schrieb

 B

School for Foreigner Students (SFS) and au pair

Robert's sister, brother and parents lived in Germany. They lived in Hannover. The sister's name was Gabi. She was twenty years old. She had learned English since she was eleven years old. When Gabi was fifteen years old, she wanted to take part in the program SFS. SFS gives the possibility for some high school students from Eurasia to spend a year in the USA, living with a host family and studying in an American school. The program is free. Airplane tickets, living with a family, food, studying at American school are paid by SFS. But by the time when she got the information about the competition date from the Internet site, the competition day had passed.

Then she learned about the program de au pair. This program gives its participants the possibility to spend a year or two in another country living with a host family, looking after children and learning at a language course. Since Robert was studying in San Francisco, Gabi wrote him an e-mail. She asked him to find a host family for her in the USA. Robert looked through some newspapers and Internet sites with adverts. He found some host families from the USA on http://www.aupair-world.net/. Then Robert

Schule für Austauschschüler (SAS) und Au-pair

Roberts Schwester, Bruder und Eltern lebten in Deutschland. Sie wohnten in Hannover. Seine Schwester hieß Gabi. Sie war zwanzig Jahre alt. Sie lernte Englisch, seit sie elf war. Als Gabi fünfzehn war, wollte sie an dem Programm SAS teilnehmen. SAS gibt Highschool-Schülern aus Eurasien die Möglichkeit, ein Jahr in den USA zu verbringen, in einer Gastfamilie zu leben und eine amerikanische Schule zu besuchen. Das Programm ist kostenlos. Das Flugticket, die Unterkunft in der Familie, Essen und das Besuchen der amerikanische Schule werden von SAS gezahlt. Aber als sie sich auf der Website über die Ausschreibung informierte, war die Frist schon abgelaufen.

Dann erfuhr sie von dem Au-pair-Programm. Dieses Programm ermöglicht es den Teilnehmern, ein oder zwei Jahre in einem anderen Land zu verbringen, bei einer Gastfamilie zu leben, sich um die Kinder zu kümmern und eine Sprachschule zu besuchen. Da Robert gerade in San Francisco studierte, schrieb Gabi ihm eine E-Mail. Sie bat ihn darum, eine Gastfamilie für sie in den USA zu finden. Robert sah Zeitungen und Websites mit Anzeigen durch. Er fand amerikanische Gastfamilien auf http://www.aupair-world.net/. Dann ging Robert zu einer Au-pair-Vermittlung in San Francisco. Er wurde von einer Frau beraten. Sie hieß Alice Sunflower.

visited an au pair agency in San Francisco. He was consulted by a woman. Her name was Alice Sunflower.

"My sister is from Germany. She would like to be an au pair with an American family. Can you help on this matter?" Robert asked Alice.

"I will be glad to help you. We place au pairs with families all over the USA. An au pair is a person who joins a host family to help around the house and look after children. The host family gives the au pair food, a room and pocket money. Pocket money may be from 200 to 600 dollars. The host family must pay for a language course for the au pair as well," Alice said.

"Are there good and bad families?" Robert asked.

"There are two problems about choosing a family. First some families think that an au pair is a servant who must do everything in the house including cooking for all family members, cleaning, washing, working in the garden etc. But an au pair is not a servant. An au pair is like an elder daughter or son of the family who helps parents with younger children. To protect their rights au pairs must work out an agreement with the host family. Do not believe it when some au pair agencies or host families say that they use a "standard" agreement. There is no standard agreement. The au pair can change any part of the agreement if it is unfair. Everything that an au pair and host family will do must be written in an agreement.

The second problem is this: Some families live in small villages where there are no language courses and few places where an au pair can go in free time. In this situation it is necessary to include in the agreement that the host family must pay for two way tickets to the nearest big town when the au pair goes there. It may be once or twice a week."

"I see. My sister would like a family from San Francisco. Can you find a good family in this city?" Robert asked.

"Well, there are about twenty families from San Francisco now," Alice answered. She telephoned some of them. The host families

„Meine Schwester ist aus Deutschland. Sie würde gerne als Au-pair bei einer amerikanischen Familie arbeiten. Können Sie mir helfen?", fragte Robert Alice.

„Natürlich, sehr gerne. Wir vermitteln Au-pairs an Familien überall in der USA. Ein Au-pair kommt in eine Gastfamilie, um im Haus zu helfen und sich um die Kinder zu kümmern. Die Gastfamilie gibt dem Au-pair Essen, ein Zimmer und Taschengeld. Das Taschengeld liegt zwischen zweihundert und sechshundert Dollar. Die Gastfamilie muss auch einen Sprachkurs für das Au-pair bezahlen", sagte Alice.

„Gibt es gute und schlechte Familien?", fragte Robert.

„Es gibt zwei Probleme bei der Wahl einer Familie. Zum einen denken manche Familien, dass ein Au-pair ein Bediensteter sei, der alles im Haus machen muss, einschließlich für die ganze Familie kochen, putzen, waschen, Gartenarbeit usw. Aber ein Au-pair ist kein Bediensteter. Ein Au-pair ist wie eine ältere Tochter oder ein älterer Sohn der Familie, der den Eltern mit den jüngeren Kindern hilft. Um ihre Rechte zu schützen, müssen die Au-pairs eine Vereinbarung mit der Gastfamilie ausarbeiten. Glaub bloß nicht, wenn Au-pair-Vermittlungen oder Gastfamilien sagen, dass sie eine Standardvereinbarung verwenden. Es gibt keine Standardvereinbarung. Das Au-pair kann jeden Teil der Vereinbarung ändern, wenn sie ungerecht ist. Alles, was ein Au-pair und die Gastfamilie machen, muss schriftlich in der Vereinbarung festgehalten werden.

Das zweite Problem ist: Manche Familien leben in kleinen Dörfern, in denen es keine Sprachkurse und wenige Orte gibt, wo das Au-pair in seiner Freizeit hingehen kann. In diesem Fall muss die Vereinbarung enthalten, dass die Gastfamilie für Hin- und Rückfahrkarten in die nächste größere Stadt zahlen muss, wenn das Au-pair dorthin fährt. Das kann ein- oder zweimal die Woche sein."

„Alles klar. Meine Schwester hätte gerne eine Familie aus San Francisco. Können Sie eine gute Familie in dieser Stadt finden?", fragte Robert.

„Na ja, im Moment haben wir etwa zwanzig Familien aus San Francisco", antwortete Alice. Sie rief ein

were glad to have an au pair from Germany. Most of the families wanted to get a letter with a photograph from Gabi. Some of them also wanted to telephone her to be sure that she can speak English a little. So Robert gave them her telephone number.

Some host families called Gabi. Then she sent them letters. At last she chose a suitable family and with the help of Alice worked out an agreement with them. The family paid for the ticket from Germany to the USA. At last Gabi started for the USA full of hopes and dreams.

paar von ihnen an. Die Gastfamilien waren froh, ein Au-pair-Mädchen aus Deutschland zu bekommen. Die meisten Familien wollten einen Brief mit einem Foto von Gabi. Manche wollten sie auch anrufen, um sicherzugehen, dass sie ein bisschen Englisch sprach. Also gab Robert ihnen ihre Telefonnummer.

Ein paar Gastfamilien riefen Gabi an. Dann schickte sie ihnen Briefe. Schließlich entschied sie sich für eine passende Familie und arbeitete mit Alices Hilfe eine Vereinbarung mit ihnen aus. Die Familie bezahlte das Ticket von Deutschland in die USA. Schließlich fuhr Gabi voller Hoffnungen und Träume in die USA.

Keys / Lösungen

Exercise 1-1
1. cat cats
2. dog dogs
3. book books
4. box boxes
5. player players
6. computer computers
7. kiss kisses
8. game games
9. tomato tomatoes
10. beach beaches

Exercise 1-2
1. baby babies
2. hair ---
3. child children
4. life lives
5. lady ladies
6. fish fish
7. wife wives
8. man men
9. woman women
10. tooth teeth

Exercise 2
1. This is a dog.
2. This is an old dog.
3. This is a book.
4. This is an old book.
5. This is some water.
6. This is a cup.
7. This is an old cup.
8. This is an apple.
9. This is a big apple.
10. This is some money.
11. This is an orange.
12. This is a big orange.

Exercise 3-1
1. This is a dog. The dog is little.
2. This is an old car. The car is clean.
3. This is an interesting book. The book is new.
4. This is some paper. The paper is white.
5. This is some water. The water is clean.
6. This is a cup. The cup is big.
7. This is an orange. The orange is little.
8. This is an apple. The apple is big.
9. This is a cat. The cat is white.
10. This is an old house. The house is little.

Exercise 3-2
1. The sun is a star.
2. The United Kingdom is in Europe.
3. The dog is an animal.
4. The Bahamas are in the south.
5. The Atlantic is a big ocean.
6. This is the right answer.
7. The sky is blue.
8. The United States are big.
9. The Federal Republic of Germany is in the European Union.
10. The hotel is on the right.

Exercise 3-3
1. The cat is a little animal.
2. I like music.
3. I learn at school.
4. I learn at a new school.
5. My birthday is in May.
6. I like Christmas.
7. I need a new car.
8. I like interesting books.

9. I need some clean water.
10. Monday is after Sunday.
11. I like breakfast.
12. It is a nice breakfast.
13. My house is in Wall Street.
14. Milk is white.

Exercise 4
1. I like this cat.
2. He likes this cat too.
3. She drinks some milk.
4. I drink some water.
5. He learns on Monday.
6. We learn on Monday too.
7. I need a book.
8. She needs a book too.
9. He runs in park.
10. They run in park too.

Exercise 5
1. He has a house.
2. I am in the park.
3. You have a house.
4. She has a house too.
5. You are in the house.
6. We are in the house too.
7. We have a cat.
8. They have a cat too.
9. She is a students.
10. I am a student too.

Exercise 6
1. The car is little. Is the car little?
2. His birthday is in May. Is his birthday in May?
3. The book is interesting. Is the book interesting?
4. The cat is white. Is the cat white?
5. The house is clean. Is the house clean?
6. The breakfast is tasty. Is the breakfast tasty?
7. This man is a teacher. Is this man a teacher?
8. This woman is a doctor. Is this woman a doctor?
9. This car is clean. Is this car clean?
10. The doctor is in the house. Is the doctor in the house?

Exercise 7-1
1. Can the cat play? The cat can play.
2. Can the dolphin read? The dolphin cannot read.
3. Can the teacher read? The teacher can read.
4. Can the dolphin swim? The dolphin can swim.
5. Can a child buy a house? A child cannot buy a house.
6. Can children drink milk? Children can drink milk.
7. Can the cat clean the house? The cat cannot clean the house.
8. Can the student read? The student can read.
9. Can a child ask questions? A child can ask questions.
10. Can the teacher use a book? The teacher can use a book.

Exercise 7-2
1. May students skip classes? Students must not skip classes.
2. May the cat drink milk? The cat can drink milk.

3. May teachers skip classes? Teachers must not skip classes.
4. May teachers go to night clubs? Teachers can go to night clubs.
5. May children go to night clubs? Children must not go to night clubs.
6. May children play? Children can play.
7. May parents play tennis? Parents can play tennis.
8. May students ask questions? Students can ask questions.
9. May children smoke? Children must not smoke.
10. May parents cook? Parents can cook.

Exercise 7-3

1. Will you read a book? I am not sure. I may not read. I may cook pizza.
2. Is Robert at home? I am not sure. He may not be at home. He may be in the park.
3. Are the children in the garden? I am not sure. They may not be in the garden. They may be in the house.
4. Will you play tennis? I am not sure. I may not play tennis. I may clean the house.
5. Will Anna cook tonight? I am not sure. She may not cook tonight. She may wash the windows.
6. Are these books new? I am not sure. They may not be new. They may be old.
7. Is this man German? I am not sure. He may not be German. He may be Italian.
8. Will you go to Spain? I am not sure. I may not go to Spain. I may go to Italy.
9. Will they buy a car? I am not sure. They may not buy a car. They may buy a house.
10. Is she in the house? I am not sure. She may not be in the house. She may be in the garden.
11. Are they Spanish? I am not sure. They may not be Spanish. They may be German.
12. Will the children drink cola? I am not sure. They may not drink cola. They may drink milk.
13. Is this woman Italian? I am not sure. She may not be Italian. She may be Spanish.

Exercise 7-4

1. Must teachers teach children? Teachers must teach children.
2. Must teachers drink milk? Teachers need not drink milk.
3. Must children learn? Children must learn.
4. Must teachers use books? Teachers must use books.
5. Must children cook? Children need not cook.
6. Can students skip classes? Students must not skip classes.
7. Can children go to a night club? Children must not go to a night club.
8. Must students go to school on weekends? Students need not go to school on weekends.
9. Must parents buy milk for children? Parents must buy milk for children.
10. Must children drink milk? Children must drink milk.
11. Must parents drink milk? Parents need not drink milk.

Exercise 8-1

1. Are there children in the park? There are not children in the park.
2. Are there books on the table? There are not books on the table.
3. Is there a table in the garden? There is not a table in the garden.

4. Is there milk on the table? There is not milk on the table.
5. Are there cars in the street? There are not cars in the street.
6. Are there cats in the school? There are not cats in the school.
7. Are there teachers in the night club? There are not teachers in the night club.
8. Is there a cup on the table? There is not a cup on the table.
9. Are there children in the room? There are not children in the room.

Exercise 8-2
1. How many children are there in the park? There are ten children in the park.
2. How many books are there on the table? There are five books on the table.
3. How many cars are there in the street? There are three cars in the street.
4. How many cats are there in the school? There are no cats in the school.
5. How many teachers are there in the night club? There are no teachers in the night club.
6. How many cups are there on the table? There are four cups on the table.
7. How many students are there in the room? There are two students in the room.
8. How many people are there in the garden? There are six people in the garden.
9. How many houses are there in the street? There are ten houses in the street.
10. How many buses are there in the street? There are no buses in the street.

Exercise 9
1. Whose children are they? They are Anna's children.
2. Whose books are on the table? They are those students' books.
3. Whose cat is in the garden? This is Tom's cat.
4. Whose computer is this? This is Otto's computer.
5. Whose bags are these? These are my parents' bags.
6. Whose cups are these? These are teachers' cups.
7. Whose car is this? This is Linda's car.
8. Whose parents are in the garden? They are this boy's parents.
9. Whose baby is this? This is that woman's baby.
10. Whose radio is this? This is this man's radio.
11. Whose house is this? This is my friend's house.
12. Whose bikes are these? These are my friends' bikes.

Exercise 10-1
1. This is my book. Give it to me, please.
2. These are their cups. Give them to them, please.
3. This is her cat. Give it to her, please.
4. This is his radio. Give it to him, please.
5. This is my computer. Give it to me, please.
6. These are our bags. Give them to us, please.
7. These are their batteries. Give them to them, please.
8. These are his bananas. Give them to him, please.
9. This is her lamp. Give it to her, please.
10. This is my pizza. Give it to me, please.
11. These are our cups. Give them to us, please.
12. These are their pens. Give them to them, please.

Exercise 10-2

1. Give me this book, please.
2. I sometimes see her.
3. Show her the garden, please.
4. I know them.
5. She understands me.
6. They sometimes help him.
7. Tell us the truth, please.
8. I sometimes invite her to play tennis.
9. Visit us on Sunday, please.
10. Ask him this question, please.
11. Trust me, please.

Exercise 11-1

1. Whose books are newer? Anna's books are newer than Linda's books. But Tom's books are the newest.
2. Whose car is faster? Otto's car is faster than Anna's car. But Robert's car is the fastest.
3. Whose cat is hungrier? Tom's cat is hungrier than Linda's cat. But Daniel's cat is the hungriest.
4. Whose computer is more expensive? Otto's computer is more expensive than Emma's computer. But Anna's computer is the most expensive.
5. Whose bags are heavier? Daniel's bags are heavier than Linda's bags. But Finn's bags are the heaviest.
6. Whose cup is bigger? Max's cup is bigger than Daniel's cup. But Otto's cup is the biggest.
7. Whose parents are friendlier? Julia's parents are friendlier than Paul's parents. But Max's parents are the friendliest.
8. Whose baby is more beautiful? Paul's baby is more beautiful than Finn's baby. But Julia's baby is the most beautiful.
9. Whose radio is smaller? Linda's radio is smaller than Emma's radio. But Finn's radio is the smallest.
10. What city is older? Milan is older than Detroit. But Luxor is the oldest.

Exercise 11-2

1. Finn is older than Emma. Tom is the eldest.
2. Tom is taller than Emma. Finn is the tallest.
3. Tom is more generous than Emma. Finn is the most generous.
4. Finn is more ambitious than Emma. Tom is the most ambitious.
5. Finn is neater than Tom. Emma is the neatest.
6. Finn is cleverer than Emma. Tom is the cleverest.
7. Finn is a better driver than Emma. Tom is the best driver.
8. Finn is happier than Tom. Emma is the happiest.
9. Finn is friendlier than Tom. Emma is the friendliest.
10. Finn is more punctual than Emma. Tom is the most punctual.

Exercise 12

1. The cat is in the room.
2. The cups are on the table.
3. The students are in the room.
4. The bus stop is at / near / close to / by the shop.
5. The dog is under the table.

6. The lamp is above the table.
7. There is a teacher among those students.
8. The shop is between the station and the school.
9. The park is to / on the left.
10. The café is to / on the right.
11. The hotel is behind the school.
12. The school is in front of the hotel.
13. The bed is in the middle of the room.
14. The park is at / near / close to / by the school.
15. The cat is under the car.
16. The balloon is above the school.
17. There is a German student among those Polish students.
18. The bus stop is between the station and the shop.
19. The school is to / on the left.
20. The park is to / on the right.
21. The shop is behind the station.
22. The station is in front of the shop.
23. The cat is in the middle of the room.

Exercise 13-1
1. I want Sam to come today. I say to him: Sam, come today, please!
2. You want Marta to lend you a book. You say to her: Marta, lend me this book, please.
3. Sam wants his mother to cook pizza. Sam says to her: Mom, cook pizza, please.
4. I want to play tennis with Marta. I say to her: Marta, let's play tennis.
5. Linda wants you to dance with her. She says to you: Let's dance!
6. Anna wants Bill to help her. She says to him: Bill, help me, please.
7. Emma wants Tom to show her the city. She says to him: Tom, show me the city, please.
8. Finn wants Linda to trust him. He says to her: Linda, trust me, please.
9. Marta wants you to have an apple. She says to you: Have an apple, please.

Exercise 13-2
1. I don't want Sam to come today. I say to him: Sam, don't come today, please!
2. Sam doesn't want his mother to cook pizza. Sam says to her: Mom, don't cook pizza, please.
3. Anna doesn't want Bill to help her. She says to him: Bill, don't help me, please.
4. Finn doesn't want Linda to trust Bill. He says to her: Linda, don't trust Bill, please.
5. Marta doesn't want you to forget it. She says to you: Don't forget it, please.
6. Tom doesn't want me to be shy. He says to me: Don't be shy, please.

Exercise 14
1. This is a cheap shop. You can buy here cheaply.
2. He is a bad player. He plays badly.
3. She is a slow worker. She works slowly.
4. This is an easy work. I can do it easily.
5. My mom is angry with me. She speaks angrily to me.
6. This girl is happy. She smiles happily.

Exercise 15
never - seldom - occasionally - sometimes - often - usually - always

Exercise 16

two years ago - three months ago - last week - yesterday - six hours ago - five minutes ago - now - soon - in five minutes - in an hour - tomorrow - in two days - next week - in three months - in two years

Exercise 17
1. I read ~~on Sundays outside~~. I read outside on Sundays.
2. The cat sleeps by day inside. The cat sleeps inside by day.
3. The cat is in the evening outside. The cat is outside in the evening.
4. The children play in the afternoon here. The children play here in the afternoon.
5. We never go at night to the park. We never go to the park at night.
6. Linda often plays tennis in the morning at school. Linda often plays tennis at school in the morning.
7. Tom works on Sundays at the station. Tom works at the station on Sundays.
8. The students are usually after the lessons in the park. The students are usually in the park after the lessons.
9. Sam is often by day at home. Sam is often at home by day.
10. Emma is always in the morning at work. Emma is always at work in the morning.

Exercise 18
1. I sometimes work outside. My work is good.
2. Can you help me? I need your help.
3. I know about her fear. She fears dogs.
4. Tom hopes to find a job. It is also Emma's hope.
5. Linda sometimes smiles to Finn. Her smile is nice.
6. This small dog often attacks other dogs. Those attacks are very short.
7. Anna's friend often visits her. She likes his visits.
8. Sam must call his mother. His calls are important to her.

Exercise 19
1. What is in the cup?
2. What is in the bag?
3. What is in the box?
4. Who is at school?
5. Where must you go in the morning?
6. When must you start your work?
7. Who is on the bus?
8. Whose cup is on the table?
9. Which car is faster, the red or the blue?
10. Whose pen is this?
11. Who can play tennis?
12. Who must do it?
13. Where is the bus stop?
14. When must Linda come home?
15. Why are you angry?
16. Why is not Sam at work?
17. How can I help you with this work now?
18. Which student is the best?
19. How is this cheese made in England?
20. How is this bread made in Germany?

Exercise 20
1. The children go to school in the morning.

2. The children come from school in the afternoon.
3. A girl comes into the café and sits down near a window.
4. Some people go out of the café .
5. I must go up to my room now.
6. Sam goes down to the kitchen in the morning.
7. My cat can jump over a small table.
8. Anna's cat runs under the table and goes into another room.
9. You can go to the station through the park.
10. Tourists go round the monument.
11. Students go to the university along a big street.
12. They go across the street near the university.
13. Students go past some book shops every morning.

Exercise 21
1. I always work outside. I never work outside.
2. How many apples can you give me? None. / I can give you no apples.
3. Every child can do it. No child can do it.
4. Somebody lives in this house. Nobody lives in this house.
5. Everything in this room is mine. Nothing in this room is mine.
6. Linda's cat can go everywhere. Linda's cat can go nowhere.
7. Finn goes somewhere at night. Finn goes nowhere at night.
8. You see a taxi everywhere in this city. You see a taxi nowhere in this city.
9. Tom always reads books. Tom never reads books.
10. There is something on the table. There is nothing on the table.
11. Emma is always angry. Emma is never angry.
12. There is somebody in the garden. There is nobody in the garden.
13. We know something about Bill. We know nothing about Bill.
14. Every student has a job. No student has a job.
15. Some children play in the park at night. No children play in the park at night.
16. How much money can you give me? None. / I can give you no money.
17. How many apples are there on the table? None. / There are no apples on the table.

Exercise 22
1. Sam friends Sam has got friends.
2. I not books I have not got books.
3. You books? Have you got books?
4. Linda free time? Has Linda got free time?
5. Finn not apples Finn has not got apples.
6. They children They have got children.
7. They a cat? Have they got a cat?
8. Marta not money Marta has not got money.
9. Bill not a job Bill has not got a job.
10. I a dog I have got a dog.
11. Emma a car? Has Emma got a car?
12. Tom not a radio Tom has not got a radio.

Exercise 23-1
1. Sam has got friends. Sam has got a lot of friends.

2. Are there books on the table? Are there many books on the table?
3. There are not apples in the box. There are not many apples in the box.
4. Linda has got free time. Linda has got a lot of free time.
5. There is not water in the cup. There is not much water in the cup.
6. There is not money on the table. There is not much money on the table.
7. There are children in the park. There are a lot of children in the park.
8. There are not dogs in the park. There are not many dogs in the park.
9. There are not big trees there. There are not many big trees there.
10. Have you got friends? Have you got many friends?
11. They drink tea. They drink a lot of tea.
12. She eats fast-food. She eats a lot of fast-food.

Exercise 23-2
1. Sam has got friends. Sam has got few friends.
2. I have got free time. I have got little free time.
3. There are shops in this street. There are few shops in this street.
4. Finn has got money. Finn has got little money.
5. There are trees in this park. There are few trees in this park.
6. Anna drinks water. Anna drinks little water.
7. I have got grammar books. I have got few grammar books.
8. Sam speaks German. Sam speaks little German.
9. There are tables in the class-room. There are few tables in the class-room.

Exercise 23-3
1. Has Sam got friends? A few.
2. Have you got free time? A little.
3. Have they got books? A few.
4. Has Tom got free time? A little.
5. Has Marta got apples? A few.
6. Has Emma got money? A little.
7. Have they got water? A little.

Exercise 23-4
1. I am happy. I have got a little money.
2. Bill is unhappy. He has got little money.
3. Sam can play tennis. He has got a little free time.
4. Emma cannot play tennis. She has got little free time.
5. Tom can cook a steak. He has got a little meat.
6. You cannot cook a steak. You have got little meat.
7. I can play football. I have got a few friends.
8. He cannot play football. He has got few friends.
9. She can learn English fast. She has got a few good books.
10. He cannot learn English fast. He has got few good books.

Exercise 24
1. Two plus three is five.
2. Four plus two is six.
3. Five plus one is six.
4. Seven minus three is four.

5. Eight plus two is ten.
6. Ten minus ten is zero.
7. Ten minus one is nine.
8. Two plus ten is twelve.
9. Twenty plus six is twenty-six.
10. Thirty plus fifty is eighty.
11. One thousand five hundred plus five hundred is two thousand.
12. Point one plus point two is point three.
13. Point six plus point four is one.

Exercise 25
1. I get up at six o'clock.
2. Linda gets up at seven o'clock.
3. She drinks a cup of coffee before going to university.
4. She studies from eight to three o'clock.
5. Linda works hard during the classes.
6. She goes to the library after the classes.
7. She usually works in the library for two hours.
8. Linda phones some of her friends while working in the library.
9. She meets her friends after working in the library.
10. They go to a café and stay there until / till seven o'clock.
11. Linda comes home at half past seven.
12. She watches TV from eight to ten o'clock.
13. She has supper while watching TV.
14. She takes a bath before going to bed.

Exercise 26
1. Sam has got some friends. I have not got any friends in this city.
2. Has Anna got any classes today? She has not got any classes today.
3. Have you got any problems with this work? Yes, I have got some problems.
4. Have they got any pets at home? They have not got any pets.
5. Are there any animals in this wood? There are some animals there.
6. Are there any big shops in this street? There are not any big shops there.

Exercise 27
1. Would you like some water?
2. I would like a banana.
3. Would you like an apple?
4. I would like a cup of coffee.
5. I would like some tea.
6. Would you like to dance?
7. I would like to play tennis.
8. Would you like to go to a café ?
9. I would like to go to the park.

Exercise 28-1
1. You live in the US. Do you live in the US?
2. You play tennis. Do you play tennis?
3. Emma speaks German. Does Emma speak German?
4. Tom can swim. Can Tom swim?
5. Bill works hard. Does Bill work hard?
6. Anna must help Bill. Must Anna help Bill?

7. This man is a bus driver. Is this man a bus driver?
8. He works on weekends. Does he work on weekends?
9. Linda likes cooking. Does Linda like cooking?
10. Linda's children like her pizza. Do Linda's children like her pizza?
11. Finn can help Linda. Can Finn help Linda?
12. Finn is Linda's friend. Is Finn Linda's friend?
13. He lives in this street. Does he live in this street?
14. Shops open at nine o'clock. Do shops open at nine o'clock?
15. Sam wakes up at seven o'clock. Does Sam wake up at seven o'clock?
16. He studies at university. Does he study at university?
17. Sam is a good student. Is Sam a good student?

Exercise 28-2

1. You live in the US. You do not live in the US.
2. You play tennis. You do not play tennis.
3. Emma speaks German. Emma does not speak German.
4. Tom can swim. Tom cannot swim.
5. Bill works hard. Bill does not work hard.
6. Anna must help Bill. Anna must not help Bill.
7. This man is a bus driver. This man is not a bus driver.
8. He works on weekends. He does not work on weekends.
9. Linda likes cooking. Linda does not like cooking.
10. Linda's children like her pizza. Linda's children do not like her pizza.
11. Finn can help Linda. Finn cannot help Linda.
12. Finn is Linda's friend. Finn is not Linda's friend.
13. He lives in this street. He does not live in this street.
14. Shops open at nine o'clock. Shops do not open at nine o'clock.
15. Sam wakes up at seven o'clock. Sam does not wake up at seven o'clock.
16. He studies at university. He does not study at university.
17. Sam is a good student. Sam is not a good student.

Exercise 29

1. Can you help me? Yes, I can. No, I cannot.
2. Can you play tennis? Yes, I can. No, I cannot.
3. Does Emma speak German? Yes, she does. No, she does not.
4. Do you live in Germany? Yes, I do. No, I do not.
5. Do they study English? Yes, they do. No, they do not.
6. Is he a student? Yes, he is. No, he is not.
7. Are they Americans? Yes, they are. No, they are not.
8. Are you happy? Yes, I am. No, I am not.

Exercise 30-1

1. I am eating an apple.
2. Finn is playing tennis.
3. Sam is helping me.
4. Anna is cooking pizza.

5. Linda is swimming.
6. Tom is working in the garden.
7. We are studying English hard today.
8. The children are playing in the park.
9. The students are having breakfast.
10. Emma is driving a car.

Exercise 30-2
1. I am (not) drinking tea.
2. I am not playing tennis.
3. The teacher is (not) helping me.
4. I am not swimming.
5. I am not working in the garden.
6. I am learning English.
7. I am not learning German.
8. It is (not) raining.
9. The sun is (not) shining.

Exercise 31
1. Does Emma teach? Yes, she does.
   Is she teaching? No, she is not.
   What is she doing? She is surfing.
2. Does Linda study? Yes, she does.
   Is she studying? No, she is not.
   What is she doing? She is cleaning a room.
3. Does Finn deliver packages? Yes, he does.
   Is he delivering packages? Yes, he is.
   What is he doing? He is delivering two packages.
4. Does Tom drive a taxi? Yes, he does.
   Is he driving a taxi? No, he is not.
   What is he doing? He is skiing.
5. Does Anna cook? Yes, she does.
   Is she cooking? No, she is not.
   What is she doing? She is riding a bike.
6. Does Sam paint houses? Yes, he does.
   Is he painting a house? Yes, he is.
   What is he doing? He is painting a wall.
7. Does Denis repair cars? Yes, he does.
   Is he repairing a car? No, he is not.
   What is he doing? He is skateboarding.

Exercise 32
1. This eating girl is my sister. She must stop eating so much.
2. This reading boy is my friend. He really likes reading.
3. Look at that dancing woman. She is crazy about dancing.
4. That singing girl has a nice voice. She dreams of singing a new hit.
5. That driving man must stop. His driving is dangerous.
6. Those surfing boys want me to surf too. But I am afraid of surfing.
7. The food of this cooking man is really tasty. He is good at cooking.
8. The food of that cooking woman is bad. She hates cooking.
9. Those swimming people are fit. Are you interested in swimming?

Exercise 33-1
1. I live in the US. I lived in Canada five years ago.
2. Anna plays tennis on Sundays. She played tennis last Monday too.
3. Bill often works in his garden. He worked in his garden yesterday.
4. Emma sometimes cooks pizza. She cooked pizza last weekend.
5. Tom can swim well. He could swim very little ten years ago.
6. Linda cleans her room weekly. She cleaned her room two days ago.
7. She washes windows every month. She washed windows last week.

8. This man is happy now. He was sad this morning.
9. This café opens at nine o'clock. But it opened at ten o'clock last Tuesday.
10. My brother wants to live in Africa. He wanted to live in China a year ago.
11. This shop always closes at nine o'clock. But it closed at eight last Friday.
12. Sam wakes up at seven o'clock. But he woke up at six o'clock last Sunday.

Exercise 33-2
1. I visited Madrid but I did not visit Barcelona.
2. Anna played tennis with Tom but she did not play with Denis.
3. Sam had some soup but he did not have a spoon.
4. Emma cooked pizza but she did not cook soup.
5. I went to the bank but I did not go to the shop.
6. Bill worked on Monday but he did not work yesterday.
7. Linda cleaned her room but she did not clean the kitchen.
8. My brother wanted to live in China but he did not want to learn Chinese.
9. You called your friend but you did not call your mom.

Exercise 33-3
1. I played golf on Sunday. And you? Did you play golf?
2. I worked on Saturday. And you? Did you work on Saturday?
3. I studied hard last week. And you? Did you study hard last week?
4. I learned German language in summer. And you? Did you learn German language in summer?
5. I cooked some soup this morning. And you? Did you cook some soup this morning?
6. I washed the windows last month. And you? Did you wash the windows last month?
7. I rode a bike in the morning. And you? Did you ride a bike in the morning?

Exercise 33-4
1. I woke up late. What time did you wake up?
2. I had my breakfast. What did you have for breakfast?
3. I looked out of the window. Why did you look out of the window?
4. I saw somebody. Who did you see?
5. I rode a bike. Where did you ride a bike?
6. I bought some apples. How many apples did you buy?
7. I paid for the apples. How much did you pay (for the apples)?
8. I met somebody. Who did you meet?
9. I came home. When did you come home?

Exercise 34-1
1. Bill was in the mountain park. He was skiing.
2. Linda was in the office. She was working.
3. Robert and Emma were on the beach. They were sunbathing.
4. Sam was in the wood. He was riding a bike.
5. Denis was in the park. He was sitting on a bench.

6. Anna was in the garden. She was working.

Exercise 34-2
1. At 6:00 she was sleeping.
2. At 7:10 she was taking a shower.
3. At 8:15 she was riding a bike.
4. At 11 o'clock she was working.
5. At 17 o'clock she was sunbathing.
6. At 18:05 she was talking with a friend.
7. At 21 o'clock she was watching television.

Exercise 34-3
1. What was Julia doing when you saw her?
2. What was mom cooking when you came home?
3. Where was Lea going when you met her?
4. Was the sun shining when you came to the beach?
5. Were you working at 10 o'clock?
6. Were you watching TV in the evening?
7. Was Emma having lunch at 2 o'clock?

Exercise 35
1. When I saw Julia she was playing tennis.
2. Tom was swimming when the rain started.
3. Mom was cooking when the children came home.
4. I closed the door and went into the garden.
5. Emma was having lunch when Sam phoned her.
6. The car stopped and a woman got out. She was wearing a white dress.
7. I saw Finn in the street. He was carrying a big red bag.
8. Anna woke up at 7 o'clock. Somebody phoned her when she was having breakfast.
9. I was playing the guitar. Lea was listening. At this moment the cat started to sing.
10. A big dog was running in the park. Some children ran home.
11. The rain started when the children were running home from the park.
12. Mom was waiting for her children when they came home.
13. They had dinner and then they watched TV.

Exercise 36-1
1. Bill is skiing.
2. Linda is working.
3. Emma is sunbathing on the beach.
4. Sam is riding a bike.
5. Denis is going to the park.
6. Anna is working in the garden.

Exercise 36-2
1. What is Julia doing on Sunday?
2. What is mom cooking tomorrow?
3. Where is Lea going next weekend?
4. What time is Sam coming?
5. Why are you working on Sunday?
6. What time is Emma having lunch?

Exercise 36-3
1. The show starts at 7 o'clock.
2. I am not playing tennis tomorrow.
3. What time does the bus arrive?
4. Who is meeting you on the station?

5. What time are you meeting Emma?
6. The café closes at 5 o'clock.
7. My cooking class finishes in December.
8. I am cooking an big Thai dish on Sunday.
9. Are you taking an English class in January?

Exercise 36-4
1. I am not going to play tennis tomorrow.
2. What time is Linda going to work in the garden?
3. How many books are you going to buy?
4. Where is Emma going to live in England?
5. When is she going to come back?
6. Tom is not going to wake up before 9 o'clock.
7. What is mom going to cook?
8. Sam is going to start a Chinese course.
9. I am going to meet Anna in the evening.
10. How much time are you going to spend in Spain?

Exercise 36-5
1. I will play tennis. I won't play tennis.
2. Tom will come. Tom won't come.
3. Emma will cook. Emma won't cook.
4. Sam will help Emma. Sam won't help Emma.
5. Bill will read the book. Bill won't read the book.
6. Lea will wash windows. Lea won't wash windows.
7. Robert will drive the car. Robert won't drive the car.
8. We will go to the park. We won't go to the park.

Exercise 36-6
1. I help you with this work, okay? **wrong** I will help you with this work, okay?
2. I sometimes help Anna. **right**
3. Tom probably comes in the evening. **wrong** Tom will probably come in the evening.
4. Tom often comes in the evening. **right**
5. I think Emma cooks pizza soon. **wrong** I think Emma will cook pizza soon.
6. Emma occasionally cooks pizza. **right**
7. We watch television tonight, okay? **wrong** We will watch television tonight, okay?
8. We always watch television in evening. **right**
9. Lea, you wash the window today after breakfast, please? **wrong** Lea, will you wash the window today after breakfast, please?
10. Lea seldom washes the window. **right**
11. I will drive the car, okay? **right**
12. My wife usually drives the car. **right**

Exercise 37-1
1. I have cooked pizza. Would you like to try it?

2. I have bought some apples. Have one, please.
3. 'Tom, are you still working?' 'No, I have finished.'
4. Look! Linda has bought a new blue bike.
5. 'Let's go to the cinema.' 'No, thanks. I have watched that film.'
6. 'Where is Emma?' 'She has gone home.'
7. Your car looks great! Have you washed it?
8. I cannot find my pen. Somebody has taken it.
9. Lea came back from Italy yesterday. Have you seen her new hat?

Exercise 37-2
1. I have corrected two mistakes in my work today.
2. I corrected five mistakes in my work yesterday.
3. I have drunk three cups of tea today.
4. I drank five cups of tea yesterday.
5. Tom has watched two shows this week.
6. Tom watched a show last week.
7. Robert and Emma have visited Emma's parents two times this year.
8. Robert and Emma visited Emma's parents three times last year.
9. My friend has sung only one short song this evening.
10. My friend sang several songs on Sunday evening.

Exercise 37-3
1. I am in Berlin. I have been in Berlin since Friday.
2. Tom lives in Boston. He has lived there for twenty years.
3. Emma works in a shop. She has worked there since June.
4. Linda has a bike. She has had it since Sunday.
5. Sam is ill. He has been ill for three days.
6. I know Anna very well. I have known her for a long time.
7. Robert and Emma are married. They have been married since April.
8. They are in London. They have been there for five days.
9. I live in the UK. I have lived here since 2005.
10. Lea works at school. She has worked there for seven years.
11. I have a cat. I have had it for two years.
12. My cat is hungry. It has been hungry since morning.
13. I know Robert and Emma well. I have known them since 2015.
14. Finn is sad. He has been sad since the start of the lesson.

Exercise 38
1. How many pages did you read yesterday?
2. How many pages have you read?
3. Tom came ten minutes ago.
4. Mom has cooked pizza.
5. When did you play tennis?
6. I have learned English since May.
7. I learned English a lot in June.
8. Have you paid for parking?
9. I paid for parking five minutes ago.
10. Finn was happy when the lesson finished.

11. Finn has been happy all day today.
12. I was hungry all day yesterday.
13. I have been hungry since breakfast.
14. Emma had a blue bike a year ago.
15. Emma has had a red bike since summer.

Exercise 39
1. I ride a bike in the park on Sundays.
2. Tom swims in the river in summer.
3. Linda cooks traditional dishes in the restaurant every day.
4. Finn writes a novel in the garden on weekends.
5. Anna drives a new car to work.
6. Sam eats two apples daily.
7. I play minigolf in the park two times a month.
8. Lea makes origami at school on Mondays.
9. Mom washes the windows every month.
10. Richard repairs his old car in the garage almost every weekend.

Exercise 40-1
1. I am hungry. - So am I. / I am not.
2. Tom is not a student. - Neither am I. / I am.
3. Emma cannot swim. - Neither can I. / I can.
4. Bill can cook. - So can I. / I cannot.
5. Sam lives in the USA. - So do I. / I do not.
6. I cooked pizza on Sunday. - So did I. / I did not.
7. Anna does not play golf. - Neither do I. / I do.
8. I did not watch television yesterday. - Neither did I. / I did.
9. I am tall. - So am I. / I am not.
10. I am not fit. - Neither am I. / I am.
11. I am happy. - So am I. / I am not.
12. I am not friendly. - Neither am I. / I am.
13. I was in Spain last week. - So was I. / I was not.
14. I will learn Spanish. - So will I. / I will not.
15. I will not go to the park next weekend. - Neither will I. / I will.

Exercise 40-2
1. I am not hungry. - Are not you? I am.
2. He likes loud music. - Does he? I do not.
3. She does not work hard. - Does not she? I do.
4. We eat more than we need. - Do you? I do not.
5. They do not speak German. - Do not they? I do.
6. Lea cannot play tennis. - Cannot she? I can.
7. Tom is not tall. - Is not he? I am.
8. Anna has got a cat. - Has she? I have not.
9. Sam has not got a bike. - Has not he? I have.
10. Bill goes to work by bus. - Does he? I do not.

11. Finn does not read much. - Does not he? I do.
12. Linda dances a lot. - Does she? I do not.
13. I will go to Italy. - Will you? I will not.
14. I will not study today. - Will not you? I will.

Wörterbuch Englisch-Deutsch

about [əˈbaʊt] - etwa
accident [ˈæksɪdənt] - der Unfall
accompanied [əˈkʌmpənid] - begleitet
accompany [əˈkʌmpəni] - begleiten
across [əˈkrɒs] - über
ad [æd] - das Inserat
address [əˈdres] - die Adresse
adventure [ədˈventʃə] - das Abenteuer
advert [ˈædvɜːt] - die Anzeige, die Werbung
afraid [əˈfreɪd] - ängstlich
after [ˈɑːftə] - nach
again [əˈgen] - wieder
against [əˈgenst] - gegen
age [eɪdʒ] - das Alter
agency [ˈeɪdʒənsi] - die Agentur
ago [əˈgəʊ] - vor
agree [əˈgriː] - einverstanden sein
agreement [əˈgriːmənt] - die Vereinbarung
air [eə] - die Luft
airplane [ˈeəpleɪn] - das Flugzeug
airshow [ˈeəʃəʊ] - die Flugschau
alarm [əˈlɑːm] - der Alarm
alien [ˈeɪliən] - der Außerirdische
all [ɔːl] - alle
all-round [ˈɔːl raʊnd] - vielseitig, alles könnend
along [əˈlɒŋ] - entlang
aloud [əˈlaʊd] - laut
already [ɔːlˈredi] - schon
also [ˈɔːlsəʊ] - auch
although [ɔːlˈðəʊ] - obwohl, trotzdem
always [ˈɔːlweɪz] - immer
American [əˈmerɪkən] - Amerikaner
and [ænd] - und
angrily [ˈæŋgrəli] - wütend
angry [ˈæŋgri] - wütend
animal [ˈænɪml] - das Tier
another [əˈnʌðə] - anderer
answer [ˈɑːnsə] - die Antwort
answer [ˈɑːnsə] - antworten, erwidern
answered [ˈɑːnsəd] - geantwortet
answering machine [ˈɑːnsərɪŋ məʃiːn] - der Anrufbeantworter
any [ˈeni] - irgendwelche
anything [ˈeniθɪŋ] - etwas, nichts
apply [əˈplaɪ] - sich bewerben

arm [ɑːm] - der Arm
arrive [əˈraɪv] - ankommen
arrived [əˈraɪvd] - angekommen
art [ɑːt] - die Kunst
artist [ˈɑːtɪst] - der Künstler
as [æz] - da, wie
as well [əz wel] - auch
ask [ɑːsk] - bitten, fragen
asked [ˈɑːskt] - gefragt
aspirin [ˈæsprɪn] - das Aspirin
asterisk [ˈæstərɪsk] - das Sternchen
at [æt] - am, beim
at first [ət ˈfɜːst] - erst
at last [ət lɑːst] - schließlich
at least [ət liːst] - wenigstens
at one o'clock [ət wʌn əˈklɒk] - um eins
attention [əˈtenʃn] - die Aufmerksamkeit
audience [ˈɔːdiəns] - das Publikum
away [əˈweɪ] - weg
back [ˈbæk] - zurück
bad [bæd] - schlecht
bag [bæg] - die Tasche
bank [bæŋk] - die Bank
barked [bɑːkt] - bellte
Bathroom [ˈbɑːθruːm] - das Bad, das Badezimmer
bath [bɑːθ] - die Badewanne
bathroom table [ˈbɑːθruːm ˈteɪbl] - der Badezimmertisch
be [bi] - sein
be ashamed; [bi əˈʃeɪmd] - sich schämen
he is ashamed [hi z əˈʃeɪmd] - er schämt sich
be sorry [bi ˈsɒri] - leid tun
beautiful [ˈbjuːtəfl] - wunderschön
because [bɪˈkɒz] - weil
bed [bed] - das Bett
beds [ˈbedz] - die Betten
beep [biːp] - der Piepton
before [bɪˈfɔː] - vor
began [bɪˈgæn] - begann
begin [bɪˈgɪn] - anfangen
behind [bɪˈhaɪnd] - hinter
believe [bɪˈliːv] - glauben
better [ˈbetə] - besser
between [bɪˈtwiːn] - zwischen

big/bigger/the biggest [bɪg ˈbɪgə ðə ˈbɪgɪst] - groß/größer/am größten
bike [baɪk] - das Fahrrad
billion [ˈbɪlɪən] - die Billionen
bird [bɜːd] - der Vogel
bite [baɪt] - beißen
black [blæk] - schwarz
blank, empty [blæŋk | ˈempti] - leer
blue [bluː] - blau
book [bʊk] - das Buch
bookcase [ˈbʊk keɪs] - das Bücherregal
bother [ˈbɔðə] - ärgern
box [bɔks] - die Kiste
boy [ˌbɔɪ] - der Junge
boyfriend [ˈbɔɪfrend] - der Freund
brake [breɪk] - die Bremse
brake [breɪk] - bremsen
bread [bred] - das Brot
break, pause [breɪk | pɔːz] - die Pause
breakfast [ˈbrekfəst] - das Frühstück
bridge [brɪdʒ] - die Brücke
bring [brɪŋ] - bringen
brother [ˈbrʌðə] - der Bruder
bus [bʌs] - der Bus
but [bʌt] - aber
butter [ˈbʌtə] - die Butter
button [ˈbʌtn] - der Knopf
buy [baɪ] - kaufen
by the way [baɪ ðə ˈweɪ] - übrigens
bye [baɪ] - tschüss
cable [ˈkeɪbl] - das Kabel
café [ˈkæfeɪ] - das Café
call on the phone [kɔːl ɔn ðə fəʊn] - anrufen
call [kɔːl] - rufen
call centre [kɔːl ˈsentə] - das Callcenter
called [kɔːld] - riefen an
came [keɪm] - kam, gekommen
can [kæn] - können
Canada [ˈkænədə] - Kanada
Canadian [kəˈneɪdɪən] - Kanadier
captain [ˈkæptɪn] - der Kapitän
car [kɑː] - das Auto
care [keə] - sich kümmern um
careful [ˈkeəfʊl] - sorgfältig
carefully [ˈkeəfəli] - vorsichtig
cash [kæʃ] - das Bargeld
cash register [kæʃ ˈredʒɪstə] - die Kasse
cashier, teller [kæˈʃɪə | ˈtelə] - der Kassierer

cat [kæt] - die Katze
catch [kætʃ] - fangen
CD [ˌsiːˈdiː] - die CD
CD player [ˌsiːˈdiː ˈpleɪə] - der CD-Spieler
central [ˈsentrəl] - Haupt-, zentral
centre [ˈsentə] - das Zentrum
city centre [ˈsɪti ˈsentə] - das Stadtzentrum
ceremony [ˈserɪməni] - die Feier
chair [tʃeə] - der Stuhl
chance [tʃɑːns] - die Chance
change [tʃeɪndʒ] - ändern
change [tʃeɪndʒ] - die Änderung
check [tʃek] - kontrollieren
chemicals [ˈkemɪklz] - die Chemikalien
chemistry [ˈkemɪstri] - die Chemie
child [tʃaɪld] - das Kind
children [ˈtʃɪldrən] - die Kinder
choose [tʃuːz] - auswählen, entscheiden für
chose [tʃəʊz] - entschied sich für
city [ˈsɪti] - die Stadt
class [klɑːs] - die Klasse
classroom [ˈklæsruːm] - das Klassenzimmer
clean [kliːn] - sauber (machen)
clean [kliːn] - sauber machen, putzen
cleaned [kliːnd] - gesäubert
clever [ˈklevə] - schlau
close [kləʊz] - schließen; nah
closed [kləʊzd] - geschlossen
closer [ˈkləʊsə] - näher
clothes [kləʊðz] - die Kleidung
club [klʌb] - der Verein
coffee [ˈkɔfi] - der Kaffee
cold [kəʊld] - kalt
coldness [ˈkəʊldnəs] - die Kälte
colleague [ˈkɔliːg] - der Kollege
college [ˈkɔlɪdʒ] - die Universität, die Uni
come, go [kʌm | gəʊ] - kommen
company [ˈkʌmpəni] - die Firma
competition [ˌkɔmpəˈtɪʃn] - die Ausschreibung, der Wettbewerb
compose [kəmˈpəʊz] - entwerfen, verfassen
composition [ˌkɔmpəˈzɪʃn] - der Entwurf, der Text
computer [kəmˈpjuːtə] - der Computer
confused [kənˈfjuːzd] - verwirrt
constant [ˈkɔnstənt] - beständig
consult [kənˈsʌlt] - beraten
consultancy [kənˈsʌltənsi] - die Beratung

consultant [kənˈsʌltənt] - der Berater
continue [kənˈtɪnjuː] - fortführen
continued to watch [kənˈtɪnjuːd tə wɔtʃ] - weiterschauen
control [kənˈtrəʊl] - die Kontrolle
Cooker [ˈkʊkə] - der Koch/die Köchin
cooking [ˈkʊkɪŋ] - kochend
co-ordination [kəʊˌɔːdɪˈneɪʃən] - die Koordination
correct, correctly [kəˈrekt | kəˈrektli] - richtig
correct [kəˈrekt] - korrigieren
cost [kɔst] - kosten
could [kʊd] - könnte, kann
country [ˈkʌntri] - das Land
course [kɔːs] - der Kurs
creative [kriːˈeɪtɪv] - kreativ
cried [kraɪd] - gerufen
criminal [ˈkrɪmɪnl] - der Verbrecher
cry [kraɪ] - weinen, schreien, rufen
crystal [ˈkrɪstl] - das Kristall
cup [kʌp] - die Tasse
current [ˈkʌrənt] - der Strom
customer [ˈkʌstəmə] - der Kunde
dad [dæd] - der Vater
daddy [ˈdædi] - Papa
damn [dæm] - verdammt
dance [dɑːns] - tanzen
danced [dɑːnst] - getanzt
dancing [ˈdɑːnsɪŋ] - tanzend
dark [dɑːk] - dunkel
date [deɪt] - das Datum
daughter [ˈdɔːtə] - die Tochter
day [deɪ] - der Tag
daily [ˈdeɪli] - täglich, jeden Tag
deadly [ˈdedli] - tödlich
dear [dɪə] - liebe
design [dɪˈzaɪn] - das Design
desk [desk] - der Schreibtisch
destroy [dɪˈstrɔɪ] - zerstören
develop [dɪˈveləp] - entwickeln
did [dɪd] - tat
die [daɪ] - sterben
died [daɪd] - starb
different [ˈdɪfrənt] - verschieden
difficult [ˈdɪfɪkəlt] - schwer
dirty [ˈdɜːti] - dreckig
do [duː] - machen
doctor [ˈdɔktə] - der Arzt

dog [dɔg] - der Hund
doll [dɔl] - die Puppe
door [dɔː] - die Tür
dorms [ˈdɔːmz] - das Studentenwohnheim
down [daʊn] - nach unten
dream [driːm] - der Traum
dream [driːm] - träumen
drink [drɪŋk] - trinken
drive [draɪv] - fahren
driver [ˈdraɪvə] - der Fahrer
driving license [ˈdraɪvɪŋ ˈlaɪsns] - der Führerschein
drove [drəʊv] - fuhr
dry [draɪ] - trocknen; trocken
DVD [ˌdiviˈdiː] - die DVD
ear [ɪə] - das Ohr
earn [ɜːn] - verdienen
earth [ɜːθ] - die Erde
eat [iːt] - essen
editor [ˈedɪtə] - der Herausgeber
education [ˌedʒʊˈkeɪʃn] - die Ausbildung
eight [eɪt] - acht
eighth [eɪtθ] - achter
either of you [ˈaɪðər əv ju] - einer von euch
elder [ˈeldə] - älter
electric [ɪˈlektrɪk] - elektrisch
eleven [ɪˈlevn] - elf
else [els] - andere
e-mail [ˈiːmeɪl] - die E-Mail
employer [ɪmˈplɔɪə] - der Arbeitgeber
energy [ˈenədʒi] - die Energie
engine [ˈendʒɪn] - der Motor
engineer [ˌendʒɪˈnɪə] - der Ingenieur
enjoy [ɪnˈdʒɔɪ] - Spaß haben, genießen
especially [ɪˈspeʃəli] - vor allem
estimate [ˈestɪmeɪt] - beurteilen
estimated [ˈestɪmeɪtɪd] - ausgewertet
etc. [etˈsetrə] - usw.
evening [ˈiːvnɪŋ] - der Abend
every [ˈevri] - jeder, jede, jedes
everybody [ˈevrɪˌbɔdi] - alle
everything [ˈevrɪθɪŋ] - alles
example [ɪgˈzɑːmpl] - das Beispiel
excuse [ɪkˈskjuːz] - sich entschuldigen
Excuse me. [ɪkˈskjuːz miː] - Entschuldigen Sie.
experience [ɪkˈspɪərɪəns] - die Erfahrung
explain [ɪkˈspleɪn] - erklären

eye [aɪ] - das Auge
eyes [aɪz] - die Augen
face [feɪs] - das Gesicht
fall [fɔ:l] - fallen
fell [fel] - fiel
fall [fɔ:l] - der Fall
fallen [ˈfɔ:lən] - abgestürzt
falling [ˈfɔ:lɪŋ] - fallend
family [ˈfæməli] - die Familie
far [ˈfɑ:] - weit
farm [fɑ:m] - der Bauernhof
farmer [ˈfɑ:mə] - der Bauer
fasten [ˈfɑ:sn] - anschnallen
favourite [ˈfeɪvərɪt] - Lieblings-
favourite film [ˈfeɪvərɪt fɪlm] - der Lieblingsfilm
feed [fi:d] - füttern
feeling [ˈfi:lɪŋ] - das Gefühl
female [ˈfi:meɪl] - weiblich
few [fju:] - ein paar
field [fi:ld] - das Feld
fifteen [ˌfɪfˈti:n] - fünfzehn
fifth [ˈfɪfθ] - fünfter
fill up [fɪl ʌp] - füllen
film [fɪlm] - der Film
finance [ˈfaɪnæns] - die Finanzwissenschaft
find [faɪnd] - finden
fine [faɪn] - gut
finish [ˈfɪnɪʃ] - das Ende; beenden
finished [ˈfɪnɪʃt] - fertig
fire [ˈfaɪə] - das Feuer
fire [ˈfaɪə] - feuern
firm [fɜ:m] - die Firma
firms [fɜ:mz] - die Firmen
five [faɪv] - fünf
flew away [flu: əˈweɪ] - flog weg
float [fləʊt] - treiben
floating [ˈfləʊtɪŋ] - treibend
floor [flɔ:] - der Boden
flow [fləʊ] - der Fluss
flower [ˈflaʊə] - die Blume
fluently [ˈflu:əntli] - fließend
food [fu:d] - das Essen
foot [fʊt] - der Fuß
on foot [ɒn fʊt] - zu Fuß
for [fɔ:] - für
forget [fəˈget] - vergessen
forgot [fəˈgɒt] - vergaß

form [ˈfɔ:m] - das Formular
forty-four [ˈfɔ:ti fɔ:] - vierundvierzig
found [faʊnd] - gefunden
four [fɔ:] - vier
fourth [ˈfɔ:θ] - vierte
free [fri:] - frei
free time [fri: taɪm] - die Freizeit, freie Zeit
freeze [fri:z] - erstarren
friend [ˈfrend] - der Freund
friendly [ˈfrendli] - freundlich
from [frɒm] - aus
from the USA [frəm ðə ˌju:ˌesˈeɪ] - aus den USA
front [frʌnt] - vorn
front wheels [frʌnt ˈwi:lz] - die Vorderräder
full [fʊl] - voll
fun [fʌn] - der Spaß
funny [ˈfʌni] - lustig
furniture [ˈfɜ:nɪtʃə] - die Möbel
further [ˈfɜ:ðə] - weiter
future [ˈfju:tʃə] - zukünftig
garden [ˈgɑ:dn] - der Garten
gas [gæs] - das Gas
gave [geɪv] - gab
German [ˈdʒɜ:mən] - der Deutsche, die Deutsche
Germany [ˈdʒɜ:məni] - Deutschland
get (something) [ˈget ˈsʌmθɪŋ] - (etwas) erhalten, bekommen
get (somewhere) [ˈget ˈsʌmweə] - ankommen
get off [ˈget ɒf] - aussteigen
get up [ˈget ʌp] - aufstehen
Get up! [ˈget ʌp] - Steh auf!
gift [gɪft] - die Begabung
girl [gɜ:l] - das Mädchen
girlfriend [ˈgɜ:lfrend] - die Freundin
glad [glæd] - froh
glass [ˈglɑ:s] - das Glas
go away [gəʊ əˈweɪ] - weggehen
go by bike, to ride a bike [gəʊ baɪ baɪk | tə raɪd ə baɪk] - Fahrrad fahren, mit dem Fahrrad fahren
gone [gɒn] - weg
good, well [gʊd | wel] - gut
goodbye [ˌgʊdˈbaɪ] - Auf Wiedersehen
great [ˈgreɪt] - super, toll
green [ˈgri:n] - grün
grey [greɪ] - grau

grey-headed [greɪ 'hedɪd] - grauhaarig
guest [gest] - der Gast
gun [gʌn] - die Waffe
guy [gaɪ] - der Junge
had [hæd] - hatte
hair [heə] - das Haar
half [hɑːf] - halb
hand [hænd] - geben
handcuffs ['hændkʌfs] - die Handschellen
happen ['hæpən] - passieren
happened ['hæpənd] - passiert
happiness ['hæpinəs] - das Glück
happy ['hæpi] - glücklich
hard [hɑːd] - schwer
hat [hæt] - der Hut
hate [heɪt] - hassen
have [hæv] - haben
he/she/it has [hi ʃi ɪt hæz] - er/sie/es hat
He has a book. [hi həz ə bʊk] - Er hat ein Buch.
have a lot of work [həv ə lɔt əv 'wɜːk] - viel zu tun haben
he [hi] - er
head [hed] - der Kopf
head, go [hed | gəʊ] - gehen
health [helθ] - die Gesundheit
heard [hɜːd] - hörte
hello [həˈləʊ] - hallo
help [help] - die Hilfe
help [help] - helfen
helper ['helpə] - der Helfer
her book [hə bʊk] - ihr Buch
here (a place) [hɪər ə 'pleɪs] - hier (Ort)
here (a direction) [hɪər ə dɪ'rekʃn] - hierher (Richtung)
here is [hɪə ɪz] - hier ist
Hey! [heɪ] - Hey
hi [haɪ] - hallo
hid [hɪd] - versteckte
hide [haɪd] - sich verstecken
hide-and-seek [ˌhaɪd n 'siːk] - das Versteckspiel
high [haɪ] - hoch
him [hɪm] - ihm
his [hɪz] - sein, seine
his bed [hɪz bed] - sein Bett
hit, beat [hɪt | biːt] - schlagen
home [həʊm] - das Zuhause

homework ['həʊmwɜːk] - die Hausaufgaben
hope [həʊp] - die Hoffnung
hope [həʊp] - hoffen
host [həʊst] - der Gastgeber
host family [həʊst 'fæməli] - die Gastfamilie
hotel [ˌhəʊ'tel] - das Hotel
hotels [ˌhəʊ'telz] - die Hotels
hour ['aʊə] - die Stunde
hourly ['aʊəli] - stündlich
house ['haʊs] - das Haus
how ['haʊ] - wie
howling ['haʊlɪŋ] - heulend
human ['hjuːmən] - der Mensch
hundred ['hʌndrəd] - hundert
hungry ['hʌŋgri] - hungrig
I ['aɪ] - ich
ice-cream [aɪs 'kriːm] - das Eis
idea [aɪ'dɪə] - die Idee
if [ɪf] - ob
immediately [ɪ'miːdiətli] - sofort
important [ɪm'pɔːtnt] - wichtig
in [ɪn] - in
incorrectly [ˌɪnkə'rektli] - falsch
individually [ˌɪndɪ'vɪdʒʊəli] - einzeln
inform [ɪn'fɔːm] - informieren, mitteilen
information [ˌɪnfə'meɪʃn] - die Information, die Angabe
informed [ɪn'fɔːmd] - informierte
inside [ɪn'saɪd] - in
instead [ɪn'sted] - stattdessen
instead of [ɪn'sted əv] - anstelle von
instead of you [ɪn'sted əv ju] - an deiner Stelle
interesting ['ɪntrəstɪŋ] - interessant
Internet site ['ɪntənet saɪt] - die Website
into ['ɪntə] - in
it [ɪt] - es
its (for neuter) [ɪts fə 'njuːtə] - sein
jacket ['dʒækɪt] - die Jacke
jar [dʒɑː] - der Krug
job [dʒɔb] - die Arbeit
job agency [dʒɔb 'eɪdʒənsi] - die Arbeitsvermittlung
join [dʒɔɪn] - kommen in
journalist ['dʒɜːnəlɪst] - der Journalist
jump [dʒʌmp] - springen
jump [dʒʌmp] - der Sprung
just [dʒəst] - einfach
kangaroo [ˌkæŋgə'ruː] - das Känguru

kettle ['ketl] - der Kessel
key [kiː] - der Schlüssel
keyboard ['kiːbɔːd] - die Tastatur
killed [kɪld] - tötete, getötet
killer ['kɪlə] - der Mörder
kilometer [kəˈlɑːmətə] - der Kilometer
kind, type [kaɪnd | taɪp] - die Art
kindergarten ['kɪndəgɑːtn] - der Kindergarten
kiss [kɪs] - küssen
kitchen ['kɪtʃɪn] - die Küche
kitten ['kɪtn] - das Kätzchen
knew [njuː] - wusste
know [nəʊ] - kennen
know each other [nəʊ iːtʃ 'ʌðə] - sich kennen
lake [leɪk] - der See
land [lænd] - landen
language ['læŋgwɪdʒ] - die Sprache
laser ['leɪzə] - der Laser
last, take [lɑːst | teɪk] - dauern
laugh [lɑːf] - lachen
leader ['liːdə] - der Führer
learn [lɜːn] - lernen
learned about [lɜːnd əˈbaʊt] - kennengelernt
learning ['lɜːnɪŋ] - lernen
leave [liːv] - verlassen
left [left] - links
leg [leg] - das Bein
less [les] - weniger
lesson ['lesn] - die Aufgabe, Lektion
let [let] - lassen
let us [let əz] - lass uns
letter ['letə] - der Brief
life [laɪf] - das Leben
life-saving trick ['laɪfˈseɪvɪŋ trɪk] - der Rettungstrick
lift [lɪft] - der Aufzug
like ['laɪk] - gefallen
like, love ['laɪk | 'lʌv] - mögen, lieben
limit ['lɪmɪt] - die Begrenzung
lion ['laɪən] - der Löwe
list [lɪst] - die Liste
listen ['lɪsn] - hören
little ['lɪtl] - klein
live [laɪv] - leben, wohnen
lived [lɪvd] - lebte
living ['lɪvɪŋ] - wohnhaft
load [ləʊd] - (be)laden
loader ['ləʊdə] - der Verlader

long ['lɔŋ] - lang
look [lʊk] - sehen, schauen, betrachten
look around [lʊk əˈraʊnd] - sich umsehen
looked [lʊkt] - sah, schaute
loose [luːs] - verlieren
lot [lɔt] - viel
love ['lʌv] - die Liebe
love ['lʌv] - lieben
loved ['lʌvd] - geliebt
machine [məˈʃiːn] - die Maschine
magazine [ˌmægəˈziːn] - die Zeitschrift
make ['meɪk] - machen
male [meɪl] - männlich
manual work ['mænjʊəl 'wɜːk] - die Handarbeit
many, much ['meni | 'mʌtʃ] - viel
map [mæp] - die Karte
mattress ['mætrɪs] - die Matratze
may [meɪ] - dürfen, können
must not [məst nɔt] - nicht dürfen
me [miː] - mich
meanwhile ['miːnwaɪl] - in der Zwischenzeit
medical ['medɪkl] - medizinisch
meet [miːt] - treffen, kennenlernen
member ['membə] - das Mitglied
men [men] - der Mann
mental work ['mentl 'wɜːk] - die Kopfarbeit
met [met] - getroffen, kennengelernt
metal ['metl] - das Metall
meter ['miːtə] - der Meter
method ['meθəd] - die Methode
microphone ['maɪkrəfəʊn] - das Mikrofon
middle name ['mɪdl 'neɪm] - der zweite Name
mine [maɪn] - mein
minute [maɪˈnjuːt] - die Minute
Miss [mɪs] - das Fräulein
mister, Mr. ['mɪstə | 'mɪstə] - Herr, Hr.
mobile ['məʊbaɪl] - das Handy
mom, mother [mɔm | 'mʌðə] - Mama, die Mutter
moment ['məʊmənt] - der Moment
Monday ['mʌndeɪ] - der Montag
money ['mʌni] - das Geld
monkey ['mʌŋki] - der Affe
monotonous [məˈnɔtənəs] - monoton
more [mɔː] - mehr
morning ['mɔːnɪŋ] - der Morgen
mosquito [məˈskiːtəʊ] - die Stechmücke

mother [ˈmʌðə] - die Mutter
moved [muːvd] - bewegte sich
much, many [ˈmʌtʃ | ˈmeni] - viel, viele
music [ˈmjuːzɪk] - die Musik
must [mʌst] - müssen
my [maɪ] - mein, meine, mein
mystery [ˈmɪstəri] - das Rätsel
name [ˈneɪm] - der Name
name [ˈneɪm] - nennen
nationality [ˌnæʃəˈnælɪti] - die Nationalität
native language [ˈneɪtɪv ˈlæŋgwɪdʒ] - die Muttersprache
nature [ˈneɪtʃə] - die Natur
nearest [ˈnɪərɪst] - nächste
nearness [ˈnɪənəs] - die Nähe
near, nearby, next [nɪə | ˈnɪəbaɪ | nekst] - in der Nähe
need [niːd] - brauchen
neighbour [ˈneɪbə] - der Nachbar
never [ˈnevə] - nie
new [njuː] - neu
newspaper [ˈnjuːspeɪpə] - die Zeitung
nice [naɪs] - schön
night [naɪt] - die Nacht
nine [naɪn] - neun
ninth [naɪnθ] - neunter
no [nəʊ] - nein
nobody [ˈnəʊbədi] - niemand
North America and Eurasia [nɔːθ əˈmerɪkə ənd jʊəˈreɪʒə] - Nordamerika und Eurasien
nose [nəʊz] - die Nase
not [nɒt] - nicht
note [nəʊt] - die Notiz
notebook [ˈnəʊtbʊk] - das Notizbuch
notebooks [ˈnəʊtbʊks] - die Notizbücher
nothing [ˈnʌθɪŋ] - nichts
now [naʊ] - jetzt, zurzeit, gerade
number [ˈnʌmbə] - die Nummer
o'clock [əˈklɒk] - Uhr
of course [əv kɔːs] - natürlich
office [ˈɒfɪs] - das Büro
officer, policeman [ˈɒfɪsə | pəˈliːsmən] - der Polizist
often [ˈɒfn] - oft
oil [ɔɪl] - das Öl
okay, well [ˌəʊˈkeɪ | wel] - okay, gut
on [ɒn] - auf
once [wʌns] - einmal

one [wʌn] - ein
one by one [wʌn baɪ wʌn] - einer nach dem anderen
one more [wʌn mɔː] - noch einen
only [ˈəʊnli] - nur
open [ˈəʊpən] - öffnen
opened [ˈəʊpənd] - öffnete, geöffnet
order [ˈɔːdə] - befehlen
other [ˈʌðə] - andere
our [ˈaʊə] - unser
out of order [ˈaʊt əv ˈɔːdə] - außer Betrieb
outdoors [ˌaʊtˈdɔːz] - draußen
over [ˈəʊvə] - über
own [əʊn] - eigener, eigene, eigenes
owner [ˈəʊnə] - der Besitzer
pail [peɪl] - der Eimer
pale [peɪl] - blass
panic [ˈpænɪk] - die Panik
paper [ˈpeɪpə] - das Papier
parachute [ˈpærəʃuːt] - der Fallschirm
parachutist [ˈpærəʃuːtɪst] - der Fallschirmspringer
parent [ˈpeərənt] - die Eltern
park [pɑːk] - der Park
parks [pɑːks] - die Parks
part [pɑːt] - der Teil
participant [pɑːˈtɪsɪpənt] - der Teilnehmer
passed [pɑːst] - abgelaufen
past [pɑːst] - nach, vorbei
patrol [pəˈtrəʊl] - die Patrouille, die Streife
pay [peɪ] - bezahlen, zahlen
paid [peɪd] - bezahlte, gezahlt
pen [pen] - der Stift
pens [penz] - die Stifte
people [ˈpiːpl] - die Menschen
per hour [pɜː ˈaʊə] - pro Stunde
person [ˈpɜːsn] - die Person
personal [ˈpɜːsənl] - persönlich
personnel department [ˌpɜːsəˈnel dɪˈpɑːtmənt] - die Personalabteilung
pet [pet] - das Haustier
pharmacy [ˈfɑːməsi] - die Apotheke
phone handset [fəʊn ˈhændset] - der Telefonhörer
phone, [fəʊn] - das Telefon
phone [fəʊn] - anrufen
photograph [ˈfəʊtəɡrɑːf] - fotografieren
photographer [fəˈtɒɡrəfə] - der Fotograf

phrase [freɪz] - der Satz
picture [ˈpɪktʃə] - das Foto
pill [pɪl] - die Tablette
pilot [ˈpaɪlət] - der Pilot
pitch [pɪtʃ] - schaukeln
place [ˈpleɪs] - legen
plan [plæn] - der Plan
plan [plæn] - planen
planet [ˈplænɪt] - der Planet
plate [pleɪt] - der Teller
play [ˈpleɪ] - spielen
playing [ˈpleɪɪŋ] - das Spielen
please [pliːz] - bitte
pocket [ˈpɒkɪt] - die Tasche
pointed [ˈpɔɪntɪd] - richtete
Poland [ˈpəʊlənd] - Polen
police [pəˈliːs] - die Polizei
poor [pʊə] - arm
position [pəˈzɪʃn] - die Position
possibility [ˌpɒsəˈbɪlɪti] - die Möglichkeit
possible [ˈpɒsəbl] - möglich
pour [pɔː] - schütten
prepare [prɪˈpeə] - vorbereiten
press [pres] - drücken
pretend [prɪˈtend] - vorgeben; so tun, als ob
price [praɪs] - der Preis
problem [ˈprɒbləm] - das Problem
produce [prəˈdjuːs] - herstellen
profession [prəˈfeʃn] - der Beruf
program [ˈprəʊɡræm] - das Programm
programmer [ˈprəʊɡræmə] - der Programmierer
protect [prəˈtekt] - beschützen
publishing [ˈpʌblɪʃɪŋ] - der Verlag
pull [pʊl] - ziehen
puppy [ˈpʌpi] - der Welpe
pursuit [pəˈsjuːt] - die Verfolgung
push [pʊʃ] - stoßen, ziehen
pussycat [ˈpʊsɪkæt] - die Miezekatze
put on [ˈpʊt ɒn] - sich anziehen
questionnaire [ˌkwestʃəˈneə] - der Fragebogen
queue [kjuː] - die Schlange
quick, quickly [kwɪk | ˈkwɪkli] - schnell
quietly [ˈkwaɪətli] - leise
quite [kwaɪt] - ziemlich
radar [ˈreɪdɑː] - der Radar
radio [ˈreɪdɪəʊ] - das Radio
railway station [ˈreɪlweɪ ˈsteɪʃn] - der Bahnhof

rain [reɪn] - der Regen
rang [ræŋ] - klingelte
rat [ræt] - die Ratte
read [riːd] - lesen
reading [ˈriːdɪŋ] - lesend
ready [ˈredi] - fertig
real [rɪəl] - wirklich
really [ˈrɪəli] - wirklich
reason [ˈriːzən] - der Grund
recommend [ˌrekəˈmend] - empfehlen
recommendation [ˌrekəmenˈdeɪʃn] - die Empfehlung
recommended [ˌrekəˈmendɪd] - empfohlen
record [rɪˈkɔːd] - aufnehmen
red [red] - rot
refuse [rɪˈfjuːz] - ablehnen
rehabilitate [ˌriːəˈbɪlɪteɪt] - gesund pflegen
rehabilitation [ˌriːəˌbɪlɪˈteɪʃn] - die Genesung, Rehabilitation
remain [rɪˈmeɪn] - bleiben
remembered [rɪˈmembəd] - erinnerte sich
report [rɪˈpɔːt] - berichten
reporter [rɪˈpɔːtə] - der Reporter
rescue [ˈreskjuː] - retten
rescue service [ˈreskjuː ˈsɜːvɪs] - der Rettungsdienst
ricochet [ˈrɪkəʃeɪ] - abprallen
right [raɪt] - rechts
ring [rɪŋ] - klingeln
ring [rɪŋ] - das Klingeln
road [rəʊd] - die Straße
robber [ˈrɒbə] - der Dieb
robbery [ˈrɒbəri] - der Diebstahl, der Überfall
roof [ruːf] - das Dach
room [ruːm] - das Zimmer
rooms [ruːmz] - die Zimmer
round [ˈraʊnd] - rund
rub [rʌb] - reiben
rubber [ˈrʌbə] - der Gummi
rubric [ˈruːbrɪk] - die Rubrik
rule [ruːl] - die Regel
run [rʌn] - rennen, joggen, laufen
run away [rʌn əˈweɪ] - weglaufen
running [ˈrʌnɪŋ] - führen
rushed [rʌʃt] - raste
sad [sæd] - traurig
safe [seɪf] - der Tresor
said [ˈsed] - sagte

sand [sænd] - der Sand
sandwich [ˈsænwɪdʒ] - das Butterbrot, das Sandwich
Saturday [ˈsætədeɪ] - der Samstag
save [seɪv] - retten
saw [ˈsɔː] - sahen
say [ˈseɪ] - sagen
school [skuːl] - die Schule
sea [siː] - das Meer
seashore [ˈsiːʃɔː] - die Küste
Season [ˈsiːzn] - die (Jahres)zeit
seat [siːt] - der Sitz
seat belts [siːt belts] - der Sicherheitsgurt
second [ˈsekənd] - zweiter
secret [ˈsiːkrɪt] - das Geheimnis
secretary [ˈsekrətəri] - die Sekretärin
secretly [ˈsiːkrɪtli] - heimlich
see [ˈsiː] - sehen
seed [siːd] - das Saatgut
seldom [ˈseldəm] - selten
sell [sel] - verkaufen
sent [sent] - schickte
sergeant [ˈsɑːdʒənt] - der Polizeihauptmeister
serial [ˈsɪərɪəl] - die Serie
seriously [ˈsɪərɪəsli] - ernst
servant [ˈsɜːvənt] - der Bedienstete
serve [sɜːv] - bedienen
set free [set friː] - freisetzen
seven [ˈsevn] - sieben
seventeen (hour) [ˌsevnˈtiːn ˈaʊə] - siebzehn
seventh [ˈsevnθ] - siebter
sex [seks] - das Geschlecht
shake [ʃeɪk] - zittern, schütteln
she [ʃi] - sie
sheet (of paper) [ʃiːt əv ˈpeɪpə] - das Blatt
ship [ʃɪp] - das Schiff
shook [ʃʊk] - wackelte
shop [ʃɔp] - der Laden
shop assistant [ʃɔp əˈsɪstənt] - der Verkäufer, die Verkäuferin
shopping center [ˈʃɔpɪŋ ˈsentə] - das Einkaufszentrum
shops [ʃɔps] - die Läden
shore [ʃɔː] - die Küste
short [ʃɔːt] - kurz
shot [ʃɔt] - schoss; angeschossen
show [ʃəʊ] - zeigen
showed [ʃəʊd] - zeigte

silent, silently [ˈsaɪlənt | ˈsaɪləntli] - leise
silly [ˈsɪli] - dumm
simple [ˈsɪmpl] - einfach
since [sɪns] - *(temporal)* seit; *(kausal)* da, weil
sing [sɪŋ] - singen
singer [ˈsɪŋə] - der Sänger
single [ˈsɪŋgl] - ledig
siren [ˈsaɪərən] - die Sirene
sister [ˈsɪstə] - die Schwester
sit [sɪt] - setzen
 sit down [sɪt daʊn] - sich hinsetzen
situation [ˌsɪtʃʊˈeɪʃn] - die Situation
six [sɪks] - sechs
sixth [sɪksθ] - sechster
sixty [ˈsɪksti] - sechzig
skill [skɪl] - die Fähigkeit
sleep [sliːp] - schlafen
sleeping [ˈsliːpɪŋ] - schlafen
slightly [ˈslaɪtli] - leicht
slowly [ˈsləʊli] - langsam
sly, slyly [slaɪ | ˈslaɪli] - schlau
small [smɔːl] - klein
smart [smɑːt] - intelligent
smile [smaɪl] - das Lächeln
 smile [smaɪl] - lächeln
smiled [smaɪld] - lächelte
snack [snæk] - der Imbiss
so [ˈsəʊ] - deswegen
solution, answer [səˈluːʃn | ˈɑːnsə] - die Lösung
some [sʌm] - ein paar, einige
somebody [ˈsʌmbədi] - jemand
something [ˈsʌmθɪŋ] - etwas
sometimes [ˈsʌmtaɪmz] - manchmal, ab und zu
son [sʌn] - der Sohn
soon [suːn] - bald
space [speɪs] - das Weltall
spaceship [ˈspeɪsʃɪp] - das Raumschiff
spaniel [ˈspænɪəl] - der Spaniel
Spanish [ˈspænɪʃ] - spanisch
speak [spiːk] - sprechen
speech [spiːtʃ] - die Rede
speed [spiːd] - die Geschwindigkeit
speed [spiːd] - rasen
 speeder [ˈspiːdə] - der Raser
spend [spend] - ausgeben, verwenden
sport [spɔːt] - der Sport
 sport shop [spɔːt ʃɔp] - das Sportgeschäft
 sport bike [spɔːt baɪk] - das Sportfahrrad

spread [spred] - übergreifen
square [skweə] - der Platz
stairs [steəz] - die Treppe
stand [stænd] - stehen
standard ['stændəd] - der Standard, Standard-
star [stɑ:] - der Stern
start [stɑ:t] - anfangen
started (to drive) ['stɑ:tɪd tə draɪv] - fuhr los
status ['steɪtəs] - der Stand
steal [sti:l] - stehlen
steer [stɪə] - lenken
step [step] - der Schritt
step [step] - treten
stepped [stept] - trat
still [stɪl] - noch, weiterhin
stinking ['stɪŋkɪŋ] - stinkend
stolen ['stəʊlən] - gestohlen
stone [stəʊn] - der Stein
stop [stɔp] - anhalten
stopped [stɔpt] - beendete
story ['stɔ:ri] - die Geschichte
strange [streɪndʒ] - fremd
streets [stri:ts] - die Straßen
strength [streŋθ] - die Stärke
strong, strongly [strɔŋ | 'strɔŋli] - stark
student ['stju:dnt] - der Student
students ['stju:dnts] - die Studenten
study ['stʌdi] - studieren
stuffed [stʌft] - ausgestopft
stuffed parachutist [stʌft 'pærəʃu:tɪst] - Fallschirmspringerpuppe
suddenly [sʌdnli] - plötzlich
suitable ['su:təbl] - passend
supermarket ['su:pəmɑ:kɪt] - der Supermarkt
sure [ʃʊə] - klar, sicher
surprise [sə'praɪz] - die Überraschung
surprise [sə'praɪz] - überraschen
surprised [sə'praɪzd] - überrascht, verwundert
swallow ['swɔləʊ] - schlucken, hinunterschlucken
swim [swɪm] - schwimmen
switched on [swɪtʃt ɔn] - machte an
table ['teɪbl] - der Tisch
tables ['teɪblz] - die Tische
tail [teɪl] - der Schwanz
take [teɪk] - nehmen
take part [teɪk pɑ:t] - teilnehmen
taken ['teɪkən] - gebracht

talk ['tɔ:k] - sich unterhalten
tanker ['tæŋkə] - der Tanker
tap [tæp] - der Wasserhahn
task [tɑ:sk] - die Aufgabe
tasty ['teɪsti] - lecker
taxi ['tæksi] - das Taxi
taxi driver ['tæksi 'draɪvə] - der Taxifahrer
tea [ti:] - der Tee
teach [ti:tʃ] - beibringen
teacher ['ti:tʃə] - der Lehrer
team [ti:m] - die Mannschaft
telephone ['telɪfəʊn] - das Telefon
telephone ['telɪfəʊn] - telefonieren
television ['telɪˌvɪʒn] - der Fernseher
tell, say [tel | 'seɪ] - sagen
ten [ten] - zehn
tenth [tenθ] - zehnter
test ['test] - die Prüfung
test ['test] - prüfen
pass a test [pɑ:s ə 'test] - eine Prüfung bestehen
text [tekst] - der Text
textbook ['teksbʊk] - das Fachbuch
than [ðæn] - als
thank [θæŋk] - danken
thank you, thanks [θæŋk ju | θæŋks] - danke
that [ðæt] - jener, jene, jenes
that (conj) [ðət] - dass
the same [ðə seɪm] - der/die/das Gleiche
their [ðeə] - ihr
then [ðen] - dann
there [ðeə] - dort
these, those [ði:z | ðəʊz] - diese
they ['ðeɪ] - sie
thief [θi:f] - der Dieb
thieves [θi:vz] - die Diebe
thing ['θɪŋ] - das Ding, die Sache
this stuff [ðɪs stʌf] - diese Dinge
think ['θɪŋk] - denken
third ['θɜ:d] - dritter
thirty ['θɜ:ti] - dreißig
this [ðɪs] - dieser, diese, dieses
this book [ðɪs bʊk] - dieses Buch
thousand ['θaʊznd] - tausend
three [θri:] - drei
through [θru:] - hindurch
ticket ['tɪkɪt] - die Fahrkarte
tiger ['taɪgə] - der Tiger

time ['taɪm] - die Zeit
tired ['taɪəd] - müde
today [tə'deɪ] - heute
together [tə'geðə] - zusammen
toilet ['tɔɪlɪt] - die Toilette
tomorrow [tə'mɔrəʊ] - morgen
too, either, also [tu: | 'aɪðə | 'ɔ:lsəʊ] - auch
took [tʊk] - nahm
town [taʊn] - die Stadt
toy [tɔɪ] - das Spielzeug
train [treɪn] - der Zug
train [treɪn] - trainieren
trained [treɪnd] - trainiert
translator [trænz'leɪtə] - der Übersetzer
transport [træns'pɔ:t] - der Transport
travel ['trævl] - reisen
trick [trɪk] - der Trick
trousers ['traʊzəz] - die Hose
truck [trʌk] - der Lastwagen
try ['traɪ] - versuchen
tried ['traɪd] - versuchte
turn [tɜ:n] - drehen
turn on [tɜ:n ɔn] - anmachen
turn off [tɜ:n ɔf] - ausmachen
turned [tɜ:nd] - drehte
TV-set [ˌti:'vi: set] - der Fernseher
twelve [twelv] - zwölf
twenty ['twenti] - zwanzig
twenty-five ['twenti faɪv] - fünfundzwanzig
twenty-one ['twenti wʌn] - einundzwanzig
twice [twaɪs] - zweimal
two ['tu:] - zwei
unconscious [ʌn'kɔnʃəs] - bewusstlos
under ['ʌndə] - unter
underline [ˌʌndə'laɪn] - unterstreichen
understand [ˌʌndə'stænd] - verstehen
understood [ˌʌndə'stʊd] - verstanden
unfair [ˌʌn'feə] - ungerecht
United States/the USA [ju'naɪtɪd steɪts ðə ˌjuːˌes'eɪ] - die Vereinigten Staaten, die USA
unload [ʌn'ləʊd] - abladen
until [ʌn'tɪl] - bis
us [əz] - uns
use ['ju:s] - benutzen
usual ['ju:ʒʊəl] - normal, gewöhnlich
usually ['ju:ʒəli] - normalerweise
very ['veri] - sehr
vet [vet] - der Tierarzt

videocassette ['vɪdiokæˌset] - die Videokassette
video-shop ['vɪdɪəʊ ʃɔp] - die Videothek
village ['vɪlɪdʒ] - das Dorf
visit ['vɪzɪt] - besuchen
visited ['vɪzɪtɪd] - besuchte
voice [vɔɪs] - die Stimme
wait [weɪt] - warten
waited ['weɪtɪd] - wartete
walk [wɔ:k] - gehen
walking ['wɔ:kɪŋ] - laufen
want [wɔnt] - wollen
wanted ['wɔntɪd] - wollte
war [wɔ:] - der Krieg
warm [wɔ:m] - warm
warm up [wɔ:m ʌp] - aufwärmen
was [wɔz] - war
wash [wɔʃ] - waschen, putzen
washer ['wɔʃə] - die Waschmaschine
watch [wɔtʃ] - die Uhr
water ['wɔ:tə] - das Wasser
wave [weɪv] - die Welle
way ['weɪ] - der Weg
we [wi] - wir
weather ['weðə] - das Wetter
week [wi:k] - die Woche
were [wɜ:] - waren
wet [wet] - nass
whale [weɪl] - der Wal
what ['wɔt] - was
What is this? ['wɔt s ðɪs] - Was ist das?
What table? ['wɔt 'teɪbl] - Welcher Tisch?
What is the matter? ['wɔt s ðə 'mætə] - Was ist los?
wheel ['wi:l] - das Rad
when [wen] - wenn
where [weə] - wo
which [wɪtʃ] - der, die, das (Konj.)
while [waɪl] - während
white [waɪt] - weiß
who [hu:] - wer
whose [hu:z] - wessen
wide, widely [waɪd | 'waɪdli] - weit
will [wɪl] - werden
wind [wɪnd] - der Wind
window ['wɪndəʊ] - das Fenster
windows ['wɪndəʊz] - die Fenster
with [wɪð] - mit

without [wɪðˈaʊt] - ohne
 without a word [wɪðˈaʊt ə ˈwɜːd] - wortlos
woman [ˈwʊmən] - die Frau
wonderful [ˈwʌndəfəl] - wunderbar
word [ˈwɜːd] - das Wort, die Vokabel
words [ˈwɜːdz] - die Wörter, die Vokabeln
worked [ˈwɜːkt] - gearbeitet
worker [ˈwɜːkə] - der Arbeiter
working [ˈwɜːkɪŋ] - arbeitend
world [wɜːld] - die Welt
worry [ˈwʌri] - sich Sorgen machen
write [ˈraɪt] - schreiben
writer [ˈraɪtə] - der Schriftsteller
wrote [rəʊt] - schrieb

yard [jɑːd] - der Hof
year [ˈjiə] - das Jahr
yellow [ˈjeləʊ] - gelb
yes [jes] - ja
yesterday [ˈjestədi] - gestern
yet [jet] - noch
you [ju] - du/ihr
young [jʌŋ] - jung
your [jə] - dein
yours sincerely [jɔːz sɪnˈsɪəli] - hochachtungsvoll
zebra [ˈzebrə] - das Zebra
zoo [zuː] - der Zoo

Wörterbuch Deutsch-Englisch

Abend, der - evening [ˈiːvnɪŋ]
Abenteuer, das - adventure [ədˈventʃə]
aber - but [bʌt]
abgelaufen - passed [pɑːst]
abgestürzt - fallen [ˈfɔːlən]
abladen - to unload [tu ʌnˈləʊd]
ablehnen - to refuse [tə rɪˈfjuːz]
abprallen - ricochet [ˈrɪkəʃeɪ]
acht - eight [eɪt]
achter - eighth [eɪtθ]
Adresse, die - address [əˈdres]
Affe, der - monkey [ˈmʌŋki]
Agentur, die - agency [ˈeɪdʒənsi]
Alarm, der - alarm [əˈlɑːm]
alle - all, everybody [ɔːl | ˈevrɪˌbɔdi]
alles - everything [ˈevrɪθɪŋ]
als - than [ðæn]
älter - elder [ˈeldə]
Alter, das - age [eɪdʒ]
am, beim - at [æt]
Amerikaner - American [əˈmerɪkən]
andere - other [ˈʌðə]
anderer - another [əˈnʌðə]
ändern - to change, [tə tʃeɪndʒ]
die Änderung - change [tʃeɪndʒ]
anfangen - to begin [tə bɪˈgɪn]
angekommen - arrived [əˈraɪvd]
ängstlich - afraid [əˈfreɪd]
anhalten - to stop [tə stɔp]
ankommen - to arrive, to get (somewhere) [tu əˈraɪv | tə ˈget ˈsʌmweə]
Anrufbeantworter, der - answering machine [ˈɑːnsərɪŋ məʃiːn]
anrufen - to call on the phone; [tə kɔːl ɔn ðə fəʊn]
rufen - call [kɔːl]
Callcenter, das - call centre [kɔːl ˈsentə]
anschnallen - fasten [ˈfɑːsn]
anstelle von - instead of [ɪnˈsted ɔv]
an deiner Stelle - instead of you [ɪnˈsted əv ju]
Antwort, die - answer [ˈɑːnsə]
antworten - to answer [tu ˈɑːnsə]
Anzeige, die - advert [ˈædvɜːt]
Apotheke, die - pharmacy [ˈfɑːməsi]
Arbeit, die - job [dʒɔb]
arbeitend - working [ˈwɜːkɪŋ]
Arbeiter, der - worker [ˈwɜːkə]
Arbeitgeber, der - employer [ɪmˈplɔɪə]
Arbeitsvermittlung, die - job agency [dʒɔb ˈeɪdʒənsi]
ärgern - to bother [tə ˈbɔðə]
arm - poor [pʊə]
Arm, der - arm [ɑːm]
Art, die - kind, type [kaɪnd | taɪp]
Arzt, der - doctor [ˈdɔktə]
Aspirin, das - aspirin [ˈæsprɪn]
auch - as well, also, either, too [əz wel | ˈɔːlsəʊ | ˈaɪðə | tuː]
auf - on [ɔn]
Auf Wiedersehen - goodbye [ˌɡʊdˈbaɪ]
Aufgabe, die - task [tɑːsk]
Aufmerksamkeit, die - attention [əˈtenʃn]
achten auf - pay attention to [peɪ əˈtenʃn tuː]
aufnehmen - to record [tə rɪˈkɔːd]
aufstehen - to get up [tə ˈget ʌp]
Aufzug der - lift [lɪft]
Auge, das - eye [aɪ]
Augen, die - eyes [aɪz]
aus - from [frɔm]
aus den USA - from the USA [frəm ðə ˌjuːˌesˈeɪ]
Ausbildung, die - education [ˌedʊˈkeɪʃn]
ausgeben, verwenden - to spend [tə spend]
ausgestopft - stuffed [stʌft]
ausgewertet - estimated [ˈestɪmeɪtɪd]
Ausschreibung, die, Wettbewerb der - competition [ˌkɔmpəˈtɪʃn]
außer Betrieb - out of order [ˈaʊt əv ˈɔːdə]
Außerirdische, der - alien [ˈeɪliən]
aussteigen - to get off [tə ˈget ɔf]
auswählen, entscheiden für - to choose [tə tʃuːz]
Auto, das - car [kɑː]
Bad, das; Badezimmer, das - bathroom; [ˈbɑːθruːm]
Badewanne, die - bath [bɑːθ]
Badezimmertisch, der - bathroom table [ˈbɑːθruːm ˈteɪbl]
Bahnhof, der - railway station [ˈreɪlweɪ ˈsteɪʃn]
bald - soon [suːn]
Bank, die - bank [bæŋk]
Bargeld, das - cash [kæʃ]

Bauer, der - farmer [ˈfɑːmə]
Bauernhof, der - farm [fɑːm]
bedienen - to serve [tə sɜːv]
Bedienstete, der - servant [ˈsɜːvənt]
beendete - stopped [stɔpt]
befehlen - to order [tu ˈɔːdə]
Begabung, die - gift [ɡɪft]
begann - began [bɪˈɡæn]
begleiten - to accompany [tu əˈkʌmpəni]
begleitet - accompanied [əˈkʌmpənid]
Begrenzung, die - limit [ˈlɪmɪt]
beibringen - to teach [tə tiːtʃ]
Bein, das - leg [leɡ]
Beispiel, das - example [ɪɡˈzɑːmpl]
beißen - to bite [tə baɪt]
bekommen - to get [tə ˈɡet]
beladen - to load [tə ləʊd]
bellte - barked [bɑːkt]
benutzen - to use [tə ˈjuːz]
beraten - to consult [tə kənˈsʌlt]
Berater, der - consultant [kənˈsʌltənt]
Beratung, die - consultancy [kənˈsʌltənsi]
berichten - to report [tə rɪˈpɔːt]
Beruf, der - profession [prəˈfeʃn]
beschützen - to protect [tə prəˈtekt]
Besitzer, der - owner [ˈəʊnə]
besser - better [ˈbetə]
beständig - constant [ˈkɔnstənt]
besuchte - visited [ˈvɪzɪtɪd]
Bett, das - bed [bed]
Betten, die - beds [ˈbedz]
beurteilen - to estimate [tu ˈestɪmeɪt]
bewegte sich - moved [muːvd]
bewusstlos - unconscious [ʌnˈkɔnʃəs]
bezahlen, zahlen - to pay [tə peɪ]
bezahlte, gezahlt - paid [peɪd]
bis - until [ʌnˈtɪl]
bitte - please [pliːz]
bitten, fragen - to ask [tu ɑːsk]
blass - pale [peɪl]
Blatt, das - sheet [ʃiːt]
blau - blue [bluː]
bleiben - to remain [tə rɪˈmeɪn]
Blume, die - flower [ˈflaʊə]
Boden, der - floor [flɔː]
brauchen - need [niːd]
Bremse, die - brake [breɪk]
bremsen - to brake [tə breɪk]

Brief, der - letter [ˈletə]
bringen - to bring [tə brɪŋ]
Brot, das - bread [bred]
Brücke, die - bridge [brɪdʒ]
Bruder, der - brother [ˈbrʌðə]
Buch, das - book [bʊk]
Bücherregal, das - bookcase [ˈbʊk keɪs]
Büro, das - office [ˈɔfɪs]
Bus, der - bus [bʌs]
mit dem Bus fahren - to go by bus [tə ɡəʊ baɪ bʌs]
Butter, die - butter [ˈbʌtə]
Butterbrot, das - sandwich [ˈsænwɪdʒ]
Café, das - café [ˈkæfeɪ]
CD, die - CD [ˌsiːˈdiː]
CD-Spieler, der - CD player [ˌsiːdiːˈpleɪə]
Chance, die - chance [tʃɑːns]
Chemie, die - chemistry [ˈkemɪstri]
chemisch - chemical [ˈkemɪkl]
Chemikalien, die - chemicals [ˈkemɪklz]
Computer, der - computer [kəmˈpjuːtə]
da, weil - since, as [sɪns | æz]
Dach, das - roof [ruːf]
danken - to thank [tə θæŋk]
danke - thank you, thanks [θæŋk ju | θæŋks]
dann - then [ðen]
danach - after that [ˈɑːftə ðæt]
dass - that [ðæt]
Datum, das - date [deɪt]
dauern - to last, to take [tə lɑːst | tə teɪk]
dein - your [jə]
denken - to think [tə ˈθɪŋk]
der, die, das (Konj.) - which [wɪtʃ]
der/die/das Gleiche - the same [ðə seɪm]
Design, das - design [dɪˈzaɪn]
deswegen - so [ˈsəʊ]
Deutsche, der; Deutsche, die - German [ˈdʒɜːmən]
Deutschland - Germany [ˈdʒɜːməni]
Dieb, der - thief, robber [θiːf | ˈrɔbə]
Diebe, die - thieves [θiːvz]
Diebstahl, der - robbery [ˈrɔbəri]
diese (Pl.) - these, those [ðiːz | ðəʊz]
dieser, diese, dieses (Sg.) - this, that [ðɪs | ðæt]
dieses Buch - this book [ðɪs bʊk]
Ding, das; Sache, die - thing [ˈθɪŋ]
diese Dinge - this stuff [ðɪs stʌf]
Dorf, das - village [ˈvɪlɪdʒ]

dort - there [ðeə]
draußen - outdoors [ˌaʊtˈdɔːz]
dreckig - dirty [ˈdɜːti]
drehen - to turn [tə tɜːn]
drehte - turned [tɜːnd]
drei - three [θriː]
dreißig - thirty [ˈθɜːti]
dritter - third [ˈθɜːd]
drücken - to press [tə pres]
du/ihr - you [ju]
dumm - silly [ˈsɪli]
dunkel - dark [dɑːk]
dürfen, können - may [meɪ]
DVD, die - DVD [ˌdiviˈdiː]
eigener, eigene, eigenes - own [əʊn]
Eimer, der - pail [peɪl]
ein - one [wʌn]
ein paar - some, a pair [sʌm | ə peə]
einer nach dem anderen - one by one [wʌn baɪ wʌn]
einer von euch - either of you [ˈaɪðər əv ju]
einfach - just; simple [dʒʌst | ˈsɪmpl]
einige - some [sʌm]
Einkaufszentrum, das - shopping center [ˈʃɔpɪŋ ˈsentə]
einmal - once [wʌns]
einundzwanzig - twenty-one [ˈtwenti wʌn]
einverstanden sein - to agree [tu əˈgriː]
einzeln - individually [ˌɪndɪˈvɪdʒʊəli]
Eis, das - ice-cream [aɪs ˈkriːm]
elektrisch - electric [ɪˈlektrɪk]
elf - eleven [ɪˈlevn]
Eltern, die - parent [ˈpeərənt]
E-Mail, die - e-mail [ˈiːmeɪl]
empfehlen - to recommend; [tə ˌrekəˈmend]
Empfehlung, die - recommendation [ˌrekəmenˈdeɪʃn]
empfohlen - recommended [ˌrekəˈmendɪd]
Ende, das - finish [ˈfɪnɪʃ]
Energie, die - energy [ˈenədʒi]
entlang - along [əˈlɔŋ]
entwerfen, verfassen - to compose [tə kəmˈpəʊz]
entwickeln - to develop [tə dɪˈveləp]
Entwurf, der; Text, der - composition [ˌkɔmpəˈzɪʃn]
er - he [hi]
er kam, gekommen - came [keɪm]

Erde, die - earth [ɜːθ]
Erfahrung, die - experience [ɪkˈspɪərɪəns]
erhalten (etwas) - to get (something) [tə ˈget ˈsʌmθɪŋ]
erinnerte sich - remembered [rɪˈmembəd]
erklären - to explain [tu ɪkˈspleɪn]
ernst - seriously [ˈsɪərɪəsli]
erst - at first [ət ˈfɜːst]
erstarren - to freeze [tə friːz]
erwidern - answer [ˈɑːnsə]
es - it [ɪt]
essen - to eat [tu iːt]
Essen, das - food [fuːd]
etwa - about [əˈbaʊt]
etwas - something, anything [ˈsʌmθɪŋ | ˈenɪθɪŋ]
Fachbuch, das - textbook [ˈteksbʊk]
Fähigkeit, die - skill [skɪl]
fahren - to drive [tə draɪv]
Fahrer, der - driver [ˈdraɪvə]
Fahrkarte, die - ticket [ˈtɪkɪt]
Fahrrad, das - bike [baɪk]
Fahrrad fahren, mit dem Fahrrad fahren - to go by bike, to ride a bike [tə gəʊ baɪ baɪk | tə raɪd ə baɪk]
fallen - to fall [tə fɔːl]
fiel - fell [fel]
Fall, der - fall [fɔːl]
fallend - falling [ˈfɔːlɪŋ]
Fallschirm, der - parachute [ˈpærəʃuːt]
Fallschirmspringer, der - parachutist [ˈpærəʃuːtɪst]
Familie, die - family [ˈfæməli]
fangen - to catch [tə kætʃ]
Feier, die - ceremony [ˈserɪməni]
Feld, das - field [fiːld]
Fenster, das - window [ˈwɪndəʊ]
Fenster, die - windows [ˈwɪndəʊz]
Fernseher, der - TV-set [ˌtiːˈviː set]
fertig - finished; ready [ˈfɪnɪʃt | ˈredi]
Feuer, das - fire [ˈfaɪə]
feuern - to fire [tə ˈfaɪə]
Film, der - film [fɪlm]
Finanzwissenschaft, die - finance [ˈfaɪnæns]
finden - to find [tə faɪnd]
Firma, die - firm [fɜːm]
Firmen, die - firms [fɜːmz]
fließend - fluently [ˈfluːəntli]
flog weg - flew away [fluː əˈweɪ]

Flugschau, die - airshow [ˈeəʃəʊ]
Flugzeug, das - airplane [ˈeəpleɪn]
Fluss, der - to flow [tə fləʊ]
Formular, das - form [ˈfɔːm]
fortführen - to continue [tə kənˈtɪnjuː]
Fortsetzung folgt - to be continued [tə bi kənˈtɪnjuːd]
Foto, das - picture [ˈpɪktʃə]
fotografieren - to photograph [tə ˈfəʊtəgrɑːf]
Fotograf, der - photographer [fəˈtɔgrəfə]
Fragebogen, der - questionnaire [ˌkwestʃəˈneə]
Frau, die - woman [ˈwʊmən]
Fräulein, das - Miss [mɪs]
frei - free [friː]
Freizeit, die; freie Zeit, die - free time [friː ˈtaɪm]
freisetzen - to set free [tə set friː]
fremd - strange [streɪndʒ]
Freund, der - friend [ˈfrend]
Freundin, die - girlfriend [ˈgɜːlfrend]
freundlich - friendly [ˈfrendli]
froh - glad [glæd]
Frühstück, das - breakfast [ˈbrekfəst]
frühstücken - to have breakfast [tə həv ˈbrekfəst]
fuhr - drove [drəʊv]
fuhr los - started to drive [ˈstɑːtɪd tə draɪv]
führen - running [ˈrʌnɪŋ]
Führer, der - leader [ˈliːdə]
Führerschein, der - driving license [ˈdraɪvɪŋ ˈlaɪsns]
füllen - to fill up [tə fɪl ʌp]
fünf - five [faɪv]
fünfter - fifth [ˈfɪfθ]
fünfundzwanzig - twenty-five [ˈtwenti faɪv]
fünfzehn - fifteen [ˌfɪfˈtiːn]
für - for [fɔː]
Fuß, der - foot [fʊt]
zu Fuß - on foot [ɔn fʊt]
füttern - to feed [tə fiːd]
gab - gave [geɪv]
Garten, der - garden [ˈgɑːdn]
Gas, das - gas [gæs]
Gast, der - guest [gest]
Gastgeber, der - host [həʊst]
geantwortet - answered [ˈɑːnsəd]
gearbeitet - worked [ˈwɜːkt]
geben - to hand [tə hænd]

gebracht - taken [ˈteɪkən]
gefallen - to like [tə ˈlaɪk]
gefragt - asked [ˈɑːskt]
Gefühl, das - feeling [ˈfiːlɪŋ]
gefunden - found [faʊnd]
gegen - against [əˈgenst]
Geheimnis, das - secret [ˈsiːkrɪt]
gehen - to walk [tə wɔːk]
gelb - yellow [ˈjeləʊ]
Geld, das - money [ˈmʌni]
geliebt - loved [ˈlʌvd]
Genesung, die; Rehabilitation, die - rehabilitation [ˌriːəˌbɪlɪˈteɪʃn]
geöffnet - opened [ˈəʊpənd]
gerufen - cried [kraɪd]
gesäubert - cleaned [kliːnd]
Geschichte, die - story [ˈstɔːri]
Geschlecht, das - sex [seks]
geschlossen - closed [kləʊzd]
Geschwindigkeit, die - speed [spiːd]
Gesicht, das - face [feɪs]
gestern - yesterday [ˈjestədi]
gestohlen - stolen [ˈstəʊlən]
gesund pflegen - to rehabilitate [tə ˌriːəˈbɪlɪteɪt]
Gesundheit, die - health [helθ]
getroffen, kennengelernt - met [met]
gewöhnlich - usual [ˈjuːʒʊəl]
Glas, das - glass [ˈglɑːs]
glauben - to believe [tə bɪˈliːv]
Glück, das - happiness [ˈhæpinəs]
glücklich - happy [ˈhæpi]
grau - grey [greɪ]
grauhaarig - grey-headed [greɪ ˈhedɪd]
groß - big [bɪg]
größer - bigger [ˈbɪgə]
grün - green [ˈgriːn]
Grund, der - reason [ˈriːzən]
Gummi, der - rubber [ˈrʌbə]
gut - good, well [gʊd | wel]
gut, alles klar - OK, well [ˌəʊˈkeɪ | wel]
Haar, das - hair [heə]
haben - to have [tə hæv]
halb - half [hɑːf]
hallo - hello, hi [həˈləʊ | haɪ]
Handarbeit, die - manual work [ˈmænjʊəl ˈwɜːk]
Handschellen, die - handcuffs [ˈhændkʌfs]
Handy, das - mobile [ˈməʊbaɪl]

hassen - to hate [tə heɪt]
hatte - had [hæd]
Haupt-, zentral - central ['sentrəl]
Haus, das - house ['haʊs]
Hausaufgaben, die - homework ['həʊmwɜːk]
Haustier, das - pet [pet]
heimlich - secretly ['siːkrɪtli]
Helfer, der - helper ['helpə]
Herausgeber, der - editor ['edɪtə]
Herr, Hr. - mister, Mr. ['mɪstə | 'mɪstə]
herstellen - to produce [tə prə'djuːs]
heulend - howling ['haʊlɪŋ]
heute - today [tə'deɪ]
hier - here [hɪə]
hierher - here [hɪə]
hier ist - here is [hɪə ɪz]
Hilfe, die - help [help]
helfen - to help [tə help]
hindurch - through [θruː]
hinter - behind [bɪ'haɪnd]
hoch - high [haɪ]
hochachtungsvoll - yours sincerely [jɔːz sɪn'sɪəli]
Hof, der - yard [jɑːd]
Hoffnung, die - hope [həʊp]
hoffen - to hope [tə həʊp]
hören - to listen [tə 'lɪsn]
hörte - heard [hɜːd]
Hose, die - trousers ['traʊzəz]
Hotel, das - hotel [ˌhəʊ'tel]
Hotels, die - hotels [ˌhəʊ'telz]
Hund, der - dog [dɒg]
hundert - hundred ['hʌndrəd]
hungrig - hungry ['hʌŋgri]
Hut, der - hat [hæt]
ich - I ['aɪ]
Idee, die - idea [aɪ'dɪə]
ihm - him [hɪm]
ihr - their [ðeə]
ihr Buch - her book [hə bʊk]
Imbiss, der - snack [snæk]
immer - always ['ɔːlweɪz]
in - in [ɪn]
in - inside [ɪn'saɪd]
in - into ['ɪntə]
in der Zwischenzeit - meanwhile ['miːnwaɪl]
Information, die; Angabe, die - information [ˌɪnfə'meɪʃn]

informieren, mitteilen - to inform [tu ɪn'fɔːm]
informierte - informed [ɪn'fɔːmd]
Ingenieur, der - engineer [ˌendʒɪ'nɪə]
Inserat, das - ad [æd]
intelligent - smart [smɑːt]
interessant - interesting ['ɪntrəstɪŋ]
irgendwelche - any ['eni]
ja - yes [jes]
Jacke, die - jacket ['dʒækɪt]
Jahr, das - year ['jɪə]
Jahreszeit, die - season ['siːzn]
jeder, jede, jedes - every ['evri]
jemand - somebody ['sʌmbədi]
jener, jene, jenes - that [ðæt]
jetzt, zurzeit, gerade - now [naʊ]
Journalist, der - journalist ['dʒɜːnəlɪst]
jung - young [jʌŋ]
Junge, der - boy, guy [ˌbɔɪ | gaɪ]
Kabel, das - cable ['keɪbl]
Kaffee, der - coffee ['kɒfi]
kalt - cold [kəʊld]
Kälte, die - coldness ['kəʊldnəs]
Kanada - Canada ['kænədə]
Känguru, das - kangaroo [ˌkæŋgə'ruː]
Kapitän, der - captain ['kæptɪn]
Karte, die - map [mæp]
Kasse, die - cash register, [kæʃ 'redʒɪstə]
Kassierer, der - cashier, teller [kæ'ʃɪə | 'telə]
Kätzchen, das - kitten ['kɪtn]
Katze, die - cat [kæt]
kaufen - to buy [tə baɪ]
kennen - to know [tə nəʊ]
kennengelernt - learned about [lɜːnd ə'baʊt]
Kessel, der - kettle ['ketl]
Kilometer, der - kilometer [kə'lɑːmətə]
Kind, das - child [tʃaɪld]
Kinder, die - children ['tʃɪldrən]
Kindergarten, der - kindergarten ['kɪndəgɑːtn]
Kiste, die - box [bɒks]
klar, sicher - sure [ʃʊə]
Klasse, die - class [klɑːs]
Klassenzimmer, das - classroom ['klæsruːm]
Kleidung, die - clothes [kləʊðz]
klein - little, small ['lɪtl | smɔːl]
klingeln - to ring [tə rɪŋ]
Klingeln, das - ring [rɪŋ]
klingelte - rang [ræŋ]
Knopf, der - button ['bʌtn]

Koch, der / Köchin, die - cooker [ˈkʊkə]
kochend - cooking [ˈkʊkɪŋ]
Kollege, der - colleague [ˈkɔliːg]
kommen - come, go [kʌm | gəʊ]
kommen in - to join [tə dʒɔɪn]
können - can [kæn]
könnte - could [kʊd]
Kontrolle, die - control [kənˈtrəʊl]
kontrollieren - to check [tə tʃek]
Koordination, die - co-ordination [kəʊˌɔːdɪˈneɪʃən]
Kopf, der - head [hed]
Kopfarbeit, die - mental work [ˈmentl ˈwɜːk]
kosten - to cost [tə kɔst]
kreativ - creative [kriːˈeɪtɪv]
Krieg, der - war [wɔː]
Kristall, das - crystal [ˈkrɪstl]
Krug, der - jar [dʒɑː]
Küche, die - kitchen [ˈkɪtʃɪn]
Kunde, der - customer [ˈkʌstəmə]
Kunst, die - art [ɑːt]
Künstler, der - artist [ˈɑːtɪst]
Kurs, der - course [kɔːs]
kurz - short [ʃɔːt]
küssen - to kiss [tə kɪs]
Küste, die - seashore, shore [ˈsiːʃɔː | ʃɔː]
Lächeln, das - smile [smaɪl]
lächeln - to smile [tə smaɪl]
lächelte - smiled [smaɪld]
lachen - to laugh [tə lɑːf]
laden - to load [tə ləʊd]
Laden, der - shop [ʃɔp]
Läden, die - shops [ʃɔps]
Land, das - country [ˈkʌntri]
landen - to land [tə lænd]
lang - long [ˈlɔŋ]
langsam - slowly [ˈsləʊli]
Laser, der - laser [ˈleɪzə]
lass uns - let us [let əz]
lassen - to let [tə let]
Lastwagen, der - truck [trʌk]
laufen - walking [ˈwɔːkɪŋ]
laut - aloud [əˈlaʊd]
Leben, das - life [laɪf]
leben, wohnen - to live [tə ˈlaɪv]
lebte - lived [lɪvd]
lecker - tasty [ˈteɪsti]
ledig - single [ˈsɪŋgl]

leer - blank, empty [blæŋk | ˈempti]
legen - to place [tə ˈpleɪs]
Lehrer, der - teacher [ˈtiːtʃə]
leicht - slightly [ˈslaɪtli]
leid tun - to be sorry [tə bi ˈsɔri]
leise - silent, silently [ˈsaɪlənt | ˈsaɪləntli]
Lektion, die - lesson [ˈlesn]
lenken - to steer [tə stɪə]
lernen - to learn [tə lɜːn]
lesen - to read [tə riːd]
lesend - reading [ˈriːdɪŋ]
liebe - dear [dɪə]
Liebe, die - love [ˈlʌv]
lieben - to love [tə ˈlʌv]
Lieblings- - favourite [ˈfeɪvərɪt]
Lieblingsfilm, der - favourite film [ˈfeɪvərɪt fɪlm]
links - left [left]
Liste, die - list [lɪst]
Lösung, die - solution, answer [səˈluːʃn | ˈɑːnsə]
Löwe, der - lion [ˈlaɪən]
Luft, die - air [eə]
lustig - funny [ˈfʌni]
machen - to make, to do [tə ˈmeɪk | tə duː]
machte an - switched on [swɪtʃt ɔn]
Mädchen, das - girl [gɜːl]
Mama; Mutter, die - mom, mother [mɔm | ˈmʌðə]
manchmal, ab und zu - sometimes [ˈsʌmtaɪmz]
Mann, der - man [mæn]
männlich - male [meɪl]
Mannschaft, die - team [tiːm]
Maschine, die - machine [məˈʃiːn]
Matratze, die - mattress [ˈmætrɪs]
medizinisch - medical [ˈmedɪkl]
Meer, das - sea [siː]
mehr - more [mɔː]
mein, meine, mein - my [maɪ]
Mensch, der - human [ˈhjuːmən]
Menschen, die - people [ˈpiːpl]
Metall, das - metal [ˈmetl]
Meter, der - meter [ˈmiːtə]
Methode, die - method [ˈmeθəd]
mich - me [miː]
Miezekatze, die - pussycat [ˈpʊsɪkæt]
Mikrofon, das - microphone [ˈmaɪkrəfəʊn]
Minute, die - minute [maɪˈnjuːt]

mit - with [wɪð]
Mitglied, das - member [ˈmembə]
Möbel, die - furniture [ˈfɜːnɪtʃə]
mögen, lieben - to like, to love [tə ˈlaɪk | tə ˈlʌv]
möglich - possible [ˈpɒsəbl]
Möglichkeit, die - possibility [ˌpɒsəˈbɪlɪti]
Moment, der - moment [ˈməʊmənt]
monoton - monotonous [məˈnɒtənəs]
Montag, der - Monday [ˈmʌndeɪ]
Mörder, der - killer [ˈkɪlə]
morgen - tomorrow [təˈmɒrəʊ]
Morgen, der - morning [ˈmɔːnɪŋ]
Motor, der - engine [ˈendʒɪn]
müde - tired [ˈtaɪəd]
Musik, die - music [ˈmjuːzɪk]
müssen - must [mʌst]
Muttersprache, die - native language [ˈneɪtɪv ˈlæŋgwɪdʒ]
nach - after [ˈɑːftə]
nach - past [pɑːst]
nach unten - down [daʊn]
Nachbar, der - neighbour [ˈneɪbə]
nächste - nearest [ˈnɪərɪst]
Nacht, die - night [naɪt]
nahe - close [kləʊz]
näher - closer [ˈkləʊsə]
nahm - took [tʊk]
Name, der - name [ˈneɪm]
nennen - to name [tə ˈneɪm]
Nase, die - nose [nəʊz]
nass - wet [wet]
Nationalität, die - nationality [ˌnæʃəˈnælɪti]
Natur, die - nature [ˈneɪtʃə]
natürlich - of course [əv kɔːs]
nehmen - to take [tə teɪk]
nein - no [nəʊ]
neu - new [njuː]
neun - nine [naɪn]
neunter - ninth [naɪnθ]
nicht - not [nɒt]
nichts - nothing [ˈnʌθɪŋ]
nie - never [ˈnevə]
niemand - nobody [ˈnəʊbədi]
noch - yet [jet]
noch einen - one more [wʌn mɔː]
noch, weiterhin - still [stɪl]

Nordamerika und Eurasien - North America and Eurasia [nɔːθ əˈmerɪkə ənd jʊəˈreɪʒə]
normal - usual [ˈjuːʒʊəl]
normalerweise - usually [ˈjuːʒəli]
Notiz, die - note [nəʊt]
Notizbuch, das - notebook [ˈnəʊtbʊk]
Notizbücher, die - notebooks [ˈnəʊtbʊks]
Nummer, die - number [ˈnʌmbə]
nur - only [ˈəʊnli]
ob - if [ɪf]
obwohl, trotzdem - although [ɔːlˈðəʊ]
öffnen - to open [tu ˈəʊpən]
öffnete - opened [ˈəʊpənd]
oft - often [ˈɒfn]
ohne - without [wɪðˈaʊt]
wortlos - without a word [wɪðˈaʊt ə ˈwɜːd]
Ohr, das - ear [ɪə]
okay, gut - okay, well [ˌəʊˈkeɪ | wel]
Öl, das - oil [ɔɪl]
Panik, die - panic [ˈpænɪk]
Papa - daddy [ˈdædi]
Papier, das - paper [ˈpeɪpə]
Park, der - park [pɑːk]
Parks, die - parks [pɑːks]
passend - suitable [ˈsuːtəbl]
passieren - to happen [tə ˈhæpən]
passiert - happened [ˈhæpənd]
Patrouille, die; Streife, die - patrol [pəˈtrəʊl]
Pause, die - break, pause [breɪk | pɔːz]
Person, die - person [ˈpɜːsn]
Personalabteilung, die - personnel department [ˌpɜːsəˈnel dɪˈpɑːtmənt]
persönlich - personal [ˈpɜːsənl]
Piepton, der - beep [biːp]
Pilot, der - pilot [ˈpaɪlət]
Plan, der - plan [plæn]
planen - to plan [tə plæn]
Planet, der - planet [ˈplænɪt]
Platz, der - square [skweə]
plötzlich - suddenly [sʌdnli]
Polen - Poland [ˈpəʊlənd]
Polizei, die - police [pəˈliːs]
Polizeihauptmeister, der - sergeant [ˈsɑːdʒənt]
Polizist, der - officer, policeman [ˈɒfɪsə | pəˈliːsmən]
Position, die - position [pəˈzɪʃn]
Preis, der - price [praɪs]
pro Stunde - per hour [pɜː ˈaʊə]

Problem, das - problem [ˈprɔbləm]
Programm, das - program [ˈprəʊgræm]
Programmierer, der - programmer [ˈprəʊgræmə]
Prüfung, die - test [ˈtest]
prüfen - to test [tə ˈtest]
Publikum, das - audience [ˈɔːdiəns]
Puppe, die - doll [dɔl]
putzen - to wash [tə wɔʃ]
Rad, das - wheel [ˈwiːl]
Radar, der - radar [ˈreɪdɑː]
Radio, das - radio [ˈreɪdɪəʊ]
rasen - to speed [tə spiːd]
Raser, der - speeder [ˈspiːdə]
raste - rushed [rʌʃt]
Rätsel, das - mystery [ˈmɪstəri]
Ratte, die - rat [ræt]
Raumschiff, das - spaceship [ˈspeɪsʃɪp]
rechts - right [raɪt]
Rede, die - speech [spiːtʃ]
Regel, die - rule [ruːl]
Regen, der - rain [reɪn]
reiben - to rub [tə rʌb]
reisen - to travel [tə ˈtrævl]
rennen, joggen, laufen - to run [tə rʌn]
retten - to rescue, to save [tə ˈreskjuː | tə seɪv]
Rettungsdienst, der - rescue service [ˈreskjuː ˈsɜːvɪs]
richtete - pointed [ˈpɔɪntɪd]
richtig - correct, correctly [kəˈrekt | kəˈrektli]
riefen an - called [kɔːld]
rot - red [red]
Rubrik, die - rubric [ˈruːbrɪk]
rund - round [ˈraʊnd]
Saatgut, das - seed [siːd]
sagen - to tell, to say [tə tel | tə ˈseɪ]
sagte - said [ˈsed]
sahen - saw [ˈsɔː]
Samstag, der - Saturday [ˈsætədeɪ]
Sand, der - sand [sænd]
Sandwich, das - sandwich [ˈsænwɪdʒ]
Sänger, der - singer [ˈsɪŋə]
Satz, der - phrase [freɪz]
sauber - clean [kliːn]
sauber machen, putzen - to clean [tə kliːn]
schauen, betrachten - to look [tə lʊk]
schaukeln - to pitch [tə pɪtʃ]
schaute - looked [lʊkt]

schickte - sent [sent]
Schiff, das - ship [ʃɪp]
schlafen - to sleep [tə sliːp]
schlagen - to hit, to beat [tə hɪt | tə biːt]
Schlange, die - queue [kjuː]
schlau - clever, sly [ˈklevə | slaɪ]
schlecht - bad [bæd]
schließen - to close [tə kləʊz]
schließlich - at last [ət lɑːst]
schlucken, hinunterschlucken - to swallow [tə ˈswɔləʊ]
Schlüssel, der - key [kiː]
schnell - quick, quickly [kwɪk | ˈkwɪkli]
schon - already [ɔːlˈredi]
schön - nice [naɪs]
schoss; angeschossen - shot [ʃɔt]
schreiben - to write [tə ˈraɪt]
Schreibtisch, der - desk [desk]
schrieb - wrote [rəʊt]
Schriftsteller, der - writer [ˈraɪtə]
Schritt, der - step [step]
Schule, die - school [skuːl]
schütten - to pour [tə pɔː]
Schwanz, der - tail [teɪl]
schwarz - black [blæk]
Schweizer - Swiss [swɪs]
schwer - difficult, hard [ˈdɪfɪkəlt | hɑːd]
Schwester, die - sister [ˈsɪstə]
schwimmen - to swim [tə swɪm]
sechs - six [sɪks]
sechster - sixth [sɪksθ]
sechzig - sixty [ˈsɪksti]
See, der - lake [leɪk]
sehen - to see [tə ˈsiː]
sehr - very [ˈveri]
sein - to be [tə bi]
sein, seine - its; his [ɪts | hɪz]
seit - since [sɪns]
Sekretärin, die - secretary [ˈsekrətəri]
selten - seldom [ˈseldəm]
Serie, die - serial [ˈsɪərɪəl]
setzen - to sit [tə sɪt]
sich anziehen - to put on [tə ˈpʊt ɔn]
angezogen - dressed [drest]
sich bewerben - to apply [tu əˈplaɪ]
sich entschuldigen - to excuse [tu ɪkˈskjuːz]
sich hinsetzen - to sit down [tə sɪt daʊn]

sich kennen - to know each other [tə nəʊ i:tʃ ˈʌðə]
sich kümmern um - to care [tə keə]
sich schämen - to be ashamed [tə bi əˈʃeɪmd]
sich Sorgen machen - to worry [tə ˈwʌri]
sich umsehen - to look around [tə lʊk əˈraʊnd]
sich unterhalten - to talk [tə ˈtɔ:k]
sich verstecken - to hide [tə haɪd]
Sicherheitsgurt, der - seat belts [si:t belts]
sie - she; they [ʃi | ˈðeɪ]
sieben - seven [ˈsevn]
siebter - seventh [ˈsevnθ]
siebzehn - seventeen (hour) [ˌsevnˈti:n ˈaʊə]
singen - sing [sɪŋ]
Sirene, die - siren [ˈsaɪərən]
Situation, die - situation [ˌsɪtʃʊˈeɪʃn]
Sitz, der - seat [si:t]
sich hinsetzen - to take a seat [tə teɪk ə si:t]
sofort - immediately [ɪˈmi:dɪətli]
Sohn, der - son [sʌn]
sorgfältig - careful [ˈkeəfʊl]
Spaniel, der - spaniel [ˈspænɪəl]
spanisch - Spanish [ˈspænɪʃ]
Spaß, der - fun [fʌn]
Spaß haben, genießen - enjoy [ɪnˈdʒɔɪ]
spielen - to play [tə ˈpleɪ]
Spielzeug, das - toy [tɔɪ]
Sport, der - sport; [spɔ:t]
Sportgeschäft, das - sport shop [spɔ:t ʃɔp]
Sportfahrrad, das - sport bike [spɔ:t baɪk]
Sprache, die - language [ˈlæŋgwɪdʒ]
sprechen - to speak [tə spi:k]
springen - to jump [tə dʒʌmp]
Sprung, der - jump [dʒʌmp]
Stadt, die - city, town [ˈsɪti | taʊn]
Stand, der - status [ˈsteɪtəs]
Standard, der - standard [ˈstændəd]
stark - strong, strongly [strɔŋ | ˈstrɔŋli]
Stärke, die - strength [streŋθ]
stattdessen - instead [ɪnˈsted]
Stechmücke, die - mosquito [məˈski:təʊ]
stehen - to stand [tə stænd]
stehlen - to steal [tə sti:l]
Stein, der - stone [stəʊn]
sterben - to die [tə daɪ]
starb - died [daɪd]
Stern, der - star [stɑ:]
Sternchen, das - asterisk [ˈæstərɪsk]

Stift, der - pen [pen]
Stifte, die - pens [penz]
Stimme, die - voice [vɔɪs]
stinkend - stinking [ˈstɪŋkɪŋ]
stoßen, ziehen - to push [tə pʊʃ]
Straße, die - road, street [rəʊd | stri:t]
Straßen, die - streets [stri:ts]
Strom, der - current [ˈkʌrənt]
Student, der - student [ˈstju:dnt]
Studenten, die - students [ˈstju:dnts]
Studentenwohnheim, das - dorms [ˈdɔ:mz]
studieren - to study [tə ˈstʌdi]
Stuhl, der - chair [tʃeə]
Stunde, die - hour [ˈaʊə]
stündlich - hourly [ˈaʊəli]
super, toll - great [ˈgreɪt]
Supermarkt, der - supermarket [ˈsu:pəmɑ:kɪt]
Tablette, die - pill [pɪl]
Tag, der - day [deɪ]
täglich, jeden Tag - daily [ˈdeɪli]
Tanker, der - tanker [ˈtæŋkə]
tanzen - to dance [tə dɑ:ns]
tanzend - dancing [ˈdɑ:nsɪŋ]
Tasche, die - bag, pocket [bæg | ˈpɔkɪt]
Tasse, die - cup [kʌp]
Tastatur, die - keyboard [ˈki:bɔ:d]
tat - did [dɪd]
tausend - thousand [ˈθaʊznd]
Taxi, das - taxi [ˈtæksi]
Taxifahrer, der - taxi driver [ˈtæksi ˈdraɪvə]
Tee, der - tea [ti:]
Teil, der - part [pɑ:t]
teilnehmen - to take part [tə teɪk pɑ:t]
Teilnehmer, der - participant [pɑ:ˈtɪsɪpənt]
Telefon, das - telephone [ˈtelɪfəʊn]
telefonieren - to telephone [tə ˈtelɪfəʊn]
Telefonhörer, der - phone handset [fəʊn ˈhændset]
Teller, der - plate [pleɪt]
Text, der - text [tekst]
Tier, das - animal [ˈænɪml]
Tierarzt, der - vet [vet]
Tiger, der - tiger [ˈtaɪgə]
Tisch, der - table [ˈteɪbl]
Tische, die - tables [ˈteɪblz]
Tochter, die - daughter [ˈdɔ:tə]
tödlich - deadly [ˈdedli]
Toilette, die - toilet [ˈtɔɪlɪt]

tötete, getötet - killed [kɪld]
trainieren - to train [tə treɪn]
trainiert - trained [treɪnd]
Transport, der - transport [træns'pɔːt]
trat - stepped [stept]
Traum, der - dream [driːm]
träumen - to dream [tə driːm]
traurig - sad [sæd]
treffen, kennenlernen - to meet [tə miːt]
treiben - floating, to float [ˈfləʊtɪŋ | tə fləʊt]
Treppe, die - stairs [steəz]
Tresor, der - safe [seɪf]
treten - to step [tə step]
Trick, der - trick [trɪk]
trinken - to drink [tə drɪŋk]
trocknen - to dry [tə draɪ]
trocken - dry [draɪ]
tschüss - bye [baɪ]
Tür, die - door [dɔː]
über - over, across [ˈəʊvə | əˈkrɔs]
Überfall, der - robbery [ˈrɔbəri]
übergreifen - to spread [tə spred]
Überraschung, die - surprise [səˈpraɪz]
überraschen - to surprise [tə səˈpraɪz]
überrascht, verwundert - surprised [səˈpraɪzd]
Übersetzer, der - translator [trænzˈleɪtə]
übrigens - by the way [baɪ ðə ˈweɪ]
Uhr - o'clock [əˈklɔk]
Uhr, die - watch [wɔtʃ]
um eins - at one o'clock [ət wʌn əˈklɔk]
und - and [ænd]
Unfall, der - accident [ˈæksɪdənt]
ungerecht - unfair [ˌʌnˈfeə]
uns - us [əz]
unser - our [ˈaʊə]
unter - under [ˈʌndə]
unterstreichen - to underline [tu ˌʌndəˈlaɪn]
usw. - etc. [etˈsetrə]
Vater, der - dad [dæd]
Verbrecher, der - criminal [ˈkrɪmɪnl]
verdammt - damn [dæm]
verdienen - to earn [tu ɜːn]
Verein, der - club [klʌb]
Vereinbarung, die - agreement [əˈgriːmənt]
Vereinigten Staaten, die; USA, die - the United States/the USA [ðə juˈnaɪtɪd steɪts ðə ˌjuːˌesˈeɪ]
Verfolgung, die - pursuit [pəˈsjuːt]
vergessen - to forget [tə fəˈget]

verkaufen - to sell [tə sel]
Verkäufer, der; Verkäuferin, die - shop assistant [ʃɔp əˈsɪstənt]
Verlag, der - publishing [ˈpʌblɪʃɪŋ]
verlassen - to leave [tə liːv]
verlieren - to loose [tə luːs]
verschieden - different [ˈdɪfrənt]
verstanden - understood [ˌʌndəˈstʊd]
versteckte - hid [hɪd]
verstehen - to understand [tu ˌʌndəˈstænd]
versuchen - to try [tə ˈtraɪ]
versuchte - tried [ˈtraɪd]
verwirrt - confused [kənˈfjuːzd]
Videokassette, die - videocassette [ˈvɪdiokæˌset]
Videothek, die - video-shop [ˈvɪdɪəʊ ʃɔp]
viel - many, much [ˈmeni | ˈmʌtʃ]
viel zu tun haben - to have a lot of work [tə həv ə lɔt əv ˈwɜːk]
viele - much, many [ˈmʌtʃ | ˈmeni]
vier - four [fɔː]
vierte - fourth [ˈfɔːθ]
vierundvierzig - forty-four [ˈfɔːti fɔː]
Vogel, der - bird [bɜːd]
voll - full [fʊl]
vor - before; ago [bɪˈfɔː | əˈgəʊ]
vor einem Jahr - a year ago [ə ˈjɪər əˈgəʊ]
vor allem - especially [ɪˈspeʃəli]
vorbei - past [pɑːst]
vorbereiten - to prepare [tə prɪˈpeə]
vorgeben; so tun, als ob - to pretend [tə prɪˈtend]
vorn - front [frʌnt]
Vorderräder, die - front wheels [frʌnt ˈwiːlz]
vorsichtig - carefully [ˈkeəfəli]
wackelte - shook [ʃʊk]
Waffe, die - gun [gʌn]
wählen, aussuchen - to choose [tə tʃuːz]
während - while [waɪl]
Wal, der - whale [weɪl]
war - was [wɔz]
waren - were [wɜː]
warm - warm [wɔːm]
warten - to wait [tə weɪt]
wartete - waited [ˈweɪtɪd]
was - what [ˈwɔt]
Was ist das? - What is this? [ˈwɔt s ðɪs]
Welcher Tisch? - What table? [ˈwɔt ˈteɪbl]

Was ist los? - What is the matter? [ˈwɔt s ðə ˈmætə]
waschen - to wash [tə wɔʃ]
Waschmaschine, die - washer [ˈwɔʃə]
Wasser, das - water [ˈwɔːtə]
Wasserhahn, der - tap [tæp]
Website, die - Internet site [ˈɪntənet saɪt]
weg - away [əˈweɪ]
Weg, der - way [ˈweɪ]
weggehen - to go away [tə gəʊ əˈweɪ]
weglaufen - run away [rʌn əˈweɪ]
weiblich - female [ˈfiːmeɪl]
weil - because [bɪˈkɔz]
weinen, schreien, rufen - to cry [tə kraɪ]
weiß - white [waɪt]
weit - far [ˈfɑː]
weiter - further [ˈfɜːðə]
Welle, die - wave [weɪv]
Welpe, der - puppy [ˈpʌpi]
Welt, die - world [wɜːld]
Weltall, das - space [speɪs]
weniger - less [les]
wenigstens - at least [ət liːst]
wenn - when [wen]
wer - who [huː]
Werbung, die - advert [ˈædvɜːt]
werden - will [wɪl]
wessen - whose [huːz]
Wetter, das - weather [ˈweðə]
wichtig - important [ɪmˈpɔːtnt]
wie - as [æz]
wie - how [ˈhaʊ]
wieder - again [əˈgen]
Wind, der - wind [wɪnd]
wir - we [wi]
wirklich - real, really [rɪəl | ˈrɪəli]
wo - where [weə]
Woche, die - week [wiːk]

wohnhaft - living [ˈlɪvɪŋ]
wollen - to want [tə wɔnt]
wollte - wanted [ˈwɔntɪd]
Wort, das; Vokabel, die - word [wɜːd]
Wörter, die; Vokabeln, die - words [wɜːdz]
wunderbar - wonderful [ˈwʌndəfəl]
wunderschön - beautiful [ˈbjuːtəfl]
wusste - knew [njuː]
wütend - angrily, angry [angrəli | ˈæŋgri]
zahlen - to pay [tə peɪ]
Zebra, das - zebra [ˈzebrə]
zehn - ten [ten]
zehnter - tenth [tenθ]
zeigen - to show [tə ʃəʊ]
zeigte - showed [ʃəʊd]
Zeit, die - time [ˈtaɪm]
Zeitschrift, die - magazine [ˌmægəˈziːn]
Zeitung, die - newspaper [ˈnjuːspeɪpə]
Zentrum, das - centre [ˈsentə]
zerstören - destroy [dɪˈstrɔɪ]
ziehen - to pull [tə pʊl]
ziemlich - quite [kwaɪt]
Zimmer, das - room [ruːm]
Zimmer, die - rooms [ruːmz]
zittern - to shake [tə ʃeɪk]
Zoo, der - zoo [zuː]
Zug, der - train [treɪn]
Zuhause, das - home [həʊm]
zukünftig - future [ˈfjuːtʃə]
zurück - back [bæk]
zusammen - together [təˈgeðə]
zwanzig - twenty [ˈtwenti]
zwei - two [tuː]
zweimal - twice [twaɪs]
zweiter Name - middle name [ˈmɪdl ˈneɪm]
zweiter - second [ˈsekənd]
zwischen - between [bɪˈtwiːn]
zwölf - twelve [twelv]

Irregular Verbs

Die unregelmäßigen Verben

Infinitive	Past Tense	Past Participle	German
abide	abode	abode	bleiben, fortdauern
arise	arose	arisen	entstehen
awake	awoke / awaked	awoke / awaked / awoken	(auf)wecken
be	was, were	been	sein
bear	bore	born(e)	gebären, ertragen
beat	beat	beaten	schlagen, besiegen
become	became	become	werden
beget	begot	begotten	erzeugen, hervorbringen
begin	began	begun	anfangen
belay	belaid	belayed	festmachen
bend	bent	bent	biegen
bereave	bereaved	bereft	berauben
beseech	besought	besought	ersuchen, anflehen
bet	bet	bet	wetten
bid	bade / bid	bidden / bid	einladen, setzen (Kartenspiel)
bind	bound	bound	binden
bite	bit	bit, bitten	beißen
bleed	bled	bled	bluten
blow	blew	blown	blasen
break	broke	broken	(zer)brechen
breed	bred	bred	verursachen
bring	brought	brought	bringen
broadcast	broadcast	broadcast	senden / übertragen
build	built	built	bauen
burn	burnt (burned)	burnt (burned)	(ver)brennen
burst	burst	burst	platzen
buy	bought	bought	kaufen
can	could	-	können

cast	cast	cast	auswerfen, werfen
catch	caught	caught	fangen
chide	chide	chidden	(aus)schimpfen, tadeln
choose	chose	chosen	(aus)wählen
cleave	clove / cloven	cleft	(zer)teilen, (zer)schneiden, (zer)spalten
cling	clung	clung	kleben, haften
clothe	clothed / clad+	clothed / clad+	(an-, be-, ein-) kleiden
come	came	come	kommen
cost	cost	cost	kosten
creep	crept	crept	kriechen, schleichen
crow	crowed / crew	crowed	a. (rum)krähen (Kinder, Hahn) / b. protzen, prahlen
cut	cut	cut	schneiden
dare	dared / durst	dared	(sich etwas) trauen, wagen
deal	dealt	dealt	handeln
dig	dug	dug	graben
do	did	done	tun
draw	drew	drawn	zeichnen, ziehen
dream	dreamt (dreamed)	dreamt (dreamed)	träumen
drink	drank	drunk	trinken
drive	drove	driven	fahren
dwell	dwelt	dwelt	wohnen, leben
eat	ate	eaten	essen
fall	fell	fallen	fallen
feed	fed	fed	füttern
feel	felt	felt	(sich) fühlen
fight	fought	fought	kämpfen
find	found	found	finden
fit	fit	fit	passen
flee	fled	fled	fliehen
fling	flung	flung	schleudern
fly	flew	flown	fliegen

forbear	forbore	forborne	unterlassen, enthalten, Abstand nehmen
forbid	forbade	forbidden	verbieten / untersagen
forego	forewent	forgone	verzichten auf; aufgeben; Abstand nehmen von
forget	forgot	forgotten	vergessen
forgive	forgave	forgiven	verzeihen, vergeben
forsake	forsook	forsaken	aufgeben, verlassen, im Stich / hinter sich lassen
freeze	froze	frozen	frieren
geld	gelded	gelt	a. kastrieren b. verschneiden
get	got	got(ten, AE)	bekommen
give	gave	given	geben
go	went	gone	gehen, fahren
grind	ground	ground	schleifen
grow	grew	grown	wachsen, anbauen
hang	hung	hung	(auf)hängen
have	had	had	haben
hear	heard	heard	hören
heave	hove	hove	heben
hide	hid	hidden	verstecken
hit	hit	hit	schlagen, treffen
hold	held	held	halten
hurt	hurt	hurt	verletzen
input	input (inputted)	input (inputted)	(Passwort) eingeben
keep	kept	kept	halten
knit	knit (knitted)	knit (knitted)	stricken
kneel	knelt	knelt	knien
know	knew	known	wissen
lay	laid	laid	legen
lead	led	led	leiten, führen
lean	leant	leant	lehnen
leap	leapt	leapt	springen
learn	learnt (learned)	learnt (learned)	lernen

leave	left	left	(weg)gehen, (ver)lassen
lend	lent	lent	leihen
let	let	let	lassen
lie	lay	lain	liegen
light	lit (lighted)	lit (lighted)	anzünden / entzünden)
lose	lost	lost	verlieren
make	made	made	machen
may	might	-	können
mean	meant	meant	meinen
meet	met	met	treffen
misunderstand	misunderstood	misunderstood	missverstehen
mow	mowed	mown (mowed)	mähen
must	had to	had to	müssen, dürfen
offset	offset	offset	ausgleichen
pay	paid	paid	(be)zahlen
put	put	put	legen, setzen, stellen
quit	quit	quit	beenden, kündigen
read	read	read	lesen
rend	rent	rent	zerreißen, zerfleischen
rewrite	rewrote	rewritten	neu schreiben / umschreiben
rid	rid	rid	befreien, loswerden
ride	rode	ridden	reiten, fahren
ring	rang	rung	läuten
rise	rose	risen	aufgehen/-stehen
run	ran	run	laufen, rennen
say	said	said	sagen
see	saw	seen	sehen
seek	sought	sought	(auf)suchen
sell	sold	sold	verkaufen
send	sent	sent	schicken, senden
set	set	set	setzen, stellen
sew	sewed	sewn	nähen

shake	shook	shaken	schütteln
shave	shaved	shaven (shaved)	rasieren
shed	shed	shed	abwerfen, haaren, vergießen
shine	shone	shone	scheinen
shoe	shod	shod	a. beschuhen b. beschlagen (Pferd)
shoot	shot	shot	schießen
show	showed	shown (showed)	zeigen
shrink	shrank	shrunk	schrumpfen
shut	shut	shut	schließen
sing	sang	sung	singen
sink	sank	sunk	sinken
sit	sat	sat	sitzen
slay	slew	slain	töten, ermorden, erschlagen
sleep	slept	slept	schlafen
slide	slid	slide	gleiten
sling	slung	slung	schleudern
slink	slunk	slunk	(weg)schleichen, davonschleichen
slit	slit	slit	(auf-, zer-)schlitzen, zerschneiden
smell	smelt (smelled)	smelt (smelled)	riechen
smite	smote	smitten	quälen, schlagen
sneak	snuck (sneaked)	snuck (sneaked)	schleichen
sow	sowed	sown	sähen
speak	spoke	spoken	sprechen
speed	sped	sped (speeded)	(mit dem Auto) rasen
spell	spelt (spelled)	spelt (spelled)	buchstabieren
spend	spent	spent	verbringen, ausgeben
spill	spilt	spilt	verschütten
spin	spun	spun	drehen, spinnen
spit	spat	spat	spucken
split	split	split	teilen, spalten
spoil	spoilt	spoilt	verderben
spread	spread	spread	sich ausbreiten

spring	sprang	sprung	springen
stand	stood	stood	stehen
steal	stole	stolen	stehlen
stick	stuck	stuck	kleben
sting	stung	stung	brennen, schmerzen
stink	stank	stunk	stinken
strew	strewed	strewn (strewed)	streuen
stride	strode	stridden	schreiten, überschreiten
strike	struck	struck / stricken	stoßen, streiken
string	strung	strung	bespannen, aufreihen
strive	strove	striven	streben, (sich) bemühen
swear	swore	sworn	schwören
sweep	swept	swept	fegen
swell	swelled	swollen	(an-, auf-)schwellen, (an)steigen
swim	swam	swum	schwimmen
swing	swung	swung	schaukeln
take	took	taken	nehmen
teach	taught	taught	unterrichten
tear	tore	torn	reißen
tell	told	told	erzählen
think	thought	thought	denken
thrive	throve	thriven	a. gedeihen b. blühen
throw	threw	thrown	werfen
thrust	thrust	thrust	stechen, stoßen (mit einem Messer)
tread	trod	trodden	treten, betreten, laufen
understand	understood	understood	verstehen
undersell	undersold	undersold	unterbieten / unter Wert verkaufen
undertake	undertook	undertaken	(Aufgabe) übernehmen
wake	woke	woken	(auf)wachen
wear	wore	worn	tragen (Kleidungsstück)
weave	wove	woven	weben, flechten
weep	wept	wept	weinen

win	won	won	gewinnen
wind	wound	wound	winden, wickeln, schlängeln,
withdraw	withdrew	withdrawn	zurückziehen
wring	wrung	wrung	(aus)wringen
write	wrote	written	schreiben

Important Ajectives
Wichtige Adjektive

ambitious [æmˈbɪʃəs] - ehrgeizig

annoying [əˈnɔɪŋ] - ärgerlich

anxious [ˈæŋkʃəs] - ängstlich

attractive [əˈtræktɪv] - anziehend

beautiful [ˈbjuːtəfl] - schön

boring [ˈbɔːrɪŋ] - langweilig

brilliant [ˈbrɪlɪənt] - geistreich

calm, quiet, silent [kɑːm | ˈkwaɪət | ˈsaɪlənt] - ruhig

careful [ˈkeəfʊl] - sorgfältig, vorsichtig

charming [ˈtʃɑːmɪŋ] - bezaubernd

cheerful, merry, gay [ˈtʃɪəfəl | ˈmerɪ | geɪ] - lustig

coarse, rude [kɔːs | ruːd] - grob

content [kənˈtent] - zufrieden

cunning [ˈkʌnɪŋ] - schlau

curious [ˈkjʊərɪəs] - neugierig

diligent [ˈdɪlɪdʒənt] - fleißig

eager [ˈiːgə] - eifrig

excellent [ˈeksələnt] - ausgezeichnet

excited [ɪkˈsaɪtɪd] - aufgeregt

experienced [ɪkˈspɪərɪənst] - erfahren

faithful [ˈfeɪθfəl] - treu

fast [fɑːst] - schnell

frank, candid [fræŋk | ˈkændɪd] - offen

friendly [ˈfrendlɪ] - freundlich

funny [ˈfʌnɪ] - spaßig

furious [ˈfjʊərɪəs] - wütend

glad [glæd] - froh

grateful, thankful [ˈgreɪtfəl | ˈθæŋkfəl] - dankbar

greedy [ˈgriːdɪ] - gierig

happy, lucky [ˈhæpɪ | ˈlʌkɪ] - glücklich

helpful [ˈhelpfəl] - hilfsbereit

helpless [ˈhelpləs] - hilflos

honest [ˈɔnɪst] - ehrlich

impudent [ˈɪmpjʊdənt] - frech

indifferent [ɪnˈdɪfrənt] - gleichgütig

intelligent [ɪnˈtelɪdʒənt] - klug

jealous [ˈdʒeləs] - eifersüchtig

loving, affectionate [ˈlʌvɪŋ | əˈfekʃənət] - liebevoll

mad, crazy [mæd | ˈkreɪzɪ] - verrückt

mean [miːn] - geizig

moderate [ˈmɔdəreɪt] - gemäßigt

modest [ˈmɔdɪst] - bescheiden

nervous [ˈnɜːvəs] - nervös

nice, kind [naɪs | kaɪnd] - nett

plain [pleɪn] - einfach

polite [pəˈlaɪt] - höflich

pretty, nice [ˈprɪtɪ | naɪs] - hübsch

punctual [ˈpʌŋktʃʊəl] - pünktlich

pure, clean [pjʊə | kli:n] - rein
reliable [rɪˈlaɪəbl] - zuverlässig
resolute [ˈrezəlu:t] - entschlossen
respectable, decent [rɪˈspektəbl | ˈdi:snt] - anständig
ridiculous [rɪˈdɪkjʊləs] - lächerlich
sad [sæd] - traurig
serious, grave [ˈsɪərɪəs | ɡreɪv] - ernst
shy [ʃaɪ] - schüchtern
slow [sloʊ] - langsam
soft [sɔft] - weich
strange, odd [streɪndʒ | ɔd] - seltsam
stubborn, tough [ˈstʌbən | tʌf] - zäh
stupid [ˈstju:pɪd] - dumm
successful [səkˈsesfəl] - erfolgreich

superficial, shallow [ˌsu:pəˈfɪʃl | ˈʃæloʊ] - oberflächlich
surprised [səˈpraɪzd] - überrascht
sympathetic [ˌsɪmpəˈθetɪk] - mitfühlend
tired [ˈtaɪəd] - müde
ugly [ˈʌɡlɪ] - häßlich
uneducated [ʌnˈedʒʊkeɪtɪd] - ungebildet
ungrateful [ʌnˈɡreɪtfəl] - undankbar
unhappy [ʌnˈhæpɪ] - unglücklich
unjust, unfair [ʌnˈdʒʌst | ˌʌnˈfeə] - ungerecht
violent [ˈvaɪələnt] - heftig
weak [wi:k] - schwach
wicked, evil [ˈwɪkɪd | ˈi:vl] - böse
wise [waɪz] - weise
youthful [ˈju:θfəl] - jugendlich

Physical qualities

Körperliche Eigenschaften

big [bɪɡ] - groß
small oder little [smɔ:l | ˈlɪtl] - klein
fast [fɑ:st] - schnell
slow [sloʊ] - langsam
good [ɡʊd] - gut
bad [bæd] - schlecht
expensive [ɪkˈspensɪv] - teuer
cheap [tʃi:p] - billig
thick [θɪk] - dick
thin [θɪn] - dünn
narrow [ˈnæroʊ] - eng
wide [waɪd], broad [brɔ:d] - breit
loud [laʊd] - laut
quiet [ˈkwaɪət] - leise
intelligent [ɪnˈtelɪdʒənt] - intelligent
stupid [ˈstju:pɪd] - dumm

wet [wet] - nass
dry [draɪ] - trocken
heavy [ˈhevɪ] - schwer
light [laɪt] - leicht
hard [hɑ:d] - hart
soft [sɔft] - weich
shallow [ˈʃæloʊ] - flach, seicht
deep [di:p] - tief
easy [ˈi:zi] - leicht
difficult [ˈdɪfɪkəlt] - schwierig
weak [wi:k] - schwach
strong [strɔŋ] - stark
rich [rɪtʃ] - reich
poor [pʊə] - arm
young [jʌŋ] - jung
old [oʊld] - alt

long [ˈlɔŋ] - lang
short [ʃɔːt] - kurz
high [haɪ] - hoch
low [loʊ] - tief
generous [ˈdʒenərəs] - großzügig
mean [miːn] - geizig
true [truː] - richtig

false [ˈfɔːls] - falsch
beautiful [ˈbjuːtəfl] - schön
ugly [ˈʌglɪ] - hässlich
new [njuː] - neu
old [oʊld] - alt
happy [ˈhæpɪ] - fröhlich, glücklich
sad [sæd] - traurig

Antonyms
Gegenteile

safe [seɪf] - sicher
dangerous [ˈdeɪndʒərəs] - gefährlich
early [ˈɜːlɪ] - früh
late [leɪt] - spät
light [laɪt] - hell
dark [dɑːk] - dunkel
open [ˈoʊpən] - offen, geöffnet
closed oder shut [kloʊzd | ʃʌt] - geschlossen, zu
tight [taɪt] - stramm, fest
loose [luːs] - locker
full [fʊl] - voll
empty [ˈemptɪ] - leer
many [ˈmenɪ] - viele
few [fjuː] - wenige
alive [əˈlaɪv] - lebendig
dead [ded] - tot
hot [hɔt] - heiß
cold [koʊld] - kalt
interesting [ˈɪntrəstɪŋ] - interessant
boring [ˈbɔːrɪŋ] - langweilig

lucky [ˈlʌkɪ] - glücklich
unlucky [ʌnˈlʌkɪ] - unglücklich
important [ɪmˈpɔːtnt] - wichtig
unimportant [ˌʌnɪmˈpɔːtnt] - unwichtig
right [raɪt] - richtig
wrong [rɔŋ] - falsch
far [ˈfɑː] - weit
near [nɪə] - nah
clean [kliːn] - sauber
dirty [ˈdɜːtɪ] - schmutzig
nice [naɪs] - nett
nasty [ˈnɑːstɪ] - gemein
pleasant [ˈpleznt] - angenehm
unpleasant [ʌnˈpleznt] - unangenehm
excellent [ˈeksələnt] - ausgezeichnet
terrible [ˈterəbl] - schrecklich
fair [feə] - fair
unfair [ˌʌnˈfeə] - unfair
normal [ˈnɔːml] - normal
abnormal [æbˈnɔːml] - anormal

Die 1300 wichtigen englischen Wörter

Days of the week Tage der Woche

Sunday ['sʌndɪ] Der Sonntag

Monday ['mʌndɪ] Der Montag

Tuesday ['tju:zdɪ] Der Dienstag

Wednesday ['wenzdɪ] Der Mittwoch

Thursday ['θə:zdɪ] Der Donnerstag

Friday ['fraɪdɪ] Der Freitag

Saturday ['sætədɪ] Der Samstag

week [wi:k] Die Woche

day [deɪ] Der Tag

night [naɪt] Die Nacht

today [tə'deɪ] heute

yesterday ['jestədɪ] gestern

tomorrow [tə'mɔrəʊ] morgen

morning ['mɔ:nɪŋ] Der Morgen

evening ['i:vnɪŋ] Der Abend

Months Die Monate

January ['dʒænjʊərɪ] Der Januar

February ['febjʊərɪ] Der Februar

March [mɑtʃ] Der März

April ['eɪpr(ə)l] Der April

May [meɪ] Der Mai

June [dʒʊn] Der Juni

July [dʒu(:)'laɪ] Der Juli

August ['ɔgʌst] Der August

September [sep'tembə] Der September

October [ɒk'təʊbə] Der Oktober

November [nəʊ'vembə] Der November

December [dɪ'sembə] Der Dezember

Seasons of the year Die Jahreszeiten

winter ['wɪntə] Der Winter

spring [sprɪŋ] Der Frühling

summer ['sʌmə] Der Sommer

autumn ['ɔ:təm] Der Herbst

Family Die Familie

aunt [ɑ:nt] Die Tante

brother ['brʌðə] Der Bruder

children ['tʃɪldr(ə)n] Die Kinder

dad Der Papa

daughter ['dɔ:tə] Die Tochter

family ['fæm(ə)lɪ] Die Familie

father ['fɑ:ðə] Der Vater

granddaughter ['græn(d)ˌdɔ:tə] Die Enkelin

grandfather ['græn(d)ˌfɑ:ðə] Der Großvater

grandmother ['græn(d)ˌmʌðə] Die Oma

grandparents ['græn(d)ˌpeər(ə)nts] Die Großeltern

grandson ['græn(d)sʌn] Der Enkel

great-grandfather [ˌgreɪt'grændˌfɑ:ðə] Der Urgroßvater

great-grandmother [greɪt'græn(d)ˌmʌðə] Die Urgroßmutter

mother ['mʌðə] Die Mutter

nephew ['nefju:] Der Neffe

niece [ni:s] Die Nichte

parents ['peər(ə)nts] Die Eltern

sister ['sɪstə] Die Schwester

son [sʌn] Der Sohn

uncle ['ʌŋkl] Der Onkel

Appearance and qualities Aussehen und Qualitäten

active ['æktɪv] aktiv

bald [bɔ:ld] kahl

character ['kærəktə] Der Charakter
clever ['klevə] klug
considerate [kən'sɪd(ə)rət] rücksichtsvoll
creative [krɪ'eɪtɪv] kreativ
cruel ['kru:əl] grausam
curly ['kɜ:lɪ] lockig
energetic [ˌɛnə'dʒɛtɪk] energetisch
fat [fæt] fett
generous ['dʒen(ə)rəs] großzügig
greedy ['gri:dɪ] gierig
hairy ['heərɪ] behaart
handsome ['hæn(d)səm] gut aussehend
kind [kaɪnd] freundlich
married ['mærɪd] verheiratet
old [əʊld] alt
plump [plʌmp] rundlich
polite [pə'laɪt] höflich
poor [pʊə] arm
pretty ['prɪtɪ] ziemlich
rich [rɪtʃ] reich
rude [ru:d] unhöflich
short [ʃɔ:t] kurz
single ['dʒen(ə)rəs] einzig
skinny ['skɪnɪ] dünn
slim [slɪm] schlank
straight [streɪt] gerade
strong [strɒŋ] stark
stupid ['stju:pɪd] blöd
tactful ['tæktf(ə)l] taktvoll
talented ['tæləntɪd] talentiert
tall [tɔ:l] hoch
thin [θɪn] dünn

ugly ['ʌglɪ] hässlich
unkind [ʌn'kaɪnd] unfreundlich
weak [wi:k] schwach
young [jʌŋ] jung

Emotions Emotionen
bored [bɔ:d] gelangweilt
confident ['kɒnfɪd(ə)nt] zuversichtlich
content [kən'tent] zufrieden
curious ['kjʊərɪəs] neugierig
ecstatic [ɪk'stætɪk] begeistert
emotion [ɪ'məʊʃ(ə)n] Die Emotion
excited [ɪk'saɪtɪd] aufgeregt
goofy ['gu:fɪ] doof
happy ['hæpɪ] glücklich
hoping ['həʊpɪŋ] hoffend
hungry ['hʌŋgrɪ] hungrig
lonely ['ləʊnlɪ] einsam
mischievous ['mɪstʃɪvəs] spitzbübisch
nervous ['nɜ:vəs] nervös
offended [ə'fend] beleidigt
sad [sæd] traurig
scared [skeəd] erschrocken
shocked [ʃɒkd] schockiert
sleepy ['sli:pɪ] schläfrig
surprised [sə'praɪzd] überrascht
thirsty ['θɜ:stɪ] durstig
tired ['taɪəd] müde

Clothes Kleider
anorak ['æn(ə)ræk] Der Anorak
belt [belt] Der Gürtel
blouse [blaʊz] Die Bluse
boots [bu:ts] Der Stiefel

bracelet [ˈbreɪslɪt] Das Armband
cap [ˈkæp] Die Kappe
cardigan [ˈkɑːdɪgən] Die Strickjacke
clothes [kləʊðz] Die Kleider
coat [kəʊt] Der Mantel
dress [dres] Das Kleid
earring [ˈɪərɪŋ] Der Ohrring
fur coat [fɜː kəʊt] Der Pelzmantel
glasses [ˈglɑːsɪz] Die Brille
glove [glʌv] Der Handschuh
hat [hæt] Der Hut
jacket [ˈdʒækɪt] Die Jacke
jeans [dʒiːnz] Die Jeans
jersey [ˈdʒɜːzɪ] Das Trikot
necklace [ˈnɛkləs] Die Halskette
nightie [ˈnaɪtɪ] Das Nachthemd
pyjamas [pəˈdʒɑːməs] Der Pyjama
raincoat [ˈreɪnkəʊt] Die Regenjacke
ring [rɪŋ] Der Ring
sandals [ˈsænd(ə)lz] Die Sandalen
scarf [skɑːf] Der Schal
shirt [ʃɜːt] Das Hemd
shoes [ʃuː] Die Schuhe
shorts [ʃɔːts] Die kurze Hose
skirt [skɜːt] Der Rock
slippers [ˈslɪpəz] Die Hausschuhe
sneakers [ˈsniːkəz] Die Turnschuhe
socks [sɔk] Die Socken
stockings [ˈstɔkɪŋz] Die Strümpfe
suit [s(j)uːt] Der Anzug
sweater [ˈswetə] Das Sweatshirt
swimsuit [ˈswɪmˌsuːt] Der Badeanzug

tie [taɪ] Die Krawatte
tights [taɪts] Die Strumpfhose
tracksuit [ˈtræks(j)uːt] Der Trainingsanzug
trousers [ˈtraʊzəz] Die Hose
T-shirt [ˈtiːʃɜːt] Das T-Shirt
umbrella [ʌmˈbrɛlə] Der Regenschirm
pants [pænts] Die Hose
watch [wɔtʃ] Die Uhr

House and furniture Haus und Möbel
alarm clock [əˈlɑːmˌklɔk] Der Wecker
apartment [əˈpɑːtmənt] Die Wohnung
balcony [ˈbælkənɪ] Der Balkon
bathroom [ˈbɑːθruːm] Das Badezimmer
bed [bed] Das Bett
bedroom [ˈbedruːm] Das Schlafzimmer
bedspread [ˈbedspred] Die Tagesdecke
bench [bentʃ] Die Bank
blanket [ˈblæŋkɪt] Die Decke
bookcase [ˈbʊkkeɪs] Das Bücherregal
carpet [ˈkɑːpɪt] Der Teppich
casket [ˈkɑːskɪt] Die Schatulle
chair [tʃeə] Der Sessel
closet [ˈklɔzɪt] Der Wandschrank
cupboard [ˈkʌbəd] Der Schrank
curtain [ˈkɜːtən] Der Vorhang
desk [desk] Der Schreibtisch
dining room [ˈdaɪnɪŋˌrʊm] Das Esszimmer
door [dɔː] Die Tür
doorbell [ˈdɔːbel] Die Türklingel
downstairs [ˈdaʊnˈsteəz] unten
furniture [ˈfɜːnɪtʃə] Die Möbel
garage [ˈgærɑːʒ] Die Garage

hall [hɔːl] Der Flur
hallway [ˈhɔːlweɪ] Der Korridor
house [haʊs] Das Haus
interior [ɪnˈtɪərɪə] Das Innere
kitchen [ˈkɪtʃɪn] Die Küche
lamp [læmp] Die Lampe
living room [ˈlɪvɪŋˌrʊm] Das Wohnzimmer
mailbox [ˈmeɪlbɔks] Der Briefkasten
mattress [ˈmætrəs] Die Matratze
mirror [ˈmɪrə] Der Spiegel
nightstand [naɪtstænd] Der Nachttisch
picture [ˈpɪktʃə] Das Bild
pillow [ˈpɪləʊ] Das Kissen
pillowcase [ˈpɪləʊkeɪs] Der Kissenbezug
roof [ruːf] Das Dach
room [ruːm] Das Zimmer
safe [seɪf] Der Safe
sheet [ʃiːt] Das Blatt
shelf [ʃelf] Das Regal
shower [ˈʃəʊə] Die Dusche
sofa [ˈsəʊfə] Das Sofa
stairs [steəˈz] Die Treppe
stool [stuːl] Der Schemel
table [ˈteɪbl] Die Tabelle
toilet [ˈtɔɪlət] Die Toilette
upstairs [ʌpˈsteəz] nach oben
window [ˈwɪndəʊ] Das Fenster

Kitchen Die Küche

burner [ˈbɜːnə] Der Brenner
cabinet [ˈkæbɪnət] Der Küchenschrank
canister [ˈkænɪstə] Der Kanister
chair [tʃeə] Der Sessel

cookbook [ˈkʊkbʊk] Das Kochbuch
dishwasher [ˈdɪʃˌwɔʃə] Der Geschirrspüler
faucet [ˈfɔːsɪt] Der Wasserhahn
freezer [ˈfriːzə] Der Gefrierschrank
kitchen [ˈkɪtʃɪn] Die Küche
kitchenware [ˈkɪtʃɪnweə] Das Geschirr
microwave [ˈmaɪkrə(ʊ)weɪv] Die Mikrowelle
oven [ˈʌv(ə)n] Der Ofen
refrigerator [rɪˈfrɪdʒ(ə)reɪtə] Der Kühlschrank
sink [sɪŋk] Das Waschbecken
sponge [spʌndʒ] Der Schwamm
stove [stəʊv] Der Herd
table [ˈteɪbl] Die Tabelle
toaster [ˈtəʊstə] Der Toaster
towel [ˈtaʊəl] Das Handtuch

Tableware Das Geschirr

bottle [ˈbɔtl] Die Flasche
bowl [bəʊl] Die Schüssel
coffeepot [ˈkɔfɪpɔt] Die Kaffeetasse
cup [kʌp] Die Tasse
fork [fɔːk] Die Gabel
frying pan [ˈfraɪɪŋˌpæn] Die Bratpfanne
glass [glɑːs] Das Glas
jug [dʒʌg] Der Krug
kettle [ˈketl] Der Kessel
knife [naɪf] Das Messer
lid [lɪd] Der Deckel
mug [mʌg] Der Becher
napkin [ˈnæpkɪn] Die Serviette
pan [pæn] Die Pfanne
pepper shaker [ˈpepəˌʃeɪkə] Der Pfefferstreuer
plate [pleɪt] Der Teller

salt shaker [sɔ:lt 'ʃeɪkə] Der Salzstreuer
saucepan ['sɔ:spən] Der Kochtopf
spoon [spu:n] Der Löffel
sugar bowl ['ʃʊgə bəʊl] Die Zuckerschüssel
tableware ['teɪblweə] Das Geschirr
teapot ['ti:pɔt] Die Teekanne

Food Essen

baked [beɪkt] gebacken
bean [bi:n] Die Bohne
beef [bi:f] Das Rindfleisch
bitter ['bɪtə] bitter
bread [bred] Das Brot
butter ['bʌtə] Die Butter
cake [keɪk] Der Kuchen
candy ['kændɪ] Die Süßigkeiten
caviar ['kævɪɑ:] Der Kaviar
cheese [tʃi:z] Der Käse
chicken ['tʃɪkɪn] Das Hähnchen
chocolate ['tʃɔklət] Die Schokolade
cocktail ['kɔkteɪl] Der Cocktail
cocoa ['kəʊkəʊ] Der Kakao
coffee ['kɔfɪ] Der Kaffee
cookie ['kʊkɪ] Das Plätzchen
croissant ['krwɑ:sɑ:ŋ] Das Croissant
cutlet ['kʌtlət] Das Kotelett
egg [eg] Das Ei
fish [fɪʃ] Der Fisch
flour ['flaʊə] Das Mehl
food [fu:d] Das Lebensmittel
fried [fraɪd] gebraten
fruit [fru:t] Die Frucht
ham [hæm] Der Schinken
ice cream [ˌaɪs'kri:m] Das Eis
jam [dʒæm] Die Marmelade
jelly ['dʒelɪ] Das Gelee
juice [dʒu:s] Der Saft
ketchup ['ketʃʌp] Der Ketchup
macaroni [ˌmæk(ə)'rəʊnɪ] Die Makkaroni
mayonnaise [ˌmeɪə'neɪz] Die Mayonnaise
meat [mi:t] Das Fleisch
milk [mɪlk] Die Milch
pancake ['pænkeɪk] Der Pfannkuchen
pasta ['pæstə] Die Pasta
pepper ['pepə] Der Pfeffer
pie [paɪ] Der Kuchen
pizza ['pi:tsə] Die Pizza
pork [pɔ:k] Das Schweinefleisch
porridge ['pɔrɪdʒ] Der Haferbrei
potato [pə'teɪtəʊ] Die Kartoffel
rice [raɪs] Der Reis
salad ['sæləd] Der Salat
salt [sɔ:lt] Das Salz
salted ['sɔ:ltɪd] gesalzen
sandwich ['sænwɪdʒ] Das Sandwich
sauce [sɔ:s] Die Soße
sausage ['sɔsɪdʒ] Die Wurst
soup [su:p] Die Suppe
sour ['saʊə] sauer
spice [spaɪs] würzen
steak [steɪk] Das Steak
sugar ['ʃʊgə] Der Zucker
sweet [swi:t] süß
tea [ti:] Der Tee
vegetables ['vedʒ(ə)təbls] Das Gemüse

Meat and fish Fleisch und Fisch

meat [mi:t] Das Fleisch
beef [bi:f] Das Rindfleisch
lamb [læm] Das Lamm
mutton [mʌtn] Das Hammelfleisch
pork [pɔ:k] Das Schweinefleisch
veal [vi:l] Das Kalbfleisch
venison [ˈvɛnɪs(ə)n] Das Wild
bacon [ˈbeɪkən] Der Speck
ham [hæm] Der Schinken
liver [ˈlɪvə] Die Leber
kidneys [ˈkɪdnɪz] Die Nieren
poultry [ˈpəʊltrɪ] Das Geflügel
chicken [ˈtʃɪkɪn] Das Hähnchen
turkey [ˈtɜ:kɪ] Der Truthahn
duck [dʌk] Die Ente
goose [gu:s] Die Gans
fish [fɪʃ] Der Fisch
cod [kɔd] Der Kabeljau
trout [traʊt] Die Forelle
salmon [ˈsæmən] Der Lachs
hake [heɪk] Der Seehecht
plaice [pleɪs] Die Scholle
mackerel [ˈmæk(ə)rəl] Die Makrele
sardine [sɑːˈdi:n] Die Sardine
herring [ˈhɛrɪŋ] Der Hering
seafood [ˈsi:fu:d] Die Meeresfrüchte
prawn [prɔ:n] Die Garnele
shrimp [ʃrɪmp] Die Garnele
mussel [ˈmʌs(ə)l] Die Muschel
oyster [ˈɔɪstə] Die Auster
lobster [ˈlɔbstə] Der Hummer

squid [skwɪd] Der Tintenfisch
crab [kræb] Die Krabbe

Fruit Die Frucht

apple [ˈæpl] Der Apfel
apricot [ˈeɪprɪkɔt] Die Aprikose
banana [bəˈnɑ:nə] Die Banane
fruit [fru:t] Die Frucht
grape [greɪp] Die Traube
grapefruit [ˈgreɪpfru:t] Die Grapefruit
kiwi [ˈki:wi:] Die Kiwi
lemon [ˈlemən] Die Zitrone
lime [laɪm] Die Limette
mango [ˈmæŋgəʊ] Die Mango
melon [ˈmelən] Die Melone
peach [pi:tʃ] Der Pfirsich
pear [peə] Die Birne
pineapple [ˈpaɪnæpl] Die Ananas
plum [plʌm] Die Pflaume

Vegetables Das Gemüse

beans [bi:nz] Die Bohnen
beet [bi:t] Die Zuckerrüben
cabbage [ˈkæbɪdʒ] Der Kohl
carrot [ˈkærət] Die Karotte
celery [ˈsel(ə)rɪ] Der Sellerie
cucumber [ˈkju:kʌmbə] Die Gurke
dill [dɪl] Der Dill
eggplant [ˈegplɑ:nt] Die Aubergine
garlic [ˈgɑ:lɪk] Der Knoblauch
onion [ˈʌnjən] Die Zwiebel
parsley [ˈpɑ:slɪ] Die Petersilie
pea [pi:] Die Erbse
pepper [ˈpepə] Der Pfeffer

potato [pə'teɪtəʊ] Die Kartoffel

pumpkin ['pʌmpkɪn] Der Kürbis

radish ['rædɪʃ] Der Rettich

tomato [tə'mɑːtəʊ] Die Tomate

vegetable ['vedʒ(ə)təbl] Das Gemüse

Beverages Die Getränke

alcohol ['ælkəhɔl] Alkohol

alcoholic beverage [ælkə'hɔlɪk 'bevərɪdʒ] alkoholisches Getränk

beer [bɪə] Das Bier

beverage ['bɛvərɪdʒ] Das Getränk

cocktail ['kɔkteɪl] Der Cocktail

cocoa ['kəʊkəʊ] Der Kakao

coffee ['kɔfɪ] Der Kaffee

drink [drɪŋk] Das Getränk

fruit juice [fruːt dʒuːs] Der Fruchtsaft

iced tea [aɪst tiː] Der Eistee

juice [dʒuːs] Der Saft

lemonade [ˌlɛmə'neɪd] Die Limonade

milk [mɪlk] Die Milch

milkshake ['mɪlkʃeɪk] Der Milchshake

orange juice ['ɔrɪndʒ dʒuːs] Der Orangensaft

soft drink [sɔft drɪŋk] Das alkoholfreie Getränk

tea [tiː] Der Tee

tomato juice [tə'mɑːtəʊ dʒuːs] Der Tomatensaft

vegetable juice ['vɛdʒ(ə)təbl dʒuːs] Der Gemüsesaft

water ['wɔːtə] Das Wasser

wine [waɪn] Der Wein

Cooking Das Kochen

add [æd] hinzufügen

bake [beɪk] backen

beat [biːt] schlagen

boil [bɔɪl] kochen

chop [tʃɔp] hacken

cook [kʊk] kochen

cooking ['kʊkɪŋ] kochend

fry [fraɪ] braten

grate [greɪt] reiben

grill [grɪl] grillen

melt [mɛlt] schmelzen

mince [mɪns] zerkleinern

mix [mɪks] mischen

peel [piːl] schälen

pour [pɔː] gießen

roast [rəʊst] braten

sift [sɪft] sieben

simmer ['sɪmə] kochen

slice [slaɪs] schneiden

stir [stɜː] rühren

wash [wɔʃ] waschen

weigh [weɪ] wiegen

whisk [wɪsk] verquirlen

Housekeeping Der Haushalt

air [eər] Die Luft

bleach [bliːtʃ] bleichen

broom [bruːm] Der Besen

bucket ['bʌkɪt] Der Eimer

cleanser ['klɛnzə] Das Reinigungsmittel

clothespin ['kləʊðzpɪn] Die Wäscheklammer

dirt [dɜːrt] Der Schmutz

dust [dʌst] Der Staub

dustpan ['dʌs(t)pæn] Die Schaufel

empty ['emptɪ] leer

garbage ['gɑ:rbɪdʒ] Der Müll

housekeeping ['haʊski:pɪŋ] Die Haushaltung

iron ['aɪən] Das Bügeleisen

ironing board ['aɪənɪŋbɔ:d] Das Bügelbrett

laundry ['lɔ:ndrɪ] Die Wäsche

laundry detergent ['lɔ:ndrɪ dɪ'tɜ:dʒ(ə)nt] Das Waschmittel

mop [mɔp] Der Mopp

rag [ræg] Der Lappen

sponge [spʌndʒ] Der Schwamm

sweep [swi:p] fegen

trash can ['træʃˌkæn] Der Mülleimer

vacuum cleaner ['vækju:mˌkli:nə] Der Staubsauger

wipe [waɪp] wischen

Body care Die Körperpflege

care [keə] Die Pflege

cologne [kə'ləʊn] Das Eau de Cologne

comb [kəʊm] Der Kamm

dental floss [ˌdentl'flɔs] Die Zahnseide

deodorant [dɪ'əʊd(ə)r(ə)nt] Das Deodorant

fan [fæn] Der Ventilator

freshener ['freʃ(ə)nə] Das Erfrischungsmittel

hairpin ['heəpɪn] Die Haarnadel

hamper ['hæmpə] Der Korb

hygiene ['haɪdʒi:n] Die Hygiene

lipstick ['lɪpstɪk] Der Lippenstift

mascara [mæ'skɑ:rə] Die Wimperntusche

mirror ['mɪrə] Der Spiegel

mouthwash ['maʊθwɔʃ] Das Mundwasser

nail polish ['neɪlˌpɔlɪʃ] Die Nagelpolitur

perfume ['pɜ:fju:m] Das Parfüm

razor ['reɪzə] Der Rasierer

scale [skeɪl] Die Waage

scissors ['sɪzəz] Die Schere

shampoo [ʃæm'pu:] Das Shampoo

shaving cream ['ʃeɪvɪŋˌkri:m] Der Rasierschaum

shower ['ʃəʊə] Die Dusche

sink [sɪŋk] Das Waschbecken

soap [səʊp] Die Seife

sponge [spʌndʒ] Der Schwamm

toilet ['tɔɪlət] Die Toilette

toothbrush ['tu:θbrʌʃ] Die Zahnbürste

toothpaste ['tu:θpeɪst] Die Zahnpasta

towel ['taʊəl] Das Handtuch

tweezers ['twi:zəz] Die Pinzette

Weather Das Wetter

breeze [bri:z] Die Brise

bright [braɪt] hell

chilly ['tʃɪlɪ] frostig

cloudy ['klaʊdɪ] bewölkt

cold [kəʊld] kalt

cool [ku:l] kühl

fog [fɔg] Der Nebel

foggy ['fɔgi] neblig

frosty ['frɔstɪ] eisig

hail [heɪl] Der Hagel

heat [hi:t] Die Hitze

hot [hɔt] heiß

lightning ['laɪtnɪŋ] Der Blitz

mist [mɪst] Der Nebel

rain [reɪn] Der Regen

rainy ['reɪnɪ] regnerisch

shower [ˈʃaʊə] Der Regenschauer

snow [snəʊ] Der Schnee

sunny [ˈsʌnɪ] sonnig

temperature [ˈtɛmp(ə)rətʃə] Die Temperatur

weather [ˈweðə] Das Wetter

wind [wɪnd] Der Wind

windy [ˈwɪndɪ] windig

Transport Der Transport

airplane [ˈeəpleɪn] Das Flugzeug

ambulance [ˈæmbjələn(t)s] Der Krankenwagen

bicycle [ˈbaɪsɪk(ə)l] Das Fahrrad

boat [bəʊt] Das Boot

bus [bʌs] Der Bus

car [kɑː] Das Auto

helicopter [ˈhelɪkɔptə] Der Hubschrauber

motorcycle [ˈməʊtəˌsaɪkl] Das Motorrad

police car [pəˈliːs kɑː] Das Polizeiauto

road [rəʊd] Die Straße

sailboat [ˈseɪlbəʊt] Das Segelboot

scooter [ˈskuːtə] Der Roller

ship [ʃɪp] Das Schiff

street [striːt] Die Straße

traffic light [ˈtræfɪk ˈlaɪt] Die Ampel

train [treɪn] Der Zug

tram [trəm] Die Tram

transport [ˌtræn(t)spɔːˈt] Der Transport

truck [trʌk] Der LKW

van [væn] Der Van

City Die Stadt

alley [ˈælɪ] Die Gasse

area [ˈɛ(ə)rɪə] Der Bereich

avenue [ˈævɪnjuː] Die Allee

bakery [ˈbeɪkərɪ] Die Bäckerei

bank [ˈbɑnk] Die Bank

bar [bɑː] Die Bar

baths [bɑːθs] Die Badeanstalt

bench [bentʃ] Die Bank

bookstore [ˈbʊkstɔː] Die Buchhandlung

bridge [brɪdʒ] Die Brücke

building [ˈbɪldɪŋ] Das Gebäude

bus stop [bʌs stɔp] Die Bushaltestelle

cafe [ˈkæfeɪ] Das Café

car park [kɑːpɑːk] Der Parkplatz

church [tʃɜːtʃ] Die Kirche

cinema [ˈsɪnɪmə] Das Kino

circus [ˈsəːkəs] Der Zirkus

city [ˈsɪtɪ] Die Stadt

coffee shop [ˈkɔfɪ ʃɔp] Das Café

corner [ˈkɔːnə] Die Ecke

crossing [ˈkrɔsɪŋ] Die Kreuzung

crosswalk [ˈkrɔswɔːk] Die Fußgängerbrücke

dentist's [ˈdentɪstz] Die Zahnarztpraxis

department store [dɪˈpɑːtmənt ˈstɔː] Das Kaufhaus

doctor's [ˈdɔktəz] Der Arzt

drugstore [ˈdrʌgstɔː] Die Drogerie

fire station [ˈfaɪəˈsteɪʃən] Die Feuerwehr

flower shop [ˈflaʊə ʃɔp] Das Blumengeschäft

flower-bed [ˈflaʊəbed] Das Blumenbeet

fountain [ˈfaʊntɪn] Der Brunnen

gallery [ˈgælərɪ] Die Galerie

gas station [gæs ˈsteɪʃ(ə)n] Die Tankstelle

gate [geɪt] Das Tor

hair salon [heəsæˈlɔːŋ] Der Friseur

hospital ['hɔspɪt(ə)l] Das Krankenhaus
hotel [həʊ'tɛl] Das Hotel
intersection [ˌɪntə'sekʃən] Die Straßenkreuzung
library ['laɪbr(ə)rɪ] Die Bibliothek
map [mæp] Die Karte
market ['mɑːkɪt] Der Markt
monument ['mɔnjʊmənt] Das Monument
movie theater ['muːvɪ'θɪətə] Das Kino
museum [mjuːˈzɪəm] Das Museum
nightclub [naɪtklʌb] Der Nachtclub
palace [ˈpælɪs] Der Palast
park [pɑːk] Der Park
parking lot ['pɑːkɪŋ'lɔt] Der Parkplatz
pavement ['peɪvmənt] Das Pflaster
pedestrian crossing [pɪ'destrɪən'krɔsɪŋ] Der Zebrastreifen
pharmacy [ˈfɑːməsɪ] Die Apotheke
picture gallery ['pɪktʃə'gælərɪ] Die Bildergalerie
police [pə'liːs] Die Polizei
pool [puːl] Das Schwimmbad
post office [pəʊst 'ɔfɪs] Die Post
restaurant ['restərɔnt] Das Restaurant
road [rəʊd] Die Straße
road sign [rəʊdsaɪn] Das Straßenschild
school [skuːl] Die Schule
seat [siːt] Der Sitz
shop [ʃɔp] Das Geschäft
sidewalk ['saɪdwɔːk] Der Bürgersteig
skyscraper [ˈskaɪˌskreɪpə] Der Wolkenkratzer
square [skwɛə] Der Platz
stadium ['steɪdjəm] Das Stadion
stall [stɔːl] Der Stall

statue ['stætjuː] Die Statue
store [stɔː] Das Geschäft
street [striːt] Die Straße
street map [striːtmæp] Die Straßenkarte
suburb ['sʌbəːb] Der Vorort
subway ['sʌbweɪ] Die U-Bahn
supermarket ['s(j)uːpəˌmɑːkɪt] Der Supermarkt
swimming pool ['swɪmɪŋpuːl] Das Schwimmbad
taxi-rank ['tæksɪræŋk] Der Taxistand
theatre [ˈθɪətə] Das Theater
town [taʊn] Die Stadt
town plan [taʊnplæn] Der Stadtplan
town square [taʊnskwɛə] Der Stadtplatz
traffic lights ['træfɪklaɪts] Die Ampeln
train station [treɪn 'steɪʃ(ə)n] Der Bahnhof
underground [ˌʌndəˈgraʊnd] Die Untergrundbahn
underpass ['ʌndəpɑːs] Die Unterführung
university [ˌjuːnɪ'vɜːsɪtɪ] Die Universität
zoo [zuː] Der Zoo

School Die Schule
backpack ['bækpæk] Der Rucksack
bell [bɛl] Die Glocke
biology [baɪ'ɔlədʒɪ] Die Biologie
blackboard ['blækbɔːd] Die Tafel
break [breɪk] Die Unterbrechung
calculator [ˈkælkjʊleɪtə] Der Taschenrechner
chair [tʃeə] Der Sessel
chalk [tʃɔːk] Die Kreide
chemistry [ˈkɛmɪstrɪ] Die Chemie
clamp [klæmp] Die Klemme
classroom ['klɑːsrʊm] Das Klassenzimmer

clip [klɪp] Der Clip

clipboard [ˈklɪpbɔːd] Das Klemmbrett

clock [klɔk] Die Uhr

correction fluid [kəˈrɛkʃ(ə)n ˌfluːɪd] Die Korrekturflüssigkeit

curriculum [kəˈrɪkjʊləm] Der Lehrplan

desk [desk] Der Schreibtisch

drawing [ˈdrɔːɪŋ] Die Zeichnung

education [ˌɛdjʊˈkeɪʃ(ə)n] Die Bildung

eraser [ɪˈreɪzə] Der Radiergummi

exam [ɪgˈzæm] Die Prüfung

examination [ɪgˌzæmɪˈneɪʃ(ə)n] Die Untersuchung

file [faɪl] Die Datei

geography [dʒɪˈɒgrəfɪ] Die Erdkunde

globe [gləʊb] Der Globus

glue [gluː] kleben

headmaster [ˌhedˈmɑːstə] Der Schulleiter

highlighter [ˈhaɪlaɪtə] Der Textmarker

history [ˈhɪst(ə)rɪ] Die Geschichte

holiday [ˈhɒlɪdɪ] Der Urlaub

lesson [ˈlɛs(ə)n] Die Lektion

locker [ˈlɔkə] Das Schließfach

map [mæp] Die Karte

mark [mɑːk] Das Kennzeichen

marker [ˈmɑːkə] Der Marker

mathematics [ˌmæθɪˈmætɪks] Die Mathematik

music [ˈmjuːzɪk] Die Musik

notebook [ˈnəʊtbʊk] Das Notizbuch

notepad [ˈnəʊtpæd] Der Notizblock

office supplies [ˈɒfɪs səˈplaɪs] Der Bürobedarf

paper [ˈpeɪpə] Das Papier

pen [pen] Der Stift

pencil [ˈpen(t)s(ə)l] Der Bleistift

pencil case [ˈpen(t)s(ə)lˌkeɪs] Das Mäppchen

physics [ˈfɪɪzɪks] Die Physik

puncher [pʌntʃ] der Locher

pupil [ˈpjuːp(ə)l] Der Schüler

pushpin [ˈpʊʃpɪn] Die Reißwecke

ruler [ˈruːlə] Das Lineal

school [skuːl] Die Schule

scissors [ˈsɪzəz] Die Schere

scotch tape [ˈskɔtʃˌteɪp] Der Tesafilm

semester [sɪˈmɛstə] Das Semester

sharpener [ˈʃɑːp(ə)nə] Der Anspitzer

stapler [ˈsteɪplə] Der Hefter

staples [ˈsteɪpls] Die Heftklammern

stationery [ˈsteɪʃ(ə)n(ə)rɪ] Die Schreibwaren

sticker [ˈstɪkə] Der Aufkleber

student [ˈstjuːd(ə)nt] Der Schüler

tape [teɪp] Das Band

teacher [ˈtiːtʃə] Der Lehrer

test [tɛst] Der Test

textbook [ˈtekstbʊk] Das Lehrbuch

timetable [ˈtaɪmˌteɪb(ə)l] Der Zeitplan

Professions Die Berufe

accountant [əˈkaʊntənt] Der Buchhalter

actor [ˈæktə] Der Schauspieler

administrator [ədˈmɪnɪstreɪtə] Der Administrator

architect [ˈɑːkɪtekt] Der Architekt

artist [ˈɑːtɪst] Der Künstler

athlete [ˈæθliːt] Der Athlet

barber [ˈbɑːbə] Der Herrenfriseur

barman [ˈbɑːmən] Der Barkeeper

bodyguard [ˈbɒdɪgɑːd] Der Leibwächter
builder [ˈbɪldə] Der Erbauer
cashier [kəˈʃɪə] Der Kassierer
cleaner [ˈkliːnə] Der Reiniger
coach [kəʊtʃ] Der Trainer
composer [kəmˈpəʊzə] Der Komponist
consultant [kənˈsʌlt(ə)nt] Der Berater
cook [kʊk] Der Koch
courier [ˈkʊrɪə] Der Kurier
dentist [ˈdɛntɪst] Der Zahnarzt
designer [dɪˈzaɪnə] Der Designer
doctor [ˈdɒktə] Der Arzt
driver [ˈdraɪvə] Der Fahrer
economist [ɪˈkɒnəmɪst] Der Ökonom
electrician [ɪˌlɛkˈtrɪʃ(ə)n] Der Elektriker
engineer [ˌɛndʒɪˈnɪə] Der Ingenieur
financier [f(a)ɪˈnænsɪə] Der Financier
fireman [-ˈfaɪəmən] Der Feuerwehrmann
guide [gaɪd] Der Führer
hairdresser [ˈhɛəˌdrɛsə] Der Friseur
interpreter [ɪnˈtɜːprɪtə] Der Dolmetscher
journalist [ˈdʒɜːn(ə)lɪst] Der Journalist
lawyer [ˈlɔːjə] Der Anwalt
librarian [ɪˌlɛkˈtrɪʃ(ə)n] Der Bibliothekar
manager [ˈmænɪdʒə] Manager
military (man) [ˈmɪlɪt(ə)rɪ] Der Soldat
musician [mjuːˈzɪʃ(ə)n] Der Musiker
nurse [nɜːs] Die Krankenschwester
photographer [fəˈtɒgrəfə] Der Fotograf
plumber [ˈplʌmə] Der Klempner
policeman [-pəˈliːsmən] Der Polizist
politician [ˌpɒlɪˈtɪʃ(ə)n] Der Politiker

postman [-ˈpəʊstmən] Der Briefträger
priest [priːst] Der Priester
profession [prəˈfɛʃ(ə)n] Der Beruf
programmer [ˈprəʊgræmə] Der Programmierer
scientist [ˈsaɪəntɪst] Der Wissenschaftler
secretary [ˈsɛkrət(ə)rɪ] Die Sekretärin
shop assistant [ˈʃɒpəˌsɪstənt] Der Verkäufer
singer [ˈsɪŋə] Der Sänger
stylist [ˈstaɪlɪst] Der Stylist
taxi driver [ˈtæksɪˌdraɪvə] Der Taxifahrer
teacher [ˈtiːtʃə] Der Lehrer
vet [vɛt] Der Tierarzt
waiter [ˈweɪtə] Die Bedienung
writer [ˈraɪtə] Der Schriftsteller

Actions Die Aktionen

bend [bend] biegen
carry [ˈkærɪ] tragen
catch [kætʃ] fangen
crawl [krɔːl] kriechen
dive [daɪv] tauchen
drag [dræg] ziehen
hit [hɪt] schlagen
hold [həʊld] halten
hop [hɒp] hüpfen
jump [dʒʌmp] springen
kick [kɪk] treten
lean [liːn] lehnen
lift [lɪft] aufheben
march [mɑːtʃ] marschieren
pull [pʊl] ziehen
push [pʊʃ] drücken
put [pʊt] stellen

run [rʌn] laufen

sit [sɪt] sitzen

skip [skɪp] überspringen

slap [slæp] schlagen

squat [skwɔt] hocken

stretch [strɛtʃ] strecken

throw [θrəʊ] werfen

tiptoe [ˈtɪptəʊ] auf Zehenspitzen gehen

walk [wɔːk] gehen

Music Die Musik

accompaniment [tuː əˈkʌmpəni] Die musikalische Begleitung

accordion [əˈkɔːdjən] Das Akkordeon

album [ˈælbəm] Das Album

bagpipe [ˈbægpaɪp] Der Dudelsack

balalaika [ˌbæləˈlaɪkə] Die Balalaika

ballet [ˈbæleɪ] Das Ballett

band [bænd] Das Band

bass [beɪs] Der Bass

bassoon [bəˈsuːn] Das Fagott

baton [ˈbætən] Der Taktstock

bow [baʊ] Der Bogen

brass instruments [brɑːs ˈɪnstrəmənts] Die Blechbläser

cello [ˈtʃɛləʊ] Das Cello

chamber music [ˈtʃeɪmbə ˈmjuːzɪk] Die Kammermusik

clarinet [ˌklærɪˈnɛt] Die Klarinette

classical music [ˈklæsɪkəl ˈmjuːzɪk] Die klassische Musik

compose [tuː kəmˈpəʊz] komponieren

composer [kəmˈpəʊzə] Der Komponist

concert [ˈkɔnsət] Das Konzert

conductor [kənˈdʌktə] Der Dirigent

cymbals [ˈsɪmbəlz] Das Becken

drum [drʌm] Die Trommel

drum sticks [drʌm stɪks] Die Trommelstöcke

flute [fluːt] Die Flöte

grand piano [grænd pɪˈænəʊ] Der Konzertflügel

guitar [gɪˈtɑː] Die Gitarre

harp [hɑːp] Die Harfe

horn [hɔːn] Das Horn

instrumental music [ˌɪnstrʊˈmɛntl ˈmjuːzɪk] Die Instrumentalmusik

loudspeaker [laʊdˈspiːkə] Der Lautsprecher

microphone [ˈmaɪkrəfəʊn] Das Mikrofon

musical instruments [ˈmjuːzɪkl ˈɪnstrəmənts] Die Musikinstrumente

musician [mjuːˈzɪʃən] Der Musiker

oboe [ˈəʊbəʊ] Die Oboe

opera [ˈɔpərə] Die Oper

operetta [ˌɔpəˈrɛtə] Die Operette

orchestra [ˈɔːkɪstrə] Das Orchester

organ [ˈɔːgən] Die Orgel

percussion [pəˈkʌʃən] Das Schlagzeug

piano [pɪˈænəʊ] Das Klavier

recital [rɪˈsaɪtl] Die Aufführung

saxophone [ˈsæksəfəʊn] Das Saxophon

single [ˈsɪŋgl] Die Single

soloist [ˈsəʊləʊɪst] Der Solist

song [sɔŋ] Das Lied

sound [saʊnd] Der Klang

string instruments [strɪŋ ˈɪnstrəmənts] Die Streichinstrumente

symphony [ˈsɪmfəni] Die Symphonie

synthesizer [ˈsɪnθɪˌsaɪzə] Der Synthesizer

transcribe [tuː trænsˈkraɪb] transkribieren

trombone [trɔmˈbəʊn] Die Posaune

trumpet [ˈtrʌmpɪt] Die Trompete

tuba [ˈtjuːbə] Die Tuba

video (clip) [ˈvɪdɪəʊ klɪp] Das Video (Clip)

viola [vɪˈəʊlə] Die Viola

violin [ˌvaɪəˈlɪn] Die Geige

virtuoso [ˌvɜːtjʊˈəʊzəʊ] Der Virtuose

wind instruments [wɪnd ˈɪnstrəmənts] Die Blasinstrumente

Sports Der Sport

aerobics [ɛəˈrəʊbɪks] Das Aerobic

athletics [æθˈletɪks] die Leichtathletik

basketball [ˈbɑːskɪtbɔːl] Das Basketballspiel

bowling [ˈbəʊlɪŋ] Das Bowling

boxing [ˈbɔksɪŋ] Das Boxen

canoeing [kəˈnuːɪŋ] Der Kanusport

cycling [ˈsaɪklɪŋ] Das Radfahren

dancing [ˈdɑːnsɪŋ] Das Tanzen

diving [ˈdaɪvɪŋ] Das Tauchen

football [ˈfʊtbɔːl] Das Fußballspiel

golf [gɔlf] Das Golf

gymnastics [dʒɪmˈnæstɪks] Die Gymnastik

hockey [ˈhɔkɪ] Das Eishockey

jogging [ˈdʒɔgɪŋ] Das Jogging

judo [ˈdʒuːdəʊ] Das Judo

karate [kəˈrɑːtɪ] Das Karate

parachuting [ˈpærəʃuːtɪŋ] Das Fallschirmspringen

ping-pong [ˈpɪŋˌpɔŋ] Das Tischtennis

racing [ˈreɪsɪŋ] Das Rennen

sailing [ˈseɪlɪŋ] Das Segeln

shooting [ˈʃuːtɪŋ] Das Schießen

skateboarding [ˈskeɪtbɔːdɪŋ] Das Skateboarding

skating [ˈskeɪtɪŋ] Das Skaten

skiing [ˈskiːɪŋ] Das Skifahren

sledding [ˈsledɪŋ] Das Schlittenfahren

swimming [swimɪŋ] Das Schwimmen

soccer [ˈsɔkə] Das Fußballspiel

tennis [ˈtenɪs] Das Tennis

volleyball [ˈvɔlɪbɔːl] Das Volleyballspiel

weightlifting [ˈweɪtˌlɪftɪŋ] Das Gewichtheben

wrestling [ˈreslɪŋ] Das Ringen

yachting [ˈjɔtɪŋ] Das Segeln

Body Der Körper

ankle [ˈæŋkl] Der Knöchel

arm [ɑːm] Der Arm

back [bæk] Der Rücken

bald [bɔːld] kahl

beard [bɪəd] Der Bart

body [ˈbɔdɪ] Der Körper

bottom [ˈbɔtəm] Das Gesäß

calf (calves) [kɑːf] [kɑːvz] Die Waden

cheek [tʃiːk] Die Wange

chest [tʃest] Die Brust

chin [tʃɪn] Das Kinn

elbow [ˈelbəʊ] Der Ellbogen

eye(s) [aɪ] Das Auge (die Augen)

eyebrow [ˈaɪbraʊ] Die Augenbraue

eyelash [ˈaɪlæʃ] Die Wimper

eyelid [ˈaɪlɪd] Das Augenlid

face [feɪs] Das Gesicht

finger [ˈfɪŋgə] Der Finger

fingernail ['fɪŋgəneɪl] Der Fingernagel
foot (feet) [fʊt] [fi:t] Der Fuß (die Füße)
forehead ['fɔ:hed] Die Stirn
glasses ['glɑ:sɪz] Die Brille
hair [heə] Das Haar
hairy ['heərɪ] behaart
hand [hænd] Die Hand
head [hed] Der Kopf
heel [hi:l] Die Hacke
index finger ['ɪndeks 'fɪŋgə] Der Zeigefinger
knee [ni:] Das Knie
leg [leg] Das Bein
lip(s) [lɪp] Die Lippe(n)
little finger ['lɪtl 'fɪŋgə] Der kleine Finger
man [mæn] Der Mann
middle finger ['mɪdl 'fɪŋgə] Der Mittelfinger
moustache [mə'stɑ:ʃ] Der Schnurrbart
mouth [maʊθ] Der Mund
neck [nek] Der Hals
nose [nəʊz] Die Nase
palm [pɑ:m] Die Handinnenfläche
pupil ['pju:p(ə)l] Die Pupille
ring finger [rɪŋ 'fɪŋgə] Der Ringfinger
shin [ʃɪn] Das Schienbein
shoulder ['ʃəʊldə] Die Schulter
stomach ['stʌmək] Der Bauch
sunglasses ['sʌnˌglɑ:sɪz] Die Sonnenbrille
thigh [θaɪ] Der Schenkel
thumb [θʌm] Der Daumen
toe [təʊ] Die Zehe
toenail ['təʊneɪl] Der Zehennagel
tongue [tʌŋ] Die Zunge

tooth (teeth) [tu:θ] [ti:θ] Der Zahn (die Zähne)
waist [weɪst] Die Taille
woman ['wʊmən] Die Frau

Nature Die Natur
beach [bi:tʃ] Der Strand
canyon [ˈkænjən] Die Schlucht
coast [kəʊst] Die Küste
desert ['dezət] Die Wüste
field [fi:ld] Das Feld
forest ['fɔrɪst] Der Wald
glacier ['glæsɪə] Der Gletscher
hill [hɪl] Der Hügel
hollow ['hɔləʊ] Die Höhle
island [ˈaɪlənd] Die Insel
jungle ['dʒʌŋgl] Der Dschungel
lake [leɪk] Die See
mountain ['maʊntɪn] Der Berg
nature ['neɪtʃə] Die Natur
ocean ['əʊʃ(ə)n] Der Ozean
plain [pleɪn] Die Ebene
pond [pɔnd] Der Teich
river ['rɪvə] Der Fluss
rock [rɔk] Der Felsen
sea [si:] Das Meer

Pet Das Haustier
cat [kæt] Die Katze
dog [dɔg] Der Hund
guinea pig [ˈgɪnɪˌpɪg] Das Meerschweinchen
hamster [ˈhæmstə] Der Hamster
horse [hɔ:s] Das Pferd
kitten [kɪtn] Das Kätzchen
pet [pɛt] Das Haustier

pig [pɪg] Das Schwein
piglet [ˈpɪglɪŋ] Das Ferkel
puppy [ˈpʌpɪ] Der Welpe
rabbit [ˈræbɪt] Der Hase

Animals Die Tiere

animal [ˈænɪm(ə)l] Das Tier
bat [bæt] Die Fledermaus
bear [beə] Der Bär
beaver [ˈbiːvə] Der Biber
bison [ˈbaɪs(ə)n] Der Bison
camel [ˈkæm(ə)l] Das Kamel
chimpanzee [ˌtʃɪmpænˈziː] Der Schimpanse
deer [dɪə] Der Hirsch
donkey [ˈdɔŋkɪ] Der Esel
elephant [ˈelɪfənt] Der Elefant
fox [fɔks] Der Fuchs
giraffe [dʒɪˈrɑːf] Die Giraffe
gorilla [gəˈrɪlə] Der Gorilla
hippopotamus [ˌhɪpəˈpɔtəməs] Das Nilpferd
horse [hɔːs] Das Pferd
hyena [haɪˈiːnə] Die Hyäne
kangaroo [ˌkæŋ(ə)ˈruː] Das Känguru
koala [kəʊˈɑːlə] Der Koala
leopard [ˈlɛpəd] Der Leopard
lion [ˈlaɪən] Der Löwe
llama [ˈlɑːmə] Das Lama
monkey [ˈmʌŋkɪ] Der Affe
moose [muːs] Der Elch
mouse [maʊs] Die Maus
panda [ˈpændə] Der Pandabär
pig [pɪg] Das Schwein
rabbit [ˈræbɪt] Der Hase

rat [ræt] Die Ratte
rhinoceros [raɪˈnɔs(ə)rəs] Das Nashorn
skunk [skʌŋk] Der Skunk
squirrel [ˈskwɪrəl] Das Eichhörnchen
tiger [ˈtaɪgə] Der Tiger
wolf [wʊlf] Der Wolf
zebra [ˈzebrə] Das Zebra

Birds Die Vögel

bird [bɜːd] Der Vogel
canary [kæˈnɛ(ə)rɪ] Der Kanarienvogel
chicken [ˈtʃɪkɪn] Das Hühnchen
crane [kreɪn] Der Kranich
crow [krəʊ] Die Krähe
cuckoo [ˈkʊkuː] Der Kuckuck
duck [dʌk] Die Ente
eagle [ˈiːg(ə)l] Der Adler
flamingo [fləˈmɪŋgəʊ] Der Flamingo
goose [guːs] Die Gans
hawk [hɔːk] Der Falke
hummingbird [ˈhʌmɪŋbɜːd] Der Kolibri
ostrich [ˈɔstrɪtʃ] Der Vogel Strauß
owl [aʊl] Die Eule
parrot [ˈpærət] Der Papagei
peacock [ˈpiːkɔk] Der Pfau
pelican [ˈpɛlɪkən] Der Pelikan
penguin [ˈpɛŋgwɪn] Der Pinguin
pheasant [ˈfɛz(ə)nt] Der Fasan
pigeon [ˈpɪdʒɪn] Die Taube
seagull [ˈsiːgʌl] Die Möwe
sparrow [ˈspærəʊ] Der Spatz
stork [stɔːk] Der Storch
swallow [ˈswɔləʊ] Die Schwalbe

swan [swɔn] Der Schwan
woodpecker [ˈwʊdˌpɛkə] Der Specht

Flowers Die Blumen
bouquet [buːˈkeɪ-] Der Strauß
camellia [kəˈmiːlɪə] Die Kamelie
carnation [kɑːˈneɪʃ(ə)n] Die Nelke
crocus [ˈkrəʊkəs] Der Krokus
daffodil [ˈdæfədɪl] Die Narzisse
dahlia [ˈdeɪljə] Die Dahlie
daisy [ˈdeɪzɪ] Das Gänseblümchen
dandelion [ˈdændɪlaɪən] Der Löwenzahn
flower [ˈflaʊə] Die Blume
gladiolus [ˈglædɪˈəʊləsɪz] Die Gladiole
iris [ˈaɪ(ə)rɪs] Die Iris
lavender [ˈlævɪndə] Das Lavendel
lily [ˈlɪlɪ] Die Lilie
lotus [ˈləʊtəs] Der Lotus
narcissus [nɑːˈsɪsəsɪz] Die Narzisse
orchid [ˈɔːkɪd] Die Orchidee
peony [ˈpiːənɪ] Die Pfingstrose
poppy [ˈpɔpɪ] Der Mohn
rose [rəʊz] Die Rose
snowdrop [ˈsnəʊdrɔp] Das Schneeglöckchen
sunflower [ˈsʌnˌflaʊə] Die Sonnenblume
tulip [ˈtjuːlɪp] Die Tulpe
violet [ˈvaɪəlɪt] Das Veilchen

Trees Die Bäume
bark [bɑːk] Die Akazie
beech [biːtʃ] Die Buche
birch [bɜːtʃ] Die Birke
branch [brɑːntʃ] Der Ast
chestnut [ˈtʃɛsnʌt] Die Kastanie
cone [kəʊn] Der Kegel
fir [fɜː] Die Tanne
forest [ˈfɔrɪst] Der Wald
leaf [liːf] Das Blatt
linden [ˈlɪndən] Die Linde
maple [ˈmeɪp(ə)l] Der Ahorn
oak [əʊk] Die Eiche
palm [pɑːm] Die Palme
pine [paɪn] Die Kiefer
poplar [ˈpɔplə] Die Pappel
root [ruːt] Die Wurzel
tree [triː] Der Baum
trunk [trʌŋk] Der Baumstamm
willow [ˈwɪləʊ] Die Weide

Sea Das Meer
alligator [ˈælɪgeɪtə] Der Alligator
cachalot [ˈkæʃəlɔt] Der Cachalot
coral [ˈkɔrəl] Die Koralle
crab [kræb] Die Krabbe
crayfish [ˈkreɪfɪʃ] Der Flusskrebs
crocodile [ˈkrɔkədaɪl] Das Krokodil
dolphin [ˈdɔlfɪn] Der Delfin
fish [fɪʃ] Der Fisch
frog [frɔg] Der Frosch
jellyfish [ˈʤelɪfɪʃ] Die Qualle
lobster [ˈlɔbstə] Der Hummer
mollusc [ˈmɔləsk] Das Weichtier
ocean [ˈəʊʃ(ə)n] Der Ozean
octopus [ˈɔktəpəs] Der Tintenfisch
otter [ˈɔtə] Der Otter
sea [siː] Das Meer
sea snake [ˈsiːˌsneɪk] Die Seeschlange

seal [siːl] Der Seehund
shark [ʃɑːk] Der Hai
shellfish [ˈʃelfɪʃ] Die Meeresfrüchte
shrimp [ʃrɪmp] Die Garnele
snail [sneɪl] Die Schnecke
starfish [ˈstɑːˌfɪʃ] Der Seestern
swordfish [ˈsɔːdˌfɪʃ] Der Schwertfisch
tortoise [ˈtɔːtəs] Die Schildkröte
turtle [ˈtɜːtl] Die Schildkröte
walrus [ˈwɔːlrəs] Das Walross
whale [(h)weɪl] Der Wal

Colors Die Farben

Yellow [ˈjeləʊ] gelb
green [griːn] grün
blue [bluː] blau
brown [braʊn] braun
white [waɪt] weiß
red [red] rot
orange [ˈɔrɪndʒ] orange
pink [pɪŋk] rosa
gray [greɪ] grau
black [blæk] schwarz

Size Die Größe

size [saɪz] Die Größe
small [smɔːl] klein
big [bɪg] groß
medium [ˈmiːdɪəm] mittel
little [lɪtl] klein
large [lɑːdʒ] groß
huge [hjuːdʒ] enorm
long [lɔŋ] lang
short [ʃɔːt] kurz

wide [waɪd] breit
narrow [ˈnærəʊ] eng
high [haɪ] hoch
tall [tɔːl] groß
low [ləʊ] niedrig
deep [diːp] tief
shallow [ˈʃæləʊ] flach
thick [θɪk] dick
thin [θɪn] dünn
far [fɑː] weit
near [nɪə] in der Nähe von

Materials Die Materialien

brick [brɪk] Der Ziegel
cardboard [ˈkɑːdbɔːd] Der Karton
clay [kleɪ] Der Lehm
cloth [klɔθ] Das Tuch
concrete [ˈkɔŋkriːt] Der Beton
glass [glɑːs] Das Glas
leather [ˈlɛðə] Das Leder
material [məˈtɪ(ə)rɪəl] Das Material
metal [mɛtl] Das Metall
paper [ˈpeɪpə] Das Papier
plastic [ˈplæstɪk] Der Kunststoff
rubber [ˈrʌbə] Das Gummi
stone [stəʊn] Der Stein
wood [wʊd] Das Holz
fabric [fəˈbrɪk] Der Stoff

Airport Der Flughafen

(air)plane [(ˈɛə)pleɪn] Das Flugzeug
airport [ˈɛəpɔːt] Der Flughafen
aisle [aɪl] Der Gang
armrest [ˈɑːmrɛst] Die Armlehne

backpack [ˈbækpæk] Der Rucksack
baggage [ˈbægɪdʒ] Das Gepäck
boarding [ˈbɔːdɪŋ] Das Einsteigen
cabin [ˈkæbɪn] Die Kabine
carry-on [ˈkærɪɔn] Das Fortfahren
cockpit [ˈkɔkpɪt] Der Cockpit
customs [ˈkʌstəmz] Der Zoll
delay [dɪˈleɪ] Die Verzögerung
destination [ˌdɛstɪˈneɪʃ(ə)n] Das Reiseziel
emergency [ɪˈmɜːdʒ(ə)n(t)sɪ] Der Notfall
flight [flaɪt] Der Flug
fuselage [ˈfjuːz(ə)lɑːʒ] Der Rumpf
gate [geɪt] Das Gate
landing [ˈlændɪŋ] Die Landung
lavatory [ˈlævət(ə)rɪ] Die Toilette
life vest [ˈlaɪfvɛst] Die Rettungsweste
liquid [ˈlɪkwɪd] Die Flüssigkeit
passenger [ˈpæs(ə)ndʒə] Der Passagier
passport [ˈpɑːspɔːt] Der Reisepass
runway [ˈrʌnweɪ] Die Startbahn
schedule [ˈʃɛdjuːl] Der Zeitplan
seat [siːt] Der Sitz
security, guard [sɪˈkjʊərɪtɪ, gɑːd] Der Sicherheitsbeamte
suitcase [ˈs(j)uːtkeɪs] Der Koffer
tail [teɪl] Das Heck
takeoff [ˈteɪkɔf] Das Abheben
terminal [ˈtɜːmɪn(ə)l] Der Terminal
ticket [ˈtɪkɪt] Die Fahrkarte
trolley [ˈtrɔlɪ] Der Wagen
undercarriage [ˈʌndəˌkærɪdʒ] Das Fahrwerk
visa [ˈviːzə] Das Visum

window [ˈwɪndəʊ] Das Fenster
wing [wɪŋ] Der Flügel

Geography Die Erdkunde

area [ˈeərɪə] Der Bereich
capital [ˈkæpɪtəl] Die Hauptstadt
city [ˈsɪtɪ] Die Stadt
country [ˈkəntrɪ] Das Land
district [ˈdɪstrɪkt] Der Kreis
region [ˈrɪdʒən] Die Region
state [steɪt] Das Bundesland
town [toʊn] Die Stadt
village [ˈvɪlɪdʒ] Das Dorf
cape [keɪp] Das Kap
cliff [klɪf] Das Kliff
glacier [ˈglæsɪə] Der Gletscher
hill [hɪl] Der Hügel
mountain [ˈmaʊntɪn] Der Berg
mountain chain - Die Bergkette / Bergkette -
pass [pɑs] Der Pass
peak [piːk] Die Spitze
plain [pleɪn] Die Ebene
plateau [ˈplætəʊ] Das Plateau
summit [ˈsəmɪt] Der Gipfel
valley [ˈvælɪ] Das Tal
volcano [vɔlˈkeɪnəʊ] Der Vulkan
desert [ˈdezət] Die Wüste
equator [iˈkweɪtə] Der Äquator
forest [ˈfɔrɪst] Der Wald
highlands [ˈhaɪlənd] Das Hochland
jungle [ˈjəŋgəl] Der Dschungel
lowlands [ləʊlənd] Das Tiefland
oasis [əʊˈeɪsɪs] Die Oase

swamp [ˈswɔmp] Der Sumpf

tropics [ˈtrəpik] Die Tropen

tundra [ˈtʌndrə] Die Tundra

canal [kəˈnæl] Der Kanal

lake [leik] Die See

ocean [ˈəʊʃn] Der Ozean

ocean current [ˈəʊʃn ˈkʌrənt] Die Meeresströmung

pool / pond [puːl pɔnd] Der Pool / Teich

river [ˈrivər] Der Fluss

sea [si] Das Meer

spring [spriŋ] Die Quelle

stream [strim] Der Strom

Crimes Das Verbrechen

arson [ˈɑːsn] Die Brandstiftung

assault [əˈsɔːlt] Der Angriff

bigamy [ˈbɪgəmi] Die Bigamie

blackmail [ˈblækmeɪl] Die Erpressung

bribery [ˈbraɪbəri] Die Bestechung

burglary [ˈbɜːgləri] Der Einbruch

child abuse [tʃaɪld əˈbjuːs] Der Kindesmissbrauch

conspiracy [kənˈspɪrəsi] Die Verschwörung

espionage [ˈespɪɑnɑːʒ] Die Spionage

forgery [ˈfɔːdʒəri] Die Fälschung

fraud [frɔːd] Der Betrug

genocide [ˈdʒenəsaɪd] Der Völkermord

hijacking [ˈhaɪdʒækɪŋ] Die Entführung

homicide [ˈhɔmɪsaɪd] Der Mord

kidnapping [ˈkɪdnæpɪŋ] Die Entführung

manslaughter [ˈmænslɔːtə] Der Totschlag

mugging [ˈmʌgɪŋ] Der Überfall

murder [ˈmɜːdə] Der Mord

perjury [ˈpɜːdʒəri] Der Meineid

rape [reɪp] Die Vergewaltigung

riot [ˈraɪət] Das Randalieren

robbery [ˈrɔbəri] Der Raub

shoplifting [ˈʃɔplɪftɪŋ] Der Ladendiebstahl

slander [ˈslɑːndə] Die Verleumdung

smuggling [ˈsmʌglɪŋ] Der Schmuggel

treason [ˈtriːzn] Der Verrat

trespassing [ˈtrespəsɪŋ] Das unerlaubte Betreten

Numbers Nummern

one [wʌn] eins

two [tuː] zwei

three [θriː] drei

four [fɔː] vier

five [faɪv] fünf

six [sɪks] sechs

seven [ˈsev(ə)n] Sieben

eight [eɪt] acht

nine [naɪn] neun

ten [ten] zehn

eleven [ɪˈlev(ə)n] elf

twelve [twelv] zwölf

thirteen [θɜːˈtiːn] dreizehn

fourteen [ˌfɔːˈtiːn] vierzehn

fifteen [ˌfɪfˈtiːn] fünfzehn

sixteen [ˌsɪkˈstiːn] sechzehn

seventeen [ˌsev(ə)nˈtiːn] siebzehn

eighteen [ˌeɪˈtiːn] achtzehn

nineteen [ˌnaɪnˈtiːn] neunzehn

twenty [ˈtwentɪ] zwanzig

twenty-one [ˌtwenɪˈwʌn] einundzwanzig

twenty-two [ˌtwenɪˈtʊ] zweiundzwanzig
thirty [ˈθɜːtɪ] dreißig
forty [ˈfɔːtɪ] vierzig
fifty [ˈfɪftɪ] fünfzig
sixty [ˈsɪkstɪ] sechzig
seventy [ˈsev(ə)ntɪ] siebzig
eighty [ˈeɪtɪ] achtzig
ninety [ˈnaɪntɪ] neunzig
one hundred [wʌn ˈhʌndrəd] einhundert
one hundred and one … einhundertundeins …
two hundred zweihundert
one thousand [wʌn ˈθaʊz(ə)nd] eintausend
one million [wʌn ˈmɪljən] eine Million

Ordinal numbers Ordnungszahlen

first [fɜːst] erste
second [ˈsekənd] zweite
third [θɜːd] dritte
fourth [fɔːθ] vierte
fifth [fɪfθ] fünfte
sixth [sɪksθ] sechste
seventh [ˈsev(ə)nθ] siebte
eighth [eɪtθ] achte
ninth [naɪnθ] neunte
tenth [tenθ] zehnte
eleventh [ɪˈlev(ə)nθ] elfte
twelfth [twelfθ] zwölfte
thirteenth [ˌθɜːˈtiːnθ] dreizehnte
fourteenth [ˌfɔːˈtiːnθ] vierzehnte

fifteenth [fɪfˈtiːnθ] fünfzehnte
sixteenth [ˌsɪkˈstiːnθ] sechzehnte
seventeenth [ˌsev(ə)nˈtiːnθ] siebzehnte
eighteenth [eɪˈtiːnθ] achtzehnte
nineteenth [ˌnaɪnˈtiːnθ] neunzehnte
twentieth [ˈtwentɪɪθ] zwanzigste
twenty-first [ˈtwentɪ fɜːst] einundzwanzigste
twenty-second [ˈtwentɪ ˈsekənd] zweiundzwanzigste
twenty-third [ˈtwentɪ θɜːd] dreiundzwanzigste
twenty-fourth [ˈtwentɪ fɔːθ] vierundzwanzigste
twenty-fifth [ˈtwentɪ fɪfθ] fünfundzwanzigste
twenty-sixth [ˈtwentɪ sɪksθ] sechsundzwanzigste
twenty-seventh [ˈtwentɪ ˈsev(ə)nθ] siebenundzwanzigste
twenty-eighth [ˈtwentɪ eɪtθ] achtundzwanzigste
twenty-ninth [ˈtwentɪ naɪnθ] neunundzwanzigste
thirtieth [ˈθɜːtɪɪθ] dreißigste
fortieth [ˈfɔːtɪəθ] vierzigste
fiftieth [ˈfɪftɪɪθ] fünfzigste
sixtieth [ˈsɪkstɪɪθ] sechzigste
seventieth [ˈsev(ə)ntɪɪθ] siebzigste
eightieth [ˈeɪtɪəθ] achtzigste
ninetieth [ˈnaɪntɪəθ] neunzigste
hundredth [ˈhʌndrədθ] hundertste
thousandth [ˈθaʊz(ə)ndθ] tausendste
millionth [ˈmɪljənθ] millionste

Appendix / Anhang

Kurze Formen

In der gesprochenen und geschriebenen Sprache finden die Kurzformen sehr häufig Verwendung.

to be (am, are, is)

bejaht		verneint	
Langform	Kurzform	Langform	Kurzform
I am	I'm	I am not	I'm not
you are	you're	you are not	you're not oder you aren't
he is	he's	he is not	he's not oder he isn't
she is	she's	she is not	she's not oder she isn't
it is	it's	it is not	it's not oder it isn't
we are	we're	we are not	we're not oder we aren't
you are	you're	you are not	you're not oder you aren't
they are	they're	they are not	they're not oder they aren't

to be (was, were)

Pronomen	bejaht		verneint	
	Langform	Kurzform	Langform	Kurzform
I, he, she, it	I was	---	I was not	I wasn't
we, you, they	we were	---	we were not	you weren't

have (got)

Pronomen	bejaht		verneint	
	Langform	Kurzform	Langform	Kurzform
I, we, you, they	I have got	I've got	we have not got	we've not got
				we haven't got
he, she, it	she has got	she's got	she has not got	she's not got
				she hasn't got

do

Pronomen	bejaht Langform	Kurzform	verneint Langform	Kurzform
I, we, you, they	I do	---	we do not	we don't
he, she, it	she does	---	she does not	she doesn't

did

Pronomen	bejaht Langform	Kurzform	verneint Langform	Kurzform
I, he, she, it, we, you, they	we did	---	we did not	we didn't

Modalverben

bejaht Langform	Kurzform	verneint Langform	Kurzform
can	---	cannot	can't
could	---	could not	couldn't
must	---	must not	mustn't
might	---	might not	---
need	---	need not	needn't
will	'll	will not	won't
would	'd	would not	wouldn't
shall	---	shall not	shan't
should	'd	should not	shouldn't
ought to	---	ought not to	oughtn't to

Index
Register

Adjektiv, 28, 61, 79, 89

Adverbien, 79, 80, 81, 82, 83

Artikel, 20, 21, 22, 23, 24, 27, 28, 62

Buchtipps, 269

Die unregelmäßigen Verben, 235

Fragesätze, 34

Fragewörter, 56, 57, 88

Futur, 161

Gegenteile, 243

Genitiv, 20, 52, 53

Gerundium, 140

Gleichheit, 63

Have got, 98

Imperativ, 74, 75

Imperfekt, 143

Infinitiv, 32, 33, 38, 121, 122, 144, 161, 162

Komparativ, 61, 62, 63

Körperliche Eigenschaften, 242

Kurzantworten, 48, 124, 125

Modale Hilfsverben, 38, 39

Much little, many few, a lot of, 99

Partizip I, 140, 170

Past Progressive versus Past Simple, 156

Perfekt, 170, 171, 172, 176

Personalpronomen, 56, 74

Plural, 15, 16, 17, 23, 28, 32, 33, 34, 39, 40, 41, 42, 56, 57, 58, 74

Präpositionen, 20, 21, 25, 56, 68, 92, 109, 111

Präsens, 32, 33, 34, 98, 120

Present Perfect versus Past Simple, 176

Present Progressive versus Present Simple, 134

Reading comprehension, 18, 30, 36, 46, 50, 54, 59, 66, 72, 77, 85, 90, 95, 102, 107, 112, 118, 126, 132, 137, 141, 147, 153, 158, 166, 173, 177, 182, 190

Some und any, 115

Superlativ, 62, 63

Too either, so neither, 186

unregelmäßige Verben, 33

Verlaufsform der Vergangenheit, 150

Verlaufsform des Präsens, 129

verneinende Wörter, 97

Wichtige Adjektive, 241

Wortartenwechsel, 87

Wortstellung, 48, 181

Would like, 117

Zahlen, 104

Bibliography / Bibliografie

Murphy, Raymond. *Essential Grammar in Use*. Cambridge: Cambridge University Press, 1990. Print.

Attribution: https://www.flaticon.com/authors/freepik Creative Commons BY 3.0

Buchtipps

Das Erste Englische Lesebuch für Anfänger Band 1
Zweisprachig mit Englisch-deutscher Übersetzung
Niveaustufen A1 A2

Das Buch enthält einen Kurs für Anfänger und fortgeschrittene Anfänger, wobei die Texte auf Deutsch und auf Englisch nebeneinanderstehen. Die Motivation des Schülers wird durch lustige Alltagsgeschichten über das Kennenlernen neuer Freunde, Studieren, die Arbeitssuche, das Arbeiten etc. aufrechterhalten. Die dabei verwendete Methode basiert auf der natürlichen menschlichen Gabe, sich Wörter zu merken, die immer wieder und systematisch im Text auftauchen. Sätze werden stets aus den im vorherigen Kapitel erklärten Wörtern gebildet. Das zweite und die folgenden Kapitel des Anfängerkurses haben nur jeweils 29 neue Wörter. Audiodateien sind auf www.lppbooks.com/English/FirstEnglishReader_audio/ inklusive erhältlich.

Das Erste Englische Lesebuch für Anfänger Band 2
Zweisprachig mit Englisch-deutscher Übersetzung
Niveaustufe A2

Dieses Buch ist Band 2 des Ersten Englischen Lesebuches für Anfänger. Das Buch enthält einen Kurs für Anfänger und fortgeschrittene Anfänger, wobei die Texte auf Deutsch und auf Englisch nebeneinanderstehen. Die dabei verwendete Methode basiert auf der natürlichen menschlichen Gabe, sich Wörter zu merken, die immer wieder und systematisch im Text auftauchen. Sätze werden stets aus den im vorherigen Kapitel erklärten Wörtern gebildet. Audiodateien sind auf www.lppbooks.com/English/FirstEnglishReaderV2_audio/ inklusive erhältlich.

Das Erste Englische Lesebuch für Anfänger Band 3
Zweisprachig mit Englisch-deutscher Übersetzung
Niveaustufe A2

Dieses Buch ist Band 3 des Ersten Englischen Lesebuches für Anfänger. Das Buch enthält einen Kurs für Anfänger und fortgeschrittene Anfänger, wobei die Texte auf Deutsch und auf Englisch nebeneinanderstehen. Die dabei verwendete Methode basiert auf der natürlichen menschlichen Gabe, sich Wörter zu merken, die immer wieder und systematisch im Text auftauchen. Sätze werden stets aus den im vorherigen Kapitel erklärten Wörtern gebildet. Audiodateien sind auf www.lppbooks.com/English/FirstEnglishReaderV3_audio/ inklusive erhältlich.

Das Zweite Englische Lesebuch
Zweisprachig mit Englisch-deutscher Übersetzung
Niveaustufen A2 B1

Das Zweite Englische Lesebuch ist ein zweisprachiges Buch für die Stufen A2 B1. Dieses Buch ist bestens für Sie geeignet, wenn Sie bereits Erfahrung mit der englischen Sprache haben. Das Buch ist nach der ALARM-Methode aufgebaut. Neue Worte werden im Buch von Zeit zu Zeit wiederholt, dadurch können Sie sich leichter an sie erinnern. Sie werden den englischen Wortschatz ohne Probleme erlernen, dabei helfen Ihnen die deutschen Übersetzungen und Paralleltexte. Audiodateien sind auf www.lppbooks.com/English/SecondEnglishReader_audio/ inklusive erhältlich.

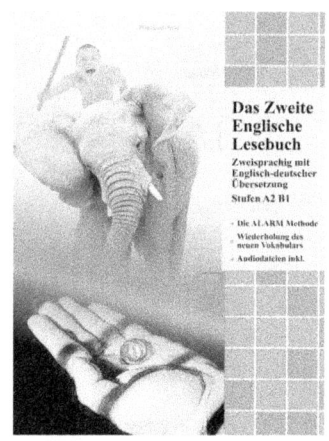

Das Erste Englische Lesebuch für Kinder und Eltern
Zweisprachig mit Englisch-deutscher Übersetzung
Niveaustufe A1

Das Buch enthält einen Anfängerkurs für Kinder, wobei die Texte auf Deutsch und auf Englisch nebeneinanderstehen. Die dabei verwendete Methode basiert auf der natürlichen menschlichen Gabe, sich Wörter zu merken, die immer wieder und systematisch im Text auftauchen. Sätze werden stets aus den im vorherigen Kapitel erklärten Wörtern gebildet. Mit dem ersten Kapitel gibt es Bilder und die ersten einfachen Vokabeln, aus welchen verschiedene Sätze gebildet wurden. Mit dem zweiten Kapitel kommen die nächsten Bilder und Vokabeln hinzu, bis im Laufe des Buches aus zusammengewürfelten Sätze, kleine Geschichten werden. Einfache Texte und ein ausgewählter und dosierter Grundwortschatz führen den Lernenden behutsam in die englische Sprache ein. Audiodateien sind auf www.lppbooks.com/English/DasErsteEnglischeLesebuchfurKinderundEltern/ inklusive erhältlich.

Das Erste Englische Lesebuch für Kaufmännische Berufe und Wirtschaft
Zweisprachig mit Englisch-deutscher Übersetzung
Niveaustufen A1 A2

Der Inhalt des Buches ist aufgeteilt in 25 Kapitel, die auf die Stufen A1 und A2 des gemeinsamen europäischen Referenzrahmen vorbereiten sollen. In jedem Kapitel wird eine Anzahl an Vokabeln vermittelt, die anschließend direkt in kurzen, einprägsamen Sätzen und Texten veranschaulicht werden. Dabei handelt es sich durchgehend um alltagstaugliches Material für Berufssituationen wie Telefonate, Besprechungen, Geschäftsreisen und Geschäftskorrespondenz. Die Übungen bauen logisch aufeinander auf, sodass die Texte allmählich komplexer werden. Audiodateien sind auf www.lppbooks.com/English/FirstBusinessReader/ inklusive erhältlich.

Das Erste Englische Lesebuch für Medizinische Fachangestellte
Zweisprachig mit Englisch-deutscher Übersetzung
Niveaustufen A1 A2

Bei diesem Lehrbuch handelt es sich um ein Lesebuch für medizinische Fachangestellte, und dementsprechend behandeln die Lektionstexte und Vokabeln auch Themen wie Patientengespräche, Diagnostik, die Beschreibung von Symptomen und vieles mehr, was man im Kontakt mit Ärzten und Patienten braucht. Die Lektionen sind in mehrere Blöcke unterteilt: Vokabelliste mit Lautschrift und Übersetzung, kurze Übungsdialoge und zweisprachige Texte und meistens im Anschluss einige Verständnisfragen zu den Gesprächsinhalten. Im Anhang finden sich Vokabellisten mit wichtigen Adjektiven, Eigenschaftswörtern, Gegenteilspaaren und irregulären Verben. Audiodateien sind auf www.lppbooks.com/English/FirstMedicalReader/ inklusive erhältlich.

Das Erste Englische Lesebuch für Studenten
Zweisprachig mit Englisch-deutscher Übersetzung
Niveaustufen A1 A2

Das Buch enthält einen Kurs für Anfänger und fortgeschrittene Anfänger, wobei die Texte auf Deutsch und auf Englisch nebeneinander stehen. Die Dialoge sind praxisnah und alltagstauglich. Die dabei verwendete Methode basiert auf der natürlichen menschlichen Gabe, sich Wörter zu merken, die immer wieder und systematisch im Text auftauchen. In jedem Kapitel wird eine Anzahl an Vokabeln vermittelt, die anschließend direkt in kurzen, einprägsamen Texten und Dialogen veranschaulicht werden. Audiodateien sind auf www.lppbooks.com/English/SuG/ erhältlich.

Das Englische Lesebuch zum Kochen
Zweisprachig mit Englisch-deutscher Übersetzung
Niveaustufen A1 A2

Lernt man eine Sprache, hilft die Bekanntheit mit einem Thema, eine Verbindung zwischen zwei Sprachen herzustellen. Das Englische Lesebuch zum Kochen stellt die Wörter und Sätze sowohl in Englisch als auch in Deutsch zur Verfügung. Fünfundzwanzig Kapitel sind in Themen und Inhalte bezüglich Kochen und Nahrung gegliedert. Rezeptanleitungen, zusammen mit leichten Fragen und Antworten, zeigen den Gebrauch dieser Wörter und Sätze. Es könnte Ihren Appetit anregen oder Englischlernenden wie Ihnen helfen, ihre Kenntnis in einem bekannten Umfeld der Küche zu verbessern. Audiodateien sind auf www.lppbooks.com/English/DELKv1/ inklusive erhältlich.

Erste Englische Fragen und Antworten für Anfänger
Zweisprachig mit Englisch-deutscher Übersetzung
Niveaustufen A1 A2

Das Buch enthält einen Kurs für Anfänger und fortgeschrittene Anfänger, wobei die Texte auf Deutsch und auf Englisch nebeneinander stehen. Die Lektionen sind in mehrere Blöcke unterteilt: Vokabelliste mit Übersetzung, zweisprachige Texte, und Verständnisfragen zu den Gesprächsinhalten. Das Buch enthält viele Beispiele für Fragen und Antworten im Englischen. Die dabei verwendete Methode basiert auf der natürlichen menschlichen Gabe, sich Wörter zu merken, die immer wieder und systematisch im Text auftauchen. Sätze werden stets aus den im vorherigen Kapitel erklärten Wörtern gebildet. Audiodateien sind inklusive auf www.lppbooks.com/English/Englische_Fragen/ erhältlich.

Das Erste Englische Lesebuch für Familien
Zweisprachig mit Englisch-Deutscher Übersetzung
Niveaustufen A1 A2

Das Buch enthält eine Darstellung der englischen Gespräche des täglichen Familienlebens, wobei die Texte auf Englisch und auf Deutsch nebeneinander stehen. Die Lektionen sind in mehrere Blöcke unterteilt: Vokabelliste für den täglichen Gebrauch, zweisprachige Texte, und Verständnisfragen zu den Gesprächsinhalten. Die dabei verwendete ALARM-Methode basiert auf der natürlichen menschlichen Gabe, sich Wörter zu merken, die immer wieder und systematisch im Text auftauchen. Sätze werden stets aus den im vorherigen Kapitel erklärten Wörtern gebildet. Audiodateien sind auf www.lppbooks.com/English/EELF inklusive erhältlich.

Thomas's Fears and Hopes
Plain Spoken English with Idioms
Bilingual for Speakers of German
Pre-intermediate Level B1

Thomas war zu seines Vaters Beerdigung nach Georgia heimgekehrt. Er wurde informiert, dass er das ganze Vermögen bekommen würde, denn er war ein Einzelkind. Da passierten einige Ereignisse, die ihm eine Furcht einjagten. Die Audiodateien sind auf www.lppbooks.com/English/PlainSpokenEnglish_audio/ inklusive erhältlich.

Fremde Wasser
Zweisprachig mit Englisch-deutscher Übersetzung
Stufe B2

Mitgründer eines Zwei-Mann-Unternehmens zu sein hat seine Vor- und Nachteile. Das kalte Wasser der Selbsttätigkeit ist aber nicht für jedermann geeignet. Die Audiodateien sind auf www.lppbooks.com/English/BusinessStartupEndeavor_audio/ inklusive erhältlich.

Das Erste Touristische Lesebuch für Anfänger
Zweisprachig mit Englisch-Deutscher Übersetzung
Niveaustufe A1

Das Lesebuch ist ein Kurs für Anfänger, wobei die Texte auf Deutsch und auf Englisch nebeneinanderstehen. Es ist der ideale Begleiter für alle, die Sprachen unterwegs lernen wollen. Das Buch enthält am häufigsten gebrauchten Wörter, einfache Sätze und Redewendungen, um sich schnell zu verständigen. Die dabei verwendete Methode basiert auf der natürlichen menschlichen Gabe, sich Wörter zu merken, die immer wieder und systematisch im Text auftauchen. Sätze werden stets aus den im vorherigen Kapitel erklärten Wörtern gebildet. Audiodateien sind auf www.lppbooks.com/English/ETLA inklusive erhältlich.

Who lost the money? Wer verlor das Geld?
First English Reader for Beginner and Elementary Level
Das Erste Englische Lesebuch für Stufen A1 A2
Zweisprachig mit Englisch-Deutscher Übersetzung

Der erste Teil des Buches erklärt mit Beispielen den grundlegenden Satzbau der englischen Sprache, wobei die Texte auf Englisch und auf Deutsch für einen leichteren Einsicht nebeneinander stehen. Der zweite Buchteil, der auch aus einfachen Sätzen zusammengestellt ist, stellt einen Krimi dar. Die dabei verwendete ALARM-Methode basiert auf der natürlichen menschlichen Gabe, sich Wörter zu merken, die immer wieder und systematisch im Text auftauchen. Sätze werden stets aus den im vorherigen Kapitel erklärten Wörtern gebildet. Die Audiodateien sind auf www.lppbooks.com/English/WLM/ inklusive erhältlich.

Unexpected Circumstance
Zweisprachig mit Englisch-Deutscher Übersetzung
Niveaustufe B2

Die forensische Wissenschaft war eine von Damien Morins Leidenschaften. Inzwischen betraf das erste wirkliche Verbrechen, dass er untersuchte, seine eigene Vergangenheit. Die Audiodateien sind auf www.audiolego.com/English/Lopez/ inklusive erhältlich.

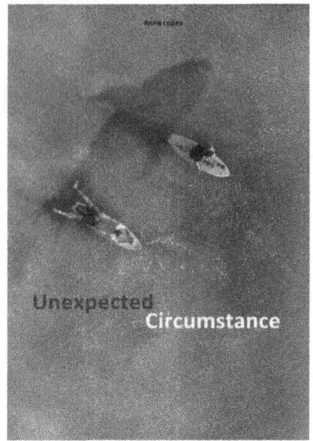

www.ingramcontent.com/pod-product-compliance
Lightning Source LLC
Chambersburg PA
CBHW081218170426
43198CB00017B/2651